The Day Lincoln Was Almost Shot

The Fort Stevens Story

Benjamin Franklin Cooling III

THE SCARECROW PRESS, INC.
Lanham • Toronto • Plymouth, UK
2013

Published by Scarecrow Press, Inc.
A wholly owned subsidary of The Rowman & Littlefield Publishing Group, Inc.
4501 Forbes Boulevard, Suite 200, Lanham, Maryland 20706
www.rowman.com

10 Thornbury Road, Plymouth PL6 7PP, United Kingdom

British Library Cataloguing in Publication Information Available

Library of Congress Cataloging-in-Publication Data

Cooling, Benjamin Franklin, III, 1938–
 The day Lincoln was almost shot : the Fort Stevens story / Benjamin Franklin Cooling III.
  pages cm
 Includes bibliographical references and index.
 ISBN 978-0-8108-8622-3 (cloth : alk. paper) — ISBN 978-0-8108-8623-0 (ebook)
 1. Fort Stevens (Washington, D.C.)—History—19th century. 2. Lincoln, Abraham, 1809–1865. 3. Maryland Campaign, 1864. 4. Washington (D.C.)—History—Civil War, 1861–1865. I. Title.
 E476.66.C849 2013
 973.7092—dc23

                                                                        2012051832

∞™ The paper used in this publication meets the minimum requirements of American National Standard for Information Sciences—Permanence of Paper for Printed Library Materials, ANSI/NISO Z39.48-1992. Printed in the United States of America.

To the memory of Peter Seaborg, 1949–1999,
proprietor of Washington's Rock Creek Bookshop and
devoted student of the Battle of Fort Stevens
and the men who fought there.

CONTENTS

CONTENTS

ACKNOWLEDGMENTS

As in previous books, much gratitude goes to Walton H. Owen, curator of Fort Ward museum and park in Alexandria, Virginia, for technical and substance assistance. For this particular volume, the author is indebted to Joseph and Sharon Scopin of Darnestown, Maryland, for the use of material from the Lewis Cass White collection in their possession. I am indebted to Steven Stanley, Gettysburg, Pennsylvania, and the Civil War Trust, Washington, D.C. (James Campi and Mary Koik), for permission to use Stanley's graphic maps. Additional thanks go to Gail Stephens, Frederick, Maryland, and National Park Service professionals Brett Spaulding and Tracy Shives Evans at the Monocacy National Battlefield for always enlightening conversations and research help at that historic site. Ron Harvey, superb National Park Service historian and interpreter when he served as such for the Fort Stevens/Battleground National Cemetery unit of Rock Creek Park in Washington, provided great insights into details of both key elements in this volume. Kym Elder and Simone Monteleone continue his efforts and have been helpful to me. One can also appreciate the efforts of the Alliance for Preservation of the Civil War Defenses of Washington (Tersh Boasburg, Susan Claffey, Loretta Neumann, Jon Fleming, and Ellen McCarthy in particular) as a support group to the National Park Service, with Fort Stevens and Walter Reed as its special focus for the sesquicentennial. Other helpmates include Michael Osborne of Osborne Books, Columbia, Maryland; Richard Sauers, Lewisburg, Pennsylvania; Frederick Ray, Asheville, North Carolina; Dr. John A. Pierce, intrepid Walter Reed historian before the base closure; Kim Holien, longtime historian of Forts Myer and McNair of the U.S. Army; Jerry McCoy, Silver Spring, Maryland, chronicler and preservationist, as are Marilyn Slatick and Loretta Vann, also of Silver Spring; Jane

ACKNOWLEDGMENTS

Freundel Levy and Mara Cherkasky of Cultural Tourism D.C.; John Emond, indefatigable National Archives researcher, Silver Spring, Maryland; Jason Hagey, Tennalytown, Washington, D.C., for Fort Reno site information; and James Johnston, who has chronicled the Loughborough family story. Gordon Berg of the District of Columbia Civil War Round Table shared insights into the Grace Church Confederates. Various other individuals, such as Ron Meininger of Antebellum Covers, Gaithersburg, Maryland; Joanna Church, Director of Collections, Montgomery County Historical Society, Rockville, Maryland; and Patricia Tyson, a moving force behind the African American Military Road School Trust, Washington, D.C., have also contributed significantly to this endeavor. Dr. John McCavitt of Rostrevor, County Down, Northern Ireland, opened new vistas on Major General Robert Ross, the man who captured Washington in 1814. Of course, the book would not have reached publication without Bennett Graff, Senior Acquisitions Editor; Jessica McCleary, Assistant Managing Editor; and old friend and associate Dr. Martin Gordon of Scarecrow Press.

INTRODUCTION

A small park exists in a northwest Washington, D.C., neighborhood. It contains the remains of a Civil War fort. That fort is called Fort Stevens. It is the place where President Abraham Lincoln was almost killed. It is also where the Union almost lost the Civil War. It is owned but forgotten by its owners—the American public. Its existence relies upon tax dollars administered by the somewhat lackluster stewardship of the National Park Service. Americans scarcely know of its existence, much less its historical importance. Several city blocks away, a small national cemetery called Battleground contains the Union dead from a battle that occurred at this spot. It, too, remains overshadowed by more popular tourist attractions downtown on the National Mall. Yet hardly another place in that horrendous saga of carnage and sacrifice to save the Union merits any more importance or recognition than here, where events and humans intertwined by fate brought them together on July 11 and 12, 1864. The near killing of the chief executive of the land, the near enemy capture of the national capital, the moment in time that might have changed the course of emancipation and American democracy in an election year are inadequately immortalized in that humble city park and cemetery. But here lies a story, forever linked as Lincoln and Fort Stevens.

What if events had happened differently? The eternal Civil War question has always been: What if Lincoln had lived, and was not assassinated at Ford's Theater on April 14, 1865? What if Booth had been stopped? How would Reconstruction have gone differently? How might an essentially new nation have developed differently thereafter? But reverse the question. What if Lincoln had been killed or maimed earlier—say, a year earlier? Who would have taken over the presidency? The innocuous Hannibal Hamlin as vice president would have taken office. Would the election of 1864 have gone to the Democrats? Would the war to restore the Union, to free the slaves, have evaporated? How would the conflict have ended if any of those scenarios had played out? This book addresses this critical, almost unknown, issue. What if President Abraham Lincoln had been shot and killed on July 11 or 12, 1864, at Fort Stevens, D.C.—as he almost was? What happened at Fort Stevens, D.C., to even beg the question?

First, this is the story of a man and a moment in time that could have changed the course of history. In another sense, it did. It is about Lincoln—reputedly the only sitting president of the United States to come under enemy fire while in office. That occurred at Fort Stevens. So the Fort Stevens story is foremost about the sixteenth president. But is that all? The book is about how Lincoln escaped a sharpshooter's bullet as he stood exposed on the parapet of a fort in northwest Washington, D.C., at a critical moment in the war, his presidency and the future of the United States. This was July 1864 in a summer before a national election. Why did he expose himself in the first place? What happened that would have affected that pivotal moment in our democracy? The story embraces more than just the man.

Second, this is also a story about the moment when the Confederacy came closest to actually capturing Mr. Lincoln's city, his capital, Washington. Here was the culmination of three years of effort on the part of Jefferson Davis, Robert E. Lee, and their armies to accomplish the supreme object of war. The story that unfolded involved their chosen instrument, the colorful Jubal Anderson Early—"Old Jube" of legend and reality. So while this book is about Lincoln's appointment with danger, it is also about Early and his army trying to take the city—the political nerve center and logistical base for the Union war efforts. The story tells of its moment of greatest danger at the hands of an enemy army. So this story embraces Mr. Lincoln, Fort Stevens, and one of the most colorful characters in the Confederacy's pantheon of generals. At the same time, it is also about soldiers and civilians, city residents—loyal and disloyal—Lincoln's composite force raked together to ward off Early and Old Jube's ragtag force that almost took the prize.

Third, the book is about "Fortress Washington." It describes the forts and defenders of Mr. Lincoln's city. It places the only battle fought within the boundaries of the District of Columbia into the context of what was called the Defenses of Washington. This term encompassed a web of forts and batteries, barracks and storehouses, roads and obstacles together with thousands of men committed to providing a sword and shield for protecting the symbol of the Union. Fort Stevens was chosen by fate to be the epicenter of the story of a decisive battle. Others on the northern defense line of the city contributed their share to that story also. Some even witnessed Lincoln's visitation before, during, and after the battle. But why were they located where they were, how were they armed, what was their individual size and shape, and what topographical features give a backdrop to the 1864 battle? How they impacted the human and physical landscape of Washington's suburbs adds texture. Moreover, why did the continuous thirty-plus miles of field fortifications nearly fail in the moment of its ultimate test?

Fourth, Fort Stevens has an aura of uniqueness to it. Remarkably, declares the eminent Civil War historian James M. McPherson, in all the literature on Lincoln, the amount of focus on his role as commander in chief "is disproportionately far smaller than the actual percentage of time he spent on that task." Nevertheless, between 2002 and today, not to speak of the past half century, there have been intense studies of that very facet of Lincoln's presidency, just not the one displayed at Fort Stevens. The intent of these studies lies with strategic leadership and command, not operational or tactical control. Even when touching, however fleetingly, upon the episode of Lincoln and Fort Stevens, analysts have skirted many useful details and vignettes. None of them plumbed the penultimate dimension of an American president at war. Lincoln functioned, for however short a time, as an actor in a tactical drama. Mystery still attends to what truly motivated him to observe, participate, and function as a military operative, not merely as a political chieftain. For history, mystery always accompanies certainty. In many ways, the book is about mysteries—Lincoln's motivation and Early's lack thereof just when he might have attained his greatest fame and accomplished his and the Confederacy's greatest feat, at Lincoln's expense. Therefore, the Fort Stevens story is one of possibilities, opportunities, success, and failure.[1]

Fifth, if this specific event was arguably so decisive, as I argue in these pages, then why has it languished in a legacy of obscurity and benign neglect for 150 years? There is always a story that continues past a moment in time. So it is with Lincoln and Fort Stevens. Almost lost numerous times to city development and expansion, the fort and land owned by a free woman of color have proven somewhat more memorable only since the civil rights focus of our own era. Even now the federally owned national parkland at Fort Stevens remains virtually unrecognized to American citizens and students of the Civil War period. It continues under threat by outside influences. Belatedly embraced years after the Civil War by survivors of the battle, their move to memorialize Lincoln's appearance makes an interesting part of the story in its own right. This was no Gettysburg, Shiloh, or even Vicksburg in American memory. It should have been, for more than a handful of survivors, those witnesses to history. Some claimed to have seen Lincoln under fire, most did not. But they recognized significance, the "might-have-been," their contribution to its not happening. So this volume concludes with a charge to the sesquicentennial generation today to ensure that future generations may better appreciate what Lincoln and his boys in blue and a fort and a city accomplished on two fateful days so long ago. It is a time gone but not lost thanks to veterans and their Lincoln "Boulder" (as they styled it) atop the Fort Stevens parapet. In a diminutive Battleground National Cemetery nearby where forty-one of their numbers sleep on fame's eternal camping ground, plus a similar burial ground a few miles away where lie seventeen immortal Confederates mark the sacrifice that Lincoln might live, the capital was saved and the nation was redeemed.

The story recounted here surpasses just two July days. It began with the British burning of public buildings during the War of 1812. Lincoln's paranoia about protecting Washington developed when he reached Washington in the winter of 1861. It continued as camps and forts broke ground in Washington's suburbs. It embraced Lincoln's mingling with garrison troops, hospital convalescents, and even city residents, and it reached its crescendo in the summer of 1864 when Lee tested the strength and determination of its defenders. The story stretches across Early's campaign from June until August and includes a preceding delaying action on the Monocacy River two days before Fort Stevens. Preeminently, the saga features Early's sharpshooters, the president watching the battle intently until nearly shot and then actually briefly directing his only battle as commander-in-chief of the nation's armed forces. In the end, Washington's defenses, Lincoln, and the defenders at Fort Stevens held against Early's breakthrough. It was this contest that reshaped the Union war effort, led to the final push of annihilation against valiant Confederate efforts elsewhere, and eventually ensured Lincoln's reelection. That was not apparent on those hot July days. Nor was Lincoln's final appointment with martyrdom—nine months in the future, ironically downtown in his capital, his city, his last home.

None of the great martial worthies of the Civil War were even present at Fort Stevens. Grant and Sherman, Lee and Jackson did not make the event. Jackson was dead, Sherman was preoccupied on the road to Atlanta, while Grant and Lee slugged it out on the Richmond-Petersburg line, one hundred miles to the south of Washington. True, minor captains orchestrated the thrust and parry involving Washington's fate at this critical point. However, only Lincoln and perhaps some of his fellow politicians on the one side and a former U.S. vice president, John C. Breckinridge, on the other presented noteworthy personalities on the scene. Otherwise, events remained in the hands of lesser-known commanders and followers, perhaps those commoners who, like Lincoln, fought the real war.

No famous landmarks such as wheat and cornfields, bloody lanes or ponds, cemetery hills or famed ridgelines were attached to the fighting at Fort Stevens. Oh, those features were there, just not accorded the fame and recognition of other battle sites. Rock Creek's valley as well as the Seventh Street artery and the country houses of some of Washington's luminaries provided some landmarks. An as-yet-unnamed rivulet traversed the battlefield, plus orchards and fields of grain dotted the landscape. They contributed little or nothing to Civil War lore—except maybe to those present who remembered them years later. In all, Fort Stevens, D.C., stands virtually absent from our pantheon of Civil War gore and glory. Simply termed *the forgotten battle* by today's stewards, the National Park Service, events here could well have changed the course of the Civil War, hence American history, more than did a dozen famous battles. The Lincoln Stone or Boulder and the restored parapet suggest that conclusion.

But why is there no National Park Service Visitor's Center at Fort Stevens, D.C.? No museum or gallery or audio-visual show interprets the two hot, steamy July days in 1864. Visitors (few as they are) have no human contact point with even the stewards of the public land. There are no human interpreters on site to inform and educate about the most important battle in the nation's struggle for survival. Infrequent on-site programs provide no substitute for permanent facilities. Here Federal troops defeated a Confederate army at the gates of the nation's capital. Here a national election hung in the balance! Here too, the president of the United States came close to death fully nine months before an assassin's bullet cut him down. Here occurred the only Civil War battle fought in the District of Columbia, and the sole marker to appreciable Confederate presence within the city's limits. Fought on soil previously owned by a free black woman who ostensibly never received payment for military confiscation of her property, the link with the African American neighborhood today seems palpable. Neither city populace nor institutions, national institutions nor citizenry seem capable of acknowledging the significance of it all. One wonders if anybody cares that emancipation and a nation could have ended right then but for this single stroke of fate called Fort Stevens!

Possibly only big battles and carnage attract Americans' attention. With casualty figures hardly approaching a thousand souls, the dust of Union and Confederate dead from this battle plus a partially restored fort in an undervalued park denote the epic significance of what took place at Fort Stevens. Any vestiges of the actual battlefield—within the former Walter Reed Army Medical Center reservation nearby or sylvan and wooded Rock Creek Park to the west—appear destined to live on in obscurity. Nothing is marked, and city development at Walter Reed threatens to obliterate altogether the battlescape associated with the fighting there. Even Lincoln's inadequate remarks during interment at the battleground resting place seem more respectful to the men and the events at the time than the respect America gives today.

After 150 years, however, the Battle of Fort Stevens and Early's campaign on Washington remain filled with vignettes and "might-have-beens." On the heavy, smoke-filled evening of July 12, as Early's ragtag legions began their recessional, Confederate major Henry Kyd Douglas stood kibitzing with Early and other officers. At one point, Old Jube said in his high-pitched drawl, "We haven't taken Washington but we've scared Abe Lincoln like hell!" Douglas disrespectfully rejoined that at some point: "I think some other people were scared as hell's brimstone." Was it true, asked John Breckinridge, Early's deputy? "That's true," Early muttered, "but it won't appear in history." How apropos to how history and posterity have treated Lincoln and the Fort Stevens story.[2]

INTRODUCTION

We have no record that Lincoln's close brush with death at Fort Stevens frightened him. But behind the bravado lies a simple fact. Early's raid, which almost captured the nation's capital, almost killed or captured Lincoln and might have forced Ulysses S. Grant to relax his stranglehold on Richmond-Petersburg had occurred during a critical moment in the life of Lincoln and the nation. All that had gone before could have been erased in a single afternoon at Fort Stevens. All that followed could have appeared quite different as a result of what might have happened. In fact, even without Lincoln as a casualty, the audacity of Confederates so near actually did alter history. But for this single, two-day engagement scarcely mentioned in Civil War literature and considered but a skirmish by people then and now, today would not be today as we know it. Early's sharpshooters came that close to accomplishing the goal of decapitating the enemy's government, changing history, and redirecting the sentiments of both the northern populace and European governments toward peace. It all traces to Lincoln's adolescent-like but calculated desire to see a battle and be seen by his soldiers fighting for the Union. As it was, even Early's ultimately unsuccessful effort—highlighted by time delays, wretched marching conditions, plus two crisp battles, one of which saw Lincoln in person conduct affairs—sublimely altered the sagas. That thought is more worthy of our remembrance, respect, and commemoration. It is the essence of Lincoln and the Fort Stevens story.

About This Volume

This book provides a detailed, if not necessarily definitive, story of Abraham Lincoln and the Fort Stevens battle. Some observers styled it "the battle of the suburbs," and I have tried to use this more inclusive portrayal where pertinent. This is the third volume of a trilogy analyzing Jubal Early's 1864 campaign to capture Washington. Additionally, it also stands fifth in recounting attempts to defend the nation's capital during the Civil War. *The Day Lincoln Was Almost Shot* replicates in research and style my previous works, *Jubal Early's Raid on Washington, 1864*, and *Monocacy: The Battle That Saved Washington*. Preceding studies, *Symbol, Sword and Shield: Defending Washington during the Civil War* and *Mr. Lincoln's Forts: A Guide to the Civil War Defenses of Washington* (with coauthor Walton H. Owen) serve as more encompassing studies of the subject. In each of these volumes, extensive words of contemporary participants have been used. They are far better than the post hoc interpretative layering by modern historians John H. Cramer, Frank Vandiver, Glenn H. Worthington, Joseph Judge, Marc Leepson, and Brett W. Spaulding, and even me. Still, they are primary sources, not the definitive word, the material from which succeeding generations may work their own conclusions. Research files from all these works are deposited in the premier study and interpretive center at Fort Ward museum and park, Alexandria, Virginia, where Wally Owen serves as curator and to whom I am forever grateful for camaraderie, technical help, and historical curiosity about men and events of an era long past.

In truth, he and I both see a mystery in what was made available through a third party to exploring the details of the truth about Fort Stevens and Lincoln. Through the good offices of Mr. and Mrs. Joseph Scopin of Darnestown, Maryland, hitherto unavailable and unpublished source material has appeared to challenge contemporary accounts, veterans' memories, and the decades of "truth" about where President Lincoln actually stood to come under Rebel sharpshooter fire and to nearly lose his life. The unpublished collection of a Pennsylvania participant, Lewis Cass White, now owned by the Scopins, contains the pointed hand-sketch description of Surgeon Crawford (wounded while standing near Lincoln that day), which suggests possible misplacement of the Lincoln Boulder now atop the Fort Stevens parapet. Or, does it? Could Crawford's account be merely one more reminiscence of an aging warrior, an artistic rendition, however unique this one piece of evidence? Our friend and fellow "post-hole" digger for truth from evidence, Peter Seaborg, would be equally intrigued and excited about revisiting such an important event in the light of such new evidence. Were he here today he would join us in agreeing with the eternal truism that history is never dead, never done, and ever worthy of new exploration.

Notes

1. James M. McPherson, *Tried by War: Abraham Lincoln as Commander in Chief* (New York: Penguin, 2008), xiv; see also Eliot Cohen, *Supreme Command: Soldiers, Statesmen and Leadership in Wartime* (New York: Anchor, 2002), chapter 2; Geoffrey Perret, *Lincoln's War: The Untold Story of America's Greatest President as Commander in Chief* (New York: Random House, 2004), 366–68; Chester G. Hearn, *Lincoln, the Cabinet, and the Generals* (Baton Rouge: Louisiana State University Press, 2010), 238–41, as well as the venerable T. Harry Williams, *Lincoln and His Generals* (New York: Vintage, 1952), 324–28.

2. Henry Kyd Douglas, *I Rode with Stonewall* (Chapel Hill: University of North Carolina Press, 1940), 296; also Fred L. Ray, *Shock Troops of the Confederacy* (Asheville, NC: CFS Press, 2006), chapter 15.

MR. LINCOLN'S CAPITAL
AS CENTER OF GRAVITY

The sun was intense; the temperature was typically hot for July in Washington. At the barren grounds of Fort Stevens out beyond the city limits, yet still within the District of Columbia, a carriage pulled up amid the flotsam of the army camp and garrison. A tall man in a black suit and his wife somewhat more colorfully attired alighted and were met by army brass. "General, I am very glad to see you," said the tall figure, speaking directly to Major-General Horatio G. Wright and extending his hand. "This looks as though we were going to do something," was his almost inscrutable comment. "Mr. President," rejoined Wright and pointing at the fort, "if you'll just come along down there with me, I'll show you one of the prettiest little fights you could wish to see." Leaving Mrs. Lincoln at their carriage, Abraham Lincoln accompanied Wright into the work, adolescent like, anxious to see what was transpiring.[1]

The pair could hear the "pop pop" of musketry and the occasional report of one of the fort's big guns. The smell and sight of black powder smoke created a haze—almost a fog—mingling with the heat and humidity. Yet general and commander-in-chief rapidly strode toward the forward parapet. "No sooner were the words out of my mouth," Wright remembered later, "than I deeply regretted having uttered them." In hindsight, he recalled, "The President's life was far too valuable to be brought into danger by any careless words of mine." But Wright took him on into danger. Lincoln "not only accepted my invitation, but insisted upon accompanying me, notwithstanding all I could say to prevent him." "When I mounted that earthwork," recalled Wright, "there he was beside me, looking out upon the scene with a great deal of interest." In full view of the enemy and their eagle-eyed sharpshooters, the president of the United States, chief executive of the government, and head of the armed forces in a war of survival, stood there wanting to see the fight. It was a

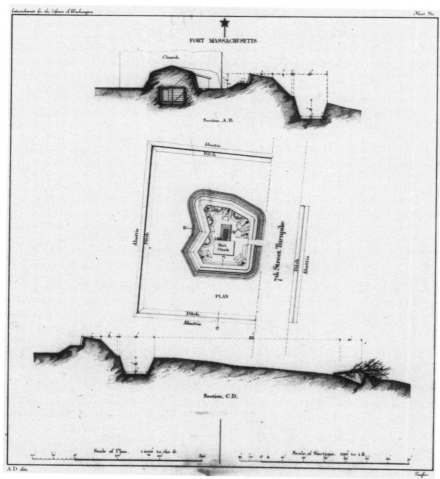

Fort Massachusetts, Engineering Drawing, 1862. *National Archives*

sight never to be repeated. One must wonder how it came to pass in the first place. Why did Lincoln willfully disregard his own safety for the opportunity to see a battle firsthand?

The Confluence of Jamie and Abe

A half-century separated the presidencies of Abraham Lincoln and James Madison. Lincoln was only five years old when the British burned Washington on August 24, 1814, during the War of 1812. Evidence suggests that Madison was present at what was dubbed the "Bladensburg races"—that ignominious defeat just outside the city that prompted the city's occupation and destruction of public buildings. Did Lincoln even know if Madison had been there and was possibly under hostile fire? Lincoln may well have not had that on his mind at Fort Stevens decades later. Yet he was surely aware of the plight of the fifth president—also an unpopular war executive and equally faced with a nation, capital, and people unprepared to cope with invasion and possible defeat. Madison and Lincoln both learned those lessons the hard way. The leap between what was discovered at Bladensburg and Fort Stevens was small. In 1814 and 1864, the United States, her seat of government, and her chief executive shared an experience that spoke to tradition—unpreparedness for the unexpected moves of an agile enemy.

Washington in 1814 was a work in progress—politically, culturally, and physically. Termed a town of houses with no streets and streets with no houses, it had not advanced much past adolescence. It was a mere village of 8,308 souls, two thousand of whom were held in bondage. Madison's wife, Dolley, and other presidential wives attempted to develop a society, while the dreams of city planners Pierre L'Enfant and Andrew Ellicott languished in the few public buildings such as the president's mansion and capitol building and randomly placed 109 "habitable" brick houses and 263 wooden abodes. Perhaps the three thousand residents (white and black, free and enslaved) had more aspirations for the unfinished city than did Americans elsewhere. The place assumed more notoriety when the nation and its leaders bumbled into a second "melancholy business of war," as Mrs. Madison termed the conflict with Great Britain.[2]

Surely other American cities had greater promise. Boston, New York, and Philadelphia, to be sure, held long-time commercial importance. Even Baltimore, the country's third most populous metropolis, could command attention if only because of her record as a haven for privateers that threatened Great Britain's maritime supremacy. Still, to declare that Washington "had no practical, strategic importance," quoting Dolley Madison's latest biographer, would seem unjust, even by Napoleonic-era standards. Any nation's governmental center and seat of policy, planning, and administration of national affairs and one boasting of logistical facilities such as an active and energetic navy yard and army arsenal—however distant from the coast and innocuous in form—suggested some strategic value. The young American government had genuflected to this fact with the construction of the modest Fort Warburton (often styled Washington), down river from the city and across the Potomac from Mount Vernon. Still, the relative security of the capital rested mainly upon wishful thinking and the conduct of the war on distant national borders, particularly with British Canada. From early 1813, His Majesty's government had opened offensive military activities in the Chesapeake region with the intent of drawing America's military focus away from Canada.[3]

About fifty miles away from Baltimore, Washington might have taken more alarm a year earlier when raiding, pillaging, and torching operations had become the British way of war in the region. Practicing offense as a good defense, Vice Admiral Sir Alexander Cochrane and Major-General Robert Ross led the campaign in the Chesapeake region. They understood the psychological importance of taking Washington as well as Baltimore even if Madison's Secretary of War, John Armstrong, interpreted the latter rather than the former as the point of danger. In fact, Armstrong would become the victim for what transpired when he pompously tried to orchestrate affairs absent more military expertise. The president himself wasn't so sure about which city faced the greatest danger, but he remained reluctant to withdraw the small, regular army from elsewhere to defend against this uncertainty close to home.

Americans' almost mystical belief in the "Minuteman" paradigm of citizen defense in response to British actions would rest with militia and civilian volunteers buttressed at best with small numbers of Commodore Joshua Barney's flotilla men and marines. On paper, perhaps ten thousand to twelve thousand Americans could be brought into the field in that fashion. But the British raider strategy kept the Americans off balance. Madison and his cabinet as well as the militia commanders began to realize Washington, not Baltimore, might be the Redcoats' target by midsummer. Still, when a more formidable expedition came ashore at Benedict near the mouth of the Patuxent River on August 20, the Americans wavered as to its intent. Were the British after Barney's troublesome mosquito flotilla of gunboats, Brigadier General William H. Winder's disputatious militia, or Washington itself? The issue remained in doubt from August 20 until 24. It became clear only by noon on the twenty-fourth when British veterans of the Napoleonic campaigns marched into Bladensburg astride the Washington to Baltimore highway and the first unprotected crossing of the Anacostia or eastern branch of the Potomac north of the capital.[4]

"The Bladensburg Races" as Precedent

There really wasn't much to the ensuing battle of Bladensburg. Upward of 6,900 American militia and regulars and eighteen guns squared off against 4,500 seasoned British veterans with only three guns but sixty intimidating rocket launchers. Winder's motley force of Maryland and D.C. militia (eventually bolstered by Barney's marines and flotilla "tars") put up a spirited fight. They took their stand first at the bridge at the edge of town and then on high ground nearly a mile to the south behind Tournecliffe's bridge over a small creek, actually quite near the fashionably notorious wooded dueling grounds. Winder, never particularly competent anyway, became flustered when the nation's high command including Madison, Secretary of

State James Monroe (thirty years out of Revolutionary War uniform but still fancying himself capable of command and control), Armstrong (another Revolutionary War officer delusional of his relevant experience and presumed right to command in the field), and even Secretary of the Navy William Jones and Attorney General Richard Rush all arrived from the city at various times. This coterie appeared to interfere rather than help battle preparations. Madison wanted to fulfill his constitutional role as commander-in-chief in the field while bolstering the backbone of the militia by presidential presence in the decisive fight. Arriving at a gallop, the presidential party rushed to the river bridge only to be saved from possible capture when a former War Department clerk now ersatz scout, William Simmons, told them that the British had arrived in town. Turning abruptly in disbelief, Madison and company rushed back to American lines seeking Winder, Armstrong, or anyone else presumed to be in authority.[5]

The battle was about to begin as the commander-in-chief, his entourage, and military commanders consulted on the state of affairs. Perhaps it was ten or eleven in the morning. The multihued American militiamen stood in some disarray, the British about to advance in desultory fashion as Ross peered through his spyglass to see hills south of the river swarming with the enemy. About this time, British rocketeer Lieutenant John Lawrence lit off a barrage of Sir William Congreve's terrifying if erratic missiles, spooking the Yankee defenders. Winder tried to rally them, but sensing the danger to the president, he suggested that the head of state and his party move back from what had become the initial battle line. Madison muttered something about letting military men handle military matters and directed, "Come, General Armstrong, come Colonel Monroe, let us go and leave it to the commanding general." At this point, Madison may have become the first president and commander-in-chief to brave enemy fire while in office—if the high-arching Congreves could be considered enemy fire. Anyway, the presidential party apparently retired to Winder's main position. By two in the afternoon, the American position at the bridge had collapsed, with the defenders streaming off on a side road to Georgetown. Winder remained with the main force on higher ground facing the oncoming British.[6]

The initial militia collapse, the confused and inept leadership of Winder and others, and the largely ineffective American defense against seasoned British veterans all set the stage for the final phase of the contest. Madison ostensibly remained to witness matters—or so claimed the D.C. banker and his friend, Jacob Barker. "The president had a full view of the conflict, and noticed the havoc made [by Barney's guns]" that winnowed British ranks. The veterans unflinchingly pressed forward, and they were soon outflanked and overrun even that second line of American defenses, said Barker later. Apparently only then did Madison as well as the other worthies break for Washington, acknowledging obvious defeat. Whether or not the fifth president of the United States actually came under British fire during this final phase of the disaster has never been proven conclusively. That he had been present at the battle, witnessed events, and was part of what became known as the "Bladensburg races" or rout of the Americans seems plausible. Attorney General Richard Rush remembered later that "the Secretary of War and commanding general were in close view of the front line, as was the President, doing what they could to encourage the resistance," however, "it soon became ineffectual." In any event, a stunned and dejected James Madison retired to the White House (his wife Dolley a half-hour ahead in flight), his army strung out all the six miles back to Bladensburg. In the end, perhaps one hundred Americans were killed and wounded in the battle, with another 100 to 120 captured. Two hundred of His Majesty's finest fell in gaining the prize—Washington, which they entered triumphantly by eight that evening.[7]

The British immediately looked to torch the city. Cockburn was all for burning the whole place. But Ross only wanted to level the public buildings in retaliation for the American destruction of British facilities in Upper Canada the previous year. The upshot was the wholesale loss of the rather inconspicuous American capitol (two freestone buildings linked only by a one-hundred-foot wooden gallery or bridge), the executive mansion, and the treasury building, although remarkably the patent office emerged unscathed. The office of an anti-British newspaper *National Intelligencer* also went up in smoke, while American commodore Thomas Tingey did the work for the enemy by blowing up the navy yard. When the British attempted to destroy stores at the army's Greenlief Point arsenal, they self-inflicted casualties in a premature explosion of gunpowder. The sudden appearance of a late summer thunderstorm with hurricane-force winds plus other signs of civil resistance further spooked the raiders. By the next evening, they left the smoldering city and marched back to their ships at Benedict. Meanwhile, a Royal Naval squadron had inched its way over the Potomac River shoals, stood by as the Fort Warburton commander blew up his own post, and then took the meek surrender of the Alexandria, Virginia, town fathers. By August 26, it was all over, and the refugees—including the Madisons—trickled back to pick up the pieces of what had been both their home and seat of government scarcely a week before.[8]

Bladensburg and the British destruction of Washington did accomplish some good. Secretary of War Armstrong left office, bearing full public scorn for the loss. He blamed just about everyone but himself. If the green troops at Bladensburg had been "faithful to themselves and country," they would have defeated the enemy and saved the capital, he claimed. The "races" notwithstanding, the disaster apparently provided a catalyst for further fighting the British (although peace negotiations were well under way) and building a sense of nationalism. Also, some locals such as Washington Federalist Rosalie Stier Calvert felt that the burning of the Capitol and the White House was the best thing that had happened in a long while. "This has finally settled the question of whether the seat of government would stay here," she declared. Such newfound confidence in the capital translated to comments within two years that "all of Washington is now jumping alive," with visitors and politicians arriving daily as everything seemed to hang upon the restored government. The British actions had cleared away "elegant skeletons, half-finished, half-dilapidated structures." This second war with the mother country and a particularly humiliating act convinced Americans that they deserved "the most splendid public edifices in the world" that were not "incompatible with the purest principles of republican government."[9]

As Calvert concluded, "In the future they will no longer keep trying to change it and as long as the union stands, the government will remain in Washington, much to the envy of other American cities." To protect a reborn nation's capital, the Madison administration sent Major Pierre L'Enfant to construct new river defenses. He did not last long, and it fell to Lieutenant Colonel Walker K. Armistead to fashion what became Fort Washington. This work provided the only defense of the city until the Civil War. Today it stands as a public park, preserved as a monument more to coastal fortification architecture and reactive recognition of vulnerability than a site for any decisive moment in protecting the capital. Most of all, this silent sentinel provides testament that officials still looked to the water threat to the capital, not the manner in which Cockburn and Ross actually got into the city, that visit notwithstanding.

Still, of Bladensburg—what a story for the future! What an unhappy precedent for generations of worry in official Washington. A U.S. president was under hostile fire, or at least in a hostile fire zone if not precisely targeted. Blatantly unmindful of the danger when dashing to Bladensburg and almost into the arms of the enemy, "little Jamie" Madison had come close to being the first casualty of an American head-of-state. Meddling and petulance by cabinet members charged with national security as well as the tactical conduct of battle also attended the affair. Lack of clear command structure surfaced before and during the disaster and was coupled with the costly reliance upon untrained citizen soldiers as the government vacillated about the danger and refused to recall regular or veteran troops from other operations. Certainly Bladensburg underscored the questionably hoary tradition of Cincinnatus or minutemen and state troops undertaking national combat responsibilities unready for the responsibility. Then, too, inadequate intelligence about the deceptive enemy (if nonetheless divided in its own Chesapeake intentions, but tactically superior to American arms) contributed to the debacle. The political basis for military appointments led to marginally qualified and incapable combat commanders defending the national capital. It was all there for the future.

Above all, in the ashes of official Washington hung the stigma of an inadequately fortified, improperly garrisoned, and an unready defense system for Washington in peace or war. Author Garry Wills declares that Great Britain's tidewater

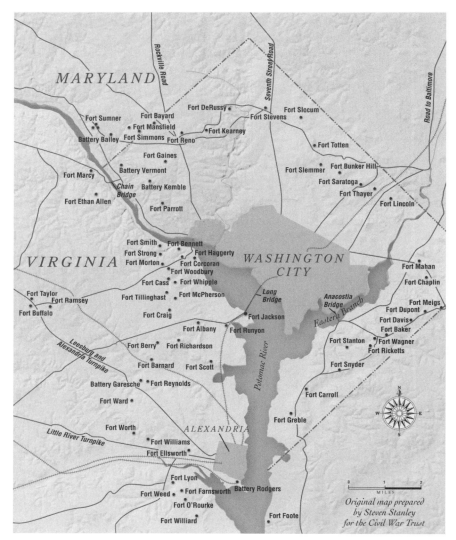

Civil War Defenses of Washington, map by Steven Stanley. *Civil War Trust*

expedition against the capital and the resulting battle at Bladensburg "amounts to a perfect study of what was wrong with Madison's conduct of the war." His "intimate involvement with every aspect of this event is unlike his more remote connection with other developments," observes Wills. His failure to save Washington "explains much about setbacks elsewhere." It begs the question of a president fifty years later and how the points advanced by Wills in regard to Madison and defending Washington might come back to haunt the conduct and oversight of the next president facing similar dilemmas. Such dilemmas included the role of the commander-in-chief on the battlefield. Abraham Lincoln would be that next president.[10]

Uncle Sam's Political Center of Gravity

Between 1814 and 1864 would come a half-century of nation and capital building. Everyone continued to scoff at a forest adorned by a city, a "Capitol" wanting a city, or even to English author Charles Dickens in 1841, "Spacious avenues that begin in nothing and lead nowhere; streets a mile long that only want houses, roads, and inhabitants; public buildings that need but a public to be complete; and ornaments of great thoroughfares which only need greater thoroughfares to ornament." He would sneer, "Some might fancy the season over and most of the houses gone out of town with their masters." It was a "monument to a deceased project," decided the English writer, although even he missed the lively social whirl that attended Washington in season when enlarged numbers of governmental and diplomatic sectors made the shabby physical city sparkle with activity. The blatant effrontery of Hiram Powers's statue *Greek Slave* on public view at wealthy financier W. W. Corcoran's gallery almost flaunted the bumptious nature of an energetic, expansive nation itself. The first railroad and telegraph came to the city and the Mexican War embroiled yet another president in controversy, but America and its capital matured ever so slowly. The fourteen thousand people of the populace in 1800 grew to 51,687 by midcentury (despite retrocession of the Virginia part of the District of Columbia back to the commonwealth). Ten years later, on the eve of the great Sectional Conflict in 1860, seventy-five thousand whites, free blacks, and slaves jostled one another on the banks of the Potomac. Washington, by this time, also enjoyed the reputation as a way station on the Underground Railroad for southern slaves escaping northward to freedom beyond the Mason-Dixon line dividing the free state of Pennsylvania from slaveholding Maryland.[11]

Washington was the symbol of a failing state by 1860. The political capital was as badly fractured as the country it represented. Author Nathaniel Hawthorne had it right: "If Washington was really the keystone of the Union, then the Union was not worth saving." As incomplete and unpolished as the Great Project itself, its one fort defended against foreign foe, not domestic insurrection. Yet that was what the government and its city faced when secession turned into rebellion and war by the winter and spring of 1861. That was the crisis faced by president-elect Abraham Lincoln when he arrived in Washington at six a.m. on February 23. Thanks to the venerable general-in-chief Winfield Scott, his younger subordinate Colonel Charles

P. Stone, who took hold of the District of Columbia militia, and a call for regular units from as far away as Carlisle Barracks, Pennsylvania, and Fort Leavenworth, Kansas, the electoral ballots were duly counted, and Lincoln took the oath of office on March 4. A rump Congress endeavored to compromise, with the continuing departure of members reflecting their states' wishes. The most acute crisis attended South Carolina's firing on Fort Sumter in April, Lincoln's immediate call for state militia to suppress insurrection, and what authors John and Charles Lockwood term the subsequent *twelve days that shook the Union*, with a supposed "siege of Washington." It was hardly that, for there was no enemy army like in 1814, and the rumored secessionist columns were just rumors, more productive for fanning the paranoia of Lincoln and his advisers before northern militia volunteers brought relief. All of this convinced the government that it needed a sword and shield to protect the symbol of the Union—Washington.[12]

Washington was now the political center of gravity for the North, the Union, and the remaining United States. Four years of war would convert the capital city into the logistical and command nerve center of the nation. In effect, an expanding city in size and function would form the Union's "symbol, sword and shield." Mr. Lincoln may have found the metropolis in February 1861 teetering on being captured by either Maryland and Virginia insurrectionists and requiring something more than a questionable local militia contingent or small coterie of marines at their barracks on Eighth Street, sailors from the navy yard, a contingent of army ordnance men at the arsenal, and a bunch of dottery, aging staff officers from the War and Navy departments adjacent to the White House. But the war would change all this—for the city, the nation, and most assuredly Mr. Lincoln. Between them, the sixteenth president, his administration, the uniformed war leaders, and the response of the people in what even he termed *a people's war* would turn Washington into something more like a "fortress." Lincoln's personal experience in February had much to do with that transition.[13]

Yet what exactly connoted a fortress? And why did America's capital city need to become one? A figure of speech from biblical entry or a professional term coined by generations of the military—that remains the question vital to our understanding. Certainly, Washington—like all cities north and south that became centerpieces in the Civil War's zones of combat—needed forts (fortifications containing troop garrisons). But would it need to become in and of itself a fortress (a fortification enclosing a town within its walls or confines)? Europeans understood the concept; they had for centuries. The great French engineer Marshal Sebastien Vauban developed a system of fortifications as, had, indeed, the ancient Romans and their successors through the Dark and Middle Ages and into the period of the so-called cabinet wars. Louisbourg in Nova Scotia as well as Luxembourg, capital of the tiny country of the same name in northwest Europe, provided early examples. Later fortresses such as Verdun and Strasbourg in play between French and German war makers defined the continental idea.

But that was Europe, this was America, land of the free and unpretentious. Necessarily protected only by random coastal forts or hinterland posts, eschewing symbols of martial pomp, military engineering might better serve the construction of, not the guarding of, a republican capital. Still, this was just what policymakers would create for Washington during the Civil War. Politicians and soldiers would surround what became the wartime political and military nerve center—a bustling command post and logistics center as well as the seat of government, with the largest array of field fortifications in North America. Under Lincoln and his generals, it became aptly termed "Fortress Washington." The president had discovered this need when he so unceremoniously slipped into the capital in the dead of a February night.[14]

Changing Mr. Lincoln's City

Not that anyone would have anticipated this in 1861. America's capital city remained more a scruffy joke. Her phoenixlike rise from the 1814 ashes had gone into constructing public buildings rather than building a majestic urban center. "Planned on a scale of surpassing grandeur, its architectural execution is almost contemptible," commented G. W. Bagby in January 1861. "There is no state in the world which possesses proportionately so small, scantily populated, and shabby a capital as the American Union," suggested J. G. Kohl about the same time. Set among wooded hills and wide panoramas of the valley of the Potomac, its low elevation on the riverbanks meant swamps, stagnant surface water, and periodic flooding. Mosquitoes and flies lifted typhoid, tuberculosis, malaria, and dysentery—even cholera—over the human landscape. Dull brick and squalid wooden buildings hovered on the edge of the few public edifices—themselves pretentious sentinels of Greco-Roman tradition. As has been noted ever since, Washington City "presented, at best, an unfinished appearance." Symbolic of and presiding over this work in progress was the imposing, incomplete Capitol building. This was the Washington that greeted Lincoln.[15]

Bagby said it best. Mr. Lincoln's Washington was a city without commerce and without manufactures. Despite the U.S. Treasury, it was "the home of everything but affluence." Houses were low, rents were high; streets were broad, crossings were narrow; and hacks were black with their horses white. Public squares were triangular, while the Capitol was oval, and the water was so soft "that it is hard to drink it even with the admixture of alcohol." It had a monument never to be finished, a Capitol "that is to have a dome, a scientific institute which does nothing but report the rise and fall of the thermometer." Two pieces of equestrian statuary—to George Washington and Andrew Jackson—"would be a waste of time to criticise." Boasting a stream dignified by the name of Rome's river, the Tiber Creek streamlet presented more the size and appearance of a "vein in a dirty man's arm." The city had a canal—"a mud puddle during one half of the day and an empty ditch during the other." Steady rain of a fortnight's duration would see a half-hour of sunlight turn the streets into dustbowls. The men were fine looking, the women homely. Still, Babgy could say that "Washington is progressing rapidly" as the advent of Lincoln, secession, and war promised change. He pronounced boldly but prophetically: "Its destiny is that of the Union."[16]

Another observer, Captain Thomas M. Woodruff of the Fifth U.S. Infantry, commented how the "dome of the Capitol had only reached to the second tier of the columns," and the House and Senate wings "were quite incomplete." The Patent Office's northern front and the Patent Office's inner court were likewise in a state of construction. The post office was only one-third finished, and only the east front of the Treasury building existed. State, war, and navy departments were housed in insignificant structures near the White House. The voluntarily subscribed Washington Monument was "at a standstill" (resulting in the clear demarcation of marble construction between prewar and postwar endeavor discernible even today). Only Pennsylvania Avenue and perhaps one mile of Seventh Street bore anything resembling paving—cobblestones—which exacerbated unpaved dust and mud edges and other thoroughfares. A newcomer to the city with the first northern militia arrivals to save Washington from capture in the spring of 1861 confused his unit's huge Sibley tent with the unfinished Capitol building![17]

There was more to Civil War Washington than just the public buildings, of course. Hotels such as the Willard (whose lobby became infamously immortalized by the later term *lobbyist*, or seeker of office, contracts, favor, and fortune), National, Kirkwood House, and St. Charles could be found on Pennsylvania Avenue or just east of the Capitol (where the famous Carroll Row had catered decades earlier to young congressman Lincoln of Illinois). A major attraction was photographer Mathew Brady's opulent art gallery on The Avenue, while City Hall was not far away, north on Fourth Street Northwest. The city's principal market stood where the National Archives dominates today. The early railroad stations of the Baltimore & Ohio and Washington & Alexandria lines hovered a stone's throw northwest of the Capitol. And citizens might partake of performances at National or Ford's theaters if so inclined.

The information nerve center for out-of-town newspapers stood just off Pennsylvania Avenue on Fourteenth Street, where today the National Press Building preserves their legacy. Hometown newspapers such as the *Evening Star* and the *National Intelligencer* had independent locations. Interspersed in this bustling city life was an aging business district predominating on F Street—residences, oyster palaces, restaurants, and seamy establishments. Elegant city churches such as Episcopal Church of the Epiphany and St. John's churches, New York Avenue Presbyterian, St. Patrick's Roman Catholic, and others jostled for space in the cityscape. Banker Corcoran's brand new art gallery intruded in 1861 before it succumbed to wartime military takeover for space. A naval National Observatory, looking remarkably like the Royal Observatory at Greenwich outside London, stood on a similar eminence, in the city's West End on the way to Georgetown. But by this point sightseers would be reaching toward the fringes of the city proper. From sketches and prints of the period, one may be sure that much of the city's marginal elegance came from the green space around public buildings.[18]

To completely appreciate the "symbol, sword and shield" appellation for Washington, however, is to venture beyond the established cityscape of the time. Confusion always attended the terms—was it Washington, the District of Columbia, and how did Georgetown and Alexandria or even tiny crossroad hamlets such as Tennallytown or Brightwood play into the original scope as separate entities? By 1861, one could identify Alexandria (as both city and county) with enemy or secessionist territory across the Potomac. But Georgetown (however divided its residents) remained within the District, as did Washington City (the urbanized area south of Boundary Street) and Washington County (the area beyond both the city and Georgetown). All were prominent parts of the Civil War story. Indeed, all of these distinguishing parts of Washington in one way or another became part of what the late historian Richard Lee termed "The Arsenal of the North." Thus, the city became not just the nation's wartime political and nerve center but also the logistical, training, and hospital complex. Naturally, this complex formed a target for the Confederacy. Greater Washington of the time would be a war zone requiring strategic focus as well as operational planning and implementation.[19]

In fact, by 1862, Washington's citizens could truthfully tell transiting Union troops that the town had "become a changed city, changed in appearance, but changed more in sentiment." Antislavery lectures would be delivered and applauded, "which before would not have been thought of, much less tolerated." Emancipation arrived first in the federal city—April 1862, to be exact. "Sages of the Capital" convened, transacted business, and engaged the attention of every cognizant man, woman, and child throughout the republic because "the destinies of unborn generations are to be affected by that august body at this critical time." Legislation for homestead aid, transcontinental railroad construction, and a new tariff protecting domestic industry development, not to speak of intrusive government actions concerning the confiscation of property and the extraction of manpower, all related to the prosecution of a war to suppress rebellion.[20]

By midwar, Washington/Alexandria became the "base headquarters of the northern armies" and central depot in particular for those involved in eastern campaigns. Everything in town now focused on the war. Campgrounds, hospitals, and a host of war workers and refugee slaves inundated the place, "adding tremendously to the public burdens." Still, one resident, Mary Clemmer Ames, remembered the place in 1862 as no great improvement over the antebellum city. Capitol Hill stretched "desolate and dreary" into "an uninhabited desert, high above the mud of the West End." Arid hills and sodden pathways showed alike "the horrid trail of war." Forts bristled from every hilltop; soldiers were entrenched at every gateway. Shed hospitals occupied acres in every suburb, while churches, art galleries, and private mansions were filled with "the wounded and dying of the American armies." She bemoaned the "endless roll of the army wagon" that never stilled, while "the rattle of the anguish-laden ambulance, the piercing cries of the sufferers whom it carried" rendered dreadful sounds morning, noon, and night. She saw the streets "filled with marching troops, with new regiments, their hearts strong and eager, their virgin banners all untarnished" as they marched up Pennsylvania Avenue, playing songs with words such as "the girl I left behind me" as if "they had come to holiday glory—to easy victory." But the thoroughfares were nonetheless filled, too, with foot-sore, sunburned, and weary veterans, "their clothes begrimed, their banners torn, their hearts sick with hope deferred, ready to die with the anguish of long defeat." Every moment "had its drum-beat, every hour was alive with the tramp of troops going, coming." From such word pictures sprang the context of Washington in the critical summer of 1864.[21]

Emergence of the Fortress

On October 16, 1861, Scottish peer Sir James Ferguson of Kilkerran jotted in his diary of North American travels how he had ridden out from Washington via "the Long Bridge" to "Upton's Hill." All along the way from the Potomac to Munson's Hill "are field fortifications of the strongest kind; on every hillock is a closed work with deep ditch, and guns mounted at the angles en barbette, and in embrasures." The bridgehead "is strongly fortified [Fort Runyon]" and "the top of the slope, half a mile in advance, has a long line of parapet eight or ten feet high, neatly finished, with steps on the interior face for the defenders." "The numerous 'lumbermen' from the Northern States" in the volunteer units had leveled woods "the whole way between the lines," thus rendering any "advance of an enemy impracticable, except by the roads, which are entirely commanded at every point." There were "undoubtedly great numbers of troops on this position"—Ferguson, as much an intelligence agent as an innocent traveler, quoted the estimates of 140,000 to 200,000—so that "here and around Washington there seem to be camps and posts enough to warrant the belief." He concluded by tweaking the quality of the Union army by stating bluntly,

"M'Clellan's [*sic*] system of fortifying every inch does not look as if he had much confidence in the steadiness of his troops."[22]

Transformation of the Washington neighborhood preceded Union general George B. McClellan by a good six months. Indeed, those six months had not been particularly promising for Lincoln and his government. The city had been a mixing bowl of rumors, fear, and uncertainty. It had no natural strength, sprawled along the riverbanks. Fort Washington downriver had been initially manned solely by a drunken caretaker ordnance sergeant. On January 5, 1861, Secretary of War Isaac Toucey sent Captain Algernon S. Taylor and forty marines "to protect public property" at the work—a phrase used by the federal government to defend forts and arsenals all over the rebellious South. Finally, sufficient northern troops rallied to the relief of Lincoln and his city, and by May, these first defenders (including loyal D.C. militiamen) filed across bridges and went by boat to brush away initial armed secessionist contingents who had finally gathered from Arlington Heights to Alexandria.[23]

The first martyr soon appeared, and the first preliminary forts were dug to defend the southern approach to the city. The two were fused when the fort on Shuter's Hill behind Alexandria was named for Colonel Elmer Ellsworth. He was Lincoln's friend from Chicago, cut down as he brazenly removed a Rebel banner in that town's business section. Thus were born the first elements of Fortress Washington—fortifications named for fallen Union heroes, located to protect greater wartime economic as well as political Washington, the port city and rail terminus to Alexandria as well. When Confederate authorities moved their own capital from Montgomery, Alabama, to Richmond, Virginia, the conflict in the east became "A Hundred Mile War" between the seats of government. This action would dictate the tempo for the war in the east. The frontier between national sections shifted to the Potomac. In turn this posed a new point of danger for the Lincoln government. A possible confrontation point developed on the southern side of the city where Confederate authorities began troop concentrations at Manassas Junction and Fairfax Courthouse, Virginia, that seemingly threatened Washington. Of course, they also blocked any Union advance to restore the Old Dominion to the Union. Before long, politicians and citizens and even the volunteer soldiery clamored "on to Richmond." Unprepared as both sides might be, battle beckoned. The way lay squarely south on the Orange and Alexandria railroad from the banks of the Potomac. The result would be two armies of citizen soldiery (militia turned volunteers) with insufficient training and stamina but great enthusiasm clashing on July 21, 1861, near Manassas at Bull Run. This first big battle between Americans resulted in another Bladensburg for U.S. forces. Unlike the 1814 disaster, however, defeated Union forces of Brigadier General Irwin McDowell did not disperse. The enemy did not capture or sack the nation's capital. Yet like the earlier catastrophe, the result catalyzed national hearts and minds, energy and resources for a greater struggle.[24]

Confederates proved incapable of mounting pursuit after their Manassas victory that might have carried them across the Potomac. The flotsam of the Union army escaped, regrouped, reorganized, and the Lincoln administration brought in a new commander to whip the boys in blue back into shape. George B. McClellan later claimed to have found "no army to command—a mere collection of regiments cowering on the banks of the Potomac, some perfectly raw, others dispirited by the recent defeat," with the city itself virtually in condition "to have been taken by a dash of a regiment of cavalry." Typical of McClellanite hyperbole, perhaps, the fifty-thousand-member infantry, less than one thousand cavalry members, and barely 650 artillerymen (nine imperfect batteries of nine guns) constituted no more than disassembled bricks with which to build a structure—the men, rudiments, or organization and the shame out of defeat. But the "Little Napoleon" (as he was styled at this point) was good at just that—assembling and making ready. Part of his bricks was the early independent forts strung out on high ground guarding the southern entre to Washington. The amassed soldiery provided the straw. Happily, even before Bull Run, Congress had looked to providing the means for building a chain of forts to protect the city, even north of the Potomac and east of the Anacostia. So McClellan blithely envisioned a "system" of linked forty-eight forts, lunettes, redoubts, and batteries for three hundred guns—all supported by the field army. Engineer major John Gross Barnard, a capable, middle-aged, quite deaf, but very dedicated soldier-scientist received the mission of oversight and construction. Over the following months, Barnard became known as the father of the Defenses of Washington for what he accomplished.[25]

Barnard felt there was no time to prepare elaborate plans or detailed estimates. He and his engineers, working with the volunteer soldiers and hired labor, quickly used the stern law of "military necessity" to fashion what McClellan had in mind. But the threat shifted by fall to an approach that defied their efforts. Confederate general Joseph E. Johnston stationed outposts as close as Fairfax and Falls Church but kept his main defense line anchored from Aquia Landing on the Potomac to Leesburg upstream from Washington. The most threatened point after October became the Potomac River—not anything affecting Fort Washington, but rather a series of Virginia shore batteries that closed the river to commerce, blockading the city. The navy supplanted the army in countermoves to keep the city from starving. The blockade was lifted only the following spring when Johnston retired as McClellan undertook a land offensive with his massive new Army of the Potomac, the maneuver force that theoretically would keep the enemy from Washington's doorsteps. Low water in the upper Potomac that late summer and autumn of 1861 fretted army officials, and a number of volunteer regiments were sent to encamp, guard, and eventually begin fortifying the back-door approaches on the north side of the capital. Passages from the aqueduct water supply downstream from the Great Falls to the Frederick-Georgetown turnpike at Tennallytown, thence eastward to a similar ingress at Seventh Street Road at Brightwood and on to the Baltimore & Ohio railroad and nearby turnpike from Bladensburg and Baltimore (frankly quite close to the infamous battlegrounds of 1814) gained attention.

Of course, the politicians soon intruded. Reflecting on the disasters of Bull Run and even more recently at Ball's Bluff in October, Congress appointed a Joint Committee on the Conduct of the War, and legislators took to instructing the military how to fortify the city. Pondering the rollercoaster fortunes of spending money, Senator Preston King reflected the thoughts of many on Capitol Hill when Barnard had asked for an additional $150,000 appropriation for "completing the defenses of Washington" on December 7. "I would not expend any additional cent on the fortifications of Washington," proclaimed King. In his opinion (and the fighting generals as well), "the best defense for Washington is the destruction of our enemies where they can be found—at a distance from Washington. What politicians and their constituents wanted was an unsheathing of the sword, not burnishing of the shield."[26]

Bladensburg in 1814 had established precedent—a harsh one at that. Then, by the end of 1861, the warring Union and Confederate governments had determined competing centers of gravity that would set the course for the Civil War in the east. They could be simply identified as national capitals of Washington and Richmond with two field armies—blue and gray—in Virginia. And all four of those centers of gravity were inextricably entwined. For the moment, Washington with its protective force backed by its fortified shield commanded the most attention. But that fact would ebb and flow among politicians and soldiers. Memories of Bladensburg and the torching of Washington by the British five decades before fell before the more immediate disaster at Bull Run. Mr. Lincoln's city experienced growth, diversified meaning, and new focus—much as did its chief executive and its protective sword and shield. Washington as symbol as well as reality remained much as it had in 1814—a target for an enemy.

Writing in January 1886 about the attack on the nation's capital that would actually occur in 1864, Vermont veteran of that event A. A. Hayes could suggest, "It is indeed hard to realize, as one walks along the splendid streets and avenues of modern Washington, where signs of peace and prosperity appear on every hand, that twenty-one years ago, it was a heavily fortified and garrisoned stronghold, and rightly so, for here were not only the seats of the civil government, but also the HQ [headquarters], the rallying point, the supply depots of the vast armies of the Union." Hayes had watched the transformation, just as he would Mr. Lincoln's city in its time of direst peril.[27]

17

Notes

1. Recounted in John Clagett Proctor, *Proctor's Washington and Environs* (Washington, DC: self-published, 1949), 350.

2. Catherine Allgor, *A Perfect Union: Dolley Madison and the Creation of the American Nation* (New York: Henry Holt, 2006), 305, also 45–62, inter alia.

3. See Christopher T. George, *Terror on the Chesapeake: The War of 1812 on the Bay* (Shippensburg, PA: White Mane, 2000), chapters 1–7; Allgor, *A Perfect Union*, 309. Two volumes appearing at the time of the bicentennial of the War of 1812 are worth notice: Troy Bickham, *The Weight of Vengeance: The United States, the British Empire, and the War of 1812* (New York/Oxford: Oxford University Press, 2012), 165–70, and J. C. A. Stagg, *The War of 1812: Conflict for a Continent* (New York/Cambridge: Cambridge University Press, 2012), 126–31.

4. George, *Terror on the Chesapeake*, chapter 7; Anthony S. Pitch, *The Burning of Washington: The British Invasion of 1814* (Annapolis: Naval Institute Press, 1998), chapter 6; Walter Lord, *The Dawn's Early Light* (New York: W. W. Norton, 1972), chapter 5.

5. The battle may be followed in George, *Terror on the Chesapeake*, chapter 8; Pitch, *Burning of Washington*, chapter 7; Lord, *Dawn's Early Light*, chapter 5, and more recently, Hugh Howard, *Mr. and Mrs. Madison's War: America's First Couple and the Second War of Independence* (London: Bloomsbury Press, 2012), chapter 7.

6. Lord, *Dawn's Early Light*, chapter 8; George, *Terror on the Chesapeake*, chapter 6; Pitch, *Burning of Washington*, chapter 7, especially page 69.

7. Ibid., George, page 104, quoting Jacob Barker, *Incidents in the Life of Jacob Barker* (Freeport, NY: Books for Libraries Press, 1970, reprint of 1858 edition), 121; John S. Williams, *History of the Invasion and Capture of Washington and of the Events Which Preceded and Followed* (New York: Harper and Brothers, 1857), 279; David S. Heidler and Jeanne T. Heidler, *Encyclopedia of the War of 1812* (Annapolis: Naval Institute Press, 1997), 56; Robert S. Quimby, *The U.S. Army in the War of 1812: An Operational and Command Study* (East Lansing: Michigan State University Press, 1997), 689.

8. George, *Terror on the Chesapeake*, chapter 9; Pitch, *Burning of Washington*, especially 113, 138–39.

9. Allgor, *A Perfect Union*, 336–37 and 169.

10. Garry Wills, *James Madison* (New York: Henry Holt, 2002), chapter 11.

11. Federal Writers' Project, Works Project Administration, *Washington: City and Capital* (Washington, DC: Government Printing Office, 1937), 53–56.

12. See Benjamin Franklin Cooling III, in *Symbol, Sword and Shield: Defending Washington during the Civil War* (Hamden, CT: Shoestring Press/Shippensburg, PA: White Mane Publishing, 1975/1991), chapter 1, and Charles Lockwood and John Lookwood, *The Siege of Washington: The Untold Story of the Twelve Days That Shook the Union* (New York: Oxford University Press, 2011).

13. The phrase *symbol, sword and shield* derives from District of Columbia Civil War Centennial Commission chairman Paul J. Sedgwick's studies of the roles played by and for Washington during the war; see his *Study in Patriotism 1861–1865* (Washington, DC: Dis-

trict of Columbia Civil War Centennial Commission, 1962, 1965) that combined separately published pamphlets bearing that rubric. On the militia of the city, see Ed Hendrickson, "Defending Washington: The District of Columbia Militia, 1861," *Washington History* 23 (2011): 37–58; Hawthorne was cited with agreement by English reporter Edward Dicey in his 1863 publication, *Six Months in the Federal States* (New York: Macmillan, 1863), and see Herbert Mitgang, editor, *Edward Dicey, Spectator in America* (Athens: University of Georgia Press, 1989/Chicago: Quadrangle Books, 1971), 65.

14. Casemate Museum Staff, Fort Monroe, Virginia, "Is It a Fort or a Fortress?" *Tales of Old Fort Monroe* 5 (January 1972): 1–4.

15. Standard works portraying Washington in this period include Ernest B. Furgurson, *Freedom Rising: Washington in the Civil War* (New York: Alfred A. Knopf, 2004); the classic book by Margaret Leech, *Reveille in Washington 1860–1865* (New York: Harper and Brothers, 1941), and Richard M. Lee, *Mr. Lincoln's City: An Illustrated Guide to the Civil War Sites of Washington* (McLean, VA: EPM Publications, 1981).

16. Contemporary commentaries in Wilhelmus Bogart Bryan, "Washington on the Eve of the Civil War," Marcus Benjamin, collector/editor, *Washington during War Time: A Series of Papers Showing the Military, Political, and Social Phases during 1861 to 1865* (Washington, DC: Committee on Literature for the Thirty-Sixth Annual Encampment of the Grand Army of the Republic, 1902), chapter 1.

17. Theodore Winthrop and Thomas M. Woodruff both quoted in Bryan, "Washington on the Eve of the Civil War," in Benjamin, editor, *Washington during Wartime*, 8–9.

18. See Lee, *Mr. Lincoln's City*, en toto but inter alia for a landscape of the Civil War downtown city.

19. Ibid., 14–18; John Kelly, "There's No 'Washington, D.C.'—But I'm Not Renaming My Column," *Washington Post*, September 27, 2009, C2.

20. Emil Rosenblatt and Ruth Rosenblatt, editors, *Hard Marching Every Day: The Civil War Letters of Private Wilbur Fisk 1861–1865* (Lawrence: University Press of Kansas, 1992), 6.

21. Mary Clemmer Ames, *Ten Years in Washington: Life and Scenes in the National Capital as a Woman Sees Them* (Hartford, CT: Queen City Publishing Company, 1873), quoted in Federal Writers' Project, *Washington: City and Capital*, 58.

22. Sir James Fergusson of Kilkerran, Ben Wynne, editor, *The Personal Observations of a Man of Intelligence: Notes of a Tour in North America in 1861* (Lambertville, NJ: True Bill Press, 2009), 134–35.

23. See Cooling, *Symbol, Sword and Shield*, chapters 1 and 2.

24. On First Bull Run (Manassas) and its aftermath, see John Gross Barnard, *A Report on the Defenses of Washington* (Washington, DC: Government Printing Office, 1871), 10.

25. Cooling, *Symbol, Sword and Shield*, 56–63.

26. *The Congressional Globe*, 2nd sess., 37th Cong., January 13, 1862, 286; Mary Alice Wills, *The Confederate Blockade of Washington, D.C., 1861–1862* (Parsons, WV: McClain Print Company, 1975), chapter 3, especially pages 96–104.

27. A. A. Hayes, "Stories of the War: The Attack on Washington, 1864," *Burlington, Vermont, Free Press*, January 4, 1886.

CHAPTER TWO
LINCOLN AND THE
ARMY COME TO THE SUBURBS

Sergeant Elisha Hunt Rhodes of the Second Rhode Island Volunteer Infantry recalled that on a very hot August 6, 1861, his regiment marched out Seventh Street from camps downtown. After passing the hotel at Brightwood, they turned onto a country road and set up camp on the farm of a Mr. Ray. Five days later they named the place "Camp Brightwood." Rhodes thought they were in Maryland, not the District of Columbia. Actually, they were close, barely a mile from the boundary line but still inside the District. The Rhode Islanders soon brigaded with the Seventh and Tenth Massachusetts and the Thirty-Sixth New York regiments under Brigadier General Darius Couch. According to Rhodes, camp life proved quite dull, and after two months at the place, he wrote in his journal, "I know every tree within two miles of camp." Perhaps that was because Brightwood itself reminded the soldiery of farms, cultivated fields, wood lots, and streamlets back home. B. W. Sulfrin wrote home disgruntledly in early October, "We are not treated half as well as any slave out here," and he opined that not half a dozen of his mates would volunteer again for army service. Still, he vowed to stick by the colors.[1]

Similarly timed letters from Camp Tenally, to the west of Brightwood at a hamlet in the District bearing that name, suggested similar activity to guard what was the main Georgetown to Rockville and Frederick turnpike. A very German-sounding A. S. Bray of the Third Pennsylvania Reserves told his brother from Tennallytown how a battle was expected. They were building a battery "werry strong and goot to protect our soldiers" that would hold about two thousand men and mounting three cannons. Almost proudly he added that "we cut down orchards with fine apple and peach trees with fine peaches and also some large corn fields" and "we have destroyed two houses that were in our way to build the battery." Landowner Giles Dwyer was certainly not impressed. William Dunlop Dixon of the sister Sixth Pennsylvania

Reserves wrote his wife how they had about finished "our earth work" with its eleven pieces of cannon, some of which overlooked the camps. "It is considered one of the strongest works about Washington City." Health at Camp Tenally was improving, and even more than at Camp Brightwood, the assembled units were already out and about, reconnoitering across Chain Bridge over the Potomac and into enemy Virginia. The camps and forts—McCall/Pennsylvania (later Reno) and Massachusetts (subsequently Stevens)—would come to play key roles over the next three years in guarding and then defending Mr. Lincoln's city.[2]

Indeed, within the year, Lincoln and the First Family would join the soldiers in the suburbs—at least for the summer. Seeking relief from the city heat and the pressures of public life, the family would retreat to the government-owned Soldiers' Home property just off the Rock Creek Church Road and less than a mile from the outer defense works at Fort Totten. They would enjoy three summers there, taking in the salubrious air and rural surroundings. The president could visit his "boys" in the fortifications as well as hobnob with the personal bodyguard from the One Hundred and Fiftieth Pennsylvania "Bucktails." Of course, he still commuted daily back to the White House with the Eleventh New York cavalry as escort. Eventually, business acquaintances, friends, and office seekers would descend on the "summer White House." Hospitals, drill camps, and even a burgeoning national cemetery at the government reservation would remind the Lincolns of wartime. There would be an additional wrinkle, however—Lincoln's vulnerability in so isolated a locale and so close to Washington's perimeter defense line. Each summer the Confederates made that vulnerability abundantly clear.[3]

Defending Crossroads and Thoroughfares, Valleys, and Hilltops

Before the Revolution, one James White had built a log cabin in the vicinity of what became Brightwood. He gained a royal patent for 536 acres of land distant from Georgetown, the colonial metropolis in this part of Maryland. One author advanced much later that White's descendants lived in the area until the 1950s, seeing "their isolated farm transformed first into a crossroads community, then finally into a suburb of the nation's capital." Indeed, Brightwood, in the beginning dubbed "Crystal Spring" (surely for a bubbling emanation nearby), appeared after the War of 1812 when a private company constructed a turnpike through what was Washington County of the District. This turnpike naturally proved controversial because of tolls, despite its benefits of conveying country products to city markets. The small community that had then spawned where today's Georgia Avenue crossed Milk House Ford Road (later called Rock Creek Ford Road) continues to define today's city neighborhood. A humble tavern/roadhouse—Moreland's Tavern—denoted the crossing at the time.

Rural landowners, both white and free blacks, constructed a two-story, log-and-frame Emory Methodist Chapel in 1832, and the turnpike company erected a tollhouse just north of the edifice to handle improvements, including planking the rutted dirt thoroughfare in 1852. Residents ultimately protested by opening traces of their own public and free "shunpike" or Piney Branch Road circumventing the tollbooth and Emory chapel property. A post office (first called Brighton, then changed to Brightwood when somebody realized there was another Brighton out further in Montgomery County, Maryland) and a racetrack drawing fans from all over the region were set up on flat land the farmers called "Crystal Spring." By this time, Emory Church itself had been improved into a larger brick "neat and commodious, splendidly equipped and furnished for its day" structure, serving fifty-nine white and thirteen black members.[4]

A county assessment in 1855 listed thirty-one property owners stretching along the turnpike from Rock Creek Church Road south of Brightwood to the District line. Here political and media mogul Francis Preston Blair constructed his sylvan country mansion, Silver Spring. It was named for the clear, crystal waters of a spring discovered by Blair and his daughter Elizabeth while out riding from their city house across from the White House downtown. Most of the landowners, however, owned small parcels; only six held more than one hundred acres. Five of the owners were free blacks, and four of them were women. The African Americans ultimately concentrated in what they styled "Vinegar Hill," west of the turnpike along Milkhouse Ford Road. Only six of the white landowners held slaves, two of whom owned more than one and all six were closely associated with business in the city. Locals such as Captain Thomas Carbery served as mayor briefly in 1822 to 1823, William Cammack maintained truck gardens for a city hotel, and John Saul used land for greenhouses and nursery beds. All of their lands would figure one way or another in events during the final year of the Civil War. That was after Brightwood had welcomed the army.[5]

Indeed, the Seventh Street Turnpike always dictated events for the hamlet. Encamped soldiery would interface with farmers and country squires such as Blair and his son Montgomery (Lincoln's postmaster general whose Falkland home rivaled that of his father's nearby). Another son, James (a midshipman prominent in the discovery of Antarctica before an untimely death at age thirty-three), left his own house the Moorings that constitutes the sole surviving family structure today. Wealthy Matthew Emery was another local who erected a summer place, just south of the Brightwood crossroads. Eminent stone-cutter entrepreneur and builder as well as local militia commander, Emery would be the District's last elected mayor after the war until the twentieth century. In the distance off to the northeast could be found Dr. Noble's place, as well as the Moreland, Pilling, and Titman farms closer to Rock Creek on the west. Nearby lay Vinegar Hill, whose offshoots of the Shamwell family of free blacks settled there in 1837. Surely most all those families north of Brightwood toward the District line felt the sting of soldiery seeking firewood, construction materials, and barnyard products as well as fraternization. Some of the civilians must have been secessionist in sentiment, possibly before the soldiers came to Brightwood. Morrison, McChesney, Reeve, Selden, Carberry, Colelazer, and Shoemaker were names on deeds and maps of the period that greeted the bluecoats who invaded their sylvan domains. Before long private property gave way to even more "military necessity" as mere camps and stations proved inadequate for defense of the Seventh Street artery into the city.[6]

Building fortifications and supporting infrastructure kept restless young men busy. The War Department and their commanders saw to that. In addition to drilling and learning about military life, as Howe Shepherd told his brother back in Massachusetts, he was "going over to the fort and shoveling three hours" every fifth day. This was in late September when Couch's brigade busily constructed independent works across the city's northern face from Fort Bunker Hill on the east to Tennallytown's forts, guarding yet another artery in and out of the city—the Rockville or Georgetown Pike at the Brookville Road merge point. Like Brightwood, Tennallytown not only featured the highway junction but also provided activities associated with such activity. John Tennally opened a tavern and inn even before the birth of the nation's capital, thus spawning a pleasant hamlet of attractive white houses when the Union soldiers arrived in 1861. Farms surrounded the hamlet, some large in size—Sarah Love's The Rest and Nathan Loughborough's Grassland (the eventual site of a Yankee fort named for logistician Edmund Gaines in this rush to occupy and fortify Washington's suburbs). Similar big farms, Clean Drinking, No Gain, and Hayes Manor, had their lanes across scrub growth and gently rolling lands to the north. In the wake of Lincoln's election, some southern sympathizers actually moved out of the city to Maryland.

Landowner Dyer logically lost his property to the burgeoning camps and fort. This unsurpassed vantage point (highest in the District of Columbia) in addition to the road junction met the "military necessity" of that moment. Young Lewis Cass White of the One Hundred and Second Pennsylvania expressed awe when he and comrades bivouacked at Tennallytown in August 1861 and went to see Fort McCall (named for the commander of Pennsylvania troops turning the earth for the fortification that would soon become Fort Pennsylvania and subsequently Fort Reno). Enamored by the wide ditch to deter cavalry and the parapets being prepared for cannon able to throw seventy-pound projectiles and pivot guns movable and elevated "at pleasure or of necessity," Cass White was struck even more by the panorama unfolding beyond the hilltop. "Saw from Ft. McCall the fortifications of the enemy across the Potomac," he jotted in his diary. Indeed, the Tennallytown vantage point would prove a godsend for reconnaissance and signalers as well as defenders of the capital in time of need.[7]

The presence of Rhode Islanders, New Yorkers, and Pennsylvanians spread across the fertile land would wreak its toll here just as in Brightwood. William Hale, a Rhode Island volunteer, wrote home in June 1862 that a few barns and "hungry looking houses straggle along a lean and hungry looking street." A tavern and blacksmith's shop "confront each other," flanked by the post office, and to the rear stood the village church, "never from appearances, a very notable structure, but now, alas, sadly dilapidated, and converted to other uses than originally intended." Indeed, the Mt. Zion Methodist Church was taken over as a guardhouse, quartermaster's storehouse, hospital, and mess hall. The Rhode Islanders' search for souvenirs desecrated the pulpit and Sabbath school library, leading Quartermaster Lysander Flagg to petition similar Sunday schools back home in Pawtucket and Central Falls for books to rebuild the Tennallytown resources. By all accounts of those soldiers stationed in the Tennallytown vicinity during the war, a pleasant climate, good water, and restful repose as well as faithful service and adoration from escaped slaves and free blacks accompanied their tour there.[8]

"There is now a perfect string of forts all around Washington so it would be almost next to impossible for the rebels to get into the city," Shepherd claimed. Rhodes added how the city was "now surrounded by a chain of forts and is considered safe from attack." Well, not quite at this stage of the war. But the fort system was extended on both sides of the Potomac and, suggested Rhodes, "we have shoveled many weary hours but feel our labor will do some good" as the city of Washington "is considered safe from attack." Rhodes and company constructed Fort Slocum (named for their first regimental colonel John S. Slocum, killed at First Bull Run) east of Brightwood. Having visited the fort, Rhodes pronounced on October 21 it "looks very warlike with its large iron guns frowning from its embrasures." But the fatigue work of the Bay Staters more directly on the Seventh Street axis was called "Fort Massachusetts." Elsewhere far to the east of Slocum and other works, they also erected Fort Bunker Hill.

The fortifications reflected military realities after Bull Run. Isolated posts, they controlled roads, creek valleys, and ravines and other features of military interest. Fort Massachusetts, for instance, seemed to straddle both the Seventh Street Road Turnpike as well as the adjacent developing "shunpike" of Piney Branch Road, according to a trained cartographer in the ranks of a Pennsylvania heavy artillery unit in 1863. For some reason its location on the west side of the road suggested that it mainly faced west/northwest overlooking broad fields toward the valley of Rock Creek. Yet despite its small size, it also covered the highway to Brookeville and provided intersecting fire with Fort Slocum to its east. Situated on less commanding ground than others in the line, observers later suggested this as its vulnerability. However, Fort Massachusetts owed its position mostly to the command of the Seventh Street Road and the tollbooth intersection with Piney Branch Road in its front. Close by, the fort literally intimidated structures owned by M. B. Beall and R. Butt. It hardly needed height to do so.[9]

By autumn, the stalemate between rival armies in Virginia allowed the War Department and the principal Union field army defending Washington to more thoroughly assess the overall defense of the city. Major General George B. McClellan had taken over both as general-in-chief of all Union armies and the eastern Army of the Potomac in particular. Threatened Confederate crossings both north and south of the city led to a Yankee concentration in southern and western Maryland as well as "some auxiliary defenses to the city itself against approaches along the northern shores." Absent Rebel or foreign warships, shallow upriver crossings proved more sensitive. Yet much maneuvering of troops and pen and ink went into the focus on secessionist-heavy southern Maryland across from Quantico, Virginia. That notwithstanding, new artillery chief William F. Barry and chief engineer John Gross Barnard cited 7,343 officers and men manning some twenty-two disconnected fortifications of the northern lines (from the Potomac north of the reservoir around to the east of the Anacostia), although a more realistic appraisal might have been perhaps half that number. The major defending force was to be the field army, not static fortifications.

The statistics nonetheless would have been consoling for a military and government trying to recover momentum after Bull Run. With that in mind, the Barry/Barnard report of October 24, 1861, enumerated Fort Gaines (105 perimeter yards, four guns, seventy-five gunners, and a 250-man garrison), Fort Pennsylvania (440 perimeter yards, twelve guns, 180 gunners, and a six-hundred-man garrison), Fort at Schwartz's house (190 perimeter yards, seven guns, 105 gunners, 250-man garrison), Fort Massachusetts (168 perimeter yards, ten guns, 150 gunners, two-hundred-man garrison), Fort Slocum (250 perimeter yards, thirteen guns, 195 gunners, three-hundred-man garrison), Fort Totten (272 perimeter yards, fourteen guns, 180 gunners, 350-man garrison), Fort Bunker Hill (205 yards, eight guns, 120 gunners, 270-man garrison), Fort Saratoga (109 perimeter yards, six guns, 120 gunners, 220-man garrison), an unnamed fort of undetermined size, later styled Thayer (four guns, sixty gunners, two-hundred-man garrison), and Fort Lincoln (446 perimeter yards, sixteen guns, 140 gunners, six-hundred-man garrison). Although the late summer/fall low water in the Potomac would always refocus the army concern for the northern front, proud engineers could point to forty-eight works encircling the city by the end of the year, built at a cost of over $344,000 ($7,000 per work on average). This translated in aggregate to thirty-seven miles of fortifications that had gone up in eight months. The extremely diligent and dedicated Barnard reported to the army's chief of engineers, Brigadier General J. G. Totten, on December 10, that since "the importance of perfect security to the capital of the United States in the present state of affairs can scarcely be overestimated," Fort Massachusetts in particular "is entirely too small for its important position."[10]

The Lincolns and Watchfires of Circling Camps

Maturing soldiers already populated Washington's suburbs by autumn 1861. Then, the onset of winter brought its own curses—freezing temperatures, muddy or frozen and snowy roads and campgrounds, and drafty, inadequate, homemade living quarters. At least some of the young soldiers had occasional experiences to regale their home folks about. One was Corporal Henry T. Blanchard of the Second Rhode Island. Fated to lose his life two years later in the Wilderness, Blanchard graphically described a reconnaissance from Camp Brightwood via Fort Slocum to Bladensburg in January 1862. They passed the old battlefield of 1814 (although he did not note it) and into the village of twelve to fourteen houses, two stores, and a blacksmith shop. In addition to the fascination with the way locals used horses and mules together in their farm teams, he was especially taken with a bill of fare posted at one tavern—"good weather and no liquor but good food; bad weather and no good grog." The place had been a gathering spot and armory for home guards before "the present trouble." Despite the mud march, Blanchard thought it a fun release from a daily diet of drills and parades, noncommissioned study and examination in both artillery and infantry tactics, and trying to whip newly arriving recruits into shape. He noted the Bladensburg dueling grounds but not the 1814 battlefield nor a glistening new fort atop Barry's hilltop defense post—named Fort Lincoln in honor of the president. But Blanchard and his squad had probably marched in via the route used by the militia to flee the earlier embarrassment.[11]

Great controversy would attend leaving Washington defenseless when McClellan took the war to the outskirts of Richmond in the spring and summer. Rhodes left with his Rhode Islanders on March 26, a cheerier young sergeant-major now declaring "so Goodbye old Camp Brightwood where we have had lots of fun and learned a soldier's duty," adding "may God bless and prosper us." They marched downtown to the Sixth Street wharf, the regiment now commanded by Lieutenant Colonel Frank Wheaton. Little did they know that two years later survivors, including the colonel and sergeant-major—both with more rank and responsibilities—would return, this time to the sounds of battle. McClellan and many comrades would be gone by then. Meanwhile, they would leave the Seventh Street Road, Fort Massachusetts, and Brightwood to others' care.[12]

Confederate battlefield success may have created a moment of greatest danger at the time of Second Manassas in late August 1862. Robert E. Lee maneuvered the conflict back to northern Virginia. Here, inept performances from the commander-in-chief, secretary of war, and general-in-chief down to field commanders Mc-Clellan and John Pope nearly destroyed Union arms once again on the Manassas Plains. But could Lee and his legions have battered their way through Washington's southern defense line anchored by even a defeated Army of the Potomac? We shall never know. The question was answered miles away by the prompt action of two New Jersey brigadiers who lost their lives in a thunderstorm while countering Lee's flank move at a forgotten farm near Chantilly or Ox Hill. Lee then turned westward into Loudon County to recoup, eventually crossing the Potomac for his first northern invasion.

All at once, the northern, not the southern, defense lines took center stage. A rejuvenated McClellan returned to inspire and reorganize the beaten Federals. Low water in the Potomac predictably threatened what was anything but a back-door approach to Washington at this point. The Confederates might have replicated 1814, but Lee turned north and west and McClellan followed out of Fortress Washington in early September. The battle for Washington this time took place on the banks of Antietam Creek in western Maryland. Once again, Washingtonians and the government breathed a sigh of relief when Union forces gained at least a pyrrhic victory that enabled Lincoln to change the strategy of the war effort to freeing slaves, not merely defeating a battle foe. McClellan and the government returned to bickering as they had for well over a year. Both parties blamed the other for the near disasters of 1862. During this time frame, the Lincoln family personally became part of the crisis of concern over the Confederate threat to the city. They had gone to the country.[13]

As early as the summer of 1861, Mary Todd Lincoln in particular had wanted to escape the heat and oppression of Washington. The Soldiers' Asylum or Home on the grounds of local banker George W. Rigg's country estate afforded great promise. Then First Bull Run intruded and the First Lady could not fulfill her wish. It would be different the following summer, as by mid-June, the president's family decamped from the White House and moved to the country. The small stucco Riggs cottage, built in the English Gothic revival style, stood adjacent to the grander stone edifice housing some 150 resident veterans. By that second summer of the war a new, burgeoning national cemetery not far away counted several thousand graves. The way out from the city also found camps of both soldiery, and the refugee, African American, so-called contraband population dotted the way. Fort Totten and the line of city defenses lay less than a mile to the north and east. At first, the sylvan reveries of the First Family seemed idyllic. Then, with the president commuting downtown to the White House daily and the growing trickle of visitors, friends, and favor seekers, even Mrs. Lincoln became frustrated that the original intent of their summer escape had become compromised. The possibility of additional compromise really struck home by the time a Rebel army came to the Washington region in August and September.

The president had busied himself that summer with McClellan and Pope, the unproductive campaigning, as well as codifying his thoughts about emancipation. Consultations and the drafting of documents during the Lincolns' respite at the summer retreat have grabbed historians' attention. But this was also the period when safety and security advanced to front rank. Whether or not Stanton, military district commander Major-General James Wadsworth (himself a New York politician and destined also to lose his life in the Wilderness), or a bevy of others first announced the presidential vulnerability remains unclear. A unit of Pennsylvania soldiery, then a New York cavalry squadron, went to both guard the summer White House and to escort the chief executive during his daily commute. Lincoln did not like such a fuss (the assassination of a president was not in America's tradition, he declared). Then he warmed to soldier companionship when his wife took their surviving younger son, Tad, off to New York (Willie had died in March, sending the family into deep bereavement; their eldest son, Robert, was off at Harvard), leaving Mr. Lincoln to his lonely task as war leader. An inquisitive president apparently climbed to the castellated tower of the Soldiers' Home building with very distant sound of cannon fire, and he ranged the camps and forts when he could. With Lincoln in the suburbs and the family's summer sojourn, military escort and presidential safety all became part of the summer agendas from 1862 on.

These events so close to the capital also occasioned another time-honored government reaction—appointment of a professional military commission to examine the state of things. John G. Barnard first pricked the balloon of Washington's self-satisfaction by pointedly addressing how incomplete, inadequate, and inappropriately armed were the defenses. The engineer took great care to describe the development of the defenses from a set of isolated works in the wake of First Bull Run to a fully improved fortification system mounting 643 cannons and seventy-five mortars a year later. The immense undertaking for a line of thirty-five to thirty-seven miles "through a country extensively wooded and of intricate topography," claimed Barnard, "was executed under the pressure of an enemy in our front, allowing no time for such thorough study" whereby "it was necessary to commence works in many cases before the woods could be cleared away enough to give that perfect knowledge of the ground essential to their best location." The field army's need for field and siege guns meant that the Washington arsenal had supplied the rather unmanageable 24- and 32-pounder seacoast guns to the local forts. And Barnard particularly cited certain works, such as Fort Massachusetts, as illustrating the problem. He declared that this "earliest work" of the northern defense line "was entirely inadequate to its most important position."[14]

Yet it had "been extensively enlarged" by the time of the report, with large quantities of timber felled in front of this position despite the generally open nature of the country. Rifle pits and some additional batteries had been constructed to support the work. "If the enemy attack Washington, it will be with a large force and numerous artillery," he predicted. The enemy "will concentrate upon the point of attack a large number of pieces; that the garrison should not be exhausted or driven out by shells, adequate bomb-proof shelter should be provided." This new construction would enlarge Fort Massachusetts during the spring and summer of 1863. And it would acquire a new name—Fort Stevens—after Isaac Ingalls Stevens, one of the fallen Jersey brigadiers who had saved the city at Chantilly.[15]

Preparing a Future Battlefield

Still, Barnard wanted more from the War Department, including five hundred freedmen or "contraband" as laborers to be sent from Fort Monroe, Virginia. Most of all he desired a full-scale study commission largely to substantiate what he thought would take $100,000 to bring "these works to a proper condition of efficiency." Secretary of War Edwin P. Stanton obliged on October 22, 1862, appointing a high-powered group including Barnard, Defenses of Washington commander Major-General Nathaniel P. Banks, the War Department's Chief of Engineers brevet Brigadier General J. G. Totten, Quartermaster General Brigadier General Montgomery C. Meigs, and brigadiers George W. Cullum and W. F. Barry. They deliberated over the next month before finalizing a report that generally approved "the lines established and of the works, and that they attach very great importance to them." Moreover, evoking "the great authority of Napoleon" as being on "record upon the necessity of fortifying national capitals," the commission cited his figure of a one to three margin between any attacking force and defenders in numbers of required garrison troops. "Had Vienna, Berlin, and Madrid been fortified and defended," they decided, "the countries of which they are the capitals would have been preserved from the fatal results of his campaigns of 1805, 1806, and 1808 against them." Moreover, "had Paris been fortified in 1814, his own Empire would have been saved from overthrow." Extrapolating to the American situation, they deduced that Washington's position, "on the very borders of the insurgent territory," exposed it to great danger in cases of serious reverse to Union forces in Virginia. "Twice already," they observed, "have its defensive works been the means of saving the capital and enabling us to reorganize our defeated armies."[16]

The commission's one new concern focused on the Potomac River threat to Washington. The concern was "an enemy's armed vessels," but more particularly, "foreign intervention would bring against us maritime forces, and we could not depend upon being always in superior naval force on the Potomac," members observed. "We are, even now, threatened with Confederate iron-clads fitted out in English ports," they contended. But Barnard in his transmittal letter highlighted more immediate realities. "The northern side of the city, between the Potomac and Eastern Branch, which had been little exposed to attack the summer before, was, in August and September of this year, the most likely to be assailed, and from the Potomac to the Seventh street road it was exceedingly weak," he advanced. During his tenure as first the defense commander and then subsequently as chief engineer, he had commenced "to strengthen this part of the line." He had "directed the enlargement of Fort Massachusetts, and laid out forts and batteries to make a complete connection between the first named work and Fort Alexander on the Potomac," while at the same time "I felled the timber to a distance of a mile in front, thus exposing the ground and making it impracticable to the enemy's movements." A cost-conscious public servant, Barnard quickly pointed out the size of expenditures and requirements for new monies for labor and supplies now that the abundance of soldier volunteers had gone from encampments around the city.[17]

The specifics of those northern lines of the defense could be best captured from details in the commission report. Left flank forts Alexander, Franklin, and Ripley were "indispensable to the security of the Chain Bridge, and protection of the receiving reservoir" for Washington's water supply. But the three unconnected works needed to be linked by parapets to avoid domination from possible enemy field batteries emplaced on higher ground to their north or front. Upgrading of the ordnance could supplement long-range fire from distant Fort Pennsylvania and smaller intervening works like Mansfield and Bayard. Fort Pennsylvania proper and a "substantially constructed" ancillary battery commanded "the three Avenues to Washington which unite at Tennallytown," as well as "the ridge of high ground in front of Forts Pennsylvania, Kearny, and DeRussy" off to the north and northeast front. Situated on the dividing ridge between the Potomac and Rock Creek, ordnance improvements included "a 100-pounder rifled gun mounted to sweep the sector from Fort Marcy [above the chain bridge on the Virginia side] to Fort Massachusetts." As across the whole northern front, intermittent unarmed batteries for field guns helped fill unprotected spaces such as the upper Broad Branch valley. DeRussy, overlooking the deep valley of Rock Creek and throwing a crossfire upon the approaches to Fort Massachusetts and (together with Fort Kearny) controlling the country roads between the Rockville Turnpike and Rock Creek, needed "the introduction of a 100-pounder, on center pintle carriage, in place of one of the 32-pounders, to sweep the sector from Fort Pennsylvania to Fort Massachusetts; the fire of which will be particularly important upon the approaches to Fort Massachusetts also." Fort Gaines, essentially "a work in second line" reserve behind Mansfield and Bayard, as well as various batteries to help supplement enfilading fire to the Arlington lines from above Georgetown, were mentioned but tangentially to the northern lines' focus.[18]

When it came to the centerpiece of the northern line—Fort Massachusetts—the commission declared that in conjunction with Fort Slocum, "it commands one of the principal avenues of approach to Washington." Ironically, they did not include Fort DeRussy with that statement, although they echoed Barnard's general feeling that "the original work was entirely inadequate to its important purpose." It had been recently "judiciously enlarged, and, with the addition, is a powerful and satisfactory work." They wanted the merlons (raised spaces between crenelations or embrasures) to be raised on the exposed front of the old work, which would, at the same time, defilade the rear and lateral faces; that the parapet of the exposed front be thickened and that bomb proofs for garrison and casemates for reverse fire at the southeast angle of the old work and at the north angle of new work be constructed. Interestingly, the commission saved its most illuminating comments to its subsequent discussion of Fort Slocum, next in line to the east of Massachusetts. "From two-thirds to a mile to 1 mile in advance of Forts Massachusetts and Slocum the country rises to heights say 20 to 30 feet higher than the crests to those works, furnishing to an enemy most advantageous emplacements for artillery." This would not be the first time that such a thought came from officialdom, conscious that the initial works had not received the proper professional engineer blessing for location the summer before. By 1864, such errors would become critical.[19]

The commission continued: "Along the dividing ridge of this high ground, between Rock Creek and the Eastern Branch, leads the seventh street turnpike road." These two works "are, therefore, exposed to the most powerful efforts of the enemy." Slocum originally had been of more respectable dimensions than Massachusetts but was still a small work and quite inadequate in strength and armament but was bomb proof. The members wanted strengthening similar to that of Slocum's sister fort, although "the high ground spoken of in advance of these works will be under the fire of the 100-pounders and other rifled guns of Forts DeRussy and Totten, besides that of the powerful batteries of the works themselves." Indeed, Totten "occupies a most commanding and strong position, and exercises a powerful influence upon the approaches from the northward and those through the valley between it and Fort Lincoln" to the east, "its 100-pounder here placed will sweep the sector from Fort DeRussy to Fort Lincoln," hence no recommendations for improvement seemed necessary. Of smaller intervening works (forts Slemmer, Bunker Hill, Saratoga, and Thayer), the commission had little to recommend except as offering crossfires for one another (Bunker Hill occupying "a very commanding position" but deficient in interior space). Members' final observations related to Fort Lincoln, whose 100-pounder could sweep the sector from Fort Slocum all the way to Fort Mahan east of the Anacostia or Eastern Branch. Fort Lincoln, they declared, "is situated on an eminence, overlooking the extensive valley formed by the Eastern Branch and its tributaries, and commanding the Baltimore turnpike, the railroad, and several minor roads, which, passing through or near Bladensburg, lead into Washington." And, they reminded readers, "at the foot of this eminence was fought the battle of Bladensburg."[20]

The commission recognized, however, that a recitation of forts alone did not tell the whole story. The group undertook analysis of what would be necessary to supplement and enhance a system of earthworks. Commission members mentioned twenty-five thousand infantrymen, computed at two men per yard of front perimeter and one man per yard of rear perimeter of works. Moreover, nine thousand artillerymen (to furnish three reliefs per gun), or a total aggregate of thirty-four thousand men, would equal a corps-size contingent. It would be "seldom necessary to keep these infantry supports attached to the works," but rather "encamped in such positions as may be most convenient to enable them, in case of alarm, to garrison the several works, and a force of 3,000 cavalry should be available for outpost duty, to give notice of the approach of any enemy." So the statistic, in reality, was not thirty-four thousand but thirty-seven thousand men permanently and formally assigned to Washington's defense. More sobering, in light of subsequent events, was the commission's conclusion with regard to the assigned artillerymen. Since their training "requires much time, having learned the disposition of the armament and computed the distances of the ground over which attacks may be looked for, and the ranges and service of their guns," they "should not be changed" but "remain permanently in the forts."[21]

The mode of operations envisioned by these senior military professionals in the event of danger to the capital would be as follows. "Whenever any enemy is within striking distance of the capital—able by a rapid march to attempt a coup de main, which might result in the temporary occupation of the city, the dispersion of the Government, and the destruction of the archives, all of which could be accomplished by a single day's possession—a covering army of not less than 25,000 men should be held in position to march to meet the attacking column." In the event of "more serious attacks from the main body of the enemy, the capital must depend upon the concentration of its entire armies in Virginia or Maryland." To Barnard and the others, "they should precede or follow any movement of the enemy seriously threatening the capital." The army only slowly acted upon such conclusions over the next two years.

Gun Drills and Doldrums, 1862–1864

Washington was no doubt a fortress city by the end of 1862. Surrounded by a chain of earthwork forts mounting the most powerful ordnance of the era, supported by an infrastructure of barracks, storehouses, repair shops, and military roads supplementing civilian thoroughfares, the national capital itself had changed greatly since Inauguration Day 1861. It even had its own army—aside from the Army of the Potomac. All of this would eventually organize as something called the Military Department of Washington or XXII Army Corps. Consistently, over the months thereafter, up to forty-thousand troops in specially allocated garrisons of trained artillery, cavalry, and infantry stood ready to man the works or take to the field in an emergency. Even the sleepy prewar southern town itself had blossomed into a bustling wartime nerve center demanding such attention. Soldiers and civilians jostled one another on the sidewalks and crowded hotel lobbies by day and night. Hackmen gouged everyone, and Congress stood in almost permanent session catering to contract seekers and lobbyists, camp followers and light-blue jacketed convalescents (the much-maligned Veteran Reserve Corps of the wounded), along with ubiquitous freed people and even occasional Rebel parolees adding to the pandemonium. The warlords of Washington presided over government offices, warehouses, and repair facilities, navy yards and arsenals, depots and convalescent hospitals. Cemeteries at Soldiers' Home and behind Lee's confiscated Arlington House received their daily quota of war dead.[22]

Out in the suburbs, forts such as Massachusetts (Stevens) and Pennsylvania (renamed for Jesse L. Reno who fell at South Mountain in September 1862) once again witnessed more earth turning as expansion and changes occupied garrisons and hired labor alike. From south of the Potomac around the northern lines to east of the Anacostia, the forts reflected changes recommended by engineers and ordnance experts. Their clay sides devoid of grass, their interiors mostly lacking shelter from the hot sun or snowy blasts, and outside environs front and rear stripped of cover save for random brush piles and stumps, these sentinels settled into a litany of oblation and drill and waiting for an unseen enemy. One newly promoted First Lieutenant at Fort Totten worried in October 1862 how he could control the mostly "Germans" in his company plus the forty Americans who had been equally unruly due to previous officers who themselves had been German. The following June, Vermont private Nat Batchelder wrote his sister gleefully how they need not clean and care for their old rough Austrian muskets that had been altered twice since issuance upon muster at Brattleboro. Using colorful patriotic stationary depicting Ellsworth's Avenger zouaves, he thought they would soon have Springfield rifles, "finished up very pretty." Drill on the heavy artillery as well as these infantry weapons indicated a duality to the Vermonters' role. Some such as B. DeWitt at Fort Simmons followed the larger pace of the war, writing to his father in Oswego, New York, on Sanitary Commission stationary at mid-May 1863 how "the conquest folks were a little too fast in celebrating the downfall of Richmond," although he thought it would fall in a few weeks. Losses like the last battle at Fredericksburg had filled Washington with wounded, and "one or two more such battles will use up both armies," in his view.[23]

CHAPTER TWO

Another Vermonter, Judson A. Lewis of the Eleventh Vermont Volunteers (soon changed to the First Vermont Heavy Artillery for duty in Washington's forts), sent dispatches back to the *Rutland Herald*, keeping homefolks informed of what was going on. In September he regaled them from Fort Lincoln, "named for President Lincoln, who is said to have thrown up the first shovel full of dirt toward its formation; and also to have raised the Stars and stripes within the parapets." It was the initial posting for the young Green Mountaineers who had been most anxious for black laborers to do the digging of rifle pits so the white volunteers might drill, gain discipline, and "fit ourselves for the more important part of warfare," which they anticipated shortly. Ironically, the Vermonters were destined to spend the eighteen months in the somnolent defenses of Washington.[24]

By October, Lewis and his compatriots were complaining that "we generally remain in one place [only] long enough to clear up our grounds, grade our streets—in short, to get comfortably settled," when the order comes to pack knapsacks and strike tents. They had done but little drilling "except what we call spade drill—that is digging rifle pits, erecting batteries, and repairing roads." Only about three miles from the city, mail call was regular, although their major complaint was the dearth of letters from home and that they had experienced their first deaths from typhoid fever. In mid-November, the big shift came with the distribution of company-sized contingents to forts Totten, Slocum, and Massachusetts.

The Vermont correspondent offered readers back home detailed portraits of how they selected the ground for permanent barracks and constructed those barracks. These weatherized structures were sixty feet long and twenty feet wide, according to military specifications, built of "stockades, or, piles eleven feet in length set in the ground, upon the tops of which the places are placed and strongly spiked." Crevices between the stockades were first caulked with moss and then plastered over nicely with Maryland mortar, which was found in abundance, especially after a rain. Rafters were put upon the plates and covered with boards. Each barrack had four windows upon each side and two doors, one at each end of the building. The interior work sported roof boards of hemlock, "but, all the nice work inside, is done off with white pine." Sleeping arrangements included three-decker bunks lining a center corridor and were similar in arrangement to those on steamboats, except lacking mattresses and pillows. The substitute for those essentials came from soldiers' knapsacks and overcoats. The soldier-correspondent assured his readers that it only took two or three months of practice to become inured to arrangements—"we think just as much of our bunks now, as we formerly did of feather beds." Writing just two days before Christmas 1862, Judson Lewis declared that the weather had been pleasant and quite warm for the previous ten days.

When off duty, men of the Eleventh/First Vermont engaged themselves reading, writing letters, discussing who was the greatest general of the war to date,

34

and even dancing to the tunes of a fiddler, who held forth from six to eight every evening. But since the unit was transiting from infantry to heavy artillery, the study of tactics also occupied their time in anticipation that "practice will be united with theory." Roll call came at 8:30, lights were out at 8:45, and "everything remains quiet for the night." Lewis further explained that three or four men from each company went out about three miles on picket duty every night. Writing from Fort Massachusetts/Stevens, he noted that the picket post was located near the "splendid residence of Post Master [Montgomery] Blair." Company C fortunately enjoyed Blair's favor, "their business being to guard his buildings and prevent their being fired." "Mr. Blair has fitted up a place for them and they have a fire and are very cozy; anything the boys wish to eat is freely given them, and no pay is ever taken in return." Anticipating recruiting from an authorized one-hundred-man infantry company to the expected 150-man heavy artillery company strength, Judson expected to remain at Fort Massachusetts through the winter, "and how much longer deponeth saith not." Brightwood remained home for Lewis and his comrades until May 1864. In May 1863, he wrote how "the 11th Vermont is as it always had been, in good spirit, and ready for any emergency which the welfare of the nation may demand." False alarms for active service and patriotism flamed anew in the young Vermonters' breasts—although apparently all of them sighed in relief that they "have thus far been exempt from the field of carnage, and have occupied other posts of trust and responsibility."[25]

Good spirits and fair health attended these "white-glove soldiers" (as field veterans dubbed the garrison troops) for all of this period. Perhaps the presence of the regimental hospital at Fort Massachusetts/Stevens in 1863 and a new surgeon as the "right man in the right place" as well as enlarged barracks to accommodate the recruits (one hundred by twenty feet, with a large mess room and kitchen) accounted for such conditions. Talk of draft resistance and shirking duty at home bothered the Vermonters who sacrificed for liberty and humanity at their Washington stations. Off-year elections in the fall of 1863 gave hope that "the war must go on till we can gain a peace which shall secure to every man his rights." Finally recruited to full strength at 1,838 men, the Vermont garrison regiment assembled before its colonel at Fort Slocum on an uncharacteristically warm late January day in 1864 to draw its new artillery state colors and pass in review. The "regiment is becoming disciplined very fast," recounted Lewis, "as the several companies are under thorough drill every day."

These fattened garrison regiments remarkably escaped calls to field service. Indeed, all the months while the Army of the Potomac campaigned miles away, only rumors of the elusive partisan John Mosby out in Loudon County, Virginia or occasional cavalry raid by Wade Hampton or J. E. B. Stuart brushed the quietude of units in Washington garrisons. True, a succession of Army of the Potomac field commanders like Ambrose Burnside, Joseph Hooker and George Gordon Meade always looked to the manpower-heavy Washington garrison for replacements to battle losses. But, the Vermonters had escaped call. When Lee again sortied north of the Potomac in the summer of 1863, foreboding and panic took over the highest halls of government as Lincoln, Stanton and Halleck cast anxious looks toward the northern limits of the city. The First Family, Lincoln at its head, once more endured the alarm over their presence at vulnerable Soldiers Home. The threat passed and Lincoln told northern citizenry that he felt Washington was safe from danger. The Commander-in-Chief continued to elude cavalry escorts and ride out to the camps and forts to mingle with the soldiery.[26]

In addition to visiting Fort Totten, a stone's throw from the cottage, the president rode out to drink from the well at his namesake, Fort Lincoln, and the adjacent Battery Jamieson, and he apparently also frequented forts Pennsylvania/Reno and Massachusetts/Stevens. Some of these visits occasioned perhaps apocryphal stories, a prominent one centering upon the enlargement of the latter work. When Massachusetts became Stevens (renamed for the sometime Washington territorial governor and New Jersey soldier Isaac Ingalls Stevens, killed on September 1, 1862, at Chantilly near Centreville, Virginia), Lincoln appeared on horseback at some point during the work's reconstitution. Soldiers and hired labor dug new ditches and parapets, laid new timber gun platforms, apparently stockaded blockage of a "shunpike" Piney Branch Road trace around the tollbooth out front, and erected a bombproof shelter for troop protection in the new part. They also raised a gabioned portion or "lookout post" where old and new forts joined as well as an additional ammunition magazine in the latter. In doing so, they tore down the free black property owner's house, perhaps using the door for entry into the new magazine. The free black property owner, Elizabeth Proctor Thomas, watched the German-speaking soldiers consummate the deed. Her memory enshrined what transpired as she recalled the desecration and privation to her and her six-month-old infant. But, she carefully added, that evening a tall man, dressed in black, came to console her with the words "It is hard, but you shall reap a great reward." Chagrined and perhaps only partially placated, she would regale veterans' gatherings decades later with this story, adding "but I never got that reward!" Still, she must have found shelter near the expanded fort. She would be present two years hence when Lincoln returned to her house site.[27]

The reward that she and a nation would receive came in 1864 at Fort Stevens when, ironically, "Aunt Betty" Thomas (as she became better known) and Old Abe once more crossed paths. The regimental historian of the Second Pennsylvania Heavy Artillery (whose men were probably the culprits in her house's destruction), subsequently bluntly declared: "Had Fort Massachusetts and Slocum remained as they were in 1862, then Jubal Early would have had no difficulty in reaching Washington on the Seventh Street Road." As it was, the expansion Aunt Betty witnessed enhanced the work from 176 to 375 perimeter yards, the ordnance from ten to nineteen guns, and added a more maneuverable siege cannon. While digging, drilling, and other tasks continued, the war proceeded elsewhere—until the spring and summer of 1864. A Fort Stevens soldier known to us only as "A.F.S." might write to a friend on the last day of January how warm weather had enabled a battalion drill in the forenoon "and in the afternoon we had to go over to Slocum and pass in review, then have dress parade then come home again and with all the travel I was considerable tired last night." Then arrival of a new player in March of 1864 promised change all the way around for those in Washington's defenses.[28]

"Butcher" Grant and Defending Mr. Lincoln's City

Lieutenant General Ulysses S. Grant took the role of general-in-chief on March 9, 1864, understanding little of the tension accorded Washington's protection in the minds of the Lincoln administration. His primary focus became Lee's army as he chose to guide the Army of the Potomac, commanded still by George Gordon Meade, hero of Gettysburg. Discussions took place between the new general, Lincoln, Stanton, and Halleck (now functioning as something of an army chief of staff), and they surely impressed upon Grant the need to protect Washington. But shades of McClellan two years before, the field army could best accomplish that task in Grant's mind. This time Lincoln seemingly acquiesced. The capital was in fact strongly defended when Grant and Meade kicked off the campaign in early May. It would not remain so forever.

Washington and Baltimore garrisons felt relatively minor impact upon their strengths at first. The principal heavy artillery units continued to perfect their servicing of heavy guns while replacements from reserve and convalescent contingents as well as dismounted cavalry fed into Washington lines without serious diminution of numbers and capabilities. Well might Attorney General Edward Bates jot in his diary on April 2: "I have no certain information, but I conjecture that [Ambrose] Burnside with his army [the independent IX Army Corps, subsequently styled the Army of the James] will be charged with the defense of this capital; and that the army of the Potomac (relieved from that embarrassing and paralyzing duty) will, henceforth be free to devote itself to all exigencies of the war farther south." All of that changed dramatically when heavy casualties from the Wilderness, Spotsylvania, North Anna, and Cold Harbor demanded replacement. Grant, compared with earlier generals, may have turned south and relentlessly marched for Richmond. But Meade and Burnside needed new men.[29]

Suddenly men, horses, and equipment in the Washington area became the focus for such reinforcements. The high command stripped the forts and garrisons to ship them to Grant. By June 7, Halleck told Grant that he had forwarded 48,265 men from the Department of Washington to the field armies since the beginning of the campaign. By the end of the month departmental strength figures dipped to 33,289 officers and men (many convalescents or hastily organized "national guard" reserves—some veterans—from the Midwest sent to serve for one hundred days). The ordnance numbered 950 heavy but thirty-nine field guns. Gone were the likes of Massachusetts, New York, and Pennsylvania heavy artillerists, now muttering about being shipped off to the fighting. Defenders of the capital feared much more any random cavalry or guerrilla raids on the perimeter. Generals Franz Sigel and David Hunter kept a lid on the Shenandoah Valley passageway northward. Were not Lee and his worn-down Army of Northern Virginia now penned up inside their own fortifications stretching from Richmond to Petersburg, everyone asked? Ironically, the moment of greatest danger to Washington arrived early in July.[30]

Shade was already becoming scarce as the heat of summer wafted over the soldiers still on guard north of the city. The raw earth overturned to expand Fort Stevens was now hidden by sod atop parapets and whitewashed revetments and gun portals. Scrub brush still cluttered neglected fields of fire and vied with farmers' fields touched with the first hints of corn or wheat. Flourishing orchards and shade trees surrounded the sprinkling of country properties owned by Washingtonians such as Francis and Montgomery Blair. The influx of soldiery in 1861 still remained, bivouacked on Brightwood's meager populace, drinking from its springs, mingling with its shadows, and guarding its roadways. Naturalist John Burroughs could declare of Washington's Rock Creek and Piney Branch valleys—"There is perhaps not another city in the Union that has on its very threshold so much natural beauty and grandeur . . . a few touches of art would convert this whole region into a park unequalled in the world." He thought they were "passages as wild and savage and apparently as remote from civilization as anything one meets with." Maybe garrisons in forts DeRussy, Stevens, Slocum, and Totten might have agreed. Sergeant "A.F.S" wrote a friend from Fort Stevens at the end of January, "Well Frank I don't think of anything interesting to you to write this morning. I don't have much chance to get news here. It's the same thing over and over every day, we have to drill and go on inspection every fair day and that is all there is to it." This was much the same as suggested back on January 21, 1863, when Evan G. Jones of the One Hundred and Seventeenth New York wrote a friend from headquarters at Fort Baker, east of the Anacostia on January 21, 1863. That location, said Jones, "is pleasantly located on the heights north east of the city across the Eastern Branch from the Navy Yard and is a strong and important position in as much as it commands the city, the navy yard and the Washington Arsenal." Headquarters to Colonel William Russell Pease, One Hundred and Seventeenth New York, "his brigade is composed of all the troops east of the Eastern Branch and includes eleven forts."

"If Washington ever falls into the hands of the enemy," Jones thought, "he will possess himself of an indefinite number of cannons for every hill top in a circle of forty miles circumference is covered with them and this number is daily increasing." Jones would prove perceptive about other sectors of Fortress Washington.

Washington "is situated in a great basin and is completely surrounded by a high ridge of hills," Evan Jones had announced. At some points "it is invulnerable." "It would be the ruin of the most desperate army in the universe to endeavor to approach the city from the direction of Poolesville or Rockville," he proclaimed. "The chain of Defenses on that side of the city from Fort Alexander to Fort DeRussey is strong in every element of strength—too much so I think for any attacking force to be successful." "If the Rebs ever attempt to cross the plains below and to the north of those fortifications they will have a taste of our Fredericksburg and I can wish them nothing worse." Suddenly, by mid-1864, all this would be put to the test. Vermonters, New Yorkers, Pennsylvanians, and others would come again to Brightwood when the imminent threat of Rebel invasion further transformed their illusion that war was simply white gloves and gun drill, repetitious and monotonous. The test would come precisely where Evans said it shouldn't![31]

Notes

1. B. W. Sulfrin to wife, son, October 4, 1861, files, Fort Ward Park, Alexandria, VA; Robert Hunt Rhodes, editor, *All for the Union: The Civil War Diary and Letters of Elisha Hunt Rhodes* (Lincoln, RI: A. Mowbray, 1985/New York: Orion, 1991), 33, 36.

2. Letters, A. S. Bray to brother, August 30, 1861, and William Dunlop Dixon to Martha, September 3, 1861, both author's collections.

3. Matthew Pinsker, *Lincoln's Sanctuary: Abraham Lincoln and the Soldiers' Home* (New York: Oxford University Press, 2003), part 1; also "The Soldiers' Home: A Long Road to Sanctuary," *Washington History* 18 (2006): 5–18.

4. Katherine Grandine, "Brightwood: From Tollgate to Suburb," in Kathryn Schneider Smith, editor, *Washington at Home: An Illustrated History of Neighborhoods in the Nation's Capital* (Baltimore: Johns Hopkins University Press, 1988), 90–91; Mary Konsoulis et al., *Battleground to Community: Brightwood Heritage Trail* (Washington, DC: Cultural Tourism DC, 2008), introduction; John Clagett Proctor, *Proctor's Washington and Environs: Written for the Washington Sunday Star (1928–1949)* (Washington, DC: self-published, 1949), 98–101, 106–09.

5. Philip W. Ogilvie, *Vinegar Hill Area 1715 to 1964* (unpublished typescript, 2002), 1–10, copy, author's files.

6. In addition to ibid., see John Gross Barnard, *A Report on the Defenses of Washington to the Chief of Engineers, U.S. Army* (Washington, DC: Government Printing Office, 1871), plate

10, and David V. Miller, *The Defenses of Washington during the Civil War* (Buffalo, NY: Mr. Copy, 1976), plate 171-100; Proctor, ibid., 107–8.

7. Lewis Cass White diary, August 31, 1861, Joseph and Sharon Scopin, Darnestown, Maryland; Judith Beck Helm, *Tenleytown, D.C.: Country Village into City Neighborhood* (Washington, DC: Tennally Press, 1981), chapters II and III; William M. Offut, "The Civil War in the Chevy Chase Area," *Chevy Chase Historical Center Newsletter* (Fall 2011): 4–5.

8. Helm, *Tenleytown*, 121–29.

9. Rhodes, *All for the Union*, 33, 38, 40; U.S. War Department, *The War of the Rebellion: A Compilation of the Official Records of the Union and Confederate Armies* (Washington, DC: 1880–1901), Series I, Volume 5, 611, 678–85, especially 682–83, hereinafter cited *ORA* with reference to series, volume, page, accordingly; Calvin D. Cowles, compiler, *Atlas to Accompany the Official Records of the Union and Confederate Armies* (Washington, DC: 1891–1895), plate 6:1, 52; R. A. Hodasevich (Chodasiewicz), "Topographical Map—1st Brigade, Defenses North of the Potomac, 4/17 to 6/27 and from 7/20 to 8/25," Map Division, Library of Congress.

10. *ORA*, I, 5, 626–28.

11. Letter, Henry T. Blanchard to brother, January 29, 30, 1862, author's collections; Lewis Cass White diary, entries, August 1861 to March 1862, Joseph and Sharon Scopin, Darnestown, Maryland.

12. Rhodes, *All for the Union*, 52–53.

13. Pinsker, *Lincoln's Sanctuary*, part 1.

14. *ORA*, I, 19, pt. 2, 391–93.

15. *ORA*, I, 19, pt. 2, 391–93.

16. *ORA*, I, 21, 916; 19, pt. 2, 461–62.

17. *ORA*, I, 21, 902–3, 915.

18. *ORA*, I, 21, 909–10.

19. *ORA*, I, 21, 911.

20. *ORA*, I, 21, 915.

21. *ORA*, I, 21, 904.

22. Noah Brooks, *Washington in Lincoln's Time* (New York: Century, 1895), 15–16.

23. Letters, John H. Guiesinger to uncle, October 26, 1862; B. DeWitt to father, May 15, 1863, and N. Batchelder to sister, June 11, 1863, all author's collections.

24. Donald H. Wickman, editor/compiler, *Letters to Vermont: From Her Civil War Soldier Correspondents to the Home Press, volume II* (Bennington, VT: Images from the Past, 1998), 123–37.

25. Ibid.; see also Aldace F. Walker Papers, Vermont Historical Society, Burlington, as cited in Benjamin Franklin Cooling, *Jubal Early's Raid on Washington, 1864* (Baltimore: Nautical and Aviation Publishing Company of America, 1989; Tuscaloosa, AL: University of Alabama Press, 2007), 129 and f.n. 1, 314.

26. Benjamin Franklin Cooling, *Symbol, Sword and Shield: Defending Washington during the Civil War* (Hamden, CT: Shoestring Press, 1975; Shippensburg, PA: White Mane, 1991), chapter 6; *ORA*, I, 29, pt. 1, 8–11, 406; Gideon Welles, *Diary of Gideon Welles* (Boston: Houghton Mifflin, 1911), I, 469–72; Pinsker, *Lincoln's Sanctuary*, part 2.

27. William Van Zandt Cox, *The Defenses of Washington: General Early's Advance on the Capital and the Battle of Fort Stevens* (Washington, DC: 1907), 4 f.n.; Bernard Kohn, "Restored Civil War Fort Is New Sightseeing Shrine," *Washington Sunday Star*, July 4, 1937.

28. George W. Ward, *History of the Second Pennsylvania Heavy Artillery* (Philadelphia: G. W. Ward, 1904), 25; Letter, "A.F.S." to "Friend Frank," January 31, 1864, copy, Peter Seaborg collection, Defenses of Washington files, Fort Ward.

29. *ORA*, I, 33, 708–9, also 472, 1047; Ward, *Second Pennsylvania Heavy Artillery*, 38–39; Howard K. Beale, editor, *The Diary of Edward Bates 1859–1866* (Washington, DC: Government Printing Office, 1933; New York: De Capo, 1971), 360–61.

30. *ORA*, I, 37, pt. 3, 3–4, 697; Delavan S. Miller, *Drum Taps in Dixie: Memoirs of a Drummer Boy, 1861–1865* (Watertown, NY: BiblioLife, 2008), 79; Edgar S. Dudley, "A Reminiscence of Washington and Early's Attack in 1864." Loyal Legion of the United States, Ohio Commandery. *Sketches of War History 1861–1865, volume I*, 107–27. Cincinnati: Robert Clarke, Co. and 1888.

31. Letters, A.J.S. to friend Frank, January 30, 1864, Seaborg Collection, Fort Ward Park, Alexandria, VA, and Evan G. Jones to friend Davis, January 21, 1863, both author's collections.

ABE'S REELECTION, OLD JUBE, AND THE MOMENT OF GREATEST DANGER

W ar is about risk—a game of cards to the great nineteenth-century Prussian war theorist Carl von Clausewitz. Poker, even a throw of the dice, could condition results. So by 1864, the outcome of the Civil War still rested with risky moves on the battlefield as well as, perhaps ultimately, the political arena. Most certainly military matters affected civilian affairs. After all, this was a national election year for the embattled Union. What Union arms did on the battlefield as well as what President Abraham Lincoln's administration did politically would condition how national will translated at the polls. If the year started with great promise, it would dramatically change by summer. Perhaps two men held the keys to direction—one in uniform, the other in mufti. Among those keys was the security of the nation's capital.

The Grand Union Plan

Abraham Lincoln and Ulysses S. Grant were the arbiters at this point. The Union centers of gravity—Washington as political command center and the field armies— numbered among the pawns. The administration brought Grant east in March from his triumphs west of the Appalachians. His previous victories boosted confidence in his abilities. Top-level consultations developed the military strategy for the coming campaign season. In "command of the Armies of the United States" (as General Order 98 read), Grant might lead from Washington or elsewhere. He chose to travel with Major-General George E. Gordon Meade's Army of the Potomac for hands-on management of that critical force. This army had never quite fulfilled its promise under previous commanders such as McClellan, Ambrose Burnside, Joseph Hooker, and really even George Meade. Truly more indicative of its name (protect the eastern frontier and the national capital) than its mission (capture the enemy capital and destroy its defending army), Grant sought to inculcate an offensive, not static, mentality in the force. The soldiery would wait and see; the Lincoln administration could not afford to do so. Lincoln no longer pressed the Washington protective mission, so confident was he in Grant's blunt enjoinder to Meade: "Lee's Army will be your objective point. Wherever Lee goes there you will go also." The commander-in-chief seemed content that those words ensured his city's security.[1]

Of course, other Union armies figured in the high command's grand strategic plan that spring. Grant's most trusted colleague, William T. Sherman, would try to capture Atlanta and destroy its Confederate defense force. More distant and less dependable, political-general Nathaniel Banks was to shift from the trans-Mississippi pursuit of cotton on Louisiana's Red River to capture the port of Mobile, Alabama. Smaller field armies were set up to assist Meade in the east. Franz Sigel's (later commanded by David Hunter) force in the Shenandoah and one that would eventually constitute something styled the Army of the James under political-general Benjamin Butler both drew together disparate forces strung out over various departments. Ostensibly, Sigel's troops would seal off the valley and thus eliminate any threat to Washington from that direction. Meade, augmented by Butler and drawing upon personnel-heavy units even from the defenses of Washington, would overwhelm Lee's Army of Northern Virginia. Offensive would offset defensive. Grant was too new to the eastern war to recognize any residue of paranoia still lingering about Washington's safety.[2]

Then there was Major-General Henry Halleck, Grant's predecessor as general-in-chief and, in fact, his superior from the earliest days of the war until now. Reassigned as "Chief of Staff of the Army, under the direction of the Secretary of War and the lieutenant-general commanding," he would still enjoy great influence. At times he doubted the efficacy of an overland campaign to Richmond from the army's winter encampments around Culpeper, Virginia. However, this was designed to unify Union actions into what would be later styled "army groups" for "co-operative action of all the armies in the field." While protecting territory already gained and occupied, such concentrations "can be practically effected by armies moving to the interior of the enemy's country" with "Lee's army and Richmond being the greater objects toward which our attention must be directed," Halleck wrote Butler on April 2. In the scheme of things, then, the Army of the Potomac held "the necessity for covering Washington." An offensive (much as McClellan and others had argued previously) would resolve the problem of protecting Lincoln's Achilles heel.[3]

The Washington Problem

It wasn't that Grant necessarily shelved the Washington protection problem in his mind or failed to see any long-range implications. Washington's protection always constrained the eastern army's flexibility. Still, a successful campaign could now put to rest that festering issue. Surely the $1 million project known as the Defenses of Washington, with its one hundred earthworks, eight hundred cannon, and upward of a corps garrison reinforced the view communicated by Assistant Adjutant General James Hardie to Halleck on March 8. "The general impression of my mind, produced by observations of the last seven days, is that the city is provided against attack with a system of fortifications calculated to inspire confidence as to the result," said Hardie. Especially when "viewing the system as intended to resist an assault of the enemy, and to compel him to resort to a siege, or to detain him until we can accumulate our resources for defense," he added. While recounting some weaknesses affording possible cavalry penetration or the unreliability of a weak picket line on the road in front of forts Stevens, Totten, Slocum, and Bunker Hill, for example, Hardie suggested "the garrison of the defenses is deemed sufficient, as to numbers, in view of the fact that the fronts not attacked may contribute the larger portion of their garrisons to the support of those threatened." Still, Secretary of War Edwin M. Stanton wanted assurance, and the next day he ordered further inspections with weekly reports detailing the "condition for defensive purposes," supplies, ammunition, forces, and especially road conditions relating from the city to the fortifications and those necessary for the military operations of those works.[4]

Further clarifying information came from Inspector General of Artillery, Brigadier General Albion P. Howe, on March 21. He noted what artillery regiments in the defenses might be organized into batteries for field service and how soon. Howe pointed out forts south of the Potomac numbered 450 guns. A full fighting complement of effective artillerymen required 9,456 men, of whom only 7,988 were present (a deficiency of 1,462). Similarly, forts north of the Potomac numbered 410 guns requiring 8,610 effective artillerymen with only 7,587 men available (a deficiency of 1,023). In Howe's view, "The Potomac River dividing the covering line would not render liable to a serious attack at the same time those portions of the line on the north and south sides of the river." Therefore, defenders could be moved more quickly than attackers to a threatened sector on either side of the river. Thus, reduction of fighting strength on one side of the river could be offset by reinforceable elements from the other, thus retaining what he called "the moral strength of the whole covering line."[5]

This arrangement would permit reduction of the full complement of the whole line of 4,305 men, or a reduction of 1,810 men from the present strength, argued Howe. He saw that the advantage of such reduction in the effective strength of any portion of the line below its full fighting complement "would depend, of course, upon the relation which the covering line bore to the operations outside of it." He felt that four heavy artillery regiments then on the covering line (numbering 6,330 effectives) would be sufficient to man forty-four field batteries (274 guns) and, within fifteen days he called for field service to "do fair light artillery service" in coordination with veteran field artillery. Howe concluded by recommending that any withdrawal of the defenses' highly skilled heavy artillerists be replaced by an equal force from the Veteran Reserve Corps and at once be instructed in the duties of that service.

Indeed, January strength statistics had shown an aggregate present total of 39,727 officers and men, 789 heavy and 246 field guns in the defenses. The defenses north of the Potomac alone—generally dismissed as the least potentially threatened sector given field operations in Virginia—counted 10,257 personnel and 334 heavy and 97 field guns. Stalwart heavy artillery units from Vermont, Pennsylvania, and New York lent strength to the figures. The spring campaign would change the statistics. Initially, buildup of Major-General Ambrose Burnside and his old IX Corps to fifty thousand took precedence on manpower demands. Grant might allow Baltimore commander Major-General Lew Wallace to retain heavy artillerists for forts guarding that always unsettled city, but Washington departmental commander Christopher A. Augur seemed particularly capable of mustering infantry out of such overstrength units as the Second Pennsylvania Heavy Artillery (1,800 white-gloved fortress garrison troops) and shipping them to the front. Those reports from Hardie led Halleck to wire Grant on the morning of March 25 that 1,800 men "can be immediately spared from the defenses of Washington," pending only a decision on whether they should be sent as heavy or light artillery. By 2 p.m., Grant had replied, "send the heavy artillery as they are; there is light artillery sufficient with the army." Halleck replied an hour and a half later that two heavy artillery regiments numbering about three thousand men would leave as soon as they could be replaced by men from other forts.[6]

Within a fortnight, Halleck reported a slightly different picture after consulting further with Augur. Writing Grant on April 17, Halleck said that despite his orders for making infantry from the Second Pennsylvania and Second New York heavy artillery units, Augur claimed this would leave his line too weak. Halleck informed Grant that the thirty-seven-mile defense line had incomplete works, and others were "injured" by the recent heavy rains and needing extensive repairs by working parties. Ten regiments and a battalion of "Heavies" garrisoned the line with thirteen thousand effectives (not counting one thousand shipped to Burnside). Of that number, "very few of these men have ever been under fire and one-third are raw recruits." He continued that public stores and buildings were exclusively guarded by Veteran Reserve Corps (VRC) invalids, while two thousand infantry, one thousand cavalry, and an artillery battery were forward positioned in the Bull Run/Occoquan gap between the southern defenses and Meade's army. Similarly, a few companies of cavalry and infantry were located north of the Potomac to guard railroads and to picket the river to the mouth of the Monocacy River south of Frederick, Maryland.[7]

Halleck further informed his superior that the artillery depot at Washington always had a number of batteries being repaired and fitted out, and there were also some four thousand dismounted cavalrymen at the Giesboro remount depot for that arm. "All these, in case of an emergency, could be armed as infantry and placed in the trenches," was his view. Halleck feared for the protection of the public stores (mostly housed in wooden sheds), for "if not well guarded would be burned by the rebels in this city and Alexandria." Citing customary board estimates of garrison figures (twenty-five thousand infantry/three thousand cavalry with a covering army; fifty thousand without), he concluded, "I think the estimates made to the President by the generals under McClellan at the time of his Peninsular campaign were about the same." Halleck reiterated his long-standing aversion to a line of defense too long ("but very able officers are of a different opinion"), and "the evil, if it exists, cannot probably be remedied now." The forts east of the Anacostia might be abandoned, but "if so, as they bear on the arsenal and navy-yard, they should be dismantled and the guns and ammunition removed."

Halleck bucked any decision on "what forces shall be assigned to General Burnside's command" to Grant. He simply enumerated Washington's heavy artillery units as

First Vermont	1,460
First Maine	1,591
Seventh New York	1,560
Ninth New York	1,322
Second New York	783
Tenth New York	1,278
First Connecticut	1,199
Second Connecticut	1,442
First Massachusetts	1,478
Second Pennsylvania	1,846
One battalion (Wisconsin)	388
Total	14,347[8]

Grant replied the next evening (April 18) that excepting the regiment Augur proposed to spare, "I did not expect to order any troops from the defenses of Washington," other than unassigned arriving troops. Even then, the Second Pennsylvania Heavy Artillery was supposed to merely move to Alexandria under Burnside's direction and relieve Army of the Potomac troops there on special duty so that they could rejoin their proper commands at the front. Meanwhile, the call had gone out to northern governors as well as military commanders from New York to the Midwest for more manpower. A perplexed Halleck reported on the afternoon of April 28, "General Augur has been stripped of almost everything available to give to General Burnside," when a temporary scare developed that Confederate general James Longstreet might interpose a force in Meade's rear along the railroad back to Alexandria. Halleck also wrote Butler at Fort Monroe that day, on the eve of the spring campaign: "Everything possible is now being done to accumulate a force in Washington from the Northern States, ready to re-enforce any weak points." Indeed, at this point, the monthly statistics for the Department of Washington still showed a paper strength of 51,874 (35,605 actually present) with 708 heavy and 308 field guns available to defend the city. Things would change dramatically within a fortnight. Grant and Meade took staggering losses in early battles in the Wilderness (eighteen thousand estimated) and Spotsylvania (another estimated eighteen thousand), but they kept moving southward, across the North Anna River (with possibly 2,600 more losses) toward Richmond. Other units in Washington forts quickly became a replacement pool for the eastern army. Grant would incur the risk of any direct threat to D.C.[9]

Any such threat to Washington appeared moot or muted at best. The ever-nettlesome activities of Lieutenant Colonel John Mosby's partisan rangers on the fringes hardly slowed the transfer of bluecoats languishing on road and bridge guards, as messengers, as roving patrols, or even the fort garrisons. Lincoln had been placated and had other things on his mind as the political season heated up. Halleck became a willing collaborator for stripping Washington of manpower, although his position gave him little choice. By May 12, Grant directed him to "send General Augur, if possible, with 10,000 of the best infantry from the defenses of Washington." Then Howe's May 17 report on the defenses provided the first glimpse of the state of things since Stanton had directed such a monthly statement.[10]

Critical Assessment on the Eve of the Storm

It was only mildly ironic that the document came from an artilleryman, not an engineer, but it was as rich in significant detail as anything the latter branch might deliver. Basically, Howe concluded, the forts "are ample in their engineering and artillery strength for the purpose for which they were intended—the defense of Washington." As to the "character and strength of the troops garrisoning the different forts, their discipline, drill, and efficiency, the kind and extent of the armament, the condition and supply of the magazines, ammunition, and implements are found in this report under the names of the respective forts." And it was with the trained artillerist's eye that Howe contributed the most to the discussion. Howe predictably devoted much attention to the south-side defenses, despite two previous campaigns north of the river. In truth, federal authorities remained fixated on south-side danger, all imagined flexibility at shifting units back and forth as needed in an emergency. Still, Howe basically found well-defended works preventing "an enemy seriously to annoy Washington with a fire from the south side of the river." They could not be carried by an assault "with an artillery strength of men sufficient to develop the fire of the forts and a proper support of infantry." Likewise, forts behind Alexandria only insofar as they protected that depot were beyond artillery range of Washington itself and "are sufficiently strong, if properly manned, to resist an assault." The greatest danger here, as around the whole line, remained surprise, since weak outposts, the malpositioning of the garrison, and the topography/road arrangement outside the works "all favor and invite a sudden and covered dash upon the works." Advance picket lines (on the south side to protect the railroad and on the north guarding river fords) seemed adequate, as did the military roads inside the defense perimeter for rapid, lateral communication or troop transfer. At least, that was Howe's assessment.

Howe did criticize the unmaneuverable heavy-caliber cannon in the river defenses as unable to prevent the Potomac passage. He wanted the completion of the lesser caliber weapons authorized for Battery Rodgers and Fort Foote. He sought improvement to forts Ward (south) and Stanton (east of Anacostia), for completion time lagged and guns remained unmounted. The forts east of the Anacostia constituted the least liable to attack, in his view, while the most important position north of the Potomac generally lay between forts Sumner and Slocum "as it covers the approaches to the city on the river line of roads" into the city from the northwest. He wanted more VRC troops supporting the northern lines overall and pilloried the Ninth New York Heavy Artillery "in point of discipline and drill (both in artillery and infantry) [as] much less efficient than any regiment in the line of defenses." The fault lay with the commanding officer, Colonel Joseph Welling, not the "generally young, active, and intelligent men." The condition of the regiment bore "unmistakable evidence that the colonel of the regiment is not fit for the command."

Howe's fort-by-fort recitation was instructive in word and meaning for what would unfold later in the season. He noted indifference among many heavy artillery units along the northern lines in terms of drill and discipline, although their arms, equipment, and supplies seemed in sufficient order. Such indifference that attended the Second, Seventh, Eighth, Ninth, and Tenth New York, First Vermont, First Maine, and First Massachusetts heavy artillery regiments may have been attributable to their imminent posting for field duty. They numbered among fifty-five contingents Halleck told Grant that he had shipped forward in May. Halleck, responding to Grant's continuing demands for manpower, indeed had stripped 48,265 replacements from the Department of Washington, including ten highly proficient "heavies" regiments. It proved a simple task to reduce Washington's protective screen to about thirty-three thousand men by the time a new Yankee disaster at Cold Harbor demanded more cannon fodder. From May 31 to June 12, thirteen thousand more Federal soldiers were added to casualty lists from the spring; a grand total estimate since the Army of the Potomac had left Culpeper winter encampments of nearly fifty-two thousand men! Little wonder Grant acquired the dubious sobriquet "butcher." Nonetheless, battle losses demanded replacements, whether trained technicians or bored garrison soldiers.[11]

Little matter that engineers such as Major-General John Gross Barnard, who had designed the fort system early in the war, protested that barely one-third of the necessary numbers actually manned the earthworks. Officials such as Halleck and Stanton found solutions to Washington's defense problems in limited-duty walking-wounded convalescents and short-term so-called 100-days men raised by northern governors. With time and drill, they might work the heavy fort guns or stand picket until Grant and Meade could dispatch a relief column in an emergency—if that became necessary. Meanwhile, besieging Richmond and Petersburg, Grant had earlier announced that he intended fighting it out on this line if it took all summer. He presumed his wily opponent thought likewise. Halleck captured the feeling and intent on May 23 when he wrote Grant: "Permit me to repeat what I have so often urged, that in my opinion every man we can collect should be hurled against Lee, wherever he may be, as his army, not Richmond, is the true objective point of this campaign." When that army is broken, he continued, then Richmond would be of very little value to the enemy. By mid-June, even Lincoln exclaimed, "I begin to see it [Grant's plan]," adding "you will succeed."[12]

Lincoln's Spring

But could Lincoln succeed politically? He had been nominated for reelection on June 8. His chances depended upon military success. War and politics had converged again. The commander-in-chief as the nation's political leader spent the first six months of 1864 doing what nineteenth-century presidents did—and then some. The previous year had ended with a short trip down the Potomac with Secretary of War Stanton to see how many of some ten thousand Rebel prisoners at the Point Lookout prison camp were ready to change sides and don Union blue. According to the *New York Tribune* they numbered about 10 percent. Then came a festive New Year's Day reception remembering Union successes of the previous year and hoping to build upon them in the coming election year. Lincoln presided over what historian Doris Kearns Goodwin coined a "team of rivals." Unpopular with many politicians as well as citizenry but equally popular with (or tolerated by) others, the sixteenth president was above all a war president—manager, cheerleader, strategist, and confident of his philosophy, policies, and programs. They would all be sorely tested in the coming weeks and months by friend and foe alike.[13]

Of course, customary paperwork—stays of military execution, additional instructions to tax commissioners, accommodation to job seekers—transited the president's desk. There were new twists for the chief executive—clarification of amnesty provisions for southern civilians and further explanation for his thoughts and actions concerning freed African Americans. He even entertained extending the ballot to black males who "have so heroically vindicated their manhood on the battle-field." By April, Lincoln was obviously pained by the reported massacre of black troops by Rebels at Fort Pillow, Tennessee. Extending volunteers' bounty payments, New York state draft quotas, and signing a new two-hundred-thousand man callup in March vied with the monitoring of military occupation in borderland Kentucky as well as secessionist Arkansas, Louisiana, Florida, and elsewhere. Diplomatic matters intruded regarding royal births and deaths and new leaders in the United Kingdom, Russia, Portugal, and Denmark—even the king of the Hawaiian Islands. Difficulties in the Americas as well as treaties with Native Americans, the illegal capture of foreign vessels by the navy, economic considerations such as reopening the Texas port of Brownsville to commerce, extending cotton-trading privileges "from within rebel lines," as well as setting transcontinental railroad termini—important to the government "for postal, military and other purposes"—similarly emerged.

The president took time to counter author James Russell Lowell's interpretation of his antebellum philosophies regarding secession, obligations, and the legal rights of citizenry under the Constitution. But in Lincoln's inimitable fashion, on January 8, he had taken a few moments to thank Mrs. Esther Stockton, an eighty-five-year-old widow of a Pittsburgh, Pennsylvania, minister who personally knitted some three hundred pairs of stockings for soldiers. At the closing of the great Sanitary Fair in Washington on March 18, Lincoln praised the women of America for their conduct and contribution to the war effort. And three years to the day from his taking the oath of office, Lincoln affirmed that "the United States Government must not undertake to run the churches," a reference to the military confiscation of church properties, the imprisonment of ministers, and other matters connected with religious denominations in the South.[14]

Above all, however, Lincoln kept a wary eye on political rivals. When he brought Grant east as top general, the president made clear that he expected Grant to publicly respond to the president's brief remarks of introduction: "First, . . . something which shall prevent or obviate any jealousy of you from any of the other generals in the service; and second, something which shall put you on as good terms as possible with the army of the Potomac." Grant dutifully complied. For one thing, it was important to retain the loyal and dedicated service of political generals such as Nathaniel Banks, Benjamin Butler, and Lew Wallace (who Lincoln specifically invited to join other general officers at an executive mansion dinner at 6:45 p.m. on March 12). He gently chided German American politician in uniform Carl Schurz about leaving his military duties to visit Washington, with obvious political intentions.

But the president mostly stood back, confident that Grant's overall team was solid and had a good plan for early success. In a manner he would never have said to any of Grant's predecessors, the commander-in-chief expressed "entire satisfaction with what you have done up to this time, so far as I understand it." "The particulars of your plans I neither know, nor seek to know," he wrote on April 30. "You are vigilant and self-reliant," he told him. "I wish not to obtrude any constraints or restraints upon you." While anxious to avoid great disaster or the capture of our men in large numbers, Lincoln promised that "if there is anything wanting which is within my power to give, do not fail to let me know it." He had made that promise to each of Grant's predecessors. By May 9, all Washington welcomed word that Grant had won a victory in the Wilderness and had moved on to Spotsylvania Court House to the south. Grant kept moving forward, and Lincoln liked that trait.[15]

Renomination and Congressional Pushback

Yet, political matters always simmered just below the surface. He reached out to the New York Workingmen's Democratic Republican association so as to keep their shoulders to the wheel. Opposition to Lincoln's renomination appeared in late February, with Secretary of the Treasury Salmon P. Chase heavily involved. Despite continuing obstacles, the nominating committee of something styled the National Union convention meeting in Baltimore notified Lincoln of his selection on June 9. Lincoln replied that day that he was gratified, certainly accepted, "yet perhaps I should not declare definitely before reading and considering what is called the Platform." He did approve the declaration favoring a constitutional amendment prohibiting slavery throughout the nation. Notwithstanding earlier difficulties with its embrace by "the people in revolt," the unconditional Union men, North and South, now saw its importance and accepted it. So he told them, "In the name of Liberty and Union, let us labor to give it legal form, and practical effect." By the twenty-seventh, Lincoln was satisfied with the platform and "gracefully accepted" the renomination, although this time his reply to the committee underscored not a slavery amendment but rather that a troublesome French intervention in neighboring Mexico and the supplanting of a republican government upon the Western continent was "menacing and threatening" to the United States. Above all, however, Lincoln and the National Union convention reaffirmed the doctrine of unconditional surrender in this war of rebellion.[16]

June was a busy month for the president and his administration. Hints of conspiracy and clandestine Confederate operations in the Midwest and the acknowledgment of the arrival of the first Midwestern "100-day" volunteer regiments "to help us in this the nation's day of trials" vied with popular patriotic expression in the Great

Central Sanitary Fair in Fairmount Park and downtown Philadelphia meetings for the president's time. His crowning political achievement came on the last day of the month when he accepted the resignation of cabinet member yet political rival, Salmon P. Chase. He had already dismissed any Grant candidacy as well as that of potential troublemakers such as John C. Fremont and others. "Of all I have said in commendation of your ability and fidelity, I have nothing to unsay," he told Chase, "yet you and I have reached a point of mutual embarrassment in our official relation which it seems can not be overcome, or longer sustained, consistently with the public service." The chief executive could no longer tolerate a "team of rivals," nor as commander-in-chief could he tolerate military intransigence preventing what he and the National Union convention had reaffirmed in their party platform—a policy of unconditional victory at the polls and on the battlefield.

Then, several matters came to a head in early July. First, Lincoln's radical opponents in Congress determined to test which branch of government would control postwar southern reconstruction. Instead of the president's reasonably moderate 10 percent repentance requirement, legislators demanded a majority for obeisance. On a stifling Independence Day, Lincoln quietly pocketed this truculent measure by senators Henry Winter Davis and Benjamin Wade. The next day he sent out two important missives over his signature. First, he suspended the writ of habeas corpus in Kentucky, teetering on the brink of disunion thanks to widespread guerrillaism and lawlessness stoked by oppressive military authority, fears of emancipation, and the enlistment of African Americans against draft quotas. The administration could ill afford to lose the affections or the vote of loyal Kentuckians. Second, equally ominous and even quite mysterious, Lincoln wired John W. Garrett, president of the vital Baltimore & Ohio railroad in Baltimore: "What does Sandy Hook [railroad officials near Harpers Ferry] say about operations of Enemy and of Sigel, doing to-day?" Conditions on the upper Potomac had caught the president's attention.[17]

Lee's Brilliant Gamble

Confederate general Robert E. Lee and his president, Jefferson Davis, were no fools. They recognized the importance of their opponents' national election year. The Rebel government stoked the incendiary flames of Union homefront discontent about war taxes, conscription, suppression of civil liberties, and war weariness. It spawned a conspiracy to separate the Old Northwest states, including borderland Kentucky, from the Union. But most of all Richmond wanted to reverse the seemingly relentless conquest of the south by Grant and Sherman. Lee's own numbers and strength declined perhaps more proportionately than Grant's in the spring battles. So the South's best soldier desperately sought a counterstroke. In fact, he had been thinking about that opportunity for some months. Subordinates such as Lieutenant General James Longstreet, even before he returned from East Tennessee in April, and the ubiquitously self-promotional Maryland brigadier Bradley T. Johnson among others advocated a raid on Washington, the capture of Lincoln, and the reversal of fortunes in Virginia. At first, Lee thought he could thus compel Meade to retire upon the capital. At some point, he apparently asked mapmaker Jedediah Hotchkiss to prepare a detailed portrayal of Washington's northern suburbs and defense line. Then, overtaken by Grant's buildup and offensive, Lee could only backpedal ever closer to the Confederate capital. Suddenly, in June, opportunity knocked when Major-General David Hunter's Yankee column coursed the Confederacy's sacred breadbasket of the Shenandoah Valley. They must be stopped and destroyed. Then the way might be open for another foray north of the Potomac.[18]

Beneath his courtly demeanor, Lee was always a risk taker. Scion of one of Virginia's first families, courtly southern gentleman, and above all, a professional soldier, the fifty-seven-year-old general was the perfect age for a senior leader. His gray hair and beard and periodic bouts with ill health while in the field generally belied a sharp mind and crisp grasp of military affairs. He was not a man to permit the enemy to seize and hold the initiative for long. He had dictated the course of events in the east for two years. Now, in 1864, he chafed inwardly that fate had awarded Grant the upper hand. Lee sought a way to regain the offensive. If Federal losses were huge, the Confederacy's own casualties were unsustainable. Manpower replacements had become difficult to find across the South. Dwindling food supplies, shortages in clothing, medicine, and equipment as well as Hunter's destructive activities in the valley weighed heavily upon him. President Davis and his principal advisor, General Braxton Bragg, sought answers from Lee while the Virginian pondered limitations. Gone were the days when his Army of Northern Virginia as a whole could make brilliant forays across the Potomac. Yet some bold counterstroke seemed necessary. Lee acknowledged to Davis on June 11 the advantage of expelling the enemy from the valley, but "the only difficulty with me is the means." Direct attack on Grant was out. If hazarding defense of Richmond by withdrawal of an army corps seemed the answer, then Lee was willing.[19]

The next day, Lee summoned his best candidate for the task to his headquarters near Cold Harbor. Frankly, the list of possibilities had diminished, and that candidate was perhaps the crustiest general in the Army of Northern Virginia. Jubal Anderson Early now commanded the old Second Corps of the immortal Thomas Jonathan Jackson. Early was much like Stonewall—but without the religion. Eccentric in his own way, Early was profane, independent, and irascible—Lee's bad, old man and, frankly, with Jackson in his grave, Longstreet and Ewell hors d'combat, there wasn't anybody else. A West Pointer and backcountry lawyer, veteran of the Seminole and Mexican wars, he had been a Unionist before Virginia's secession brought him back in uniform. He had risen through regimental and division command and had proven himself on the battlefield.

Nicknamed "Old Jube," he once faced off with Jackson when queried why his chief had discovered stragglers behind Early's marching men. Because, said Early, Jackson had been riding there. Never as dear to Rebel hearts as Stonewall, the ranks, claimed George McCullough Mooney, Company H, Fifth Virginia, referred to Early as "old lop ear, his ears were so big." His predecessor, the crippled Dick Ewell, always thought Early had politicked for his job, something Old Jube denied vehemently. There was bad blood between them. Nonetheless, Lee told President Davis on the fourteenth: "If the movement of Early meets with your approval, I am sure it is the best that can be made," although adding wearily that the limited extent of his own knowledge "to perceive what is best." In any event, Early was to save Lynchburg and the Valley from the clutches of "Black Dave" Hunter. Barring Grant's suddenly becoming active before Richmond/Petersburg, Early's force would move rapidly down the Shenandoah, cross the Potomac, and capture (or at the very least threaten) Washington. Jackson had talked about the idea in 1861. An attack on Washington might cause Grant's recall.[20]

Hunter's people had practiced "hard war" as they marched up the Valley before turning east to Lynchburg. War production facilities, storehouses, even civilian property felt the bluecoats' wrath. They had torched the famed Virginia Military Institute and Virginia governor John Letcher's home in Lexington—arguably public property related to the rebellion but raising southern ire to the point that Lee wanted to punish Hunter. Ironically, a crisp but arduous march and rail trek by Early's nine thousand hard-bitten veterans from June 13 to 17 not only reinforced Kentuckian John C. Breckinridge's eleven thousand defenders holding Lynchburg but also so completely unnerved Hunter that a brief confrontation saved the city and sent the Yankees scurrying back to the valley. But instead of retiring whence he had come, back down the valley, or as he had originally intended, to move on and join Grant and Meade, Hunter retired into the West Virginia mountains.

Fearing Early's pursuers would block the valley route, Hunter sought his Potomac supply base via Salem (June 21), Lewisburg (June 26), Charleston (June 30), and Parkersburg on the Ohio River. What Early did not do to Hunter, guerrillas, hunger, fatigue, and demoralization did. Hunter might think his command was in "excellent heart and health" having been "extremely successful, inflicting great injury upon the enemy." But at least Chaplain William Walker of the Eighteenth Connecticut indicated otherwise. The twenty-mile-per-day forced march was one of the most "difficult and dangerous retreats of the war," in the face of heat, starvation, and death. More to the point, Hunter's move opened Early's next move in Lee's scheme. Years later, Lee told Hunter how gratified he had been that the Federal "had preferred the route through the mountains to the Ohio." At the time, Lee merely felt

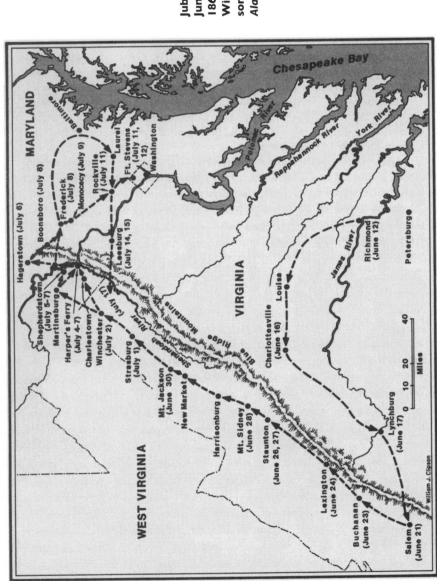

Jubal Early's Raid, June 12–July 18, 1864, map by William J. Clipson. University of Alabama Press

Hunter "has not been much punished except by the demoralization of his troops and the loss of some artillery." Lee was winning the game of risk in Virginia. Grant appeared clueless.[21]

Early's Raid to Washington

Early's march on Washington began immediately after his Lynchburg victory. Lee momentarily fretted when Federal pressure at Petersburg built by midmonth. He telegraphed Early on the eighteenth to strike Hunter quickly so that he could either return to help the main army or go forward with the original plan. By June 21, Early was moving "in accordance with original instructions." A relieved Lee ensured that Davis still concurred with the operation. But by this time Early's men were already swinging jauntily down the valley pike, headed north to adventure and anticipated success. At first, men in the ranks such as Lieutenant Leonidas Lafayette Polk of the Forty-Third North Carolina had thought Grant "like the whole Yankee nation," and Lee intended a long stay in the trenches for the summer. The move to Lynchburg suggested otherwise, he wrote his wife. She should not be surprised to hear that he and the army might have gone to Maryland and Pennsylvania, even Ohio "or any-where else" on a "sort of independent wild goose chase" with no telling where they might finish up. Early knew where he was going, for Lee had definitely told him to "threaten Washington and if I find an opportunity—to take it."[22]

The march to Staunton was almost triumphal. There would be stops and de-lays, and the drought of summer dictated periodic rest. Early's men took time for a pilgrimage to Jackson's grave and to view the ruins of VMI and Letcher's home at Lexington. A stop at staff officer Sandie Pendleton's home to feast on cold ham, lettuce, rice, and raspberries permitted his mother to regale the party with lurid tales of Yankee insults and depredations, thus raising more Rebel hackles. Many of the soldiers, however, were barefoot and in tattered uniforms. Many were on sick call thanks to months of marginal diets as well as the rugged marching and debilitating fighting. So when the force reached Staunton, Early called a halt and allowed many of the troops to wander off to visit local friends or relatives and to forage in ripe orchards and fields. Consultation with commissary chief Major Wells J. Hawks de-veloped a woeful tale of slow resupply, so Early decided to reorganize what would be styled a new "Army of the Valley District." He would strip unnecessary baggage and excess wagons from the entourage and hold officers and men to strict accounting for only the necessities of weapon, equipment, and toilet. When Father James Sheeran of the Fourteenth Louisiana protested to the general several days later at Winchester about "the manner in which you have treated me," the crusty army commander re-joined that even he had only one pair of underdrawers "and had to do without them whilst they were being washed."[23]

Early's reorganization was most important. First off, what was to be done with Major-General John C. Breckinridge, the forty-three-year-old veteran of many battles east and west and former vice president of the United States? The Kentuckian had melded his Lynchburg defense force with Early's command so that now he became a supernumerary corps commander and second-in-command of the new army. Forty-one-year-old Lynchburg native and valley veteran John Echols replaced an ailing and not especially effective Major-General Arnold Elzey, who returned to local defense chores at Richmond. Echols was a key player since so many of the troops under his command were locals and had to be carefully watched as their patriotic ardor evaporated the further northward the campaign carried. Breckinridge's status also resolved a disruptive situation between Early and his crack division commander, Georgia two-star general John B. Gordon. The pair were high-spirited fighters, often at odds, and they suffered fools badly. Gordon's division held equally disruptive Louisiana "Tigers" Harry Hays, Leroy Stafford, and Zebulon York (the latter a transplant from Maine). Early trusted Breckinridge's steadying hand.

Happily, the other two divisions under thirty-five-year-old Robert Rodes (another Lynchburg native and VMI graduate) and North Carolinian Stephen Dodson Ramseur promised less disciplinary problems. Ramseur, a balding twenty-seven-year-old newlywed anticipated news of a firstborn child. As Southern historian Douglas Southall Freeman noted in retrospect, these major-generals "could operate advantageously together because a strong personal affection and the fullest confidence existed between them." As for the artillery and cavalry support echelons, thirty-nine-year-old Armistead Long took control of six batteries of forty guns organized into three battalions comprising mostly 12-pounder Napoleon bronze smoothbore cannon. Early's mounted arm was the most troublesome. Part of the problem was Old Jube, who regarded anything on horseback as merely "a Buttermilk ranger" more apt to forage and wander off than do good service. At least one of those "rangers" returned the compliment, contending Early was unfit to command a separate army by virtue of his personal habits, "even had he possessed the qualifications." Robert Ransom, a thirty-six-year-old Tar Heel, commanded the cavalry with brigade commanders of mixed quality. Marylander Bradley T. Johnson and Virginians W. L. "Mudwall" Jackson, John D. Imboden, and John "Tiger John" McCausland were those subordinates with Captain Thomas E. Jackson's battery of four guns in support. Together they had performed, but marginally thus far in the valley. Their spirits were freewheeling, their equipment questionable, and their discipline even worse. But Early would have to rely on his horsemen both for scouting as well as battlefield support. Frankly, they were much better at raiding in what had become the best traditions of Confederate cavalry. On the other hand, a gigantic raid was what Early's move was all about anyway.[24]

In one final bold, if controversial, decision, Early disbanded all Valley District reserve units. Secretary of War James Seddon told Davis and Lee that the general had exceeded his authority. But Early felt these men would do better staying home and harvesting crops so that civilians and soldiers alike might eat the following winter. While true, this move left Lynchburg and valley towns devoid of protection except for invalids and erratic home guards. Nevertheless, with Hunter safely pushed aside there seemed little likelihood of any Federals returning to the region any time soon. Early's offensive would provide the requisite defense. With that, Early's refreshed army, evoking the spirit and name of Jackson's famed "foot cavalry," marched swiftly out of bivouacs shortly before 3:00 a.m. on June 28. There may have been as few as fourteen thousand infantry and four thousand cavalry, or there may have been upward of twenty thousand men in the column together with fifty to fifty-five cannon and sixty or more wagons rolling down the Valley turnpike headed north to the Potomac. Early told Lee that his soldiers "are in fine condition and spirits, their health greatly improved." He anticipated no supply difficulties, and "if you can continue to threaten Grant, I hope to be able to do something for your relief and the success of our cause shortly." He promised, "I shall lose no time." One thing was certain—the Yankees had nary an inkling of what was coming.[25]

Notes

1. U.S. War Department, *The War of the Rebellion: A Compilation of the Official Records of the Union and Confederate Armies* (Washington, DC: 1880–1901), Series I, Volume 33, 669, 827–29, hereinafter cited *ORA* with reference to series, volume, page, accordingly; also author's *Symbol, Sword and Shield: Defending Washington during the Civil War* (Hamden, CT: Shoestring Press, 1975/Shippensburg, PA: White Mane, 1991), 181–84.

2. *ORA*, I, 33, 828.

3. *ORA*, I, 33, 663, 669, 794–95.

4. John Gross Barnard, *A Report on the Defenses of Washington* (Washington, DC: Government Printing Office, 1871), Appendix H, especially 123; *ORA*, I, 33, 660–61, 664, 673.

5. *ORA*, I, 33, 708–09.

6. *ORA* I, 33, 3, 4, 33, 373, 472–73, 678, 685, 729, 730, 733, 734, 803, 864.

7. *ORA*, I, 33, 887–88.

8. *ORA*, I, 33, 888.

9. Frances H. Kennedy, editor, *The Civil War Battlefield Guide* (Boston: Houghton Mifflin, 1998 edition), 285, 286, 289; *ORA*, I, 33, 770, 803, 826, 838, 864, 897, 940, 945, 955, 956, 992, 994, 1002–3, 1009, 1013, 1047–53, especially 1047.

10. *ORA*, I, 33, 708–9 and 36, pt. 2, 883–97.

11. *ORA*, I, 33, 685, also 36, pt. 1, 3, pt. 2, 652, 825, and pt. 3, 245; Grant's correspondence may be used conveniently from John Y. Simon, editor, *The Papers of Ulysses S. Grant*

(Carbondale and Edwardsville: Southern Illinois University Press, 1967–), volumes 10 and 11 as relevant; Kennedy, editor, *The Civil War Battlefield Guide*, 292.

12. *ORA*, I, 36, pt. 3, 393; 33, 114, 879–88, 897.

13. In addition to Doris Kearns Goodwin, *Team of Rivals: The Political Genius of Abraham Lincoln* (New York: Simon & Schuster, 2005), three other recent works outline Lincoln's critical 1864 year, including Charles Bracelen Flood, *1864: Lincoln at the Gates of History* (New York: Simon & Schuster, 2009); David E. Long, *The Jewel of Liberty: Abraham Lincoln's Re-election and the End of Slavery* (Mechanicsburg, PA: Stackpole Books, 1994), and John C. Waugh, *Reelecting Lincoln: The Battle for the 1864 Presidency* (New York: Crown, 1997).

14. Roy P. Basler, editor, *The Collected Works of Abraham Lincoln, volume III* (New Brunswick, NJ: Rutgers University Press, 1953), 95–382 inter alia and, for example, the Fort Pillow massacre, 345–46.

15. Basler, ibid., 234–35, 241, 262–63, 268, 324–25, 334.

16. Basler, ibid., 380–82, also 200–1, 259–60, 383, 384.

17. Basler, ibid., 385–426 inter alia, especially 386–88, 424, 425–26.

18. *ORA*, I, 32, pt. 2, 541–42, 566–67, and 37, pt. 1, 627, 707–58 inter alia, 767, 806; Bradley T. Johnson, "My Ride around Baltimore in Eighteen Hundred and Sixty Four," *Journal of the United States Cavalry Association* I (September 1889): 250–60.

19. Clifford Dowdey and Louis Manarin, editors, *The Wartime Papers of Robert E. Lee* (New York: Brammel House for Virginia Civil War Commission, 1966), 774–75.

20. Jubal A. Early, *War Memoirs* (Bloomington: Indiana University Press, 1960), 371; *ORA*, I, 37, pt. 1, 346; John W. Daniel, "Jubal A. Early," in Edward Daniel, compiler, *Speeches and Orations of John W. Daniel* (Lynchburg, VA: J. P. Bell Co., 1911), 520; Henry Kyd Douglas, *I Rode with Stonewall* (Chapel Hill: University of North Carolina Press, 1940), 33; G. Moxley Sorrel, *Recollections of a Confederate Staff Officer* (Jackson, TN: McCowat Mercer, 1958), 50; Terry L. Jones, editor, *Campbell Brown's Civil War: With Ewell and the Army of Northern Virginia* (Baton Rouge: Louisiana State University Press, 2001), 259–60; Lee A. Wallace, *Fifth Virginia Infantry* (Lynchburg, VA: H. E. Howard, 1988), 60.

21. Dowdey and Manarin, *The Wartime Papers of Robert E. Lee*, 201, 206–7; Douglas Southall Freeman, *R. E. Lee, A Biography, volume 4* (New York: Scribners, 1935), 240–41; Frank Vandiver, *Jubal's Raid: General Early's Famous Attack on Washington in 1864* (Lincoln: University of Nebraska Press, 1992), 32–55, esp. 37–38; *ORA*, I, 7, pt. 1, 93–160 inclusive.

22. Letter, Jubal A. Early to Robert E. Lee, June 28, 1864, Civil War Folder #100, Civil War Collection, Huntington Library, San Marino, CA; Telegram, R. E. Lee to Jubal A. Early, June 26, 1864, Folder II, Telegraph Book, R. E. Headquarters papers, 241, Virginia Historical Society, Richmond (VHS); Early, *War Memoirs*, 371; *ORA*, I, 37, pt. 1, 346, 766–67; Leonidas L. Polk to wife, June 16, 1864, Southern Historical Collection, University of North Carolina, Chapel Hill (SHC/UNC).

23. Joseph T. Durkin, editor, *Confederate Chaplain: War Journal of Rev. James B. Sheeran, C.SS.R. Fourteenth Louisiana, CSA.* (Milwaukee: Bruce Publishing, 1960), 93. For other Confederate accounts of this period of Early's raid, see William Allan, "Reminiscences," 20, 21, 22, Allan papers and J. Kelly Bennette diary, June 4, 20, 21, 27, 1864, both SHC/UNC;

J. Stoddard Johnston, "Notes of March of Breckinridge's Corps from Lynchburg June 19 to Leesburg July 15," entries June 20, 21, 22, 1864, New York Historical Society (NYHS); Letter, Richard Colbert to Mrs. E. M. Potts, July 24, 1864, Archives of North Louisiana Historical Association, Centenary College, Shreveport, Louisiana (NLHA); "Draft Report of Twentieth North Carolina Regiment," July 1, 1864, Thomas F. Toon papers, North Carolina Department of History and Archives, Raleigh (NCHA); G. W. Nichols, *A Soldiers Story of His Regiment* (Kennesaw, GA: Continental Book Company, 1961 edition), 168–69; W. G. Bean, *Stonewall's Man: Sandie Pendleton* (Chapel Hill: University of North Carolina Press, 1959), 203–5; Douglas, *I Rode with Stonewall*, 291–92; Susan P. Lee, *Memoirs of William Nelson Pendleton, D.D.* (Harrisonburg, VA: Sprinkle Publications, 1991), 343–61; Robert E. Park, "Diary," *Southern Historical Society Papers* I (1876), 375; W. W. Scott, editor, "Diary of Capt. H. W. Wingfield," *Bulletin of the Virginia State Library* 16 (July 1927), 42; Richard W. Iobst, *Bloody Sixth: The Sixth North Carolina Regiment* (Gaithersburg, MD: Olde Soldier Books, 1987), 213–15; John H. Worsham, *One of Jackson's Foot Cavalry* (New York: Neale, 1904; Jackson, TN: McCowat Mercer, 1964), 149; James I. Robertson, *The Stonewall Brigade* (Baton Rouge: Louisiana State University Press, 1963), 230; George H. Lester, Georgia Division, "War Record of the Tom Cobb Infantry," in United Daughters of the Confederacy, *This They Remembered* (Washington, GA: Washington Publishing Company, 1965), 104; W. H. Runge, editor, *Four Years in the Confederate Artillery: Diary of Private Henry Robinson Berkeley* (Chapel Hill: University of North Carolina Press, 1961), 84–85; Robert Park, "Diary," 374–75, and "The Twelfth Alabama Infantry, Confederate States Army," *Southern Historical Society Papers* 33 (1905), 326; J. E. Green diary, June 17–July 12, 1864, Stephen D. Ramseur—wife, June 27, 1864, Ramseur papers, Allan, "Reminiscences," 24, all SHC/UNC; *ORA*, I, 37, pt. 1, 763 and 43, pt. 1, 602.

24. Vandiver, *Jubal's Raid*, 67–68; Douglas S. Freeman, *Lee's Lieutenants: A Study in Command* (New York: Scribner, 2001), III, 525–26, 558; Alexander Hunter, *Johnny Reb and Billy Yank* (New York: Neale Publishing Company, 1905), 649; *ORA*, I, 37, pt. 1, 776.

25. *ORA*, I, 51, pt. 2, 1028–29, also I, 37, pt. 1, 703–4, 769.

SIGEL, WEBER, AND DELAYS ON THE UPPER POTOMAC

W e may never know precisely how many men Early took with him to Washington. His own strength estimates came long after the fact, suggesting a total force of twelve thousand to thirteen thousand for the campaign. He claimed to have left Lee on June 13 with only nine thousand effectives. Various computations by Lee's chief of staff Colonel W. H. Taylor and Colonel William Allan (Early's ordnance chief) suggest a low of 9,570 infantry alone in a total force of thirteen thousand to fourteen thousand at the time of Lynchburg. Composite figures integrating Breckinridge's units provide plausible figures of 16,943 to 17,830, although one recent count adds Virginia Military Institute cadets and 1,900 home guardsmen at that point for a total of 20,443. This new count suggests that on June 28, Early really went forward to the Potomac with 13,561 infantry, 4,250 cavalry, and 990 artillerists for a total of 18,801. Figures cited by federal authorities such as Major-General John G. Barnard, Grant's chief engineer and architect of the defenses of Washington, generously claimed 22,420 Rebel officers and men appearing before the city in mid-July. Certainly none of this mattered to local farmers and their families flocking to the roadside to cheer their butternut heroes as they marched down the Shenandoah Valley. Everyone rejoiced that Early was taking the war to the enemy. It would have mattered had federal authorities known, however.[1]

Northward across the Potomac

Early's progress was slow at first. Distractions of exhilarating scenery, cheering bystanders, and diversions to pick berries or to capture some of Hunter's lurking stragglers accounted for covering less than a desired twenty miles per day. Then, breathing deeply, Early's men jogged a lusty twenty-four miles on June 29. Rumors swirled about going north again to Pennsylvania or even capturing Lincoln and Washington. Passing the "classic ground" of Jackson's earlier victories at Port Republic and Cross Keys inspired Louisiana brigadier Zebulon York as did New Market where, six weeks before, the VMI cadets had bested a Yankee lot under Franz Sigel. Early wrote Lee from that town at 9:30 a.m. on June 30 how "the wheat and grass crops in the Valley from Salem to this place are very fine and abundant; but little damaged by the enemy." Reserve troops were securing them. The telegraph to his rear was being repaired slowly and extended west from Lynchburg to Liberty and possibly north to Salem. This was the missive where he promised to "lose no time." Privately, however, he began to fret about encountering Federal outposts as he got closer to the Potomac. A contingent of scouts under Captain George W. Booth, adjutant of Colonel Bradley Johnson's Maryland cavalry, uncovered the first Federal opposition only near Winchester.[2]

When the army passed through that often-fought-over town on July 2 and 3, Alabama captain Robert Park discovered "the good people of W. received us ever kindly and enthusiastically." Certainly pro-Confederate Laura Lee and her family did. Not so for crosstown unionist Julia Chase. Having watched the marching Rebel host, she recorded in her journal for July 2, "We are only too much afraid that our leaders are not aware of this move, and the next thing we shall hear is that the rebs have entered Maryland, or torn up the R. Road." Still, the majority in the region were like Lucy Buck, a Front Royal Rebel, who was "enraptured" when she learned from local young men that "Early twenty thousand strong" was marching upon Martinsburg. The Forty-Third North Carolina was especially happy, recalling how terrorist-abolitionist John Brown had been tried and hung in Charlestown and that every household seemed to give up milk, butter, bread, and other delicacies not normally found in the army's diet. Fanning out above Winchester to Smithfield, Leetown and Charlestown began to dent Early's timetable when his troops encountered the first Yankee opposition.[3]

Scraps of information and rumors fed the conclusions of Winchester civilians Laura Lee and Julia Chase. Matching Lee's delight at the return of male friends and relatives in Early's array, her family home soon glowed with entertaining Early, his generals, and their staffs. Unionist Chase, meanwhile, remarked, "What a change 24 hours or even less than that has brought about." Arrests of her kind by Maryland cavalryman Harry Gilmor challenged equanimity in the town. Of course, this was only fair-play turnabout for Hunter's similar harassment of Rebels earlier. Chase thought the neighbors of the unionists "are the cause again of all this trouble, and there are some such despicable creatures in our town that they do not care what becomes of the Union people." If they could have their way, all loyalists "should be shot or hung, & yet Southern people call themselves such praying people, that they are more righteous & holy than the Northern people." Apprehensively, she anticipated "the coming anniversary of our Nation's independence." "Oh, God," she exclaimed, "may thy right hand lead us, and if it please thee give success to our National Arms." By July 3 and 4, the two diarists had secured more solid news.[4]

Chase counted heads, artillery pieces, and stands of colors. She recorded, "It is said between 25 to 30,000 troops & their object to destroy the Bal. & Ohio Railroad, probably also to enter Maryland & Pennsylvania." She asserted that "we shall expect to hear of much destruction of property in retaliation of the property destroyed by our generals in recent raids." Hopefully, Union defenders would be prepared and, my, how she wished "that this war was at an end, and Peace declared." But apparently a conversation between Early and an arrested Unionist disclosed that Old Jube was perfectly convinced "that the South would never be subjugated" and remained assured "of the South's Independence being declared," concluding that "time alone will determine these things." Laura Lee was more airy in her diary, recording only how Early and his staff came to tea on Saturday afternoon, followed by other swains in Rebel gray, while at 4:30 the next morning her family awakened to military bands and marching feet. Early and his coterie had resumed their march. So civilians cheered their knights ("in the finest spirits, though very shabby after their incessant marching and fighting for two months"), and by ten o'clock they had all vanished. Ruefully she noted the next day that with the army crossing into Maryland at Shepherdstown and Harpers Ferry, "already people are talking of their returning in a few days and leaving us again to the Yankees." No news passed the lines, and Chase's intelligence could not be sent to alert the national cause. Even Miss Lee found "we hear very little which is reliable from either side," the official communication being by signal "as there is no telegraph nearer than New Market."[5]

Early's difficulties now began to surface. Additional orders arrived from Lee to hold in the lower valley "until everything was in readiness to cross the Potomac." He especially wanted the Baltimore & Ohio railroad destroyed west of Harpers Ferry. The railroad was a direct link to the Ohio valley from the Chesapeake region. It provided a vital logistical link in the Union war effort and the means by which Hunter would return to the game board. Early would claim in his memoirs (unverifiable since the original document was apparently lost) that Lee's dispatch confirmed his previous set of priorities. But his provisions now ran short. Any rapid advance on Washington via the Virginia side of the river would entail stopping to thresh wheat, and one suspects that negotiations with local partisan ranger chief John Mosby in Loudon County reflected little enthusiasm on the latter's part to have a large army traipsing through his special domain, disrupting civilian comity, and perhaps souring the locals on a scavenging horde. Better, noted Early, that they take a more circuitous route across the river, seizing "provisions from the enemy" before descending on Washington from that angle. Hindsight or contemporary reality aside, friendly civilian providers and captured enemy supplies resolved his dilemma. Still, Early and his army lost valuable time exiting the lower valley. Moreover, the enemy had discovered them.[6]

If Grant remained skeptical that any sizable body of Rebels was descending the valley toward the Potomac, Henry Halleck was remarkably prescient. He had become sensitive to Washington's Achilles heel—the Shenandoah—especially from 1862 when both Jackson's campaign as well as Lee's subsequent Maryland campaign had unhinged the Union's grand drive on Richmond. Writing to the general-in-chief early on the afternoon of the first day of July 1864, Halleck speculated, "It certainly would be good policy for [the Confederates] (while Hunter's army is on the Kanawha) to destroy the Baltimore and Ohio Railroad and make a raid in Maryland and Pennsylvania." Sigel had few resources upriver, and Halleck worried about what he could send for reinforcements. Moreover, under Grant's order, artillery at Washington had been stripped of horses and put into the city's forts. Three batteries had been remounted subsequently and sent to the field army. "This leaves very little in the forts, except militia," Halleck continued, "who are not sufficiently instructed to work the guns." Sounding like a worrywart, perhaps, it may have been too early for Washington officials to react to multiple rumors when "some say that Breckinridge and Pickett are following the cavalry, which has just made a raid on the Baltimore and Ohio Railroad, while others say they are not in the Valley at all." Nevertheless, Halleck sensed potential mischief.[7]

Local Federal commanders, however, outnumbered and prone to panic at the thought of any large body of graycoats, would have to dispute whatever was coming their way. It was as simple as that. Facetious comments in Rebel ranks had John Pope and Franz Sigel commanding rear echelon railroad and depot guards. They scoffed that neither general could stand up to Jackson's veterans. But the Second Manassas campaign was past; Pope long departed to subdue Indians in Minnesota. The German émigré Sigel was indeed in charge in that district. Commanding something styled as the Reserve Division in Hunter's Department of West Virginia, Sigel had at his disposal 9,500 officers and men with thirty-four heavy and forty-four light artillery pieces. More realistically, he and his subordinates probably counted five to six thousand soldiers protecting Martinsburg, the Baltimore & Ohio, and Harpers Ferry. Yet another émigré brigadier, Max Weber, led dispersed garrisons all along the railroad from the Monocacy River on the east to Sleepy Creek in the Alleghenies to the west. Part of Sigel's and Weber's problem was this dispersion and how to concentrate without uncovering specific locations such as Duffield's Depot that was, indeed, soon captured and destroyed by Early's outriders. Weber could scarcely scare up 108 effective men and one effective battery when queried by Sigel's assistant adjutant general on July 2 about protecting Harpers Ferry and cooperating with a third German American brigadier, Julius Stahel, in countering Early's advance on Martinsburg.[8]

Sigel took charge of clearing out Martinsburg warehouses for shipment by wagon back to Frederick or burning on-site while Colonel John Mulligan battled the oncoming Rebels. Railroad agents kept Baltimore management, other officials up and down the line, and, frankly, the military apprised of the unfolding situation. By July 2, they all knew that this was no mere raid. Heavy fighting, scouts, and refugee reports all suggested "strong indications of a movement of the enemy in force down the Valley." Those were the very words Sigel telegraphed the adjutant-general of the army in Washington that day while Frederick, Maryland, provost marshall Major J. L. Yellott wired him that a lady in the small city had received information that her husband would be part of a Rebel army that would most certainly destroy the railroad between Martinsburg and Harpers Ferry on Sunday, July 3. Over the next three or four days, with communications to Hunter severed by rail and telegraph disruption to the west, Sigel continued to inform Washington while B&O agents told railroad Baltimore headquarters of the unfolding situation.[9]

Thus, B&O president John Garrett and master of transportation William Prescott Smith particularly underscored the concern for their railroad and matters unfolding on the upper Potomac. An ever-sensitive Halleck wired Grant late on the third about the threat but dismissed any deterrence by Sigel, Stahel, and Weber as marginal, relying upon Hunter to return to properly defend the sector. Of course, few at Grant's City Point, Virginia, headquarters credited anything more than another upcountry scamper helped by enemy cavalry raiders. Grant wired Halleck at 5 o'clock that no major force had left Lee's lines and that Hunter simply "ought to get back on the Baltimore and Ohio as soon as possible." Hunter (unaware of the threat due to downed telegraph lines along the railroad) tried to return to the playing field from Wheeling, West Virginia. He anxiously wanted an audience with Secretary of War Edwin Stanton. Grant wished to personally meet him at City Point and "in the meantime your troops should be so stationed as to prevent any serious raids by the enemy now in the valley." Just two days before the supreme commander had expected Hunter to move against the railroad and canal at Charlottesville, Virginia. Now, events were clearly moving beyond that idea. Early, however, hamstrung by Lee's message to linger for railroad destruction, intended to bag all Yankees upriver before either Hunter or Washington could intervene.[10]

The record remains unclear whether Sigel precipitously evacuated Martinsburg or was chased out by Early. "Cattle-Show doesn't come but once a year," voiced one Massachusetts soldier assigned to the provost marshal's office at Harpers Ferry, adding "neither does a 'Harper's Ferry skedaddle.'" The first information "of the close proximity of the Rebels, was on Sunday, the 3rd inst.," claimed one member of the Third Battalion, Fifth Maryland (Heavy) Artillery stationed on heavily fortified Maryland Heights across from the ferry. "Our scouts brought intelligence of a force of between six and seven hundred mounted men at Charlestown," apparently after Twelfth Pennsylvania cavalry horses, he suggested. Charles H. Moulton of the Thirty-Fourth Massachusetts (sending home newspaper columns under the nom de plume "Rambling Jour") observed that Independence Day in the town "presented a lively aspect, everybody packing up, knowing that it was time for the yearly 'skedaddle' which is as sure to come as Christmas itself."[11]

Certainly nativist prattle about panicky German American generals, self-covering reports by commanders on both sides, and the fog of actual events dot the historical record as historians accentuate the negative over the positive concerning Sigel and company. No doubt Early's cavalry plus local partisan ranger groups once more wrecked portions of Garrett's railroad from Harpers Ferry all the way to Patterson's Creek west of the mountains. Mosby's band even moved out of their Loudon County lair to cross the Potomac on the Fourth of July and disrupt rail and wire service from Point of Rocks toward Frederick. Local railroad as well as Frederick logistics officials and citizenry at first panicked, rushed to evacuate the sick, wounded, and the stores as well as to dispatch personal bank accounts to places of safekeeping. Then, they settled down to await developments. Early failed to snag Sigel, Weber, and Stahel or their supply train. By July 4, Sigel had safely retired to Maryland Heights, clustered under protective heavy guns of Fort Duncan and other batteries, and he invited Early's attention. Greatly criticized in so doing, Sigel and Weber effectively blocked passage on both the railroad and highway eastward through Point of Rocks to Frederick. The German Americans never received credit for that feat.[12]

Transiting Central Maryland

Early was stuck. He needed to gain the hardpan National Road, so familiar from the Maryland campaign two years before and the principal east-west highway through the region. Getting across South Mountain to the Jefferson-Frederick Road was another option. Everything depended upon reaching the road hub of Frederick City. Here, Early would hold the key to moving further against either Washington or Baltimore. Heavy artillery exchanges and skirmishing failed to dislodge the Yankees from Maryland Heights, and they blocked the Harpers Ferry river crossings, finally burning the bridges. So Early had to turn to the familiar path of two years before—north through Shepherdstown, Sharpsburg, the Antietam battlefield, and Keedysville thence to Boonsboro, where gaining the National Road meant a fast pace over South and Catoctin mountains to Frederick. Robert Rodes moved to Rohrersville on July 7 from the Sharpsburg area to prevent Sigel's escape. The more direct route from Harpers Ferry via Knoxville was Jefferson—Frederick might have gained a few extra hours and perhaps saved a bit of wear and tear on the men. It could have discomforted the Federals sooner since they were basically unprepared for any Confederate appearance beyond Harpers Ferry and vicinity. Sigel's stand on Maryland Heights and the burning of bridges across the Potomac at Harpers Ferry therefore shut down that option. Moreover, Sigel remained behind Early's troops awaiting Hunter's arrival by rail. Their unified force could close off Early's escape route in that direction.[13]

The boys in butternut and gray blissfully enjoyed the sumptuous Independence Day feasts left by evacuating Yankees at Martinsburg and Harpers Ferry. In a way, they lost as much time and advantage in that fashion as being denied march routes. In any case, Early's men took to the road again by July 5. At this point they could celebrate some good fortune. Having marched nearly two hundred miles since leaving Richmond, they had beaten Hunter back from Lynchburg, swept the enemy from the Valley, and captured quantities of desperately needed supplies. Scouts reported cooperation from local partisan bands for an advance into Maryland and a wildly enthusiastic populace that swelled pride in the ranks. How pleased both Early and Lee would have been if they knew that the fog of war completely engulfed the other side, much as it had two years earlier. On the other hand, did either of them recognize the inherent contradiction in Lee's directives?

If merely creating a diversion on the upper Potomac and some sort of raid into Maryland was the intent to draw Federals away from Richmond/Petersburg, then time was not a factor. Nor had success been obtained at this point. Grant and Meade had not taken the bait. But if threatening and capturing the Yankee capital in an election year was the principal goal, then time was vital. Delays ripping up railroads and eating oysters in Yankee camps on the Fourth of July while tweaking Sigel and Weber were impediments to success. Lee's multitasking (which would only get worse) carried the seeds of its own defeat. Moreover, it placed Early on the horns of a dilemma. By Independence Day afternoon, Federal authorities began to awaken. Grant wired Halleck and special war department official Charles A. Dana telegraphed Secretary of War Stanton simultaneously at 4 p.m. saying how a Sixty-First Virginia deserter had informed interrogators that "Ewell's" corps was not in Lee's lines and had gone north. Grant still dismissed a deserter's word but suggested the national capital region take precautions. Halleck would manage matters there, although Grant still looked to his old friend and mentor Hunter to "concentrate against any advance of the enemy."[14]

Early was no doubt slow in crossing the Potomac. Then, his raiding force lost verve transiting central Maryland. The weather was hot and dry; the jaded Rebels needed more rest stops than two years before with Stonewall Jackson. True, eating green corn did not decimate their ranks as it had in September 1862. But straggling and desertion took their usual toll, and Early even sent contingents back to Winchester to collect foragers there until the expedition's return to Virginia. Other detachments stopped to guard captured stores at Martinsburg and Harpers Ferry. Local boys such as Bott's Grays of the Second Virginia were permitted to wander off to visit families and to reoutfit themselves at home. Loyal staffer and Maryland Confederate major Henry Kyd Douglas even persuaded Early, Breckinridge, Gordon, and Ramseur to dine, however briefly, at his family home, Ferry Hill, outside of Shepherdstown on the way to Sharpsburg, where they then toured the ill-fated field of the previous Maryland campaign.

While bands once again played "Maryland, My Maryland" crossing the Potomac and John Worsham remembered how the sharp stones in the river bed "stuck in my feet at every step," Early himself embarked on a bit of "hard war" retaliation, sending Brigadier General John McCausland's troopers to extract $200,000 from Hagerstown burghers while he subsequently demanded $5,000 at Middletown. In both cases, he threatened to torch the communities upon nonpayment. McCausland bungled his assignment, misreading the decimal point and getting a tenth of the necessary cash. Early, too, only secured $1,500 at Middletown. Everyone fared better at Union warehouses and local clothing stores in Hagerstown. Rodes, after blocking Sigel at Rohrersville, moved speedily through Crampton's Gap to Jefferson and hurried on toward Frederick.

Early, like Lee earlier, issued strict orders against pillaging. On July 5, he reminded both officers and men that they were not on a marauding expedition and were not making war on the defenseless and unresisting. Strict discipline was in order, with supply requisition under the direction of chiefs of various departments and payment made accordingly. That proved fruitless as the bedraggled Rebels soon looked more like a circus than an army, eventually accumulating a nine-mile vehicular train of wagons, buggies, livestock, and other spoils of war. By this time, too, local contingents of Federals such as battle-tested veterans of the Eighth Illinois Cavalry under Lieutenant Colonel David R. Clendenin began nipping at Early's flanks and advance. A new wrinkle arose on the afternoon of July 6, when Lee's son, Captain Robert E. Lee Jr., rode into Early's camp near Sharpsburg. He bore a vague additional mission from his father.[15]

The Davis government and Lee in particular had become interested in a well-stocked Union prison camp at Point Lookout, Maryland, where the Potomac flowed into Chesapeake Bay. Intelligence had upward of fifteen thousand to twenty thousand Confederates held captive there. They invited release and return to Lee's ranks before Petersburg. Richmond wanted Early to send Maryland brigadier and Frederick native Bradley T. Johnson with his cavalry brigade on a circuitous raid toward Baltimore (ripping up rail and telegraph lines north of the city as well as between Baltimore and Washington) and then transit the one hundred or so miles to Point Lookout. They would liberate the captives (helped by an additionally cobbled-together naval force under Captain/Colonel John Taylor Wood) and march the whole bunch back up to

Washington and reunite with Early's main force, supposedly by then besieging or actually occupying the Federal capital. The elder Lee had saluted the scheme and sent his son as messenger to what would be an obviously perplexed Early. By this time, the expeditionary commander had so many conflicting, overlapping, and handicapping missions as to be on the cusp of losing focus as much as his men. For the moment, and until he got to Frederick, Early could do little but accept the order and mumble under his breath. Perhaps he began to question the success of the mission altogether.[16]

Early dutifully pushed his men on. As Federal resistance stiffened closer to Frederick, the timetable seemed to slip further. Clendenin's 250 men, bolstered by scattered local squadrons such as Colonel Henry Cole's Independent Maryland Cavalry, not only picked at the advancing Rebels but also countered any ancillary aid coming from the likes of Mosby's partisans. Moreover, harder intelligence added to the scattered reports of railroad operators as well as Sigel and Weber (the telegraph remaining intact from Harpers Ferry east on the B&O through Frederick to Baltimore). In fact, Early and company may have thought resistance came merely from militia as they caught sight of the "clustered spires" of Frederick (a phrase resonating from John Greenleaf Whittier's inspirational poem "Barbara Frietchie" marking Lee's incursion two years before). In fact, this resistance came from a series of coalescing factors involving railroad officials and the departmental commander in Baltimore as well as Washington officials and even Grant. To be sure, the general-in-chief still seemed out of touch, tepidly offering "if the enemy cross into Maryland or Pennsylvania I can send an army corps from here to meet them or cut off their return south." This was hardly a robust response to the oncoming storm.[17]

The Fog of War

Grant, and for that matter Lee, could only follow developments at a distance. Grant, of course, had a technical advantage, for City Point headquarters linked with Washington as well as field commands by the fragile wires of the telegraph. But the wartime confusion, the time lag in message traffic, and Grant's apparent cavalier attitude toward the capital city's safety were compounded by the technology of the device itself. Scarcely twenty years old, this communications marvel was complex, its operators often underperforming and, moreover, it was tied to railroad rights-of-way, in reality its reason for being in the first place. In that sense both railroad and telegraph as instruments of war had strategic and tactical value to friend and foe. Secretary of War Edwin M. Stanton jealously guarded control of the telegraph in Washington, Grant had no direct access to the secret ciphers for sending messages, and perhaps only Lincoln enjoyed ready access to the telegraph corner in the War Department at Seventeenth and Pennsylvania Avenue, N.W.

Beyond the capital, the wires ran beside the tracks to Baltimore, thence to places like Harpers Ferry and the west and northward to the rest of the nation. Army Signal Corps stations provided supplemental contact with the armies in the field, but resources remained a problem. Lieutenant Amos M. Thayer, acting signal officer for operations around Harpers Ferry, reported he had fifty-eight men and two officers who, with one exception, "were recruits who had seen no active service and were of necessity inexperienced in everything pertaining to the operations of a signal party in the field." Thayer did his best to instill "careful instructions in all the different codes," and it became more a problem of getting superiors to use their talents. Still, his crew became indispensable to ascertaining Early's route via Sharpsburg to Boonsboro, thence to Frederick, all of which Sigel dutifully reported to higher authority, meaning ultimately Washington and City Point. How long it took for such information to reach its intended recipient so as to be actionable was another matter.[18]

Problems soon developed beyond those basics. To reach City Point, communication had to take a circuitous route to ensure security. Telegrams went north to Wilmington, Delaware, then down the eastern shore of Chesapeake Bay to Cherrystone Inlet, across a twenty-mile stretch of underwater cable, overland via Fort Monroe to Williamsburg on the peninsula, southward to the James River, again underwater to Fort Powhatan, and then above ground to City Point. The four-hundred-mile circuitous route was often broken by saboteurs, and Grant himself complained about such breaks during Early's movements in Maryland. Delays of twenty-four, even thirty-six hours were common, thus affecting response to threats such as unfolded that July. If that were not enough, command and control problems with the new arrangement for the general-in-chief remained unresolved. Halleck's new role as "chief of staff" to his former subordinate now superior, Grant, was a work in progress. Additionally, as "military adviser" to Stanton and Lincoln (a function that he had traditionally held when he was general-in-chief), meant that Old Brains, not Grant, remained the principal military official in Washington. Designed "to keep things from getting into a snarl," Halleck admitted that he "must obey and carry out what they decide upon whether I concur in their decisions or not." Some, such as Secretary of the Treasury Salmon P. Chase and Secretary of the Navy Gideon Welles, doubted Halleck could make a decision at all. But Halleck sounded pretty determined when on July 5 he assured Governor John Brough of Ohio that "in no event will troops be withdrawn from General Grant." To further confuse things, with confidence in Sigel at low ebb and frustration with Hunter just the opposite, there were questions about yet a third general who was about to enter the picture. Fortunately for the Union, one civilian harbored no doubts about him.[19]

Frederick, the Railroad, and the Monocacy

The two new players were John C. Garrett, president of the Baltimore & Ohio railroad, and Major-General Lew Wallace (a prewar Democrat in politics and scapegoat for some of Grant's questionable actions at Shiloh two years before in Tennessee). Wallace now commanded the Middle Department—VIII Corps—and like B&O headquarters it was located in Baltimore. The entrepreneurial Garrett had been worried about his often-damaged rail line and turned Washington heads with an alert telegram that reached the War Department on the early afternoon of June 29. He was satisfied, he said, "the operations and designs of the enemy in the Valley demand the greatest vigilance and attention." Official response over the next week hardly pacified Garrett, especially when Stanton told him late in the afternoon of July 3 that measures had been taken "as far as within my power" to meet the emergency. The great difficulty "is to know the exact truth, and to avoid being misled by stampede and groundless clamor, or being surprised by real danger." Halleck icily told the railroad executive that if he had "any source of truthful information you had better resort to it." And Garrett did so, laying out to Washington all the data at hand from his own company employees and telegraphers on the rail line west. But War Department officials dithered, awaiting clearer word from Sigel, Hunter, and virtually anyone else. Statistically, upward of seventy-five thousand men could be arrayed from West Virginia across the northeast to defend the capital region, if necessary. Realistically, less than half that number could be concentrated against a threat. So Garrett eventually acted on his own. At some point, July 5 if Wallace recalled correctly, Garrett strode into the general's office and bluntly asked what was being done about the situation.[20]

Wallace acknowledged the uncertainty and how "the strength of the invading column, by whom it was commanded, what its objects were, the means provided to repel it, everything in fact connected with it" as being "on my part, purely conjectural." Later he reported, "All that I was certain of was that my own department was seriously threatened." With the onus of Shiloh still hanging over him, Wallace had been shunted earlier to command at Cincinnati and thence to Baltimore mainly to enforce law, order, and logistics in the rear of the fighting armies. Yet not completely stripped of initiative, Wallace at Garrett's prompting and support seized upon the situation in western Maryland to "concentrate that portion of my scanty command available for field operations at some point on the Monocacy River, the western limit of the Middle Department." Sense of duty and responsibility, dreams of redeemed combat glory—who knows Wallace's motive for such alacrity at a distance of a century and one half. In any case, Lew Wallace, future author of the famous *Ben-Hur: A Tale of the Christ*, acted while others waited. He was determined to create opportunity and to manage those developments, as he sent his second-in-command, Brigadier General Erastus Tyler, with some 2,500 troops to the line of the Monocacy.[21]

Tyler's task—ascertain what was going on. What seemed to be going on in the Frederick neighborhood was confusion. Railroad officials helped the army evacuate convalescents and supplies from the city while husbanding their own locomotives and rolling stock to also support troop reinforcements ordered by the War Department to Harpers Ferry. About this time, Washington sent three dismounted artillery batteries—Battery A, Maryland artillery, Battery F, Independent Pennsylvania artillery, and Battery G, First Pennsylvania artillery, all originally scheduled for Grant—under Brigadier General Albion Howe to stiffen Sigel and Weber. Wallace told Tyler to unload them at Monocacy, but Howe insisted on pushing on. Halleck ordered Wallace to assist him in doing so, and by 3 a.m. on the sixth, Howe and his men were bottled up with Sigel and Weber on Maryland Heights. The next day, Howe superseded Sigel and Stahel, although he subsequently proved no more proactive against Early than that pair. Halleck continued to assure Grant as late as 10:30 p.m. on July 5 that he saw no need to interfere with Petersburg operations. "If Washington or Baltimore should be seriously threatened as to require your aid, I will inform you in time; I have no apprehensions at present about the safety of Washington or Baltimore, Harper's Ferry or Cumberland," he claimed, as "raids cannot effect any damage that cannot soon be repaired." He did think dismounted cavalry could be used effectively if Grant could send any.[22]

However much modern communication technology helped inform all parties, it also created confusion. Time lapses in transmittal and receipt, physical breakdowns, and disruption of lines and equipment and the rapidly changing circumstances in the field were all culprits. Halleck's 1 p.m. missive on July 4 indicated a more serious crisis, although he relied on Hunter to correct whatever was wrong upriver. Halleck told Grant that if estimated enemy strength was twenty thousand to thirty thousand men, then "we cannot meet one half that number in field until Hunter arrives" for "we have almost nothing in Baltimore and Washington except militia, as you are aware." In between Halleck's two telegrams to Grant, however, the general-in-chief himself decided to act. He directed Meade to send an infantry division and dismounted cavalry at once, although he disclaimed any intention of sending a corps until "there is a greater necessity for it." Logistical preparations (marching men to embarkation points, collecting transports, and departing) all consumed time. At least six to eight hours elapsed, and it wasn't until early afternoon on the sixth that Brigadier General James B. Rickett's estimated five thousand infantry and four thousand cavalry (the figures varied and so provided false comfort to any recipient) were on the water en route to Washington. They were sent without teams and wagons and only the ammunition they carried in their bullet pouches. Furthermore, no field artillery went along either. Grant anticipated their rapid return to the Potomac army as Meade himself complained that "this made nearly 9,000 men sent from this army, which I trust will meet the exigency." "I should be reluctant to spare any more," he whined. Grant, for his part, still placed faith in Hunter's annihilating "Ewell, Breckinridge, etc." so as to "move through to Charlottesville and destroy railroad and canals without the help of troops from here."[23]

Wednesday, July 6, found affairs at a standstill in Washington. Erstwhile military adviser, old major-general Ethan Allen Hitchcock, badgered Halleck and Stanton about the threat from up the Potomac. Their seemingly detached response prompted Hitchcock to take the issue to Lincoln. Hitchcock doubted anybody from Grant to the War Department truly sensed the urgency. If Stonewall Jackson were still living and in command of the invaders, "in my opinion," he told the commander-in-chief, "he would be in Washington in three days." A placid president promised to speak to his war secretary about it. Actually, anxiety suddenly gripped both Washington and Richmond. Halleck wired Grant at 5 p.m. on the sixth that a supine Sigel seemed to be guessing at the enemy's strength variously from "7,000 to 30,000" with other estimates in the twenty thousand to thirty thousand range. Make no mistake, this was an "invasion of formidable character," he implied. He enumerated Ewell, Breckinridge, Imboden, William L. "Mudwall" Jackson, and Mosby's commands in array. He wanted Grant to send a major-general to command in the field pending Hunter's return.[24]

Anxiety also surfaced one hundred miles to the south. Lee sounded a similar alarm, signaling President Davis on July 7 that twelve troop-laden transports of Yankees had separately departed with three still boarding more. When taken with his reading of the *New York Herald* of July 4 about Sigel's retirement to Harpers Ferry and Hunter's mustering on the Kanawha, "I fear the troops reported descending the James River are on their way to Washington." "It is so repugnant to Grant's principles and practice to send troops from him that I had hoped before resorting to it he would have preferred attacking me." The probabilities were that the troops were bound for Washington, and if Hunter was "brought up the Ohio and around by railroad, Early may be opposed by a force too large for him to manage." Lee offered little solution, merely comment. It appeared that from the fifth to the seventh, Washington was beginning a cordon of containment around Early's raiders. With Hunter and Sigel in the Confederate rear, Pennsylvania governor Andrew Curtin's calling out militia to block any northward thrust into his state, and Wallace taking some sort of delaying position near Frederick, pieces began to come into place. A scratch force from garrisons, remount facilities, hospitals, government offices, and emergency units would have to hold the capital. Questions remained. How strong were the invaders, and what really was their destination?[25]

By this time, Curtin had informed Washington that the invaders' direction was Baltimore or Washington, not Pennsylvania. Halleck admitted to Grant that "Early and Breckinridge are unquestionably on this raid, which is probably larger than we first supposed," but "their special object is not yet developed." He scrambled to find the most suitable general to lead the effort pending Hunter's arrival. Darius Couch (at Harrisburg), E. O. C. Ord from Petersburg, or Quincy A. Gillmore (awaiting assignment) were candidates, the latter preferable to Halleck. Of course, Wallace thought he had the principal responsibility for clearing up the mystery of enemy intentions. His little command concentrated near the Monocacy railroad junction, covering the principal road and rail crossings northward past the B&O blockhouses, several smaller fords to the National Road at "Jug" Bridge. Then, notwithstanding early trepidations over the limits of his jurisdiction and pending clarification from Washington, Wallace sent infantry and artillery to cooperate with Clendenin west of Frederick City. The first of Rickett's troops, Colonel William H. Henry's Tenth Vermont, joined them. They soon encountered Early's advance guard moving east from Middletown but held their own so nicely that Wallace wired his chief-of-staff at Baltimore, "Think I have had the best little battle of the war" insofar as his intrepid band had repulsed the enemy three times in an early evening contest for Frederick's possession. This little fray on the western edge of the city, dubbed "the battle of Frederick," further slowed Early.[26]

Eventually, however, Confederate pressure and shortage of ammunition and rations caused Wallace to withdraw back through the city. "Learning that the enemy's position on our front was merely a feint to cover his movement on Urbania [sic] and thence to Washington," read one communiqué to the New York Tribune, General Wallace withdrew his forces and evacuated Frederick City at 10 o'clock Friday night. It appears to have become a common assumption at Wallace's headquarters that Early was now headed for the capital. Wallace personally sent a wire to Halleck from Frederick at 8:00 p.m. "Breckinridge, with strong column, moving down the Washington pike toward Urbana; is within six miles of that place," it read. "I shall withdraw immediately from Frederick City and put myself in position on the road to cover Washington, if necessary." Here was the crucial communiqué of the campaign thus far.[27]

What spooked Wallace into writing that wire? Had Rebels actually gotten behind the Union line on the west side of Frederick? Was a 7:05 p.m. telegram from his own aide, Lieutenant Colonel Lynde Catlin, commanding the Monocacy post, what triggered Wallace? Catlin stated three deserters reported that not only was Breckinridge with twelve thousand men marching on Harpers Ferry but also that "a rebel advance is on the Buckeystown road" and the enemy "is on the road between Point of Rocks and Berlin in strong force" and "moving this way." The latter may have been Rodes moving from Harpers Ferry via Crampton's Gap in South Mountain thence to Jefferson and on into the southwestern edge of Frederick. Perhaps it was new activity by Mosby's partisans in the Point of Rocks and Adamstown area. Or, possibly McCausland may have already been on the move as Early had directed. Early claimed in postwar memoirs that he had ordered Tiger John (as McCausland was called) "to move to the right, in the afternoon, and the next day cut the telegraph and railroad between Maryland Heights and Washington and Baltimore—cross the Monocacy, and, if possible, occupy the railroad bridge over that stream, at the Junction near Frederick." Whatever the cause, in the words of Lew Wallace's biographer, Gail Stephens, "Why Wallace thought Washington was the goal is probably again his own intuition and his belief, which he articulated in his autobiography, that he had to make Halleck do something." "It was a gutsy move and he would truly have been finished if he had been wrong." Wallace was certainly taking a big chance (given his track record with Halleck), and "he lucked out." The Hoosier warrior was that kind of general; suggests Stephens, "In this case, it worked."[28]

Wallace's Frederick dispatch should have alarmed Washington and the Lincoln government. It did finally cause Halleck to wire Grant by 10:30 that Friday evening, "latest dispatches state that a heavy column of the enemy has crossed the Monocacy and is moving on Urbana." Early and Breckinridge were in command. Using estimates supplied by Sigel and Couch, he cited twenty thousand to thirty thousand in number, one-third of Lee's entire army, with three thousand to four thousand cavalry. Until more veterans arrived from Petersburg lines, "we have nothing to meet that number in the field." Militia would not even reliably hold the fortifications at Washington or Baltimore. None of the cavalry promised earlier by Grant had arrived, and Halleck wanted everything now sent to the capital, not Baltimore, anyway, "if you propose to cut off this raid and not merely to secure our depots." "We must have more men," since Hunter was "too far off and moves too slowly." "I think, therefore," said Grant's chief-of-staff rather bluntly, "that very considerable re-enforcements should be sent directly to this place," meaning Washington![29]

Thus, by late evening on July 8, Federal authorities had sufficient information to deduce that Washington—not Baltimore or Pennsylvania—was Early's target. Still, until Early actually got to Frederick and disclosed his next move, the issue remained somewhat in doubt. So that night, Wallace withdrew all his men, hungry and weary, back behind the Monocacy where they might regroup and gain rations from supplies brought up from Baltimore as well as reinforcements. The wreck of a locomotive on the branch from the junction into Frederick had stymied evacuation of the sick and wounded for a time that day until it was cleared. Eventually the situation calmed, awaiting developments at dawn. Yet matters remained in doubt even the next morning. When the first Confederates arrived in the city, under Old Jube's orders, Rodes's division moved eastward on the National Road toward the "Jug" Bridge crossing while McCausland, Ramseur, and Gordon swung south out of town on the main thoroughfare to Washington. Bradley Johnson's cavalry column departed out by the Libertytown Road headed for Baltimore and Point Lookout. Early preoccupied himself in town, refreshed by a warm reception from some of the city's closet secessionists. He expected little further resistance from what he took to be mere militia harassing his passage to Washington. The unexpected then occurred as something beyond mere militia soon mounted resistance at the Monocacy crossings. Early was about to suffer more delays. Lew Wallace would see to that.[30]

It seems ironic that the subsequent delaying battle of Monocacy would be fought in part on an antebellum slave plantation in Unionist central Maryland. Some conventional wisdom has that action as the pivotal event saving Washington. Was it? There had been other delays for Jubal Early's legions on the upper Potomac. Certainly Lee's earlier holding order to Early in the valley plus resulting railroad destruction, the impact of summer marching, and the Fourth of July revelries of Early's men and most assuredly actions of Sigel, Weber, and Stahel all impacted the timetable. The hot, tiresome trek across South and Catoctin mountains, then Wallace and Clendenin's probing harassment outside Frederick, played their part. Diversionary tribute demands at Hagerstown and Middletown, the Antietam battlefield excursion, and finally Lee's Baltimore/Point Lookout order sapped Early's time and purpose. In part, they were preliminaries to some culminating event. One thing was sure, Early detached his crack cavalry squadrons under Johnson at the very moment he would need them on the Monocacy. Johnson, as a Frederick native, knew the terrain south of town, and that terrain became critical to quickly enabling Early's continued march to the capital.

The Fourth of July weekend was a strange one in Washington. The Lincolns moved back to the Soldiers' Home summer cottage, but concerns about military affairs, the country's financial solvency, and turbulence in the administration shadowed the citizenry. The recent departure of Secretary Salmon P. Chase from the Treasury was the talk of the town, as was the heat and yellow dust. Explosion of the cartridge department at the Washington Arsenal that had killed seventeen female workers and injured scores of others created its own pall. Seemingly only Washington's African American community conducted a festive party on Monday, Independence Day. With permission, they held a grand Sunday-school picnic on the lawn between the White House and War Department. The well-dressed, festive crowd caused staring white spectators to react at this unprecedented scene, "some with laughter, some with curses, some with shrugs of resignation to the processes of revolution," recounted Pulitzer Prize winner Margaret Leech eight decades later. The city was alive with less fortunate refugee slaves (contraband) and poor vagabonds who looked at the spectacle with equal dismay. A seamier side to the revolution as well as the state of the country came about the same time. Military officials grew even more apprehensive of President Lincoln's safety after a couple of mysterious, threatening episodes, and Washington departmental commander Christopher C. Augur on the third formed an enhanced military escort. Wrote the president in reply curtly, "I believe I need no escort, and unless the Sec. of War directs, none need attend me." And that was that.[31]

That Monday, President Lincoln journeyed to the Capitol signing last-minute legislation before congressional adjournment. He authorized many things from a little room set aside for such purposes; one establishing the office of a Commissioner of Immigration and one repealing certain provisions of the Enrollment Act. But one bill he simply pocket vetoed. That was the controversial Wade-Davis legislative version for the reconstruction of the seceded states. Lincoln subsequently explained publicly that he remained unready to support congressional reconstruction, especially when slavery could only be abolished constitutionally. Affairs in Kentucky and the annoyance of *New York Tribune* editor Horace Greeley also troubled him—Lincoln would treat with anyone but only when peace had to be based on restoration of the Union and ending slavery. Mostly, however, the president wanted to focus on military affairs.[32]

Aware that things were not right on the upper Potomac, thanks to reading War Department telegrams, the nation's leader directly wired B&O president John Garrett on July 5. Since the telegraphic communication had been reestablished with Sandy Hook, according to Garrett, Lincoln asked, "Well, what does Sandy Hook say about operations of Enemy and of Sigel, doing to-day?" The crisis was beginning to come into focus even for the White House. Whatever was going on upcountry, whoever the Rebel leader, and whatever the strength, the threat to the national government, the presidency, and the city had become palpable. By the end of that first week in July 1864, Jubal Early was a potential terminator for Abraham Lincoln's plan to reconstitute the divided nation.[33]

Notes

1. Given all of Early's postwar statements, perhaps he only had an approximate idea of his actual strength following the Staunton reorganization. See Jubal A. Early, Frank Vandiver, editor, *War Memoirs* (Bloomington: Indiana Univesity Press, 1960), 49, and "The Advance on Washington," *Southern Historical Society Papers* 9 (July/August 1881), 301–2; W. H. Taylor and William Allan computations, Folder R, Strength of the Army of Northern Virginia at Various Times, Lee Headquarters Papers, Virginia Historical Society, Richmond (VHS); William C. Davis, *Breckinridge: Statesman, Soldier, Symbol* (Baton Rouge: Louisiana State University Press, 1974), 143, f.n. 15, citing Field Report of Second Division, Breckinridge's Corps, June 28, 1864, Field Return of the Regiments and Battalions composing the different Brigades of the lst Division, Breckinridge's Corps, n.d. [June 24 to June 26, 1864], Field Return of Troops Commanded by Major General Breckinridge, July 15, 1864, all in James W. Eldridge collection, Huntington Library, San Marino, CA (HL); also Everard Hall Smith III, "The General and the Valley: Union Leadership during the Threat to Washington in 1864," unpublished doctoral dissertation, University of North Carolina, Chapel Hill, 1977, 231–32, f.n. 50 and 239–40, f.n. 64; John G. Barnard, *Report on the Defenses of Washington* (Washington, DC: Government Printing Office, 1871), 121, also 119–20.

2. Zebulon York, Official Report, July 22, 1864, Eldridge collection, Huntington Library (HL); W. W. Scott, editor, "Diary of Captain H. W. Wingfield," *Bulletin of the Virginia State Library* XVI (July 1927): 43; W. H. Runge, editor, *Four Years in the Confederate Artillery: Diary of Private Henry Robinson Berkeley* (Chapel Hill: University of North Carolina Press, 1961), 85; Manly Wellman, *Rebel Boast: First at Bethel—Last at Appomattox* (New York: Henry Holt, 1956), 164–67; George Wilson Booth, *Personal Reminiscences of a Maryland Soldier* (Baltimore: by private subscription, 1898; Lincoln: University of Nebraska Press, 2001); *ORA*, 51, pt. 2, 1028–1929.

3. Robert E. Park, "Diary," *Southern Historical Papers* I (1876): 377. William P. Buck, editor, *Sad Earth, Sweet Heaven: The Diary of Lucy Rebecca Buck during the War between the States* (Birmingham, AL: Cornerstone, 1973), 265; Michael G. Mahon, editor, *Winchester Divided: The Civil War Diaries of Julia Chase and Laura Lee* (Mechanicsburg, PA: Stackpole Books, 2002), 151–53; John G. Young diary, July 4, 1864, North Carolina Department of History and Archives, Raleigh (NCHA).

4. Mahon, *Winchester Divided*, 151–52.

5. Ibid., 153.

6. Early, *War Memoirs*, 382–83.

7. *ORA*, I, 37, pt. 2, 4.

8. *ORA*, I, 37, pt. 1, 174–76, 701, 703; pt. 2, 6, and 11.

9. Miscellaneous letters, July 1–3, 1864, Volume 2, Letters and Telegrams, 1861–1864, William Prescott Smith papers, Ekstrom Library, University of Louisville, Louisville, Kentucky, and William E. Bain, *B&O in the Civil War: From the Papers of Wm. Prescott Smith* (Wichita, KS: Boxcar Books, 1966 edition), 89–104.

10. *ORA*, I, pt. 1, 688–89; pt. 2, 3–34; Howard K. Beale, editor, *The Diary of Edward Bates* (New York: Cambridge Scholars Publishing, 1971 reprint), 382.

11. Lee C. Drickamer and Karen D. Drickamer, compilers/editors, *Fort Lyon to Harper's Ferry: On the Border of North and South with "Rambling Jour," the Civil War Letters and Newspaper Dispatches of Charles H. Moulton (34th Mass. Vol. Inf.)* (Shippensburg, PA: White Mane, 1987), 192–96; William B. Styple, editor, *Writing and Fighting the Civil War: Soldier Correspondence to the* New York Sunday Mercury (Kearny, NJ: Belle Grove Publishing Company, 2000), 274.

12. Bain, *B&O in the Civil War*, 98–100; Miscellaneous telegrams, July 4, 5, 1864, Volume 2, Letters and Telegrams, 1861–1864, William Prescott Smith papers, Ekstrom Library, University of Louisville, Louisville (ULL).

13. Meysenburg, "Notes on Battles around Martinsburg, VA," July 2, 1864 entry, Perkins Library, Duke University Library (DUL); Virgil Carrington Jones, *Ranger Mosby* (Chapel Hill: University of North Carolina Press, 1944), 185; Samuel Clarke Farrar, *The Twenty-Second Pennsylvania Cavalry* (Pittsburgh: Regimental Association, 1911), 254–56; Millard K. Bushong, *Old Jube: A Biography of General Jubal A. Early* (Boyce, VA: Carr, 1955), 195; Harry Gilmor, *Four Years in the Saddle* (New York: Nabu Press, 1866), 182–87; Letter, R. G. Coleman to wife, August 2, 1864, copy, Defenses of Washington files, Fort Ward Museum and Park, Alexandria, VA (FWP); Wellman, *Rebel Boast*, 167; Runge, *Four Years in the Confederate Artillery*, 377; Bennett diary, July 5, 1864, SHC/UNC; Park, "Diary," 377; George H.

Lester, "War Record of the Tom Cobb Infantry," in United Daughters of the Confederacy, *This They Remembered* (Washington, GA: Washington Publishing Company, 1965), 105.

14. *ORA*, I, 37, pt. 2, 33.

15. John H. Worsham, *One of Jackson's Foot Cavalry* (New York: Neale, 1914; Jackson, TN: McCowat Mercer, 1964), 233–34; Henry Kyd Douglas, *I Rode with Stonewall* (Chapel Hill: University of North Carolina Press, 1940), 293; Robert Park, "Diary," *Southern Historical Society Papers* I (1876): 378; Runge, *Four Years in the Confederate Artillery*, 85; John N. Opie, *A Rebel Cavalryman with Stuart and Jackson* (Chicago: W. B. Conkey, 1899), 244–45; Young diary, July 6, 1864, NCHA; Wilmington (NC), *Daily Journal*, July 27, 1864; Lester, "War Record of the Tom Cobb Infantry," 106; Wellman, *Rebel Boast*, 169; John O. Casler, *Four Years in the Stonewall Brigade* (Dayton, OH: Morningside Bookshop, 1971), 227; *ORA*, I, 37, pt. 2, 593.

16. *ORA*, I, 37, pt. 1, 767–68; Early, *War Memoirs*, 384–86; Edward J. Stackpole, *Sheridan in the Shenandoah: Jubal Early's Nemesis* (Harrisburg: Stackpole Books, 1961), 53; George Wilson Booth, *A Maryland Boy in Lee's Army: Personal Reminiscences of a Maryland Soldier in the War between the States, 1861–1865* (Baltimore: privately published, 1898/Lincoln: University of Nebraska Press, 2000), 126–27; Robert E. Lee Jr., *Recollections and Letters of Robert E. Lee* (New York: Doubleday Page, 1904), 131–32; Douglas Southall Freeman, editor, *Lee's Dispatches: Unpublished Letters of General Robert E. Lee to Jefferson Davis and the War Department of the Confederate States of America, 1862–1865* (New York: G. P. Putnam, 1957), 269–71; Clifford Dowdey and Louis Manarin, editors, *The Wartime Papers of Robert E. Lee* (New York: Brammel House for Virginia Civil War Commission, 1966), 807–8; R. G. Coleman to wife, July 6, 1864, Mary E. Schooler papers, Perkins Library, Duke University (DU); Bushong, *Old Jube*, 197; Park, "Diary," 377; Young diary, July 4, 1864, NCHA; William Beavens diary, July 4, 5, 1864, Southern Historical Collection/University of North Carolina, Chapel Hill (SHC/UNC); Wellman, *Rebel Boast*, 166–67.

17. *ORA*, I, 37, pt. 2, 58; J. Thomas Scharf, *History of Western Maryland* (Baltimore: Regional Publishing Company, 1968), 286–87; Middletown, *Valley Register*, July 22, 1864; Bennette diary, July 1–8, 1864, SHC/UNC; "A Brief Sketch of Cole's Independent Maryland Volunteer Cavalry," n.d., 7, 8, Maryland Historical Society, Baltimore (MHS); *ORA*, I, 37, pt. 1, 170, 1943–45 and 51, pt. 1, 1171–74; Bradley T. Johnson, "My Ride around Baltimore in 1864," *Journal of the United States Cavalry Association* II (September 1889): 252; Edward Y. Goldsborough, *Early's Great Raid* (New York: Nabu Press, 2010), 6–12.

18. Adam Badeau, *Military History of Ulysses S. Grant* (New York: D. Appleton, 1885), II, 444; Everhard H. Smith, "The General and the Valley," 136–42; John Emmet O'Brien, *Telegraphing in Battle: Reminiscences of the Civil War* (Scranton: Nabu Press, 1910), 142–50; especially 150–51; William R. Plum, *The Military Telegraph during the Civil War* (Chicago: Jansen, McClurg 1882), I, 137–38 and II, 130–32, 260–61; Bruce Catton, *Grant Takes Command* (Boston: Little, Brown, 1968), 314; *ORA*, I, 37, pt. 1, 180–85.

19. *ORA*, I, 32, pt. 2, 408, 34, pt. 3, 333, 36, pt. 2, 329 and 37, pt. 2, 70; Beale, *The Diary of Edward Bates*, 385; Gideon Welles, *Diary* (Boston: Houghton Mifflin, 1909), I, 180, 373; W. A. Croffut, editor, *Fifty Years in Camp and Field: Diary of Major General Ethan Allen Hitchcock* (New York: Putnams, 1909), 463–64; Lew Wallace, *Autobiography* (New York:

Harper, 1906), II, 577–80; Ella Lonn, *Foreigners in the Union Army and Navy* (Baton Rouge: Greenwood Publishing Group, 1951), 179–80.

20. *ORA*, I, 37, pt. 1, 174–75, 193, 644–45, 650–51, 664, 670, 673, 674, 677, 687, 689, 694–95; pt. 2, 3, 16–18, 33, 58–60, 65; Telegram F. N. Haskett (Sandy Hook) to W. C. Quincy, 5:25 p.m., July 5, 1864, Mss. 18690, MHS; Bain, *B&O in the Civil War*, 99–101; miscellaneous telegrams, July 5, 6, 1864, William Prescott Smith papers, ULL.

21. *ORA*, I, 37, pt. 2, 14, 55, 59, 60, 104.

22. Miscellaneous telegram July 5–8, 1864, William Prescott Smith papers, ULL; Bain, *B&O in the Civil War*, 101–4, 113–20.

23. *ORA*, I, 40, pt. 1, 34, pt. 3, 31, 32; 36, 44, 49, and 37, pt. 2, 60, 80.

24. Croffut, *Fifty Years in Camp and Field*, 463–64; *ORA*, I, 37, pt. 2, 79.

25. *ORA*, I, 37, pt. 2, 593–94.

26. *ORA*, I, 37, pt. 2, 109–10.

27. *ORA*, I, 37, pt. 2, 127; Bain, *B&O in the Civil War*, 124; Telegram, "Dr." Sidney H. Gay, July 9, 9:45 a.m., 1864, miscellaneous telegram, Smith papers, ULL.

28. E-mail exchanges between author and Gail Stephens, December 28, 29, 31, 2011, and January 4, 5, 2012, all author's files; Jubal A. Early, *A Memoir of the Last Year of the War for Independence: In the Confederate States of America* (Toronto: Lovell and Bigson, 1866: Columbia: University of South Carolina Press, 2001), 56–57; *ORA* I, 37, pt. 2, 127; 51, pt. 1, 1174.

29. *ORA*, I, 37, pt. 2, 119–20. The author is indebted to Mrs. Gail Stephens, former intelligence analyst and currently a Monocacy battlefield park volunteer, for emphasizing this round of communication as the key to understanding just when—even before the Monocacy battle—that Washington had been clearly identified as Early's target, Wallace's subsequent arguments notwithstanding.

30. *ORA*, I, 37, pt. 1, 171, 172, 173, pt. 2, 98, 100, 101, 104, 108, 110, 111; Benjamin Franklin Cooling, *Jubal Early's Raid on Washington 1864* (Baltimore: Nautical and Aviation Publishing Company of America, 1989; Tuscaloosa: University of Alabama Press, 2007), 60–61, and *Monocacy: The Battle That Saved Washington* (Shippensburg, PA: White Mane, 2000), 76–77; miscellaneous telegram, July 8, 1864, Smith papers, ULL.

31. Roy P. Basler, editor, *The Collected Works of Abraham Lincoln, volume III* (New Brunswick, NJ: Rutgers University Press, 1953), 422–23; Margaret Leech, *Reveille in Washington, 1860–1865* (New York: Harper and Brothers, 1941), 329; Matthew Pinsker, *Lincoln's Sanctuary: Abraham Lincoln and the Soldiers' Home* (New York: Oxford University Press, 2003), 127–30; Frederick Hatch, *Protecting President Lincoln: The Security Effort, the Thwarted Plots, and the Disaster at Ford's Theater* (Jefferson, NC: McFarland, 2011), 25–34.

32. E. B. Long, *The Civil War Day by Day: An Almanac, 1861–1865* (Garden City, NY: De Capo Press, 1971), 534, 535–36; Basler, editor, *Collected Works of Lincoln*, VII, 425–27, 433–36; Allen C. Guelzo, *Fateful Lightning: A New History of the Civil War and Reconstruction* (New York: Oxford University Press, 2012), 456–57; William C. Harris, *Lincoln and the Border States: Preserving the Union* (Lawrence: University Press of Kansas, 2011), chapter 7; Doris Kearns Goodwin, *Team of Rivals: The Political Genius of Abraham Lincoln* (New York: Simon & Schuster, 2005), 639–40; Tyler Dennett, *Lincoln and the Civil War in the Diaries and Letters of John Hay* ((New York: Dodd, Mead, and Company, 1939), 204–5, 207.

33. Basler, *Collected Works of Lincoln*, VII, 424.

CHAPTER FIVE

MONOCACY, A SECRETARY'S SON, AND THE ROAD TO WASHINGTON

Wwithin weeks of the great battle at Gettysburg, one of Baltimore & Ohio railroad president John W. Garrett's correspondents had written to him from Washington. "Our next battle will be fought in Maryland," said Rutherford Worster, for "there can be no doubt that the great fight will be in repelling an attempt to cut occupation of your road between this & Baltimore." "Only an enemy, more determined than before, and they are rendered still more ferocious by the fall of Vicksburg and Port Hudson," the sixty-four-year-old Nova Scotia–born physician, inventor, and author observed. "I regard Washington in more danger, than ever, at this time." It took another year, and Jubal Early was now Lee's instrument to do just that. Ironically, on July 9, 1864, as citizen-soldier Lewis "Lew" Wallace tried to uncover the Rebel raiders' trajectory and target and at the same time protect Garrett's almost sacred iron and stone railroad bridge near Frederick, the general's Baltimore headquarters exempted Garrett's three horses from seizure by the army. Others would not be so lucky when the Rebels liberally requisitioned and exacted tribute on their way to capture Washington. At that moment, however, major battle, not foraging, seemed the key to Early's activities.[1]

Buying Time

Fighting began again on Saturday, July 9, this time east and south of Frederick. Confederate brigadier Robert D. Lilley's brigade of Major-General Robert Rodes's division opened the action. Between 6:00 and 8:00 a.m., the dusty, bedraggled Johnnies probed eastward toward the Jug Bridge crossing of the Monocacy River on the National Road to Baltimore. They soon encountered resistance from the One Hundred and Forty-Fourth and One-Hundred and Forty-Ninth Ohio, specifically

81

recruited for "one hundred days" of service but often including veteran soldiers from earlier campaigns of the war. Upriver at Linganore's Mill, a mounted troop of the One Hundred and Fifty-Ninth guarded the flank. Sparring between these forces would continue all day, as it became apparent that this was not the main axis of Early's advance. Still, Rodes effectively pinned down Federals desperately needed to stop the main Confederate thrust to the south. Wallace dared not relinquish his principal escape route to Baltimore. So the Jug Bridge sector—virtually forgotten and unincorporated today in the Monocacy National Battlefield Park, remains an important part of the Monocacy story. Similarly, Reich's and Crum's fords between this sector and the Washington road and railroad bridge crossings also required protection. They, too, diluted what Wallace could bring to bear in the vicinity of Frederick or Monocacy junction. But it was here, in those same early hours of a beautiful midsummer day in Maryland, that unfolded what is termed the "battle that saved Washington." Here Wallace uncovered the main intent of Jubal Early's plan. These events coupled with Old Jube's preoccupation with extracting money from Frederick's Unionists affected the result.[2]

Union pickets exchanged the first shots in this main combat sector with Major-General Stephen Ramseur's men, perhaps a mile north of the junction. Here, a smaller but quite passable road to Buckeystown and Point of Rocks broke off to the right from the main turnpike south to Washington. On Simon Cronise's property, and very soon to the south on a larger so-called Best Farm, the Rebels took their first prisoners. They learned that these were not mere militia but, indeed, veterans of the much-respected VI Corps, the Army of the Potomac. Captive hospital steward W. G. Duckett of the Ninth New York Heavy Artillery helped deceive the enemy of Wallace's true strength. When brought before Confederate brigadier John G. Echols, the general muttered: "Damn that 6th corps, we meet them wherever we go." The plucky Duckett responded that the Rebels would soon find the whole corps there to welcome the general and his men "with bloody hands to hospitable graves." Later he would remember: "I believe they were more cautious than they would have been had they known our real strength, and we were saved from greater disaster." Desultory fighting soon intensified as elements of the First Maryland Potomac Home Brigade and the Tenth Vermont joined the New York skirmishers holding back the gray tide on undulating farmland that once comprised a vast slave planta-tion belonging to French Haitian exile Madame Mangan de la Vincendiere and her family. The ground that was now washed with the blood of blue and gray had seen earlier violence, apparently, for the harsh treatment of the black labor force (thanks to memories of revolutionary atrocities in that island country) had been notorious in local lore. In 1862, Lee's famous "Lost Order" that so affected the Antietam cam-paign had been found on this farm.[3]

Some of the Vermonters such as the regimental surgeon and chaplain had determined to have breakfast in Frederick that morning. Furthermore, Lieutenant T. H. White of Company G and two comrades had decided on an early morning bath in the Monocacy. Bullets and artillery rounds dissuaded all such activity just as the rather unexpected resistance north of the Monocacy slowed the Rebel initiative. As more and more of the southern army passed through Frederick, traffic backed up south of town. Wallace had only one battery manned by Captain Frederick W. Alexander's Baltimore reservists, but they sent shells crashing but three feet above the heads of Captain George E. Davis's feisty skirmishers in the fields north of the stream. The Federal guns eventually drew the wrath of thirty veteran guns on the Confederate side. But where were the Confederate decision makers, the generals who could direct a thrust past Wallace's roadblock? Brigade and division commanders could not do so on their own. Where was Early?[4]

Ransoming Frederick

Many Frederick residents had shuttered their blinds and sent away personal wealth and horses at the Rebel approach. Military quartermasters hustled away stores and convalescents, banks secreted their funds, the Internal Revenue collector dispatched $70,000 to Washington, and Garrett's railroaders withdrew all locomotives and rolling stock for safekeeping far to the east. Any local sons in Confederate gray might snatch time at home (Bradley Johnson was an exception, much to his chagrin, for he soon departed on his own mission). The army commander wined, dined, and slept at the home of secessionist-sympathizing Dr. Richard Hammond on the northwest corner of Second and Market Street. Still, while Early relaxed, he had given his supply chiefs hard-boiled instructions to meet with city fathers, to ransom the city, or to burn it down. He expected more of the rich treasure trove of Martinsburg, Harpers Ferry, Hagerstown, or even little Middletown. He would make the middle Marylanders feel the hint of harsh war. Perhaps he remembered the tepid reception accorded Lee's army two years before when it had bivouacked south of town awaiting an upsurge of sympathizing Marylanders that never came. His wrath certainly resulted "in retaliation for similar acts by the Federal forces within our borders," he told his supply officers.[5]

Early's representatives dutifully tried to carry out his instructions. Ordnance chief Lieutenant Colonel William Allan, commissary chief Major W. J. Hawks, Quartermaster Major John A. Harmon, and Chief Surgeon Dr. Hunter McGuire presented the $200,000 "assessment" demand "in current money or the use of the army," or $50,000 in material goods at current prices plus five hundred barrels of flour and six thousand pounds of bacon. A strong cohort of soldiers stood ready to burn the city for noncompliance. But Mayor William G. Cole and the town fathers balked, perhaps as Allan later argued, stalling "until the issue of the battle with Wallace should be ascertained." That was hindsight, as the people's representatives pointed out the city population of barely eight thousand, a tax base of but $2,200,000, and an annual corporate tax revenue of only $8,000 could hardly bear the imposition. Citing Hagerstown's tribute as only one-tenth that amount (news had come quickly despite the Confederate clamp-down on civilians passing through the lines), Cole's group asked Early to reconsider. He would not, said Allan and company. Indications are that if they had presented that request to Old Jube at the time, he might have done so. In any case, negotiations took time.[6]

By early afternoon (possibly sensing the trend in Wallace's battle), the civilians relented. Local bankers from the Farmers and Mechanics, Franklin Savings, Frederick County, as well as the Fredericktown Savings Institute produced the requisite cash as a "loan to the city." Major J. R. Braithwaite, the only bonded quartermaster officer in Early's whole army, accepted the cash and reputedly hauled it away in a basket much like some medieval robber baron receiving payment from his serfs. Local lore (according to prominent lawyer and Democratic Party activist Alton Y. Bennett) told the story that a free black, John Murdock, who worked for Bennett's grandfather, a wheelwright at the time, was selected to carry the money to Early. Early told Murdock to spread the money on a blanket so that he might count it, did so, and muttered, "This is $2.35 short." The free man turned out his pockets and found enough coins to make up the difference, so saving the city from destruction— or so Murdock proclaimed for years afterward. Whatever the story, the city would repay half of the total principal debt in 1868 through the issuance of bonds, the final maturity being retired in 1951. Further reimbursement came through a slight reduction of city taxes that continued through 1986. But Frederick City itself would never recover money from the U.S. government despite repeated attempts in Congress.[7]

Delays in Crossing the Monocacy

Wherever Early was that morning, haste did not attend his movements. His twenty-four-year-old aide, Lieutenant Colonel Alexander (Sandie) Pendleton, managed at some point to ride in from the battlefield to find out about the ransom negotiations only to stray off to a champagne and ice cream social with friends prior to returning to duty. Urgency dogged no one's footsteps, it seemed. Surely by noon Early had become aware of the delays attending the passage of the Monocacy. Unsure of the locale and terrain, Bradley Johnson's presence might have made the general aware that the Buckeystown Road provided a way to cross the Monocacy downstream, circumventing Wallace's roadblock at the bridge and junction. As shown on Isaac

Bond's 1858 Frederick County map, a map surely known to Johnson, lay a crossing near Michael's Mill (south of Buckeystown) that afforded an alternative to any roadblock on the Washington Road. Early had already ordered his other cavalry brigade leader, Brigadier General John McCausland the day before to move in a fashion that might have uncovered this route. But McCausland had focused on the railroad bridge and apparently missed the full possibilities offered by the Buckeystown Road. The next afternoon, his horsemen clattered down that very road, found the McKinney-Worthington farm ford where Ballenger Creek flowed into the larger stream near the Mackall house, and sought to outflank the stiffening Federal resistance on both sides of the river. But for Johnson's departure that morning for Baltimore and Point Lookout, the ensuing bloody battle might have been avoided.[8]

Lieutenant Colonel David Clendenin's Eighth Illinois horsemen initially stymied McCausland. From a command post situated on bluffs just east of the railroad bridge and from the site of one of two protective blockhouses and earthworks guarding the junction, Wallace spotted increasing dust clouds beyond the immediate skirmishing north of the river. This perceived Confederate flanking movement caused the Hoosier to send Ricketts word to move "your whole command to the left of the railroad, with your front to the Monocacy, with a view of guarding the approaches on the Washington road." The VI Corps veterans would fuse with Brigadier General Erastus B. Tyler's thinly stretched line upriver. Ricketts's men were to carry three days of rations, permit no citizenry to pass the lines except for intelligence-gathering purposes, and Ricketts was to personally report his strength and ammunition conditions. He responded at noon that he had sent four regiments "under an officer well acquainted with the country to meet the column of the enemy reported advancing." He promised to make the best disposition he could to meet the enemy's advance and suggested moving all available artillery to the west or left of the Washington Road, "as there seems to be no further necessity for it on our right." Artillery would prove Wallace's weak point. Only Alexander's six-gun, three-inch rifle Baltimore artillery battery plus a howitzer at the blockhouse could offset nine Rebel batteries moving into position on the Best Farm north of the river. The howitzer ultimately jammed, and ammunition replenishment became problematic as Alexander had been providing fire support for Clendenin and Tyler for two days as well as the skirmishers north of the river that morning. Rationing a dwindling supply became necessary as the battle heated up by afternoon.[9]

A Three-Phased Battle

Tenth Vermont colonel William W. Henry told his state's adjutant and inspector general nearly thirty years after the war that Monocacy had comprised "three distinct battles that day: from about 8:30 to 10 a.m.; from 11 a.m. to 1 p.m.; and the last one from 3 to nearly 5 p.m. when we barely escaped over the iron bridge of the B&O R.R. which had no roof or superstructure it being all open, with no framework above the track, and was forty feet above the river." The morning standoff kept intrepid Vermont and Maryland skirmishers pinned down as Henry implied, but increasing pressure by early afternoon caused Wallace and Ricketts to fire the wooden highway bridge to Washington across the Monocacy. Wallace particularly agonized over sacrificing the skirmishers to enemy capture. "To burn the structure looked like a deliberate sacrifice of the gallant Vermonters—or rather like a wicked desertion," Wallace thought. "I argued, Ricketts may be driven before Davis can be retired; if I retire Davis the enemy will follow on his heels; and then (and this nerved me) if the bridge was allowed to stand Early would be en-route for Washington, it might be in an hour." "To Save Davis was to lose *Washington* [Wallace emphasis]. I gave the word, and in five minutes the eastern end of the old crossing was a whirl of flame and black smoke. With a last look at my skirmish line—it was still fighting—I rode away."[10]

Later, during the night of July 9, Wallace would learn that Davis and a portion of his men had escaped. Yet until he read Vermonter Lucius E. Chittenden's 1891 recollections of time serving Lincoln as Treasury registrar in which Davis's feat was recounted, the Hoosier claimed he never knew the full story. "That Davis would attempt to cross the river by the rail road bridge stepping from tie to tie, under fire at close range, and forty feet in the air never entered my mind," observed Wallace. It "was one of the bravest things of the war." But "riding off the field, I imagined him dead or on the road to Libby [Virginia prison]," but now [in 1893] Wallace "put my hand on his shoulder, and asked Vermont the mother of so many men stout in their courage and loyalty to do him honor." And honor they would give as Davis received a belated Medal of Honor (one of two awarded Vermonters after the war for bravery at Monocacy). On the afternoon of July 9, however, such bravado and daring counted for little in the battle's result, only the escape of Davis and his skirmish line from north of the Monocacy.[11]

Ultimately gaining access to the south bank, McCausland's Rebels confidently rode up past John Worthington's comfortable farmhouse, where the owner's young son hid in the cellar. Young Glenn Worthington watched what was transpiring and eventually penned the earliest account of the pivotal battle in his yard. Dismounting and swinging southeast as if on parade, McCausland's people were buffeted by the rest of Clendenin's defenders and then were stopped cold by Ricketts's veterans mustered on the adjacent farm Araby. A second advance by the southern horsemen accomplished little, either, and Confederate commanders knew that they faced veterans, not militia or reserve troops. Ostensibly Breckinridge commanded on the field, and he ordered John B. Gordon's crack infantry to cross and break Ricketts's position while at the same time Ramseur's pressure caused Wallace and Ricketts to burn the highway-covered bridge. Gordon took position about midafternoon and proceeded to crack Ricketts's bent-back line as Rebel cannon north of the river and four guns in Worthington's front yard completely suppressed Alexander's over-worked guns. The young captain twice limbered up and started to the rear without orders only to incur Ricketts's wrath "that if he limbered up again without order, he would shoot him." Ricketts subsequently declined to charge Alexander "owing to his extreme youth and mental distress, it being his first engagement," as leniency was "justified by his subsequent commendable conduct." At the time, however, Wallace saw Ricketts's predicament and told him "hold the crest [of high ground on the Araby farm] if the cannonading is not too enfilading" when the brigadier frantically asked for instructions.[12]

Eventually Ricketts could not hold, especially against Gordon's final charge of a skirmish and three battle lines in full array. Still, he would retire only under Wallace's written order, he claimed. This came six hours after the Confederates should have been well down the pike to Washington. The graycoats finally clustered around the junction and Gambrill's mill south of the Monocacy by early evening, cheering their tactical victory. Wallace's battered and demoralized army evaporated over the railroad and hills to the north en route to the Baltimore retreat route. Louisiana brigadier general Zebulon York, a transplanted "Down Easterner" from Maine, declared a fortnight later that "the victory was perfect, the rout was disgraceful as the Yankee army could make—they ran like sheep having no shepherd." Equally disgraceful, however, were two other incidents on the Union side. Much earlier, the junction telegraph operator had fled with the last train out of the battle zone so nobody in Washington or Baltimore had news of the disaster. A "missing" por-tion of Ricketts's second brigade—about nine hundred men under Colonel John F. Staunton (slow to come up from Baltimore) had stopped at Monrovia and New Market, miles to the east, for rations and never reached the battlefield. They might have made a difference. As it was, the Pennsylvania colonel was court-martialed and cashiered.[13]

Small consolation came from a sharp little cavalry action by Clendenin at Urbana after the close of the battle. A Confederate flag was captured from the "Nighthawk Rangers." Still, Wallace's losses stood at approximately 1,300 killed, wounded, and captured. Early's men suffered five hundred killed and five hundred badly wounded and left at Frederick. Three thousand more wounded "who either walked away or were brought away in their trains," Vermont colonel (later brigadier) William H. Henry told Medal of Honor winner George Davis in 1884. That figure came upon the good authority of Horatio Trundle, a native Virginian living near Leesburg, who had gained such numbers directly from conversation with Early once the Confeder-ates returned to the Old Dominion later. York claimed he lost "more than ¼ of the numbers I took into the fight with me." He told someone else the numbers were forty-five killed and 118 wounded. Gordon told Robert E. Lee three years after the war that Monocacy "was one of the severest ever fought by my troops." He claimed to have lost "one third of my command." Terry's brigade counted thirteen killed, seventy-eight wounded, and twenty-one missing. Years later two foeman who fought against one another that day but later found themselves members of the same church congregation compared notes. Claiming his side had thirty thousand to thirty-three thousand on the field, the former Confederate thought his enemy had numbered at least twenty thousand. He concluded, "Our losses were out of all proportion if you had no more engaged than [6,000]." No matter, the hot day may have netted Old Jube his $200,000 tribute from town fathers and a tactical victory, but it cost him easily twelve hours or more in the race for the capital. He had expended much ammunition and bloodied his best fighting division. Moreover, he alerted Washington as to the true axis of his advance.[14]

That night, Early's exhausted troops slept on the battlefield while details buried the fallen. Logisticians figured how to get the wagon train and artillery across the river at a ford adjacent to the burnt-out covered bridge. His artillery tried to batter down the iron railroad span but to no avail. Since prisoners numbered Army of the Potomac veterans as well as Wallace's garrison troops, Early knew that his movements were now apparent to Grant and Washington. That was quite in line with what Lee intended. Still, Early wanted more, to pull off the greatest prize of all—capturing Washington. Yet far from his line of communications back in the Shenandoah Valley, presumably threatened by David Hunter's reentry into the theater, burdened with a fast tiring, battle-worn army, and much of his "eyes and ears" cavalry sent by Lee's orders on some wild-goose chase beyond his control and burdened with a miles-long booty and supply train as well as nearly six hundred prisoners requiring guards, food, and special care that he did not want (and so after the war claimed that was the reason he did not chase Wallace after the battle), Early faced a quandary. How was he going to get this menagerie to Washington? How would he get it back to Virginia? That indeed was something to ponder that sultry night.[15]

Monocacy in Perspective

When Lew Wallace finally reached safety at Ellicott's Mills close to Baltimore, he telegraphed an initial battle report to Halleck at 2:05 p.m. on July 10. Ricketts had been overwhelmed by four lines of Gordon's infantry and enfiladed by artillery, yet the VI Corps veterans "bore the brunt of the battle with a coolness and steadiness . . . not exceeded in any battle during the war." The men of that Third Division "were not whipped, but retired reluctantly" under Wallace's orders. He did not see himself "seriously beaten," for not a gun or flag had been lost. The Rebels captured no stores, and in the face of "overwhelming force, I brought off my whole command, losing probably not over 200 prisoners," although he admitted the 100-days men had straggled badly. He admitted to heavy casualties, but they "cannot possibly equal that of the enemy, as they charged several times in close lines, and with a recklessness that can be justified only upon the ground that they supposed my command consisted of raw militia." He wildly estimated eighteen thousand men engaged on the left flank with two thousand more skirmishing north of the river.[16]

More edifying for Halleck, who sent the report on to Grant by evening, Wallace laid out his purpose in fighting in the first place—keeping rail communication open to Harpers Ferry, covering the roads to Washington and Baltimore, and last, "to make the enemy develop his force." He admitted failure in all but the last, as he told Washington that from what he discerned, "the enemy must have two corps of troops north of the Potomac." He based that judgment on the column operating in the Hagerstown and Harpers Ferry sectors and the one he had battled on the Monocacy. At no time did he specifically identify Early as in command but rather relied upon the words of a dying Rebel officer on the field to one of Ricketts's staff "that Lee was managing these operations in person, and would shortly have three corps about the Potomac for business against Washington and Baltimore." Fearing the incredulous nature of this information, Wallace protested "this circumstance is true; give it what weight you please." Subsequent affairs prevented Wallace from penning a fuller report until August. By then, little had changed, but more details were added. He now admitted 1,649 total casualties for Ricketts's veterans, 1,968 for Tyler. But these statistics soon dropped under recount to 1,294 total. Wallace remained adamant, however, that Rebel losses exceeded his own, learning that four hundred wounded had been left in the hospital in Frederick. In a literary flourish apropos to his postwar literary career, Wallace noted that orders had been given to "collect the bodies of our dead in one burial ground on the battle-field suitable for a monument upon which I propose to write: 'These men died to save the National Capital, and they did save it.'" At the time of his first report, the day after the battle, Lew Wallace could not be so sure. Nor, for that matter, could his opponent![17]

Might Monocacy have turned out differently? There would always be the question of detaching Johnson's cavalry on the Baltimore–Point Lookout mission, thus handicapping reconnaissance and action. Then, too, Early surely dispersed his strength, too heavily feinting at Jug Bridge when Rodes's men might have added weight to break Wallace's defense at the railroad/highway crossings on the Washington Road sooner. Rodes might have pressed the situation by storming Jug Bridge, occupying the Baltimore Road, and actually annihilating Wallace's army. Wasting time with ransom demands and not pushing lackadaisical infantry subordinates also slowed events. The whole affair could have been over by noon or quickly thereafter with plenty of daylight for less-fatigued and bloodied Johnnies to press on down the road to the nation's capital that afternoon. For Wallace's part, had he more artillery, ammunition, or that missing brigade of VI Corps veterans, he might have held out even longer or punished McCausland and Gordon even more severely. As it was, the dilatory Staunton with the Sixty-Seventh Pennsylvania, Sixth Maryland, and part of the One Hundred and Twenty-Second Ohio finally arrived only in time to throw a rear guard across the National Pike at New Market ten miles east of the battlefield and to cover the Union retreat. Supposedly slow to arrive by boat at Baltimore, they needed three days of rations and proceeded west on the B&O troop trains about 4:00 p.m., only to meet two mysterious scouts who informed them of Wallace's defeat. Whether they were possible outriders from Johnson's raiders or bona fide scouts from Sigel's command—we simply don't know. No matter, the trains stopped, the regiments alighted and rested, while Wallace and Ricketts paid for this lapse. The faux pas cost the colonel his command despite a completely disingenuous calendar report of his actual presence on the battlefield. So whatever damage was done, Monocacy turned out as it did.[18]

By contrast, two Vermonters eventually received honors for their actions at Monocacy. Corporal Alexander Scott and First Lieutenant George E. Davis, both of Company D, Eleventh Vermont, would be awarded Medals of Honor in the 1890s. Scott would be cited on September 28, 1897, for simply but heroically saving the national flag of his regiment under heavy fire following the collapse of Ricketts's line on the Araby farm. Davis's citation on May 27, 1892, was more descriptive of really what Wallace overall had accomplished—"While in command of a small force, held the approaches to the two bridges against repeated assaults of superior numbers, thereby materially delaying Early's advance on Washington." Of course, at the time, neither man really understood that was the effect of their actions. Another fellow Vermonter thought he did several weeks later when, returning to the area from chasing Early, the Green Mountain boys took a day or two of rest at Frederick and halted a short time at Monocacy to look over the battlefield. Lieutenant T. H. White visited the site where Captain George Milledge's Georgia Battery had attempted to go into position. "We found forty-four graves," claimed White, and Milledge had apparently told ladies at a neighboring house that "his battery had been in a great many of the hardest fought battles of the war but had never been so terribly cut up as here." White concluded, "Our two guns worked by the Maryland boys and Capt. Davis's skirmishers had done their work well." On July 9, however, the best that a weary and nonplussed Lew Wallace could wire railroader John Garrett at 8:33 p.m. was "I did as I promised, Held the bridge to the last. They overwhelmed me with numbers. My troops fought splendidly. Losses fearful."[19]

Monocacy evoked various impressions from contemporaries. Colonel Joseph Warren Keifer, erstwhile commander of the Second Brigade, Third Division, VI Corps, who had missed the action due to wounds suffered earlier in the Wilderness, always fretted about Staunton's cashiering for malingering. "It is highly probable that if he had peremptorily brought up the detachment of troops in his command, the disaster that fatal day, would have been saved," he claimed. There never would be many "what ifs" about Monocacy over the years, but this was one of them. Three weeks after the action, Assistant Regimental Surgeon Benjamin A. Fordyce of the Sixtieth New York wrote his daughter Abbe from a quiet campsite beside the river. "It is a lovely romantic place surrounded with hills and mountains," he noted, and the stream itself brimmed with little friendly fishes that nibbled at his toes and legs when bathing. Wallace used similar romantic word pictures in his memoirs recalling the scenic landscape before death and destruction wrought their will on the farmland. Eyewitness Glenn Worthington always termed it the "battle that saved Washington," but then he was pardonably biased in elevating the significance of the carnage that took place in his family's yard.[20]

Vermont medal of honor recipient Davis brashly wrote Ricketts in 1873 with two blunt questions. One involved the section of Alexander's guns that inadequately supported VI Corps infantry in the afternoon of the battle. The other question was far more evocative. Davis wanted Ricketts's opinion, "if the Third division could not have saved Washington had we retreated toward Washington instead of going toward Baltimore, even if the balance of the Sixth Corps had not arrived as they did." Ricketts, by then in comfortable retirement in the nation's capital and suffering from war wounds, answered circumspectly. In his opinion "the 3d Division, 6th Corps could have interposed 'Early' before Washington, on July 12th if necessary, being however the only reliable body of troops at hand, its retention was very important to Baltimore, while the other two Divisions of the 6th Corps were arriving 'in time' due to the heroic conduct of the 3d Division, 6th Corps at the Battle of Monocacy, which crippled and delayed the enemy—but for this obstinate stand against fearful odds, Washington would have fallen and the whole character of the War changed." "This is the truth," Ricketts proclaimed, but would go no further. The basic question has remained unanswerable ever since.[21]

Through Heat and Dust to Washington

Monocacy that night reflected detritus from battle—crushed grain in the fields, firearms, munitions, equipment strewn with the dead and wounded. Nearby Mackall and Arcadia farms north of the river as well as Worthington and Araby farmyards and Gambrill's mill south of the stream counted as dressing stations and makeshift field hospitals. The seriously wounded eventually were left back at former Yankee hospital facilities in Frederick, which would be quickly reopened by Federal doctors when pursuing elements of Hunter's army liberated the town. Assistant Adjutant General A. S. "Sandie" Pendleton's signed order to Breckinridge had Rodes's division stepping off smartly at 3:30 a.m. the next morning when temperatures would be at their coolest. A battery from brigadier Armistead Long's artillery battalion would come immediately after the division's first brigade. The rest of the battalion would follow the remainder of Rodes's division, then Ramseur's division, another artillery battalion followed thereafter by Gordon's division, the army's wagon trains with Echol's division accompanied by Rufus King's artillery bringing up the rear. McCausland's battered command rode point down the pike to Washington. The railroad bridge destruction order delayed Ramseur's departure and "were annoyed also somewhat by the enemy's cavalry." Despite Monocacy, remnants of Clendenin's force plus oncoming riders of Hunter's army were fast closing on Early's column.[22]

Heat, dust, sweat, and periodic harassment by shadowy Yankee outriders such as the Twenty-First New York Cavalry from Julius Stahel's mounted force with Franz Sigel's Reserve Division now harassed the marching Rebels. Still, the rear guard always managed to beat them back. Colorful little hamlets such as Urbana, Hyattstown, and Clarksburg brought out both "Secesh" as well as loyal Unionists. One North Carolina reporter in the ranks thought supportive locals were abundant, while another Tar Heel recalled how young women supposedly rode miles just to catch a glimpse of their southern heroes. A heavy Union conscription quota leveled in the area may have contributed a few recruits to the ranks, but not many. Union Monocacy prisoners ostensibly found tubs of water and barrels of crackers set out for their pleasure at Columbus Winsor's place in Urbana, while one Clarksburg senior realized many of the begrimed figures were "our men! Why Union men, of course," bringing forth cheers from the dejected captives. Actually, the constant cry from Rebel officers to "close up" irritated friend and foe alike in the ranks. As Virginia cavalryman Alexander Hunter recalled there was little "dog trotting" or "running" from the Monocacy south to capture Washington. The battle and subsequent march were deterrents. Both prisoners and captors happily dropped by the road to sleep once the sun set on the day's tramp. Early was a day behind schedule, fast losing even more time: a result of Monocacy, Glenn Worthington never ceased to point out.[23]

Sunday night found the Confederates strung out from well north of Gaithersburg southward almost to Rockville. The army straggled badly, and so much of the overnight hours went to rounding them up and snatching snippets of rest. One principal concentration point seemed to be the farm of Ignatius Fulks and his family that attracted 1,800 cavalrymen and soon yielded up carcasses of butchered livestock to attest to Rebel appetites. Also, John T. De Sellum and his Summit Hill farm just south of town hosted Early and his generals as "guests." De Sellum, a prominent slave-owning farmer and respected bachelor in the community, was no stranger to controversy and may have had his place singled out for retaliation because of his well-known unionism and involvement with local draft enforcement. He and his spinster sister had listened to the distant gunfire at Monocacy and watched as some of Major William Fry's Sixteenth Pennsylvania cavalry had deployed Sunday afternoon out in front of their property in anticipation of the Rebels' arrival. De Sellum engaged his Confederate visitors in lively political discussion over dinner, opining that the South should be "whipped back under the Constitution, Union and Government of the United States with the rights and privileges she had before the war." Some hotheads among Early's staff took umbrage, with one named Lee declaring to De Sellum, "You are an abolitionist—it is no use to blame the devil and do the devil's work." Early and Brigadier General Arnold J. Elzey restored civility and "prevented a serious termination of the conversation." But De Sellum's hospitality and slave ownership failed to save him from Early's scavengers.[24]

De Sellum was a man of means and prestige in Montgomery County, Maryland, a locale of distinctly divided loyalties. Although the Presbyterian Church trustee, he had donated land to the construction of the little frame Episcopal Church nearby. He served as an agricultural and scientific adviser in Washington as well as on the board of the Gaithersburg Milling and Manufacturing Company. One can appreciate the squire promptly confronting Early on Monday morning about the plundering of his horses, beef, cows, bacon, hay, and corn barrels. Frankly, he and his sister thought "our lives were in imminent danger," as he bluntly asked Early "if he intended to give me up to be indiscriminately plundered." The battle-hardened Early replied with equal bluntness that since De Sellum appeared to have no sympathies for the Confederacy, "you can't expect favour or protection." However, he did sign an order leaving De Sellum and his sister with two barrels of corn. When grubby Rebel privates searched Summit Hill house for money and arms, De Sellum's plucky sister secreted $3,000 and U.S. government bonds under her dress. Later, when the visitors had left the area, De Sellum hid three southern soldiers from pursuing Federals but observed caustically, "How many of Early's men I directed to the North Pole or how many left by crossing the Potomac southward I only know by the large number of abandoned muskets left around my house." By that time, McCausland's horsemen, having skirmished with Fry's men at nearby Gerrardsville before brushing past Summit Hill, took the action southward to the streets of Rockville and inexorably toward the nation's capital via the Rockville turnpike.[25]

The initial sparring for Washington had already begun by the time De Sellum confronted Early in his front yard that warming Monday morning. Random bands of Rebels and Yanks clashed all over the county as the southerners tramped southward. One forager, twenty-one-year-old William D. Scott from Greenbrier County in southwest Virginia, was mortally wounded in a brush near Clopper's Mill, crawled to the Clopper farm Woodlands, and was succored by the family and their family doctor. He did not survive and lies buried in front of the St. Rose of Lima Church, unknown until a more salubrious postwar climate in the area allowed the United Daughters of the Confederacy to erect a suitable headstone over his grave. The fourth of seven children, Scott had three other brothers serving the Confederacy. Refugees began to precede the advancing Rebels, and Fry and Captain Levi Wells's squadron from Clendenin's Eighth Illinois (cut off from its parent unit after a brisk skirmish just after Monocacy at Urbana) were dislodged by McCausland's horse artillery on a hill just south of Rockville late Sunday. Residents realized they were now in a war zone. Young Virginia Campbell Moore recalled years later how she and her family had just come out of a church service that Sabbath to learn from a dusty, blue-clad trooper, "Get these horses away from here and get to your homes—the Rebs are coming." For the next few days the family "slept in Confederate lines, breakfasted in Federal lines, dined in those of the Confederates and so on." War had come to Washington's Maryland suburbs.[26]

Stock Taking at Week's End

This was roughly the situation as one week ended and another began. Mary Green-how Lee started her July 9 diary entry, "the end of a busy week," gloating that "Early is floating about in Maryland and has his face turned towards Baltimore," as well as dismissing "sensationalists" who had "got up a rumour that the Yankees who were hemmed up at Harpers Ferry would make a raid into Winchester." Cut off from reliable news of any kind, Rebel Lucy Buck in Front Royal, Virginia, could only recount how she and her parents had been turned back by besieging Confederates when they attempted a sightseeing excursion to Harpers Ferry. They had witnessed some fighting, and she marveled at the "sides of the green purple mountain and the white tents of the Yankee camp about the summit" while "thinking of all the various incidents connected with this classic ground of our . . . history." Her counterpart Laura Lee in Winchester, who had less excitement in her life, noted hearing nothing but rumors from Maryland as all communications were cut off while Hunter supposedly was "following Early rapidly." "This suspense is almost as terrible as what we endured a few weeks ago," she noted, adding that a report had Early recrossing the river at Leesburg. Winchester Unionist Julia Chase, however, jotted in her diary how July 10 was "a very noisy day, great many wagons are passing up & down," with cavalry going to Martinsburg, "which looks like the whole of Lee's army pushing this way, more troops about then we had any idea of, and we fear the report of the Federals being at Martinsburg and other points is incorrect." Reports from southern Pennsylvania had squads of Rebel cavalry infesting the mountains from Monterey to

Frederick, stealing horses, and creating great alarm. But then, the same might have been said of affairs generally to the eastward toward Baltimore.[27]

Reports from southern Pennsylvania had squads of enemy cavalry infesting the mountains from Monterey to Frederick, stealing horses, and creating great alarm. The same could be said of affairs eastward to Baltimore. William Farquhar of Sandy Spring in Montgomery County years later extrapolated from his wartime diary that news had come that "the Rebels hold Frederick and the line of the Monocacy." On Sunday, men were arriving from New Market "fleeing with their horses from the danger." "Accounts of the progress and near approach of the Rebels crowd upon us," he added. Uncertainty and chaos reigned throughout the region.[28]

Wallace and Ricketts failed to intercept Bradley Johnson's expedition. His riders roamed at will that weekend against the Northern Central railroad and telegraph lines north of Baltimore. A portion under local bon vivant Harry Gilmor moved to likewise disrupt traffic on the Wilmington and Baltimore line by burning the bridge over Gunpowder River. On the way, Gilmor stopped off to visit his family home at Glen Ellen, and Johnson soon partook of friend and distant cousin John Merryman's festal board at Hayfields—all in what author Joseph Judge aptly terms "the emerald valleys to the northwest of Baltimore." Merryman was the local militiaman infamous for interfering with the passage of Pennsylvania troops through Baltimore en route to Washington in 1861. His resultant incarceration in Fort McHenry led to a celebrated legal standoff between judicial and executive branches of the Federal government as to who had the right to suspend common law protection of citizens under habeas corpus. A general application of overbearing military control to much of the state to keep it in the Union won over few Marylanders to the Lincoln administration. One suspects there could be little doubt as to the trend of conversation between Merryman and Johnson over cordials that afternoon. Perhaps the Maryland scions remained conscious of Early's timetable for the Point Lookout as well as Baltimore missions; perhaps not. Johnson recalled later how "the charming society, the lovely girls, the balmy July air, and the luxuriant verdue" of the Hayfield estate was mostly an escape to yesteryear. Forty-odd miles to the southwest, Early certainly knew nothing of Johnson's reveries. He would not have been pleased.[29]

Much further south, from Petersburg headquarters, Robert E. Lee sent President Jefferson Davis a newspaper on July 10. By custom, Lee read Yankee mail, that is to say, the *New York Herald* on this occasion, and he fairly beamed that Davis "will see the people in the U.S. are mystified about our forces on the Potomac." The expedition "will have the effect I think at least of teaching them they must keep some of their troops at home & that they cannot denude their frontier with impunity." That was not going to win the war, however, although "it seems also to have put [the Federals] in bad temper as well as bad humour." Lee saw from the news that "they are removing the prisoners from Point Lookout." That was less favorable to his scheme, but there was little he might do directly at that stage. More telling, "gold you will see has gone as high as 271 & closed at 266 ¾"—indication in Lee's mind of the economic and political effects of Early's operation, especially as time drew closer to northern fall elections.[30]

Old Jube's ragtag army was only a hair's breadth from achieving the greatest Confederate triumph of the war—the taking of Washington. Early could only rely upon what he actually knew that Sunday night while dining at De Sellum's place. Pursuers pestered Ramseur's rear guard that finally closed with the main army before midnight. The rugged nineteen-mile march on the hot and grimy Sabbath had nearly broken his army. If Early received any fleeting reports of Johnson's actions around Baltimore, he still dreamed of success. His destination now clear to friend and foe alike, Early still counted success from both the results at Monocacy as well as subsequent progress toward the capital on Sunday. Whatever he learned from refugees and scouts indicated the prize was still within reach. One last dash and they would be there. What Early did not know for sure was the strength of Washington's defense lines and whether any veterans from the Army of the Potomac had arrived to man those defenses. That the initiative was even then passing from southern to northern hands might be inferred from an official Yankee telegram to which Early was not privy. At 4:00 a.m. on the tenth, Wallace had telegraphed his own Baltimore headquarters from Ellicott's Mills that since being defeated he was not pursued by the Confederates; "I infer they are marching on Washington." He urged the word be passed to Halleck in Washington. Three hours later Grant's chief-of-staff had it on his desk. The fate of the capital and perhaps the nation now rested in his hands.[31]

Sometime that Saturday, Patent Office examiner Horatio Nelson Taft wrote in his diary that a week before, he had intended being back with his family at Sag Harbor, Long Island. But the press of business kept him at his desk. His family and the Lincoln children had been playmates until Willie Lincoln's death in February 1862. Then the two families had parted company due mostly to Mrs. Lincoln's psychotic behavior. At any rate, "Judge" Taft now remained alone in the city concentrating upon his beloved patent work. Today, however, "I would not like to leave the City while the rebels are threatening it." These were very "'exciting times' just now in Maryland and in Pennsylvania," with the enemy "estimated at all numbers from five thousand to thirty thousand," reportedly even occupying Frederick, Maryland. Some squads of Rebel cavalry had even reached within fifteen miles of Washington over the previous two or three days "on this side of the Potomac." "It is supposed that they will make an attempt upon this City or Baltimore," next he penned. "This raid is supposedly to draw Grant away from Richmond to Defend Washington," he concluded. "But that 'ruse' will not do," according to Taft. "I think that will be done without Grant." One man's opinion remained to be proven on the hot Washington weekend of July 9 and 10.[32]

There remained another man's opinion that counted, perhaps above all. That was President Lincoln. He could read the military message traffic and query his chief military advisor Henry Halleck or the secretary of war. But apparently unsatisfied, perhaps even hearing (as many claimed) the sounds of some distant gunfire far in the distance from the Soldiers' Home retreat or because of family concern for the fate of Secretary Seward's son, the commander-in-chief wired his civilian friend John Garrett. "What have you heard about a battle at Monocacy to-day," he queried the railroad magnate. "We have heard nothing about it here except what you say," referring to earlier messages on the army's wires. Young William Henry Seward Jr. had been unhorsed and injured early in the battle while commanding a portion of the Ninth New York Heavy Artillery fighting as infantry with Ricketts. He was presumed captured or worse. Eventually he would turn up safely, but the president's cabinet circle did not know this at the time. Garrett's 7:15 p.m. reply contained no news on that count but was disheartening enough. Information relayed through the Monrovia telegraph operator had Wallace's aide reporting that "'our troops at Monocacy have given way, and that General Wallace has been badly defeated,' the bridge having been abandoned." Lincoln must have been nonplussed by that information. It had been a long day. He had written an unpleasant letter to Horace Greeley about peace commissioners, and now there was defeat on the Monocacy.[33]

Notes

1. Letter, Rutherford Worster to John W. Garrett, July 29, 1863, and Middle Department/VIII Army Corps order, July 9, 1864, both in Folder July–December 1863, Box 123, Robert Garrett family papers, Library of Congress (LC), Washington, DC; *Star Almanac*, 1882.

2. For the fullest coverage of the battle at Monocacy, in addition to earlier works on Early's raid generally, see the author's *Monocacy: The Battle That Saved Washington* (Shippensburg, PA: White Mane, 2000); Glenn H. Worthington, *Fighting for Time: Or, the Battle That Saved Washington and Mayhap the Union* (Baltimore: Day Printing Company, 1932; Shippensburg, PA: Burd Street Press, 1985); and Brett W. Spaulding, *Last Chance for Victory: Jubal Early's 1864 Maryland Invasion* (Frederick, MD: Thomas Publications, 2010), chapters 4–7.

3. Karen Gardner, "Digging History," Frederick *News-Post*, May 2, 2002; Paula Stoner Reed, "The Hermitage on the Monocacy," *Catoctin History* I (Fall 2002): 18–21; Joy Beasley, "Archeology on the Best Farm," *Catoctin History* I (Fall 2002): 16–17; David Snyder, "Digging Up Grim Past," *Washington Post*, November 9, 2003; and Michael E. Ruane, "A Record of Humanity Held in Brutal Captivity," *Washington Post*, August 26, 2010; on "Lost Order" see Wilbur D. Jones Jr., *Giants in the Cornfield: The 27th Indiana Infantry* (Shippensburg, PA: White Mane, 1997), 229–30.

4. T. H. White, "Tenting on the Old Camp Ground," 22, July 8, 1892, Bradford, Vermont *Opinioner*, July 8, 1892, folder 6, George E. Davis collection, Monocacy National Battlefield; see also G. G. Benedict, *Vermont in the Civil War, A History of the Part Taken by the Vermont Soldiers and Sailors in the War for the Union, 1861–1865, volume II* (Burlington, VT: Free Press Association, 1886), 307–18; E. M. Haynes, *A History of the Tenth Regiment, Vermont Volunteers* (Rutland, VT: Tuttle, 1894), chapter 5.

5. William R. Quinn, editor, *The Diary of Jacob Engelbrecht 1818–1878* (Frederick, MD: Historical Society of Frederick County, 1976), 271–72, 274; Worthington, *Fighting for Time*, 282–89; Thomas Scharf, *History of Western Maryland* (Philadelphia: L. H. Evarts, 1882, and Baltimore, 1968: Genealogical Publishing Company), 288–89; Edward Delaplaine, "General Early's Levy on Frederick," in Frederick County Civil War Centennial, *To Commemorate the 100th Anniversary of the Battle of Monocacy* (Frederick, MD: Frederick County Civil War Centennial, 1964), 48–54.

6. A useful account appears in Steven Bernstein, *The Confederacy's Last Northern Offensive: Jubal Early, the Army of the Valley and the Raid on Washington* (Jefferson, NC: MacFarland, 2011), 38–40.

7. William Allan journal, 29–30, Southern Historical Collection, University of North Carolina, Chapel Hill; Nancy F. Whitmore and Timothy L. Cannon, *Frederick: A Pictorial History* (Norfolk: Donning Company, 1981), 56–57; Scharf, *History of Western Maryland*, 289; Delaplaine, "General Early's Levy," 50–54; Millard Bushong, *Old Jube: A Biography of General Jubal A. Early* (Boyce, VA: Carr, 1955), 197.

8. Jubal Early, *War Memoirs* (Bloomington: Indiana University Press, 1961), 386; Isaac Bond, *Map of Frederick County* (Baltimore: Maryland State Archives, 1858).

9. U. S. War Department, *War of the Rebellion: Official Records of Union and Confederate Armies* (Washington, DC, 1880–1901), Series I, Volume 51, part 1, 1175–76, hereinafter cited *ORA*, with appropriate series, volume, part, and page.

10. Lew Wallace testimonial, Kenilworth Inn, Biltmore, North Carolina, March 30, 1893; Copy Letter, William W. Henry to T. S. Peck, April 15, 1892, both folder 13, George E. Davis collection, Monocacy National Battlefield.

11. L. E. Chittenden, *Recollections of President Lincoln and His Administration* (New York: Harper and Brothers, 1891), 393, 394, 399, 400.

12. *ORA*, I, 51, pt. 1, 1176; Letter, James B. Ricketts to George E. Davis, May 17, 1873, and Davis note to file, undated, folder 6; S. J. Barber to Davis, February 17, 1886, Folder 12, all George E. Davis collection, Monocacy National Battlefield; William C. Davis, *Breckinridge: Statesman, Soldier, Symbol* (Baton Rouge: Louisiana State University Press, 1974), 445.

13. Letters, Zebulon York to B. R. Welford, July 18, 1864, and York to R. W. Hunter, July 22, 1864, in York collection, Huntington Library, San Marino, CA; Floyd King to Sister, July 15, 1864, in Thomas Butler King papers, Southern Historical Collection, University of North Carolina, Chapel Hill (UNC); William Terry Report, July 12, 1864, Chicago Historical Society, Chicago IL (CHS); Buckner McGill Randolph diary, July 9, 1864, Virginia Historical Society (VHS); on Staunton, see court-martial proceedings at http://67thpa.wordpress.com/post-your-soldier-information/col-john-f-staunton/court-martial-proceedings/.

14. Miscellaneous notes, folders 2 and 6, Davis collection, Monocacy National Battlefield.

15. *ORA*, I, 51, pt. 1, 195–99.

16. *ORA*, I, 51, pt. 1, 191–92; S. J. Barber to George E. Davis, February 17, 1886, Folder 12, Davis papers, Monocacy.

17. *ORA*, I, 51, 193–202, especially 200–202.

18. *ORA*, I, 37, pt. 1, 139, pt. 2, 274; Samuel P. Bates, *A History of Pennsylvania Volunteers* (Harrisburg: B. Singerly, 1869–1871), Volume II 639.

19. *ORA*, I, 37, pt. 2, 139; U.S. Cong., 96th, lst Sess., Senate Committee Print 3, Committee on Veterans' Affairs, United States Senate. *Medal of Honor Recipients 1863–1978* (Washington, DC, 1979), 69, 212; T. H. White, "Tenting on the Old Camp Ground," Column Number 25, Bradford, Vermont *Opinioner*, September 23, 1892.

20. Letter, J. Warren Keifer to wife, September 11, 1864, Joseph Warren Keifer papers, Manuscript Division, Library of Congress, Washington, D.C.; Lydia P. Hecht, editor, *Echoes from the Letters of a Civil War Surgeon* (Long Boat Key, FL: Bayou Publishing, 1994), 185.

21. Letter, James B. Ricketts to George E. Davis, May 17, 1873, and Davis file memo, both Folder 13, George E. Davis collection, Monocacy National Battlefield.

22. *ORA*, I, 37, pt. 2, 594; Henry Kyd Douglas, *I Rode with Stonewall* (Chapel Hill: University of North Carolina Press, 1940), 294; J. Stoddard Johnston, "Notes of March of Breckinridge's Corps," June 19–July 15, 1864, entry July 10, 1864, New York Historical Society (NYHS), New York, NY; E. N. Atkinson, "Report of Evan's Brigade," July 22, 1864, Eldridge Collection, Huntington Library (HL), San Marino, CA.

23. Alexander Hunter, *Johnny Reb and Billy Yank* (New York: Neale Publishing Company, 1905), 650; George Perkins, *A Summer in Maryland and Virginia Campaigning with the One Hundred and Forty-Ninth Ohio Volunteer Infantry* (Chillicothe, OH: Sholl Printing Company, 1911), 52–53; J. Cutler Andrews, *The South Reports the Civil War* (Pittsburgh, PA: University of Pittsburgh Press, 1970), 408–9; Sergeant Major John G. Young, diary, North Carolina Division of History and Archives (NCHA), 39–40, and W. W. Scott, editor, "Diary of Captain H. W. Winfield," *Bulletin of the Virginia State Library* XVI (July 1929): 43; John C. Bonnell Jr., *Sabres in the Shenandoah: The Twenty-First New York Cavalry 1863–1866* (Shippensburg, PA: White Mane, 1996), 103.

24. John T. De Sellum, narrative reminiscence, copy, n.d., 46–48, and "Farm Family in County Had 1,800 Troops as 'Guests,'" undated clipping, both Montgomery County Historical Society, Rockville (MCHS); Hunter, *Johnny Reb and Billy Yank*, 650; Perkins, *A Summer in Maryland and Virginia*, 52–53.

25. De Sellum, ibid., 49–52; also see Joseph Judge, *Season of Fire: The Confederate Strike on Washington* (Berryville, VA: Rockbridge Publishing Company, 1994), 219–21.

26. Virginia Campbell Moore, "Reminiscenes of Life along the Rockville Pike during the Civil War," *Montgomery County Story* XXVII (November 1984): 137; Clay Hamilton and Charles T. Jacobs, "Greenbrier Civil War Soldier Buried in Maryland," Lewisburg, West Virginia, *Daily News*, October 11, 1983; *ORA*, I, 37, pt. 1, 236, 239, 248, 249; pt. 2, 166–67.

27. Eloise C. Strader, editor, *The Civil War Journal of Mary Greenhow Lee (Mrs. Hugh Holmes Lee) of Winchester, Virginia* (Winchester, VA: Winchester Historical Society, 2011), 379; William P. Buck, editor, *Sad Earth, Sweet Heaven: The Diary of Lucy Rebecca Buck during*

the War between the States (Birmingham, AL: Cornerstone, 1973), 265–67, and Michael G. Mahon, editor, *Winchester Divided: The Civil War Diaries of Julia Chase and Laura Lee* (Mechanicsburg, PA: Stackpole Books, 2002), 152–55.

28. William H. Farquhar, *Annals of Sandy Spring, Or Twenty Years History of a Rural Community in Maryland* (Baltimore: Cushings & Bailey, 1884), 12–13.

29. Mahon, *Winchester Divided*, 154; Buck, *Sad Earth, Sweet Heaven*, 267; Bradley Johnson, "My Ride Round Baltimore in Eighteen Hundred Sixty-Four," *Journal of the United States Cavalry Association* (September 1889): 251–54; Harry Gilmor, *Four Years in the Saddle* (New York: Nabu Press, 1866), 190–93; Judge, *Season of Fire*, 212–13; *ORA*, I, 37, pt. 22, 155–57, 166–67; 170–90 inter alia.

30. Clifford Dowdey and Louis H. Manarin, editors, *The Wartime Papers of Robert E. Lee* (New York: Brammel House for Virginia Civil War Commission, 1966), 818–19.

31. *ORA*, I, 37, pt. 2, 174.

32. Diary of Horatio Nelson Taft, July 9, 1864, volume 3, Library of Congress, Washington, D.C.

33. Roy P. Basler, editor, *The Collected Works of Abraham Lincoln, volume VII* (New Brunswick, NJ: Rutgers University Press, 1953), 434, 435, and *ORA* I, 37, pt. 2, 138; Frederick W. Seward, *Reminiscences of a War-Time Statesman and Diplomat* (New York: G. P. Putnam's Sons, 1916), 246–47; Alfred Seelye Roe, *The Ninth New York Heavy Artillery* (Worchester, MA: Author, 1899), 132–33; Gideon Welles, *Diary* (Boston: Houghton Mifflin, 1909), II, 71.

BLINDNESS OR STUPIDITY ON A HOT WEEKEND

The issue was very much in doubt that weekend. On Saturday, Charles M. Yocum, a member of the Fifty-Second Ohio National Guard and one of the 100-day regiments sent to guard the capital early in the summer, wrote to his friend Bella from Fort Reynolds on the southern defense line. He had passed the previous day "on a visit to Washington City—and many times when I beheld the monuments of the illustrious, the paintings illustrative of renowned assemblies and a thousand things in which a great people once felt a sacred and common interest, I could but lament with sad feeling of the deepest regret that the people are now cursed with a Civil and Fratricidal war." He had "traveled through the Smithsonian Institute with a thousand things to excite the minds and admiration of the most careless and superficial eye," and he thought she, too, would have enjoyed that experience. Then he got down to the immediate crisis. "Just now the boys are passing jokes about leaving as the report has come that we are under marching orders," he suggested. "They say we are going to Harpers Ferry" and "there is considerable excitement about Frederick as they are having some fighting there." He personally wanted to go to Harpers Ferry, Yocum decided. "Just now we hear the constant booming of heavy artillery which is undoubtedly the cannonading of an engagement, and I should not wonder if we move in a little while." Whatever comes, so be it, he concluded. He and the Fifty-Second would not move anywhere, but others protecting Washington would as Monocacy took effect.[1]

Lincoln and His City on the Brink of Crisis

President Abraham Lincoln had avoided dabbling in day-to-day military operations that summer as he had done two years before with George B. McClellan. Perhaps he should have done so now. But other affairs intruded on the chief executive.

Moreover, telegrams and dispatches from general-in-chief Ulysses S. Grant's field headquarters at City Point, Virginia, kept the president generally well apprised of the war's progress. Moreover, matters seemed sufficiently satisfactory for Lincoln to leave the war to the generals. Still, by early July, the national capital's own region seemed on the cusp of something but knew not what. Major-General David Hunter's rebuff at Lynchburg and his mysterious retirement into the western Virginia mountains left Washington vulnerable once more. Then, on July 2, Franz Sigel wired the adjutant general in Washington that "there are strong indications of a movement in force down the Valley." Refugees reported Early and three divisions were moving in that direction. Was this merely a raid? Washington and the high command all chose to regard it as the customary summer move by Rebels—and watchfully waited. Over the next week, this watchful waiting expanded beyond the red brick walls of the War Department and telegraph office. Trepidations increased especially when Lew Wallace sent a final definitive wire outlining his defeat that reached the War Department about twenty minutes before midnight.[2]

Retreating "with a foot-sore, battered, and half-demoralized column," the Hoosier warrior reported forlornly having been overwhelmed by numbers of the enemy in severe fighting. The Union high command including Lincoln, Stanton, and Halleck knew this already from various intervening reports from Garrett. But particularly chilling must have been Wallace's stark warning: "You will have to use every exertion to save Baltimore and Washington." Whatever watchful waiting, preliminary preparations, and communication between Washington and Grant, the scare in Maryland now assumed dire overtones. Not surprisingly, the heretofore hands-off commander-in-chief would soon emerge at the center of affairs.[3]

The president's docket for the previous month had included not just the usual soirees and audiences attending office or even the customary requests for jobs, amnesty, and other favors. He had gone to Philadelphia to deliver speeches in conjunction with the Great Sanitary Fair in that city. He also attended to international matters such as affairs in Mexico, Colombia, and the Hawaiian Islands. But what concerned Lincoln most of all were domestic issues. He signed a Pacific railroad bill on the second, designed to cross the continent with modern communication, a sign of hope for a more tranquil postwar America. Yet he and the nation had to get through the conflict first, and that was certainly in doubt. A rising tide of discontent pervaded Kentucky and the Midwest largely over the never-ending war and local military enforcement of administration war policies affecting civil liberties, conscription, and the enlistment of African Americans. In the loyal border Bluegrass, unaffected by his previous year's Emancipation Proclamation, times were so turbulent that Lincoln suspended the writ of habeas corpus on July 5, just about the time he began to think about some mysterious reports of Rebels apparently rummaging about in the lower Shenandoah. Proclaiming a national day of humiliation and prayer for the first Thursday in August, the president then confronted the Capitol Hill insurgency over reconstruction. Newspaperman Horace Greeley resumed his meddling about meeting representatives of the Confederate government concerning peace overtures. No wonder the president and his family looked to weekend quiet at Soldiers' Home.[4]

Summer in Washington before the advent of air conditioning could be brutal. People left town in droves—if they could. Congress adjourned at the very time Early's minions supped on Independence Day fare at Harpers Ferry and Martinsburg. Even the Blair family of old Francis Preston and one son, Postmaster General Montgomery, left town for cooler climes in the mountains of Pennsylvania and the New Jersey seashore. The president settled for the gray stucco and brick Gothic Revival cottage on the grounds of an incomplete asylum for veterans set three hundred feet above the city's zero sea level. Rolling acres of oak, beech, meadows, and pastures near little Rock Creek Episcopal parish as well as garrison camps at nearby forts Slemmer, Totten, and Slocum reminded the Lincolns of both war and peace. The president remained on call and in contact with downtown Washington, the nerve center for winning the war. Precautions were already afoot, with Assistant Secretary of the Navy Gustavus V. Fox ordering a steamer ready to evacuate government records, even the president, should the emergency become dire. Lincoln's bodyguards became more edgy as refugees from upcountry began filtering through northern defense lines with their possessions and prized farm animals spreading tales of Rebel plunder and villainy that quickly turned into street rumors. The city's secessionist "fifth column" began to gather data to pass on to an advancing enemy.[5]

War Department officials kept mum, dismissing such unworthy information. More discretely, the military began scrambling to organize resistance from city militia, invalids, and dismounted cavalrymen awaiting remounts at Camp Stoneman over the Anacostia River on Giesboro Point. Short-term 100-day enlistees and whatever remained of Washington's normal fort garrisons and administrative troops tried to sort out just who might be in command. Convalescing sergeant J. D. Bloodgood of the One Hundred and Forty-First Pennsylvania led forty lads for two weeks of duty at the Central Guard House, thus freeing others to march to the sound of the guns. Newspapers upped the decibels from "idle scare" to serious threat, and carping cabinet members such as Attorney General Edward Bates wondered how an enemy could get so close while deciding "Wallace and Seigel [sic] et cetera are helpless imbeciles." The first family remained blissfully detached from the crescendo of turmoil passing across the city and region.[6]

Meanwhile, Lincoln received a telegram from five prominent Baltimore citizens sent from Camden Station in that city Saturday evening. Authorized by Mayor John Lee Chapman (who together with Governor Augustus Bradford had declared the city in imminent danger and called out five loyal Union League–officered local-defense contingents to help defend the place), Thomas Swann, Evan T. Ellicott, William E. Hooper, Thomas S. Alexander, and Michael Warner asked the president for reinforcements. Frantically they begged, "It is too late to organize the citizens to any extent before the enemy will be upon us?" Lincoln patiently replied from the military telegraph office at 9:20 a.m. on July 10 that "I have not a single soldier but whom is being disposed by the Military for the best protection of all." Furthermore, by that time, the latest account had the enemy moving on Washington anyway. "They cannot fly to either place," he observed a bit peevishly it seemed, adding quietly, "Let us be vigilant but keep cool," for "I hope neither Baltimore or Washington will be sacked." The president was equally calm in communication with his military men.[7]

Street talk, wires from frantic citizenry in an adjacent city, and tight-lipped officials all notwithstanding—just when did official Washington decide the Rebel host was seriously headed its way? The scares in upper Maryland and Sigel's notice of Confederates in the valley perhaps even when Early reached Frederick could hardly excite more than watchful waiting. Wallace's frenetic sounding July 8 evening dispatch to Halleck about "Breckinridge, with a strong column, moving down the Washington pike toward Urbana" seemed hardly conclusive, although perhaps it was a warning flag. In fact, nothing definitive might be cited, until the spate of dispatches confirming the Monocacy defeat and open route to the capital as well as the droves of anxious refugees actually appeared at Washington's doorstep. If so, was War Department and army response tardy in the absence of definitive intelligence? From Lincoln, Stanton, and Halleck to Grant, not to mention asides to political colleagues such as the governor of Pennsylvania, the Union high command had been trying to find, muster, and deploy resources appropriate to a perceived level of disturbance, however vague, until the very last minute. It has all seemed so clear over subsequent generations. It was not at the time.[8]

The Knowns and the Unknowns

As of July 3, Grant and Meade maintained that no Confederates had left the Petersburg-Richmond front other than to defend Lynchburg. There was some question, however, as to whether such a column had actually returned from that task. Lee's subterfuge worked perfectly. Then Sigel's warnings, Garrett's confirmations, and the onset of fighting in the lower Shenandoah funneled through Washington led to efforts to begin to reinforce the upper Potomac Federals awaiting Hunter's return to the fray. Any reinforcements directed by the Union high command, however, were destined for Harpers Ferry at this point, and it was the concern of Baltimore & Ohio president John Garrett for his railroad that triggered Wallace and his Middle

Department to push forward a column to defend Monocacy River crossings as early as that first week in July. Such actions suggest that some people might have fretted about Washington and looked to deploy a customary forward defense posture for protecting the city.

Indications, however, were that this was merely some upcountry raid. As the threat intensified, the question shifted to how much would be sufficient to stop the intruders, where would resources come from, and how soon could they be moved into position—to protect either Baltimore, Washington, or both. Still, as of the afternoon of Independence Day, City Point was only beginning to sift through the fog of war. Both Assistant Secretary of War Charles A. Dana and Grant caught sight of a deserter report that Ewell's corps "has not returned here, but is off in the Valley with the intention of going into Maryland and Washington City." This was only the report of a deserter, added Grant, and "we have similar authority for it being here and on the right of Lee's army." Watchful waiting continued, and Albion Howe with dismounted artillerists went forward by rail from Washington through Baltimore en route to reinforce Harpers Ferry. Wallace's subordinate Erastus B. Tyler fortified and maintained the vital Monocacy crossing.[9]

Finally, shortly after noon on July 5, Grant signaled his intent. "If the enemy crosses into Maryland or Pennsylvania," Grant could "send an army corps from here to cut off their return south." He wanted Halleck to order the quartermaster to send transportation. In turn, Halleck then brought his superior up to date on the situation, still seemingly anything but dire. He may have inadvertently contributed procrastination or delay in confronting matters up front. Responding within the half-hour to Grant, Halleck talked about breakdowns in communication. Sigel successfully withdrew to Maryland Heights, but the Confederate capture of Harpers Ferry exaggerated enemy strength figures (between twenty thousand and thirty thousand), which even "if one-half that number we cannot meet" in the field without Hunter's return. Grant was no doubt aware that "we have almost nothing in Baltimore or Washington except militia, and considerable alarm has been created by sending troops from these places to reinforce Harper's Ferry." He advised Grant to send all dismounted cavalry to Washington to be reequipped as infantry. Learning later by reopened telegraph that Hunter was still out of supporting position at Parkersburg in western Virginia, Halleck wired Grant again at 10:30 that night that he still did not think Grant's operations against Lee directly should be imperiled by sending troops to Washington. In two sentences bordering on contradictory or unrealistic, Halleck told Grant, "If Washington and Baltimore should be so seriously threatened as to require your aid, I will inform you in time." While most of the forces were "not of a character suitable for the field (invalids and militia) yet I have no apprehensions at present about the safety of Washington, Baltimore, Harper's Ferry or Cumberland."[10]

Halleck and the War Department still focused on raids that could be contained and damage repaired. Grant responded at 11:30 p.m. on July 5 that he had dispatched dismounted cavalry and a division of infantry, "which will be followed by the balance of the corps if necessary." It was important, said the senior commander, to "crush out and destroy any force the enemy have sent north," and reinforcements from Petersburg "can be spared from here to do it." That very afternoon, Meade confirmed that Jubal Early's two divisions of Ewell's old corps, Breckinridge's command, and other contingents were "making an invasion of Maryland with a view of capturing Washington, supposed to be defenseless." An infantry division was on the way from the Army of the Potomac, but "no artillery need be sent," Grant instructed the Potomac army commander George G. Meade. Grant told him, "I will not send an army corps until there is greater necessity for it." In Washington, however, lethargy attended the formal defense of the city to the extent that Major-General John Gross Barnard, chief engineer for the department, reported brush overgrowing the approaches to the works "in such quantities as to militate against the proper use of the means of defense given to them." So departmental commander Major-General Christopher Augur instructed that commencing at Fort Sumner on the western edge of the northern line, available men would be employed in "removing the cover alluded to." Still at this point, expectations rested with Howe's expedition helping to conduct the forward defense of the capital at Harpers Ferry while Hunter still had primary responsibility "to take such measures as may be proper to meet the emergency."[11]

Indeed, to this point all eyes had focused upon the Harpers Ferry region. The Washington high command could be seen parrying the possibility of another move farther north into Pennsylvania by calling upon Pennsylvania and New York governors each for twelve thousand 100-days men drawn upon the militia. Major-General John A. Dix in New York City was tapped for more Veterans Reserve corps. Halleck ordered an engineer review of Washington bridge defense. Wallace also sought to strengthen guards on the Baltimore & Wilmington railroad at the Bush, Back, and Gunpowder river crossings north of Baltimore while tapping eastern shore contingents as well as skulkers from Sigel's force at Annapolis to bolster his meager resources. Loyal Union League Marylanders mustered to bolster morale and homefront response in Baltimore city. Augur increased patrols in southern Maryland based upon rumored attempts to raid the Point Lookout prisoner of war camp. Much depended upon a coordinated response in all this, and Washington would have to take the lead. With little doubt attending the knowledge that Early was on the upper Potomac with a sizable force by July 6, Grant still talked more about another raid up the Shenandoah Valley to destroy Rebel stores and communications. He envisioned Hunter moving rapidly on Charlottesville, destroying rail and canal links to Lee's army once "Ewell, Breckinridge &c." had been destroyed. There was no reason that reinforcements from Petersburg lines should take "teams, ambulances, or ammunition, except what they carry in boxes" to Maryland. He expected their quick return. Besides, he thought there were about six hundred teams ready for issue in Washington depots anyway. By time of writing, Major-General James Ricketts's Second Division, VI Corps (five thousand infantry), had left southern Virginia for Harpers Ferry via Baltimore. Cavalry chief Philip Sheridan had transferred three thousand dismounted cavalry for refitting at the big Giesboro, D.C., remount facility. Sheridan really only sent 2,496 sick cavalrymen, sans arms, not fit veterans. Field chieftains still thought marginal reinforcement would contain the threat.[12]

Grant and Meade spent time wondering about Lee's whereabouts and whether he had taken the majority of his army on a raid north. Monocacy notched upward the immediacy of the crisis. "There is great alarm in Washington," Grant finally told Meade on Sunday, the tenth, as Wallace had been "whipped at Monocacy bridge, and driven back in great confusion." Grant now was sending back two more divisions of the VI and one of the XIX corps to form a junction with Hunter ("who must be at Harper's Ferry tonight") and "for them to follow up in the enemy's rear." Everything looked favorable to Grant, "but I want to avoid the possibility of Lee getting off with a great part of his force without taking advantage of it." Grant and Meade remained too closely focused on what to do about Lee while matters were coming apart 150 miles to the north. In Washington, filtering the news and innuendoes from all over middle Maryland and southeastern Pennsylvania about the whereabouts and activities of the Rebel raiders consumed time, attention, and reply. To some people, it still looked more like a foraging expedition bent on taking horses and property from Maryland farmers than any attack on Washington.[13]

Calculating Resources

To show how detached different theaters of the war were from one another despite the advantage of telegraphic communication, western commander Major-General William T. Sherman that very Sunday morning sent Halleck a wire from north Georgia en route to Atlanta. "If General Grant has nothing particular for Hunter, Crook and Averell to do, and if they be in the Kanawha Valley, as is reported, they could be well employed by going to Abingdon, smashing up things in that quarter, and then going over in North Carolina." This may have occasioned a sardonic laugh at the War Department given the more imminent disaster impending for Washington. The key to action now lay with the War Department leadership of Halleck and Stanton. Time had passed for half measures. The actual scene of operations moved inexorably eastward and then southward toward the nation's capital from July 7 to 10. Questions of rear echelon militia and short-service contingents, garrison detachments, underequipped relief forces, unsupported infantry, and yet-to-be-remounted cavalry filled the messages passing back and forth between Washington and City Point. Halleck told the chief of the Cavalry Bureau to organize all employees of that bureau and men at Giesboro depot into companies and regiments armed and prepared for the defense of that critical logistics facility. Some twelve thousand XIX Corps veterans were anticipated at City Point, Virginia, from action on the Gulf Coast, and available for emergency duty at Washington.

A July 10 abstract from Augur's trimonthly Department of Washington report cited 23,500 officers and men present for duty (from some 39,440 on the rolls) with 944 heavy and thirty-five field guns available to directly defend the city. Admittedly, these figures drew upon the June report of 25,667 officers and men present for duty (33,289 aggregate present, 38,906 aggregate present and absent) with 950 heavy and thirty-nine field guns. Discrepancies and accounting differences notwithstanding, the real question was one of positioning, as it had been ever since the outset of the war. While the more sophisticated and integrated system of fortifications lay on the Virginia side of the city, the weight of numbers for manpower and guns had shifted to the north side by 1864. Not by much, perhaps six thousand troops and twenty-four pieces of heavy artillery, was still evidence of a new ration of field guns of twenty-two cannon north to six south. And complicating the definition of available garrison forces also derived from troop assignments. Discounting department headquarters, forces north of the Potomac included an artillery camp of instruction (twenty-two guns), the Giesboro cavalry facility and a cavalry division (with seven companies of the Eighth Illinois deployed in the field), the District of Washington provost and other contingents, hospital guards, and the Fort Washington garrison as well as a distinct St. Mary's district in southern Maryland supplied guards for the Point Lookout prison camp and did stabilization and occupation work in that secessionist area. Only roughly four thousand men under Lieutenant Colonel J. A. Haskin actually did fort duty in those lines. The situation was just as sketchy south of the Potomac. There, District of Alexandria provost units, a Rendezvous of Distribution training camp, and provisional brigades including cavalry took manpower, with only Brigadier General Gustavus A. DeRussy's division actually manning the sector's forts. Clearly, Fortress Washington relied upon defenders who were little more than guards for a vast political and logistical enterprise as Jubal Early's army bore down on the place that hot July weekend.[14]

As such the defenses of Washington had never been designed as anything more than a deterrent and to singularly cope with anything more than partisan raiders and inner-city subversives. The fortifications provided a base for operations. But such operations against a besieging force of the size Early was bringing would come from the field army. At least that was the theory, and it had been so for over two years. The Union's strategy rested squarely upon mobilizing a counterstrike force from the main Army of the Potomac should Washington come under enemy attack. Washington's shield—sixty plus forts, ninety-three or more unoccupied field gun batteries, miles of interlocking entrenchments, the support roads, buildings, camps, and other infrastructure would always be just a base, a hinge from which a field army would move like a grim reaper to destroy the attacker. That was dogma and exactly the thinking up and down the chain of command in July 1864. In this case, whatever Grant and Meade sent back to counter the enemy threat now in Maryland would join forces to cooperate with Hunter to destroy the raiders. A good defense of Washington was always preeminently a good offensive in army eyes. Dispatches to a point underscored that approach.

Halleck's message to Grant late in the evening of July 8 sounded alarmist. Intelligence from mid-Maryland indicated a force estimated at twenty thousand to thirty thousand Rebels moving south from the Monocacy directly toward Washington. Halleck was advancing Wallace's sincere, if a bit premature, prognosis. The next day's battle on the Monocacy provided truth to the contention. But Halleck conveyed the belief that "one-third of Lee's entire force is with Early and Breckinridge, and that Ransom has some 3,000 to 4,000 cavalry." A now panicky chief-of-staff debunked the notion that militia or even Hunter's tardily arriving force could counter the threat. None of Grant's proffered cavalry had arrived yet, nor "do we get anything from Hunter." Troops sent from the James should come to Washington, not Baltimore, said Halleck, for they could not be supplied at the Maryland city. Without heavy reinforcement, "if you propose to cut off this raid and not merely to secure our depots we must have more forces here," meaning Washington.[15]

Grant took precautions. He postponed a massive assault he had planned at Petersburg and ordered the remainder of the VI Corps and a division of the XIX Corps (arriving from service in the Gulf) to Washington, while noting "forces enough to defeat all that Early has with him should get in his rear south of him, and follow him up sharply, leaving him to go north, defending depots, towns etc., with small garrisons and the militia." Worried now that perhaps James Longstreet's corps had departed north, Grant and Meade had Army of the Potomac veterans on the march to embarkation points by midevening on July 9. A race to see who reached the nation's capital—Union or Confederate veteran troops—was now on. Perhaps for the first time since the onset of the emergency, Grant began to stir to the crisis. "If the President thinks it advisable that I should go to Washington in person I can start in an hour after receiving notice, leaving everything here on the defensive," he wired Halleck at 6:00 p.m. that day. The War Department received the telegram only early the next afternoon. At the moment of dispatch, and unknown to everyone, Wallace's shattered command was streaming toward Baltimore in precipitous retreat. The way to Washington lay wide open.[16]

Enter the president of the United States at this point. By 2:30 p.m. that steamy and unsettled Sunday, the commander-in-chief weighed in on the situation. Back to Grant he wired, "referring to what I may think in the present emergency." He carefully outlined the situation on the ground—no force fit to go to the field, 100-days men and invalids capable of defending Washington but scarcely Baltimore, Albion Howe not very reliable, Hunter approaching Harpers Ferry "very slowly" with uncertain numbers, while Wallace "with some odds and ends and part of what came up with Ricketts, was so badly beaten yesterday at Monocacy that what is left can attempt no more than to defend Baltimore." "What we shall get in from Pennsylvania and New York [militia] will scarcely be worth counting," he added. Now what he thought, said the president, was that Grant "should provide to retain your hold where you are, certainly, and bring the rest with you personally, and make a vigorous effort to destroy the enemy's force in this vicinity." He thought "there is really a fair chance to do this if the movement is prompt." This was what Lincoln thought, he told Grant, upon the general's suggestion to Halleck, "and is not an order." Was Lincoln relapsing into suggestive direction much as he had with previous commanders? Or did he retain unbridled confidence in the man from the west? Did this particular moment demand stronger leadership? Was not this particular crisis the most critical moment in the war when his presidency, his capital, and the nation in an election year tottered in doubt? That hot Sunday afternoon on the tidal Potomac—that fateful hour—demanded that soldier and statesman-politician needed confidence and trust in one another as the nation's future hung in the balance. Neither man shirked his constitutional responsibility. Yet Grant was not on the scene; Lincoln was.[17]

Mustering for the Critical Moment

Late Sunday brought a new sense of urgency for the Lincolns at the summer White House. After telegraphic exchanges with Grant and other consultations, the president and his escort ventured back out to Soldiers' Home only to have a squad of blue-coated soldiers awaken the first family near midnight. The officer in charge presented a dispatch from Secretary of War Stanton (some accounts claimed the cabinet official came in person) to the effect that the situation was so dire, the commander-in-chief's safety so threatened by Early's arrival, that the first family must return to the White House. Just a few days before Abe had rebuffed the Department of Washington commander's suggestion for a personal escort by saying only if the Secretary of War directed it. Now, Stanton demanded it, although an obviously chagrined Lincoln complained and only reluctantly returned downtown that night through the oppressive darkness. By eight the next morning, he would be back in the telegraph office wiring Grant his latest thoughts. But that night, the thin line of defenses stretching from forts Slemmer and Totten to Slocum was simply too undermanned to chance some raiding party of Rebels knifing through and carrying off the most important man in the land.[18]

Lincoln's 8:00 a.m. wire to Grant on July 11 would express his satisfaction with the general's previous late-evening response. Yet the president sounded strangely detached, commenting merely, "The enemy will learn of Wright's arrival, and then the difficulty will be to unite Wright and Hunter south of the enemy before he will recross the Potomac." He noted some firing between Rockville and the city. The president still left it to the high command to get the nation out of this latest predicament. And so Halleck, and also Assistant Secretary of War Charles A. Dana, would now step in to more fully inform yet press Grant who, in turn, was badgering Meade to find out who had left Confederate lines for Maryland, and then execute a major assault on Lee's remaining force at Petersburg. "If they [meaning the Confederates] have gone to Washington we will try to carry Petersburg before detaching further from this army," he decreed, micromanaging just how Meade might accomplish that task in some detail. Ironically, at that very moment, Lee (learning from a scout of Union waterborne movements down the James River) told his own commander-in-chief, Jefferson Davis, how it was "repugnant to [Grant's] principles and practices to send troops from him [and] that I had hoped before resorting to it he would have preferred attacking me." Such thoughts seemingly contradicted the Confederate commander's own strategy of forcing withdrawal of the besieging enemy by sending Early's diversion northward in the first place. By July 11, Lee would reiterate this new preference that Grant attack him directly rather than respond to Early's threat, and he admitted his own inability to attack the besieging Federals in turn but possibly to send reinforcements to help Early. Intelligence derived from "deserters, prisoners, scouts and citizens," plus Lee's ubiquitous reliance on the *New York Herald*, gave him a pretty good idea of the order of battle of those troops sent back to defend Washington. He began to fear Early's being caught in a pincer between those forces and Hunter's returning army from the west.[19]

Meanwhile, Washington could only look to first defenders. Veteran Major-General Alexander McCook had reported to the War Department promptly on the morning of July 10. Directed to find Halleck, McCook soon found himself assigned to the Department of Washington with orders to set up a reserve camp near the Piney Branch tributary that flowed into Rock Creek near the T. Blagden place and Crystal Spring, about midway between the city and the northern defense line at Fort Stevens. Together with Defenses of Washington engineer lieutenant colonel Barton S. Alexander, McCook proceeded to scope out the camp and the northern fortifications. The pair found that Colonel Charles M. Alexander's Second District of Columbia, Lieutenant Colonel Robert E. Johnston's Ninth Veteran Reserve Corps,

Captain Frank C. Gibbs's Battery L, and First Ohio Light Artillery and Captain Albert W. Bradbury's First Maine Battery had already encamped. Later that afternoon, as other troops were alerted across the Department of Washington, convalescing Colonel J. M. Warner, First Vermont Heavy Artillery, was told to "move without delay" the companies occupying batteries Cameron, Parrott, Kemble, and Vermont (positioned to provide 100-pounder enfilading distance fire across the Potomac to help forts Ethan Allen and Marcy defend Chain Bridge). Warner was to occupy a frontline from forts Simmons and Mansfield and "place them in such weak points in your line" as he thought advisable. A small guard was left for the batteries.[20]

Soon, department headquarters tapped south-side contingents such as Captain Wallace M. Spears's Battery A, First Wisconsin Heavy Artillery; Lieutenant Frank S. French's Battery E, First U.S. Artillery; and Captain Henry D. Scott's Sixteenth Massachusetts Light Battery from Fort Lyon below Alexandria to transfer to Martin D. Hardin, the amputee veteran general officer at Tennallytown, who himself had arrived about midnight from the city. They could call upon the quartermaster's office for transportation, "either by rail or water," to the city, such was the urgency. "We were just getting up quite a scare at Ft. Lyon," Bay State gunner John Easley remembered to tell a friend later, having doubled the pickets and fort guards when the order to move arrived. Left behind were only Ohio 100-days' men. Easley and company took the train into Washington, arriving at the depot at 11:00 p.m. and marching to Tennallytown, getting there at 3:00 a.m. They immediately shifted eastward to Fort Kearny. At this same time, the intrepid guerrilla fighter, Colonel Charles R. Lowell, was ordered to withdraw his Second Massachusetts Cavalry from screening Mosby's guerrillas out in Falls Church, Virginia, and likewise join what seemed to be increasingly the point of possible danger—the Tennallytown position on the Rockville-Georgetown Turnpike.[21]

Distinguished veteran, four times wounded, and now an amputee, Major-General Martin D. Hardin took command at Tennallytown just before midnight. He would be joined on the morrow by Warner of the First Vermont Heavy Artillery. There were no signs yet that the Rebels were rushing in on the turnpike from Rockville or anywhere else according to reconnaissance in that direction, while Hardin deployed wounded warriors of the Veteran Reserve Corps (VRC)—a national organization (although credited against state quotas for manpower) amalgamated from the old Invalid Corps but in some cases dressed in a distinctive uniform of light blue cloth with dark blue trim—almost a giveaway that these were marginal, light-duty troops. Formed under General Order 111 in March from men able to wield a musket and perform guard, depot, and similar duties, it constituted two battalions, and they were ideal for duty in the forts. Many learned how to sight, range, and handle the heavy artillery as well as those units specifically recruited for that duty from states throughout the northeast. Present at the time of Early's raid, the First, Sixth, Ninth, Twelfth, Nineteenth, Twenty-Second, and Twenty-Fourth VRC regiments would number among the first defenders against that threat to the city. A Tenth VRC regiment went to Baltimore to help there during the emergency. Hardin would find he had Colonel G. W. Gile's First Brigade of the VRC and later added Major James W. Snyder's battalion of the Ninth New York Heavy Artillery, Battery I, Second U.S. Artillery and a company of the One Hundred and Fifty-First Ohio National Guard from the "river batteries to the front line," all of whom "this night bivouacked at the guns and along the rifle-pits."[22]

In addition to these preparations, humble as they seemed, the situation had been developed by Major William H. Fry, Sixteenth Pennsylvania Cavalry, who had taken a five-hundred-man detachment from Camp Stoneman at Giesboro out the pike to Rockville. There, about 11:00 a.m., his five squadrons met an ailing and weary Captain Levi Welles's squadron of Lieutenant Colonel David Clendenin's Eighth Illinois Cavalry that had been cut off during withdrawal from the Monocacy. They had hovered on Early's flank coming down through Barnesville, past Sugar Loaf Mountain. Together these Yankee horsemen moved about five miles north on the turnpike from Rockville, where they encountered McCausland's advance guard at a small village called Gerardsville. The Confederate weight of numbers pushed the Federals back again through Rockville, and Fry's dismounted stand on a hill about a mile from town was abruptly terminated when McCausland brought artillery into play. At least the hitherto lackluster performance of Union intelligence gathering had begun to secure a more precise trajectory for Early's move to the capital. But it still remained imprecise. Just before midnight, Major Walter Cutting wired Department of Washington headquarters that Fry reported "all quiet," with no enemy in sight. In the Pennsylvania major's own words, "I dismounted the men at midnight and let them rest, but did not unsaddle nor permit the horses to leave the line." There would be hot work on the morrow.[23]

Patent Office examiner Horatio Taft claimed he passed a quiet Sunday on George-town Heights with family and friends but "could hear the Drums beating most of the day in Washington." On his return about 8:00 p.m. by horse car, he could see the street was nearly full of people and soldiers. "We met five Regiments going west or through Georgetown and it was quite an impressive sight to see so many bright bayonets gleaming in the dim gaslight and listen to the measured tread upon the pavement." Newspaper extras issued at 4:00 p.m. and three hours later proclaimed Early's raiders within fifteen miles of Baltimore, with a fight for that city anticipated the next day. "It is said that the rebels are at least 20,000 strong." They must be greatly outnumbered by our troops, "but [the latter] are mostly raw troops." The invaders were marching on Washington, too, the excited bureaucrat jotted in his diary, so "this is making the matter more interesting still." It promised lively times "here tomorrow," and must have accounted for the troop movements Taft witnessed. He supposed "our wise men here know what they are about and have taken sufficient precautions to ensure the safety of the City," he added somewhat facetiously. After all, "this demonstration on the part of the Rebels is just what might have been expected if it was possible for them to make it and should have been provided for if it has not been." Taft himself had predicted this happening from the moment Grant crossed the James River. Now, "I have no idea how many men there are in the fortifications around the City," but he offered that "there should never have been less than thirty or forty thousand in and around the City, at any time."[24]

Another detached observer, Hunter's chief of staff and loyal Virginian from Martinsburg in the valley, Colonel David Strother, penned in his diary on July 11: "The military aspect is serious," as "this movement of the enemy is truly the energy of despair but what may be the result who can tell." "The great financial crash which is rapidly approaching and the despairing fury of the Rebel armies may yet accomplish our ruin, and there is no great man to take the helm and guide us through." Twenty-two years later, a Vermont veteran of Early's raid, A. A. Hayes, would recall for the *Burlington Free Press*, "In Washington they do not seem to have been 'stampeded' (to use the happy and expressive phrase) until they heard on the ninth of Gen. Wallace at Monocacy." The city heard that news by Sunday. So downtown was rife with rumors but little hard data on the threat. Refugees driven before the Rebel storm spread dire tales, but Fry's information was better, if still imprecise. L. E. Chittenden, register of the Treasury, readied his family at the Willard Hotel for Monday's train trip to New England "to pass the season of oppressive heat." So, too, did Major-General William B. Franklin, transiting the city from consultations with Grant at City Point and then the capital bent on catching the 8:30 a.m. Monday train, suspicious from rumors of Rebel raiding of wire and rail in the Baltimore area. He told his sister later that he thought by taking the earliest train he would gain an hour "at the dangerous end of the road." Fate would prove otherwise. Franklin would be captured by Harry Gilmor's raiders at Magnolia Station north of Baltimore, although he eventually escaped from his fatigue-laden captors. The Blair family had already left their Silver Spring and Falkland country mansions beyond the District line on the Seventh Street Road, the women destined to enjoy the sea air at Cape May, New Jersey, the men folk for a Pennsylvania fishing trip. Some wags wondered later that they would leave their stylish country mansions in the path of Early's hooligans.[25]

In retrospect, the Washington correspondent for the *Sacramento Union*, Noah Brooks, may have best captured the atmosphere of the moment. The news was brought to the city (from whatever "lodged" at the War Department) "by the panic-stricken people from Rockville, Silver Spring, Tennallytown, and other Maryland villages," he suggested. They flocked into the city by the Seventh Street Road, with their household goods "flying in wild disorder. We understood in a general way that Washington was cut off at the north and east, and that the famine of market-stuff, New York newspapers, and other necessaries of life" was due to the cutting of railroads north, he noted. For two or three days no mail, no telegraphic messages, and no railway travel was the norm, the only "communication with the outer world was by steamer from Georgetown, D.C. to New York." "Washington was in ferment; men were marching to and fro; able-bodied citizens were swept up and put into the District militia; and squads of department clerks were set to drilling in the parks."

To Brooks, it was an odd sight to see men so impressed into public service, dressed in linen coats or in partial uniform, being put through martial paces by "an impromptu captain, who in turn was coached by his orderly sergeant (a messenger employed in the War Department)." For Lucius Chittenden, during Saturday and Sunday, "the Confederate sympathizers in Washington were anxiously listening for the sound of Early's guns." They "knew his purpose, his strength, and the weakness of the city," of which "he was expected to take possession without much resistance." Of all this, he observed later, the week closed on Saturday without the loyal citizens imagining that the city was in any danger, or that any thought for their personal safety was necessary. Overnight the situation had changed. "The night of Sunday, the Tenth, I have always believed the city might have been captured had the enemy followed up his advantage," recalled Lincoln's portrait artist, F. B. Carpenter, three years later. These were "the dark days of 1864," indeed, using Noah Brooks's phrase.[26]

Notes

1. Letter, Charles M. Yocum to Bella, July 9, 1864, author's collection.
2. U.S. War Department, *The War of the Rebellion; The Official History of Union and Confederate Armies* (Washington, DC, 1880–1901), Series I, Volume 37, Part 2, 138, 174–75.
3. *ORA*, I, 37, pt. 2, 137–39, 145, 174–75.
4. Roy P. Basler, editor, *The Collected Works of Abraham Lincoln, volume VII* (New Brunswick, NJ: Rutgers University Press, 1953), 383–435 inter alia; Charles Bracelen Flood, *1864: Lincoln at the Gates of History* (New York: Simon & Shuster, 2009), 174–78.
5. Matthew Pinsker, *Lincoln's Sanctuary: Abraham Lincoln and the Soldiers' Home* (New York: Oxford University Press, 2003), 127–31, 134.
6. J. D. Bloodgood, *Personal Reminiscences of the War* (New York: Hunt and Eaton; Cincinnati: Cranston and Curts, 1893), 186–88.
7. *ORA*, I, 37, pt. 2, 140; Basler, *Collected Works of Abraham Lincoln*, 437–38.
8. *ORA*, I, 37, pt. 2, 127.
9. *ORA*, I, 37, pt. 2, 14–58 inter alia.
10. *ORA*, I, 37, pt. 2, 58–60.
11. *ORA*, I, 37, pt. 2, 60–62.

12. *ORA*, I, 37, pt. 2, 63–118 inter alia.

13. *ORA*, I, 37, pt. 2, 131, 157–59.

14. *ORA*, I, 37, pt. 1, 697, 698–701; pt. 2, 171.

15. *ORA*, I, 37, pt. 2, 119–20.

16. *ORA*, I, 37, pt. 1, 697, also 698–701; pt. 2, 133–35, 119–20, 159, 171.

17. *ORA*, I, 37, pt. 2, 155.

18. Joseph Judge, *Season of Fire: The Confederate Strike on Washington* (Berryville, VA: Rockbridge Publishing, 1994), 224.

19. *ORA*, I, 37, pt. 2, 593–94, 594–95.

20. *ORA*, I, 37, pt. 1, 239, 251, and pt. 2, 164, 165, 168–70.

21. *ORA*, I, 37, pt. 2, 170; Letter, John Earley to Sanborn, August 7, 1864, author's files.

22. *ORA*, I, 37, pt. 2, 236, 239; Jack E. Schairer, *Lee's Bold Plan for Point Lookout: The Rescue of Confederate Prisoners That Never Happened* (Jefferson, NC: McFarland, 2008), chapter 25.

23. *ORA*, I, 37, pt. 1, 248–49 and pt. 2, 164–67; see also Carol Bundy, *The Nature of Sacrifice: A Biography of Charles Russell Lowell Jr., 1835–1864* (New York: Farrar, Straus and Giroux, 2005), 394–96; James McLean, *California Sabers: The 2nd Massachusetts Cavalry in the Civil War* (Bloomington: Indiana University Press, 2000), chapter 6; Thomas J. Parson, *Bear Flag and Bay State in the Civil War: The Californians of the Second Massachusetts Cavalry* (Jefferson, NC: McFarland, 2001), chapter 8.

24. Diary of Horatio Nelson Taft, July 10, 1864, Volume 3, Library of Congress, Washington, D.C.

25. L. E. Chittenden, *Recollections of President Lincoln and His Administration* (New York: Harper and Brothers, 1891), 404; A. L. Hayes, "Stories of the War: The Attack on Washington, 1864," Burlington (VT) *Free Press*, January 4, 1886; George H. Davis collection, Monocacy National Battlefield; Cecil D. Eby Jr., editor, *A Virginia Yankee in the Civil War: The Diaries of David Hunter Strother* (Chapel Hill: University of North Carolina Press, 1961), 279.

26. F. B. Carpenter, *Six Months at the White House with Abraham Lincoln: The Story of a Picture* (New York: Hurd and Houghton, 1867), 301; Noah Brooks, *Washington in Lincoln's Time* (New York: Century, 1895), 172–74; Chittenden, *Recollections*, 403–4; Albert Gallatin Riddle, *Recollections of War Times: Reminiscences of Men and Events in Washington 1860–1865* (New York: G. P. Putnam's Sons, 1895), 286–87; Franklin quoted in Mark A. Snell, *From First to Last: The Life of Major General William B. Franklin* (New York: Fordham University Press, 2002), 326.

FIRST DEFENDERS TO THE FRONT: LINCOLN AT FORT STEVENS, JULY 11

The Rebels are upon us," Secretary of the Navy Gideon Welles recorded in his diary on Monday, July 11. Indeed, some officials in Washington were aghast at such developments. "How an army so great could traverse the country, without being discovered, is a mystery," pronounced Attorney General Edward Bates. He feared "the most supine negligence—or worse." Welles had learned on Sunday that Rebel scouts were "on the outskirts of Georgetown, within the District lines" and had captured a neighbor's son. But the War Department rebuffed him when he asked what was going on. Welles's concern was genuine, as his son, Thomas G., had just joined Major-General Alexander McCook's staff on the defense perimeter. "I regret his passion for the service and his recklessness and youth," opined the father. Sensing the truth that "the forts around Washington have been vacated and the troops sent to General Grant who was promised reinforcements to take Richmond," the elder Welles laid the problem at the general-in-chief's feet.[1]

Grant had been in the vicinity of the Confederate capital for a month, had expended much blood getting there, and had not displayed any strategy, "resting apparently after his bloody march," said the crusty secretary. Meanwhile, "Lee has sent a force threatening the National Capital, and we are without force for its defense." The gruff, Connecticut Yankee captured the sentiments of many in the public community. Starting on Saturday, Welles chronicled what he took to be the ignorance, neglect, and inattention of Secretary of War Edward Stanton and Chief of Staff Henry Halleck. He decided that "it is a scheme of Lee's strategy," asking rhetorically, "but where is Grant's?" For the next century and one half, historians and students of the war have posed the same question.

By Monday the eleventh, Welles concluded that there would be no attack on the city. "The whole demonstration is weak in numbers but strong in conception that the Rebels have but a small force." He was satisfied that the enemy had lost a remarkable opportunity. "On our part there is neglect, ignorance, folly, imbecility, in the last degree," he ranted. The Confederates were making a show of fight while they stole horses and cattle throughout Maryland. "They might easily have captured Washington as Stanton, Halleck, and Grant are asleep or dumb." While the waste of war was terrible, "the waste from imbecility and mismanagement is more terrible and more trying than from the ravages of the soldiers," declared the bureaucrat. He felt that it was impossible for the country to bear up under these monstrous errors and wrongs. Such sentiments pervaded many quarters of the nation's capital. At a lower level, and in retrospect, as Captain A. B. Beamish of the Ninety-Eighth Pennsylvania decided in 1886, "It was only a question who should reach the goal" of capturing—or saving—Washington.[2]

The First Defenders Move

Monday would dawn clear, hot, and still. The thermometer would hover in the mid-nineties for the next few days. Friend and foe alike had to be up and out of bivouac early just to accomplish anything before the extreme heat of midday. The Ohio National Guard 100-day pickets brushed with scattered Rebel outriders on the Virginia side of the Potomac at first light, then scampered back to Fort Marcy near Chain Bridge. All that was diversionary. Confederate goals lay north of the river. Their opponents' mission included uncovering the axis of Jubal Early's approach, preparing the defense, and countering any attack. Wild rumors still flourished, as seen in an Eighth Illinois cavalry captain's report to Washington departmental and XXII Corps commander, Major-General Christopher Augur from Seven Oaks, Maryland. One local Unionist, a John Stone's nephew, "had last evening conversed with a brother belonging to the rebel army." The brother told him that their advancing army numbered seventy-five thousand to one hundred thousand commanded by Lee in person. Other intelligence said six thousand alone had already passed through Rockville "with the intention of moving to attack Washington in the morning." Early and his generals had dined comfortably at the Montgomery House in that little county seat.[3]

Federal authorities spent the overnight trying to organize their resources and even deciding who might command various portions of the defense line. There seemed to be a plethora of generals, many of dubious distinction. When one brigadier J. R. West announced his availability to the War Department from the comfortable confines of the Fifth Avenue Hotel in New York, Henry Halleck shot back, "We have five times as many generals here as we want, but are greatly in need of privates." Anyone volunteering in that capacity would be welcome. So the field command situation seemed fluid on Sunday night. Even Assistant Secretary of War Charles A. Dana admitted confusion in a 10:00 p.m. dispatch to Grant. Augur had been told to organize the overall defense effort. Capable enough and assisted by Colonel Moses N. Wisewell, military governor of the city, Augur was then undermined in authority by Halleck, who with Grant's blessing assigned Major-General Quincy A. Gillmore to that task. In the course of events, Gillmore in turn would eventually be relegated to merely commanding a section of the actual northeastern fortifications while collecting arriving XIX Corps reinforcements. Then, Secretary of War Stanton introduced Major-General Alexander McCook to the equation, as this general specifically took charge of the northern defense line. Apparently Grant had intended still another supernumerary two-star, E. O. C. Ord, for this mission, but the Monocacy disaster sent him to rally Baltimore and organize a counterstrike force from there. In truth, the general on the ground that night was really convalescing amputee Martin D. Hardin, possibly the most decorated and battle scarred of the lot.[4]

Hardin was thrust overnight to the point of greatest danger—that portion of Washington's defenses most likely to be attacked by Early's army at the Tennallytown heights where turnpike and country roads joined. Hardin found Augur inspecting the poorly kept earthworks stretching from Fort Reno eastward to Fort Stevens where the Seventh Street Road passed the lines. Hardin counted a "division" of scarcely 1,800 infantry, perhaps a similar number of artillerists, and but sixty cavalrymen including four companies of the One Hundred and Fifty-First Ohio National Guard and five or six companies of light artillery, including one of U.S. regulars all under Colonel J. M. Warner of the First Vermont Heavy Artillery. His eleven forts west of Rock Creek were in themselves strong enough, mounting some one hundred guns ranging in size from 24- and 32-pounder seacoast cannon to 100-pounder Parrott guns.

Further along the line, Lieutenant Colonel Joseph A. Haskin had possibly 1,250 men of the One Hundred and Fiftieth, One Hundred and Fifty-First, and One Hundred and Seventieth Ohio National Guard and two companies of volunteer heavy artillerists plus VRC invalids to defend the expanse of line eastward from Rock Creek to the Anacostia River. Some 126 heavy fortress guns counted in this sector. Hardin soon tapped into less-threatened forts south of the Potomac to get Company A, First Wisconsin Heavy Artillery, dispatched from Fort Lyon, below Alexandria. Colonel Benjamin Rosson's One Hundred and Fifty-Seventh Ohio National Guard that had just been shuttled back to Fort Ethan Allen at Chain Bridge after a month manning positions from forts Reno to Stevens also returned north of the Potomac. It moved to Augur's reserve camp at Crystal Spring (south of Fort Stevens toward Piney Branch Creek on the Fourteenth Street road). Augur also had several District of Columbia militia regiments that could muster six hundred muskets as well as bits and pieces of units on provost duty in the city and other mobilizable citizen soldier contingents. Maybe four thousand more men and muskets could be brought up for the emergency—disparate bodies lacking discipline to stand against veterans. They might be expected to fight from behind earthworks, though.[5]

Defending the city was a daunting task. Intrepid war correspondent and part of Grant's inner circle, Sylvanus Cadwallader, had sniffed crisis early in the game. He took a steamer from City Point twenty-four hours ahead of the VI Corps reinforcements and arrived at Washington's wharves about 10:00 a.m. on Monday. Quickly mounting a rented horse, he toured the northern line of forts. "They were all in a deplorable condition," he thought. The armament was insufficient, their ordnance supplies limited, "and all of them so weakly manned as to make any protracted resistance impossible" on a line that generally ran "about six miles out from the heart of the city." By the time "I reached Fort Stevens, on the Crystal Springs [Fourteenth Street] road, Early's army was emerging from the timber and going into position in plain view from where I sat on horseback," he wrote in postwar memoirs. A regular line of battle was extended right and left, "running across farms, through orchards and dooryards, and batteries planting their guns to open on our fortifications," he declared. The Rebels "stacked arms up and down the line as far as I could see, built fires, cooked and ate their dinners deliberately," and "I have always wondered at Early's inaction throughout the day."[6]

Truth was that Monday morning, Federal authorities desperately sought every possible advantage in the emergency. At dawn, Colonel Charles R. Lowell Jr. and the Second Massachusetts Cavalry started again to reconnoiter out of Rockville Pike, where Major William H. Fry, Sixteenth Pennsylvania Cavalry, was posted in reserve with a provisional cavalry regiment. Fry and a residue of the Eighth Illinois Cavalry under captains A. Levi Wells and Malcom H. Wing once again joined the effort against advance elements of Brigadier General John McCausland's vanguard of Rebels coming in the Frederick-Georgetown turnpike from the north. Another Federal squadron similarly departed on the river road to picket a post five miles out. Additional parties took the Brookeville Road from Tennallytown to observation points at Leesborough. Federal intelligence gathering ranged eastward to Laurel on the Baltimore & Ohio railroad. About all anyone discovered was that Brookville may have witnessed some of Bradley Johnson's outriders passing through and that wild rumors circulated about Robert E. Lee heading the invasion himself with seventy-five thousand to one hundred thousand men. Meanwhile, XXII Corps headquarters fretted that assorted bands of invaders might try to enter the capital east of the Anacostia River and ordered all crossings closely guarded and boats confiscated. Union field commanders mostly worried that whatever the Rebels' strength, they would deviate only slightly east or west from the axis from Rockville to Tennallytown.[7]

Fry and Lowell got no farther than Old Tavern (modern Bethesda) on Monday morning before encountering McCausland. "We fell back, skirmishing constantly, until within two miles of Tennallytown, where a dismounted skirmish line was formed and held, the enemy never succeeding in driving us away," Fry reported. Altogether he registered about five hundred troopers, greatly outnumbered by the Rebels again and supported by a rifled gun. The fortress artillery soon came into play, endangering friend as much as foe, and the dust, the flies, and the heat as well as escalating skirmishing became annoying to all involved. However, Lowell took a few moments to pen a brief note to his wife, Ellen, in which he told her "there is no end of confusion out here, a very little known of the enemy." He recorded his horse, Rush, several others, and two men as wounded. But his important comment was "They are reported approaching similarly on the Seventh St. road,—it looks at present more like a move to mask heavier movements than like a serious effort against this part of the fortifications." From about 9:50 a.m., McCausland probed the Yankee lines from forts Reno west to Bayard, Simmons, Mansfield, and Sumner. Action was sufficiently brisk, and Hardin sent back an anxious message near noon, asking for thirty-two thousand more Burnside and Sharps carbine rounds and forage for 450 horses. Lowell had done well providing "accurate and reliable information." Yet Confederate intent remained unclear. It had been difficult for any Federals to get close to Early's column.[8]

The Federals should have had sufficient "eyes and ears." Between Wells's Eighth Illinois Cavalry, Major De Witt C. Thompson's troopers from the Muddy Branch cavalry camp west of Rockville, Lowell's men shifted from Falls Church perimeter duty in Virginia, and Fry's five hundred men scooped from the Giesboro depot as a provisional regiment (supposedly reflecting every mounted unit in the Army of the Potomac), Augur and the others had enough intelligence gatherers. Cavalry told the Union high command that Early's rear guard had cleared Urbana and was even now pressing toward the Tennallytown lines. But something more was needed, and that came from a group of signalers and telegraphers organized around the defense perimeter to take this cavalry-provided intelligence and send it downtown to the War Department and back out to field headquarters for action. Thus, it fell to these professionals in Fort Reno at Tennallytown—the highest point in the District at three hundred feet above sea level—to decipher the latest Confederate intentions. By late morning, all the signalers needed to see was a huge dust cloud in the distance to understand enemy marchers were shifting eastward from Rockville toward Leesborough, where they could take the Seventh Street Pike into the city. So Hardin wired Augur, "The enemy are seen very plainly moving down the Leesborough road in direction of [Fort] Stevens." Infantry, wagons, and ambulances could be seen through field glasses, and confirmation soon came from an additional Fort Reno dispatch— "the enemy's line of march clearly indicates that the main attack will be to the right

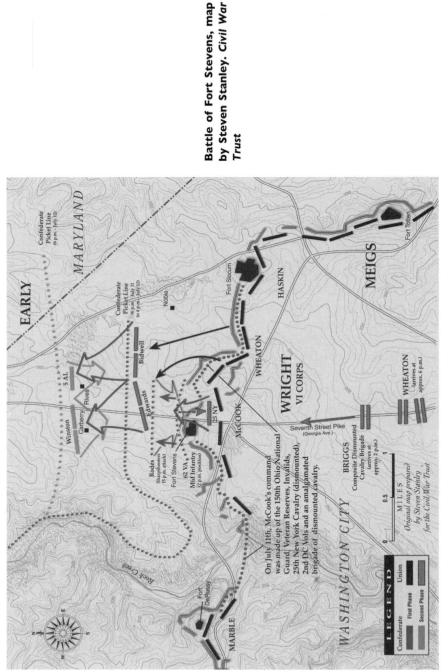

**Battle of Fort Stevens, map
by Steven Stanley.** *Civil War
Trust*

of this point." McCook was alerted. Even the extreme right of the line toward the Baltimore rail and road connection at Bladensburg seemed threatened. Colonel James A. Hardie at headquarters urged Augur to move reserves to the front.[9]

Discovering Early's Every Move

Was McCausland's strong reconnaissance a feint? Or was it a serious effort to discover the strength of the forts at Tennallytown? Could "Tiger John," as he was known, actually have breeched the Union lines west of the high stronghold? Two miles of cleared fields of fire on open farmland and meager woodlots seemed most uninviting for direct assault. Guns from Fort Sumner (843 perimeter yards and thirty cannon) commanded the Chesapeake and Ohio canal, towpath, and aqueduct into the city, field gun batteries Bailey and Benson covered Powder Mill Branch valley, Battery and Fort Mansfield (220 perimeter yards, eleven guns) as well as Fort Simmons (177 perimeter yards, eight guns) dominated the farms of the Unionist Shoemaker and Dean families (upon whose land they rested). The River Road axis that had heard the tramp of English general Edward Braddock's men on their way to an appointment with disaster in western Pennsylvania a century before was but marginally presided over by little Fort Bayard (123 perimeter yards, six guns) forward of the major Tennallytown ridge (where further west the early Fort Gaines now was little more than an unattended reserve post). Only at Fort Reno with its twenty-seven heavy guns (including a long-range 100-pounder Parrott) and fused Battery Reno (both of which commanded the Rockville pike and country lane out to Brookeville, Maryland, where the fleeing President James Madison had sought shelter in 1814) could the defenses have been thought impregnable. Surely, McCausland communicated that fact to Early. And McCausland's demonstrations adequately pinned down defenders in this sector for the next two days. But Hardin and the signalers had done their job well. Topography, fortifications, and a corporal's guard stymied McCausland. They conveyed a message. Washington would be defended.[10]

Monday morning witnessed a Herculean effort by Early and his commanders to roust dirty, tired, and jaded soldiery from makeshift bivouacs and back out on the road again. His army stretched by the wayside from Rockville well beyond Gaithersburg. Stragglers were all over the map. Soon, whomever Early could muster made their way past dead horses from the previous day's cavalry fight in strongly secessionist Rockville. Union prisoners from Monocacy enjoyed some succor from one Unionist woman, who offered to write and send letters to their homefolks telling of their fate. Less solicitous, however, their guards drew the Yanks into line and relieved them of their valuables—"the chief object of rebel cupidity." These captives then paraded before Major-General John C. Breckinridge, Early's second-in-command. One New Yorker wondered years later if this former vice president "might and ought to be in a better business than seeking to destroy the place where, for four years, he had been the recipient of so many honors." As sounds of distant gunfire diverted the captors' attention, random Confederates rushed past the down-trodden Federals to be among the first to enter "and loot the city" of Washington. One of the guards announced the sound of those heavy fortress guns was the sweet-est music on earth to him, for they had finally arrived at their goal. Ohio captive William Browning, however, shot back that before any Rebels would get into the nation's capital, they would be accommodated with plenty more such sweet music. Browning later taunted returning stragglers as to why had they not taken the city. The begrimed Confederates admitted, "We would, only the cursed Yankees are throwing flour barrels at us," alluding to those very fortress guns that had previously announced their arrival. Battle sounds then shifted eastward as Early searched for an alternate route to the city.[11]

A thermometer eventually reached 94 degrees that day out at W. H. Far-quhar's Lonesome Hollow farm near Sandy Spring, not that far from Early's labor-ing column. Men, animals, and equipment became enveloped in dust clouds, caus-ing further discomfort and delay. Coursing eastward on New Cut Road, the army passed Samuel Viers's gristmill on upper Rock Creek (which eventually wandered south through the Union defense perimeter and on to the Potomac at Georgetown). Although strung out for miles, the Rebels reached Mitchell's Crossroads and Lees-borough (modern Wheaton) and eventually Sligo Post Office (today's Silver Spring). Robert Rodes's division led the van, then Stephen Ramseur, John B. Gordon, the army train with Echols in the rear, and Brigadier General Armistead Long's artillery interspersed between the infantry divisions. Georgian G. W. Nichols recalled how comrades fell out left and right from exhaustion and sunstroke. But, he claimed later, "we pulled on the best we could," with officers riding up and down urging haste so as to capture "Old Abe" in the White House. Virginian John Worsham with Gor-don scoffed that it had little effect, for "our division was stretched out almost like skirmishers." Early used the term *suffocating*, with no air circulation, and how "it became necessary to slacken our pace." The crushed flint stone turnpike base might have been invaluable in mud and snow but hard on poorly clad feet and lungs of the foot soldiers. Ramseur wrote his wife, "Our men could not possibly march further." That had a telling effect on what was to come.[12]

Onward the Confederates advanced, very slowly. The ranks hardly noticed a little wooden Grace Episcopal Church and various country houses before they got to Sligo Post Office. But Early did, apparently, or at least posterity would say so when victims of the ensuing battle were buried in the churchyard. Captain James F. Berry's Eighth Illinois troopers, like the Fort Reno signalers, tracked Early's progress from their postings midway between the District line and Leesborough. They reported what they saw to McCook's headquarters at the Mooreland Tavern in Brightwood, just behind Fort Stevens. The Rebel onslaught pointed directly at that fortification. When McCook's men filed into places in the frontlines, "there never was before a command so hereogeneous [*sic*], yet so orderly," claimed McCook. Ranks filled with soldiers, invalids, government clerks, veterans, and 100-day men, "each working with a singleness of purpose and willing to discharge any duty imposed upon him." Worried about a tempting entry point via the Rock Creek valley between forts Stevens and DeRussy, Union commanders ensured the declivity was filled with fallen timber and brush. This creek valley effectively separated Early's main effort from all secondary maneuvers westward to Tennallytown. Arrival of the first dismounted troopers from the Army of the Potomac went into slashing at the creek and drove back the advance elements of Confederates fully a mile and one-half, cited M. B. "Smokey" of the Veteran Reserve Corps participants. Eventually, full contact between antagonists in this "battle of the suburbs" would stretch across the northern reaches of the District of Columbia from the Potomac to the Anacostia. Fort Stevens in the center, DeRussy to the west, and Slocum and Totten to the east would provide the focal point aside from the Tennallytown action. "Smokey" grabbed a much-prized Spencer repeating carbine from a fallen cavalryman and "made it hot with a Johnny," who had been giving him and a comrade trouble.[13]

Early described precisely making a thirty-mile march via Rockville and turning east when he told Lee about the operation later. Yet, was this somehow preordained by Jedediah Hotchkiss's map prepared mysteriously in the spring? Or was the move the more immediate result of McCausland's observations or even word from spies, local secessionists, or other scouts? Was it merely Early's scheme for edging closer to a linkage with Bradley Johnson's returning column from the Baltimore/Point Lookout raid? At any rate, while McCausland pushed hard up to a point at Tennallytown, the main army turned east and onto the Seventh Street Road by noon. This lengthened both distance and time to get on target. Actionable intelligence came only to the fortified Federals at Tennallytown. McCook recorded hearing from Captain Berry about 10:00 a.m. "that the enemy was advancing in force with infantry, artillery and cavalry." But no screening Federal cavalry harassed Early's march. As Hardin told the story later, "General McCook was notified, the skirmish line strengthened from Fort Reno to Rock Creek, and a proper disposition of the infantry supports made." Skirmishing only before the fortifications would then occupy the afternoon.[14]

Country squire Francis Preston Blair's overseer told his patron later that the advance guard of Early's army had arrived at the Silver Spring farm about 2:00 a.m., "kept quiet till daylight," then began ransacking Blair's house, cellar, buildings, and fields. They had killed cattle and sheep in the course of their orgy as well as robbing his cellar of a large and very valuable stock of rare wines and whiskey and got drunk, was his claim. They then proceeded during the morning to violate personal chambers of the women of the household, said the overseer, even donning their apparel and cavorting about. Many years after the war, Lieutenant George D. Jewett of the Thirteenth Michigan Battery wrote Color Sergeant Lewis Cass White of the One Hundred and Second Pennsylvania—old comrades from Early's storied visit to Washington—that there had been a Union picket post in the woods just south of the Blair property that was driven in "soon after daylight." They had retired to Fort Stevens and reported "that the enemy were in force out beyond." Word was sent to Washington and, according to Jewett, this prompted President Lincoln's appearance by late morning as he and McCook, together with some other officers, would stand on the parapets "watching that strip of woods through their field glasses anxiously for some time." Finally, "there appeared, a thin line of skirmishers stretching out both sides of the [Seventh Street Road], creeping slowly along, and after they had advanced a little ways, another line appeared, much stronger than the first." Jewett theatrically concluded, "Then, it was, that President Lincoln and Gen. McCook almost thought we were, or rather Washington was doomed."[15]

The *Washington Star* on July 15, 1864, carried an account of J. E. Turton of the city "who enjoyed superior opportunities for observation, having been in the hands of the rebels at Silver Spring during their entire stay there." Filling a remodeling job at Montgomery Blair's Falkland, "he was surprised by the appearance of six rebels who dropped down upon him as if from the skies" about 11:00 o'clock. Asking whose house it was, and learning it belonged to Lincoln's postmaster general, "the leader of the gang exclaimed to the others 'this house must go up.'" Turton claimed the house was locked, so they proceeded to break open doors and despoil it, scattering books of which "they seemed to have an indifferent opinion, and papers around in every direction and carrying off whatever they deemed would be of use to them." They did the same at the Silver Spring mansion, he told the newspaper. There they discovered "what they deemed an excellent prize, an excellent county map of the state of Maryland." This map was spirited away and "for many hours afterward a corps of rebel draftsmen, occupying the house of Thomas Gettings at the third tollgate, was busily employed over it making sketches and copies."[16]

In the interim, "We made as good a show as possible with the material we had, in front of the Fort, but it was a sickly attempt, after the enemy had advanced their lines in some ways," Jewett concluded about the morning's ensuing events. Alexander Kingsland of the Second District of Columbia wasn't quite so negative. Having come over from a Virginia posting on Sunday and witnessing the first push of Rebel skirmishers between forts Stevens and Slocum at ten o'clock Monday, "Our Regt. was the first in the rifle [pits] and at Eleven O'clock we was ordered out on the advance skirmish line." The Confederates were very bold, but they held the line until about 8:00 p.m., "when we were relieved by another Regt and we went back to the entrenchments for [sector to the right of Fort Stevens brigadier

Halbert E.] Paine 'said we was worth more there than any troops he had.' They would lay on their arms all night expecting to be attacked every moment but they did not push our line."[17]

By noon, however, the dismounted Twenty-Fifth New York cavalrymen interrupted such frolic. These veteran horsemen had mustered at Saratoga Springs and Hart's Island in New York Harbor in the late winter and spring of 1864. They had been assigned provost duty with the Army of the Potomac and happened to be back in D.C. looking for new mounts when the Confederates appeared. Transported to Baltimore from City Point, they had then been hustled aboard a cattle and baggage train to Washington, arriving about 6:00 a.m. Saturday. Transferring to old quarters at Camp Stoneman at Giesboro Point, and feeling like coming home, "we had determined to take things easy, and make ourselves comfortable until we got our horses and equipments, which we were told would be very soon," recounted "B.O.B." Alas, the bugle sounded at midnight Sunday, and they marched through confusion in the city where "white lips and pale cheeks were announcing that 'the Rebels were right at hand in great force.'" Sergeant A. G. Jacobs of Company B, Sixth Ohio Cavalry, had similar memories about packing up quickly and "hoofing it" through Washington "without our breakfasts as we were on the move," but "we were well supplied with bread and butter and other eatables by citizens who thronged the route with baskets." They all went past Crystal Spring and were about a mile from Fort Stevens when a squad of mounted men "came dashing down from the city." The advance guard shouted 'Give the road for the President,'" and the president and others trotted past in a carriage. "Five minutes later," said Jacobs, "an order came to us to double-quick" to the fort. "We got to the fort between ten o'clock and noon." It would always be a source of controversy and pride as to who first redeemed the situation at Fort Stevens—Veteran Reserve Corps, Army of the Potomac dismounted cavalry, or arriving VI Corps veterans.[18]

No matter at the time, all of them were eventually thrust out in front of Fort Stevens, their fading blue uniforms still covered with red Virginia dust lent a veteranlike appearance to these first-responders. They probably comprised contingents first spotted by Lincoln, as he supposedly told one of their junior officers, "Our Capital is in a critical condition and upon you and your good men depend the safety of the Capital; but should any of your command be captured, say nothing about the situation of Washington, and if they ask whose command you belong to, say the advance of the Sixth Corps." The New Yorkers had hardly deployed in skirmish lines when "the Rebels were soon coming down the opposite hill, a perfect cloud of skirmishers" in their own right.[19] However, as noted, Confederate commanders had a strong line of skirmishers moving through, and the Union cavalrymen plus 100-day men of the One Hundred and Fiftieth Ohio National Guard were ordered "to fall back slowly fighting, until they reached the rifle-pits."

The strengthening Rebel host opened fire at various points along the northern lines, and it appeared they were massing for major attack. The first shots were exchanged; Ohio private William Leach became the first casualty, wounded and borne away to die four days later. At some point, remembered Blair's overseer, Early and another Confederate general, probably John C. Breckinridge, "came up and he was indignant that his men had not attacked Washington at once" upon arrival as he ordered, referring to the unnecessary delay in pillaging the Blair properties. Turton also recalled conversing with all the Rebel generals, John B. Gordon particularly querying him as to the number of troops in the city. Turton evaded the question by saying he had not been in Washington for some days. In turn, the officers did not tell Turton whether they intended to attack Washington, "but the men talked quite freely of what they would do if they got possession of Washington."[20]

By this point, curious sightseers also began to trickle out from downtown. *Chicago Evening Journal* reporter Benjamin Taylor portrayed the scene as if they had come with map in hand. "Taking either Seventh or Fourteenth street," he told readers much later, "you leave the city, cross the old stamping ground of McClellan [on Meridian Hill], pass beautiful residences, gardens and groves, and so, up hill and down dale, until you reach a 'Uriah Heep' of a tavern [Mooreland Tavern at Brightwood], squatted by the road-side—the headquarters of General McCook." Just beyond stood Fort Stevens, "ragged to look at, with an abattis of dry branches of trees under its chin, like a scraggy whisker, but a strong piece of War's solid geometry for all that." You were now three miles from the border of Washington City, looking north. Fort DeRussy stood to one's left, Slocum to your right, and slightly closer to the city, while Totten lay "further to the east; Lincoln more distant still, and beyond it to the northeast is Bladensburg." "This fan-like section of the northern defenses fronted the hostile apparition [of Early's advance]," Taylor eloquently waxed. "A heavily undulating sweep of landscape is before you," he continued, "while descending away from the Fort [Stevens], you have a little shallow valley, three-fourths of a mile broad, then a roll of land, with a depression beyond, and then a swelling ridge, perhaps a mile and a half distant, that bounds the horizon." Finally, wrote Taylor, "It is confused with shrubbery, sprinkled with trees, dotted with homes." This would be the principal ground for the Battle of Fort Stevens, July 11–12, 1864.[21]

Lincoln Welcomes His Boys

A pleasant and outwardly confident Lincoln (claimed his secretary John Hay) fretted only that the Confederates might escape. He and Stanton soon rode through the city streets in an open carriage to stiffen panicky civilians. Irritated perhaps that a warship stood ready in the Potomac to evacuate both him and the public treasury, the chief executive worried about arrival of Grant's reinforcements. From an upstairs White House window, he peered down the Potomac through a spyglass looking for the relief. Before long he spotted what he sought, rushed downstairs to his carriage, and journeyed to the Sixth Street wharves to greet off-loading men in faded blue. Waiting with other eager, unofficial greeters, the commander-in-chief had prepared one of his quips for the initial arrivals. "You can't be Late if you want to get Early," he laughed.[22]

The president's humor may have amused only Lincoln himself, we don't know. But the well-tanned, businesslike "Greek Cross fellows" (as the Rebels always styled John Sedgwick's (now Horatio Wright's), VI Corps Federals, arrived with arms at the ready, their corps emblems adorning headgear, refreshed by Chesapeake breezes on the trip from the Petersburg trenches. They had just finished a hot and grimy raid to Reams Station, southwest of that city, where they ripped up and bent rails before returning to embark for Washington. Lewis Cass White of the One Hundred and Second Pennsylvania recalled arriving somewhere around noon on the eleventh aboard the steamer *Dictator*. They had lain off Mount Vernon an hour before until space at the wharves could be found for the first of some ten thousand arrivals. He never mentioned seeing Lincoln, but rather a convalescing comrade Martin P. Hays, who feverishly told him "there is great excitement in Washington and the rebels were just outside." White and company were part of Brigadier General Frank Wheaton's brigade (Ninety-Third, Ninety-Eighth, One Hundred and Second Pennsylvania, and Sixty-Second New York), who would bear the brunt of much of what would become styled the "Battle of Fort Stevens" over the next two days. White actually may have been with the vanguard arriving before Lincoln made it down to the docks from the executive mansion.[23]

New Yorker George T. Stevens of the Seventy-Seventh volunteers from the Empire State recounted how at two o'clock they docked their little steamer *Escort*. Colonel Daniel Bidwell's brigade staff and brigade band, part of the Forty-Ninth New York, as well as one hundred horses in addition to the Seventy-Seventh awaited their turn due to "some immense sea steamers," crowded with XIX Corps troops just arrived from New Orleans. Since "the process of disembarking occupied but little time," claimed Stevens, what caught everyone's eye was President Lincoln standing there "chatting familiarly with the veterans, and now and then, as if in compliment to them, biting at a piece of hard tack which he held in his hand." It seemed like a homecoming party as the ranks in column marched away from the river, up Seventh Street past familiar sites of the Smithsonian Institution, the patent and post offices. Bystanders shouted "Hurrah for the Sixth," "These are the men who took Mayre's Heights," "The danger is over," and "You better hurry if you want to catch Jubal Early!" We never before realized the hold that the corps had upon the people's affection, Stevens thought later. The city "an hour before was in a panic; now as the people saw the veterans wearing the badge of the Greek cross marching through their streets, the excitement subsided and confidence prevailed."[24]

Thirty years after the war, Thomas Scott of Company B, Forty-Third New York, remembered certain details that colored his own experience that day. The attempt to capture Washington "had thrown the population into a state of great excitement," he observed, so they greeted the arriving VI Corps "heartily, and brought ice water to them without limit." The weather, he said, was "intensely warm," and as the men had been two days closely packed on the transports "with very bad water to drink," such "kindly acts of the grateful citizens" caused hundreds to fall out on the march to the fortifications, Scott claimed. Still, "God bless you," and "You will save us," greeted the sweltering troops as they passed through the streets. Cass White of the One Hundred and Second thought "the citizens were very kind to us as we came through Washington having bread, water, coffee and other things for our refreshment." Fellow shipmate Captain A. B. Beamish of the Ninety-Eighth Pennsylvania also remembered their arrival. Having been packed aboard the *Dictator* like sardines in a box, "I do wish our good Uncle Samuel, or Sam would charter gutta percha boats that would expand." Soon other things took precedence.[25]

Beamish and comrades reached Washington about 11:00 a.m., "each one asking 'whats up.'" From the Sixth Street wharf, they soon found out for "upon landing an old gentleman grasped me by both hands, saying 'for God's sake make haste and save the capital the rebels are within five miles of us!'" Beamish "thought the old gent had been to the commissary and had his canteen filled with corn juice, to bath his head or take a bath in, said juice affecting his brain." It was not long, however, before Beamish and others "found out that the old gent was not filled with corn juice, but fear." "Cheer after cheer went up from men, women and children," he recalled, "as the flag bearing the cross of the old VI corps passed up Pennsylvania Avenue, followed by those brave men who have made the old corps a pride to themselves and an honor to our army." Moving via Seventh Street, "a good portion of the way double quick," was the result. Beamish would always remember "the scenes of distress as the terrified families in their flight towards the city, passed us" as the troops marched to the battlefront. "Men, women, and children, with part of their furniture, crowded into farm wagons, the farmer driving his stock in straggling herds," thought Beamish, "the sharp crack of the rifle hastened them towards the city, while the troops pressed forward to meet the danger of battle that awaited them."[26]

At first, Wright merely followed orders. Halleck had dictated a concentration on the extreme northwest area of the defense line. The VI Corps would prepare for a counteroffensive on Early's flank and rear. That fit with the War Department plan for relieving the besieged city. So the dusty VI Corps headed in the direction of Chain Bridge until somebody on the sidewalk yelled, "What in the name of heaven are you marching this way for? Why the devil don't you get out to Fort Stevens? Hell's popping out there and the lid's off." Halleck reversed himself about 1:40 p.m. Augur's chief of staff, Lieutenant Colonel Joseph Taylor, caught the column turning left up Pennsylvania Avenue and more politely if just as emphatically redirected Wheaton and Bidwell to continue toward what now were clear echoes of gunfire. Wheaton promptly acceded via Eleventh Street. Wright passed the column en route and ordered a rendezvous at Crystal Spring racetrack a half-mile or so behind the DeRussy-Stevens sector of the endangered line near the rendezvous camp. And tagging along, it seemed, was the president and his clattering mounted guard of Black Horse cavalry. Sabers drawn and resting over their shoulders, they shouted, "Give the road to the President," probably to the irritation of the marching infantry as well as the crowd of civilian spectators anxious to watch veterans chase away the Johnnies. The VI Corps veterans took until late afternoon to move into bivouac in a grove behind Fort DeRussy. As author Joseph Judge later captured the scene so well, "It seemed the whole town, including Abraham Lincoln himself, was on its way to war."[27]

Anxious for action, Wright seemed perplexed that his veterans were placed in reserve while the earthworks continued to fill with invalids, government clerks, and various dismounted cavalrymen. He penned a quick note to Augur late in the afternoon asking permission to send a brigade out against a very light enemy skirmish line, as "General McCook's men are not as good as mine for this purpose." But Augur was unready for offensive action, deeming it unwise "to make any advance until our lines are better established; perhaps tomorrow." Similarly, Halleck merely ordered arriving elements of the XIX Corps out the Bladensburg Road to the area of Fort Saratoga and assigned them to the temporary command of Major-General Quincy A. Gillmore. The idea was to develop the situation out in front of the fortifications and only use Wright's (and presumably Gillmore's) people to reinforce areas immediately threatened by a Confederate breakthrough preparatory to a pincerlike counterattack (always seemingly on senior commanders' minds if not always apparent in retrospect).

Union actions seemed quite lethargic and unappreciative of the crisis. Since shortly after noon, active skirmishing and sharp shooting indicated the arrival of the Confederates as Early tried to arrange a full-scale attack. Beckoning both sides were shade tree shelter from dust, heat, and fatigue, sylvan crystal waters of Silver Spring, or the more sluggish waters of Rock and Sligo creeks or whatever liquor could be purloined from houses and country stores at Sligo Post Office north of the Blair properties. Lieutenant Colonel David Long led the van of Colonel George H. Smith's Sixty-Second Virginia Mounted Infantry down Seventh Street Pike with Early personally not far behind. Somewhere at the ridgeline just north of what by the next century would become the Walter Reed Army Medical Center, Early

131

with his binoculars peered at the Yankee lines less than a mile distant. Escalating small arms fire in the fields and wood lots suggested the Rebels had arrived before Washington's defenses. Lincoln and the veterans were not there yet. A ragtag band of defenders were.[28]

The Time of Greatest Danger

The moment of greatest danger to the national capital—at any point during the four years of war—came during the noon hour on July 11, 1864. The only troops directly in front of Early's advance on the Seventh Street Road registered Company K, One Hundred and Fiftieth Ohio National Guard (100-day men), and a portion of the dismounted Twenty-Fifth New York Cavalry on the picket line with a small number of artillerists in the fort and Veteran Reserve Corps personnel plus Quartermaster employees and the Second District of Columbia Volunteers manning adjacent rifle puts. Under such conditions—"or rather disorganization as was at the time possible," commented a somewhat smug Captain Beamish later—any combat between Confederate veterans and the few raw and inexperienced Union troops "could have but one result, namely, the capture and possible destruction of the capital." "The Confederate force was certainly rife and eager for anything desperate," he observed, "too much credit cannot well be given to the really unorganized Union troops that opposed them, fighting them step by step to within 150 yards of the fort, and at some points not more than 50 yards from our works."[29]

Heavy artillery opened from Fort Stevens, "with the destructive shot and shell compelling [the attackers] to fall back some distance," claimed Beamish. Nonetheless, morning skirmishing had been carried on by only the Rebels' advance guard. "Subsequently they showed signs that they were about to attack in force, and from appearances at a point considerably weaker than the immediate vicinity of Fort Stevens," said Beamish, citing a smaller and considerably weaker work about a mile to the left. Bottom line—"by Monday Noon the main portion of the rebel army reached the vicinity and began manouvring [sic] toward our works. Never, during the whole rebellion, was our government and the capital in actual greater peril of capture and destruction than at this hour."[30]

The Second Pennsylvania Heavy Artillery cannoneers in Fort Slocum to the east claimed honors for firing the opening artillery salvoes of the battle. Skilled and sarcastic veteran gunners at nearby Fort Totten noted: "A body of Confederate cavalry rode aimlessly to and fro along the edge of a wood, about five miles from our fort" completely undeterred by such show of Yankee firepower. Captain Norris of the Second Keystone heavies at Fort DeRussy and Colonel John M. C. Marble of the One Hundred and Fifty-First Ohio National Guard who commanded both that fort, Fort Kearny to the west, and all intervening works such as batteries Smeade and Terrill reported heavy skirmishing west of Rock Creek by Colonel George W. Gile's Veteran Reserve brigade. Confederates tried to infiltrate the debris-filled Rock Creek defile while sharpshooters in Claggett's and other farmhouses to the front of the works began taking their toll of men in the fortifications. Gunners sent one-hundred-pound shells crashing at targets four thousand or more yards away, beyond Silver Spring, as well as time, percussion, and case shells in the direction of the Rebel footmen at 1,700 to 2,800 yard range.

Further west, Fort Reno artillerists also plied McCausland's rear as far out in modern Bethesda as the farm where today stands the new Walter Reed National Military Medical Center. Skeptical Rebels might claim that Yankee shells "which made a roaring noise like the passing of a railroad train" simply passed over their heads at "great altitude and burst to our rear, doing no damage to any one." A more perceptive Georgian, I. G. Bradwell, determined that the enemy fire was intended for Confederate wagon trains. Yet he, too, dismissed the shelling as producing nothing more than "a great contempt for the 'melish.'" But John Earley of the Sixteenth Massachusetts battery later claimed that "some of the heavy artillery corps which came down with us [from Fort Lyon to Fort Kearny the night before] got the credit of some excellent shots from [Fort DeRussy's] hundred pounder Parrott, one shell fired at a wagon train three miles off, a scout reporting to have knocked over three wagons."[31]

North Carolina sergeant major John G. Young still pronounced the salvoes of "nail kegs" to be "very unhealthy." Colonel John M. C. Marble declared in his official report: "We are assured by citizens . . . that the enemy was surprised at the accuracy of our fire at such distance, and from information since obtained we are led to conclude that the accuracy and activity of our artillery and skirmish line contributed largely to deter them from making the intended assault on Monday night." Lieutenant Frank Wilkeson, Battery A, Fourth U.S. Artillery, temporarily assigned to Fort Totten, pithily announced the shooting overall to be the worst he ever saw and echoed Bradwell's comments that it was all the militia and departmental clerks' doing and that the enemy "did not pay the slightest attention to it." Nevertheless, Confederate general John B. Gordon was sufficiently annoyed to order up a battery of Parrott rifles, which one observer said "unlimbered in front of the brigade out in the open field in full view of the Yanks about four hundred yards away, and replied, knocking up the red dirt around the muzzles of the big fellows in the fort, while the enemy continued to aim at the moon and stars."[32]

Newsman Cadwallader remembered that battery as planted in his brother-in-law's dooryard. He and Edward A. Paul were owners of the *Milwaukee Daily News* back home in Wisconsin. Paul was now a captain serving with Brigadier General William W. Averill's cavalry, but his family supposedly remained in the Seventh

Street Road house, where they became part of the battle landscape. The house was often struck by missiles, Cadwallader observed, "but no inmate was killed." Of course, such a structure with others in the area soon became haven for nests of sharpshooters, hence the target of Union counterfire over the next two days. Cadwallader noted that the main body of Confederates "were about a mile distant from Fort Stevens, across open plantations, affording a fine view of all that was done." He contended that both sides developed a spirited cannonading until nightfall, Rebel gunners "plunging shot and shell into our forts and earthworks," while "our guns replied with as much vigor as possible." One New Yorker, perhaps from the Twenty-Fifth Cavalry now appearing on the skirmish line, was somewhat apprehensive lest "some droppings fall on us." Nonetheless, this banging away by artillery and musketry at one another soon stabilized matters. Six hundred more dismounted cavalrymen of the Army of the Potomac's Second Division of the Cavalry Corps drove back the Rebels and reestablished McCook's picket line some 1,100 yards in front of the works at about 1:30 p.m.[33]

The "handsome manner" in which the cavalrymen performed "elicited the warmest commendations from all witnesses and set it in a high niche in the estimation of the people of Washington." But "B.O.B" of the Twenty-Fifth New York Cavalry still found room to criticize as the few officers of the regiment who went on the field behaved commendably but "on the line, where the shoulder-straps should have been there were many, many vacancies." Still, one leader, Major Samuel W. MacPherson, "raised himself considerably in the estimation of the men by his conduct during these few days, as they had supposed he was too much of a martinet in camp to show much fight in the field." The *Mercury* correspondent was "happy to say that he has belied this opinion." It remained his impression, however, even after the next day's continuing sharp combat, that "we have very few men; very, very few officers, and very d-d few of those who are with us will be found on the battle-field, although the regiment has some noble exceptions." As a whole, decided that veteran of the Fort Stevens fight, "the line of shoulder-straps is exceedingly of the 'dead beat' order," as this would always be the case "where money, not merit, is the keystone of the arch that leads to preferment." The Twenty-Fifth New York Cavalry would sacrifice nine killed and seventeen wounded to reach such conclusions in their Fort Stevens experience.

Stabilizing the Situation

Renewed Rebel pressure by late on July 11 required insertion of VI Corps veterans when they got to the front between 4:00 and 5:00 p.m. The initial VI Corps reinforcements from the D.C. wharves hove into view. "The first indication the skirmishers of the enemy had was the hurried movements of troops in rear of our works," said Beamish, "and the appearance a little distance in front of the same, of a number of mounted men." Frank Wheaton and his staff plainly displayed the square blue corps flag with a white cross, the emblem of the Second Division of that organization. The first brigade arrived at the double-quick, explained Beamish, "and probably at that time stretched out to appear to the astonished Johnnies at least treble its actual strength." No doubt many a one of them asked himself or his neighbor, "J . . . L, What's that coming?"[34]

In a few minutes, commented Beamish, "a column filed out of the works, advanced about 100 yards, filed to right, formed line and displayed as skirmishers, the left of the regiment on Seventh Street and at once advanced in as nonchalant a style as drilling on a parade ground to the music of the band." But instead of actual band music, the shrieking Yankee shells and "buzzing rifle balls which the enemy sent as their first compliments, accompanied the deployment of VI corps veterans." Without stopping the steady advance of the boys in blue, excepting eight of his company wounded, determined Beamish, "the Johnnies found it safer to vacate considerable ground, leaving here and there scattered over the field some of their comrades to make a closer acquaintance with the Union surgeons and their tools."

The advance and retreat of Union and Confederates "kept on until the latter reached the crest of a hill north [south] of the late Hon. Montgomery Blair's residence—a very strong position for them." Part of the Union line "was not fifty yards from the now hastily strengthened rebel line, who tried again and again to drive our boys back from their position." Despite the bolstered Confederate skirmish line, said Beamish, "the boys in that [Union] line were not to be driven back, knowing that they and their actions were closely watched through any number of field glasses by high and low military and civic officials and citizens from comparatively safe points in the forts and breastworks." He felt justified years later "in stating that every man in that line was determined not to retreat a single step from the position once taken unless ordered by their officers to prevent a too reckless exposure to the enemy where a more covered position could be taken." They all knew only too well from experience "that after a fight a live Dutchman was always better than many dead heroes." Of course, the line of blue coats "that dawned so importantly on the rebel's vision was soon extended to meet the necessity of the situation."

The first unit to advance had been his own, said Beamish, commanded by Colonel John Ballier. Out front reconnoitering, "the occasion requiring immediate, prompt, and decisive action, he, for reasons best known to himself at that time, selected his own regiment to lead," later joined by other regiments of the brigade (Ballier having been verbally placed in command by Wright rather than Wheaton, the division commander), detailed Beamish. Ballier's regiment was to lead, later to be joined by the other sister units of the brigade, "namely the 139th deployed on our right, on the left of 7th Street, the 102nd, joined on its left by the 93rd, all Pennsylvania Veteran Volunteer regiments," outlined Beamish. "I yet often imagine that I see the confused expression of a captured Reb as we passed him in advancing and he asked, as he recognized the 6th corps badges on our caps, 'where in the d . . . l did you uns come from, anyway?'" Beamish did not stop to give him the desired information at that time. Losing eight men wounded "relieving a portion of the home guards who from the way they retired were well pleased to be promoted to the rear," observed Beamish, "was about 4 p.m." Six hours later, "the commissary sergeant of Early's corps rode into our lines," he noted. He was surprised when ordered to dismount and give the countersign and more surprised to find himself a prisoner "of the 6th army corps, who he thought was in front of Petersburg." The astonished Johnny concluded, "If the Holy Cross of Christ fellows are here, Gen Early had better give up the idea of taking Washington." Indeed, by evening, as occasional picket shots continued to ring out, Old Jube was beginning to think the same thing. Neither he nor the Confederacy realized it, but the highwater mark in their history had been reached that day.

Thomas Scott of Company B, Forty-Third New York, also remembered the day many years later. His brigade had arrived at Fort Stevens, hurriedly passed outside the fortifications, and deployed "taking distance on the advance in a manner that elicited the applause of the President, military commanders, and the principal members of Congress, who had come out to the front to witness the engagement." A double skirmish line had been thrown out, and in a brief time Rebel skirmishers were sent reeling back on their reserves. Artillery from forts Stevens and DeRussy then "sent their compliments to the enemy, who were rapidly moving forward a line of battle." These Confederates made "a decided stand" about two miles out on the main road. He surmised that "it was the intention of the commander, no doubt, to draw the rebels on to a general engagement, as the troops were so well concealed that the enemy did not discover them lying in line of battle expecting a general attack." Scott thought it a "desperate engagement between this double skirmish line with their small reserves and a line of battle of the enemy."[35]

Immediately in front of the Forty-Third as well as One Hundred and Twenty-Second New York and Sixty-First Pennsylvania, "a strong force of the enemy lay behind a board fence." "Their fire was well-directed," and in the gathering darkness—"for it was getting dark at 8:30"—"our men were directed to concentrate their fire on the lower board of the fence at short range." Still, Union ranks were thinning as the men "protected themselves as best they could and poured such an incessant fire on the prostrate enemy that it compelled them to retreat in disorder." This was "a double skirmish line of disciplined troops, well officered, that met and drove back, after a severe engagement, a full line of battle." In no other engagement "of our three year's service," Scott commented, "did we witness so many acts of individual valor and daring," and particularly, he boasted, among the men and officers of his own regiment. He admitted "the gallant, but hasty, Lieutenant Colonel James D. Vischer lost his life by his own imprudence." Each regiment seemed to vie with the others to hold their ground and force back the enemy. Scott felt that "Early got enough of the Sixth corps that evening to induce him to get out of Maryland at once."

A Near Miss in Shimmering Heat

Scott most memorably recounted "one of the most tragic scenes of the war" at this point. He had taken a safe position at a point where the enemy's lines were in easy range and with a companion "lay down behind a low pile of cedar posts and directed our fire on the heads of the enemy as they raised up to take aim." Here was life in the Petersburg lines all over again—a personal contest between marksmen. Suddenly, five men of the Sixty-First Pennsylvania joined him despite remonstrance that "the firing of so many would call forth a concentrated fire from the enemy," to which they paid no heed. They fought well for a time, and in the darkness "that gradually settled down on the contest like a funeral pall," the New Yorkers did not notice that the Pennsylvanians' guns were silent "and the five lay as if asleep." Indeed, Scott recalled, "they were all asleep, in the sleep 'that knows no wakening here,'" as he found with horror upon trying to rouse them to action. Placing his hand on the head of the man to his right, the touch of oozing blood and brain told "the wound of the deadly minie ball." Reaching over to the others, Scott found that they too were dead. Hastily rising to leave this sickening scene and wondering how he had escaped the fate that befell his comrades, Scott, too, received a disabling wound in the arm that sent him to the rear. Returning at daybreak, Scott visited the pile of posts riddled with bullets. "My escape the night before was owing to a large flat stone leaning against the posts, scarred by many bullets." Pondering the meaning of this terribly personalized experience in his twilight years, Scott could but suggest "the historian dwells but briefly on this engagement, but no movement of the war had a greater stake at issue." And he had been a witness.

Union forces had achieved a special victory by the afternoon of July 11. At 2:30 p.m., Signal Officer Lieutenant Asa T. Abbott in Fort Stevens telegraphed Augur that he had just received the message: "The enemy is within twenty rods [120 yards or 330 feet] of Fort Stevens." The little tollhouse at the corner of Seventh Street and Piney Branch roads at this time became the "highwater mark" of Early's invasion, hence the Confederacy. Whether or not it was McCook's somewhat unusual ploy of putting out a motley skirmish line in front of the fortifications as he would a normal line of battle, the artillery support (however accurate or inaccurate) or the bolstering of the picket line by VI Corps veterans like Beamish and White—the fact is, they contained Early's momentum. Whether Ohio 100-day volunteers, walking convalescents, civilians mobilized in mufti, dismounted veteran horsemen, or garrison reserves—whoever, they rose to the occasion. McCook would sing their praises in his official report two weeks later. The hour of greatest danger had been met and won by Mr. Lincoln's army, however randomly thrown together.[36]

Artillerists like Captain John Norris, Second Pennsylvania Heavy Artillery, told of effectively throwing Early's teamsters and wagon train into disarray 4,500 yards out as they transited across his front on the Brookville and Seventh Street roads. Union commanders used their advantage of interior lines to shift reinforcements toward the shifting, threatened areas of the fighting. This enabled Colonel John M. C. Marble commanding the One Hundred and Fifty-First Ohio National Guard to counter infiltrating Rebels in the Rock Creek defile where felled tree entanglements did better service than adjacent unarmed field gun batteries manned only by infantry. In fact, Buckeyes were stretched out along a skirmish line from Fort Kearny and Battery Smeade all the way east to Bladensburg, claimed Marble's counterpart, Colonel William H. Hayward, who commanded the sister One Hundred and Fiftieth regiment. Yet Lieutenant Colonel John N. Frazee of that regiment (directly commanding Fort Stevens) contended that his garrison of Captain Charles Dupont's Thirteenth Michigan Battery, aided and assisted by convalescents and infantry, had used predetermined target ranges for the big guns to effectively hit the Rives's house at 1,050 yards and Carberry's house across the Seventh Street Road at 1,078 yards, flushing sharpshooters who were badgering Union skirmishers. They also directed counterbattery fire against Gordon's deployed guns, using 30-Parrott and 24-pounder percussion shells and solid shot even nearly 2,075 yards, totally disrupting Confederate momentum that afternoon.[37]

So it was more than merely Yankee signalers catching sight of Early's flank movement. Whether veterans or novices, the first defenders on the skirmish line and in the earthworks won the day for the Union. As James G. Crawford with scraped-together cavalry, infantry, and artillery provisionals told his father two weeks later, "When our Brigade marched in they [thought] we were the militia and thinking we would run but no instead of running we stood up and fought like men for our country and flag. Long may she wave." And they had done this under the watchful eyes of national government officials, he implied, including their commander-in-chief, Abraham Lincoln. Of course, it wasn't over yet. But whether invalids, provisionals, or veterans, the first defenders had contained Early's quest for fame and glory on July 11 for Mr. Lincoln and the nation.[38]

Taking Stock of the Situation

Just what had Jubal Early achieved at this point? He subsequently told Robert E. Lee that when "we reached the sight of the enemy's fortifications the men were almost completely exhausted and not in condition to make an attack." The march that started from the earliest hour had slackened as the dust became so dense that his men dropped by the wayside in droves. In fact, their general may have lost invaluable time trying to simply gather them together or at least to prevent them from dribbling off to ransack neighborhood properties such as those of the Blairs and lesser folk. Nonetheless, he reported officially that he pushed forward skirmishers "to the vicinity of the fortifications" that "we found to be very strong and constructed scientifically." For Lee's benefit, Early claimed they consisted of "a circle of inclosed forts, connected by breastworks, with ditches, palisades, and abates in front, and every approach swept by across-fire of artillery, including some heavy guns." Whether or not Early determined those facts immediately that July afternoon or over the course of the next twenty-four hours cannot be determined. They went into Early's official report written on July 14, and it remained his litany for the remainder of his life. J. D. Bloodgood, late sergeant of Company I, One Hundred and Forty-First Pennsylvania, and a postwar minister, declared in his own 1893 reminiscences, "I haven't any doubt that Early could have captured and burned the whole city if he had made an energetic assault when he first came on it." Such sentiments echoed through the years to become part of the historical litany. Early did not believe his army was ready to seize that opportunity.[39]

The time sequence can never be determined with precision. The fact was that McCook concluded that the enemy was not "developing any force other than their skirmish line." So a broiling sun shone unrelentingly upon jaded Confederate marchers and the scratch force of defensive Federals, unshaded either in the works or on the skirmish line, and Early lost his chance. He had gotten a small portion of his force inside the firing fields before the works. At some point, J. G. Telford at Fort Reno told headquarters, "Enemy's skirmishers signaled inside of target of Fort Stevens and DeRussy." Similarly, Lieutenant A. T. Abbott at the Soldiers' Home signal station alerted Augur that he had just received a message, "The enemy is within twenty rods of Fort Stevens." That translates to 110 yards! Ohio guard commander Frazee claimed it was within "150 yards of our immediate front and 50 yards of our right." But they got no further. Still, they achieved truly the highwater mark of the Confederacy! They stood that July afternoon inside the District of Columbia—Mr. Lincoln's city—and capital of the Union. They came just beyond the length of a modern football field of breaching the greatest fortification system of the time. Yet Early and his men could not bring closure. Still trying to muster strength, to ascertain the situation, and to gain traction for a decisive attack, their commander may have bungled his chance in history. Unable or unprepared to press the moment, perhaps he had no alternative. Yet there will always be that "might have been," the "what if" of Jubal Anderson Early at Fort Stevens.

For the moment, soldiers on both sides did as soldiers always do (orders from on high notwithstanding). They reacted to conditions. They hunkered down in the blazing sun. Rodes's men, the first Rebels on the scene, could do little more than send skirmishers across the fields and through farm orchards of the Carberry, Shoemaker, and Reeves families. Perhaps they thought they were still conducting defensive skirmishing in force as they had at Jug Bridge on the Monocacy two days before. Sharpshooters dropped off to occupy houses and outbuildings and would bedevil the Yankees in the forts over the next day or so. Union pickets "were ordered to fall back slowly, fighting, until they reached the rifle pits" fronting Fort Stevens, reported McCook. They took casualties, gathered their numbers, and made for key points such as the "Chestnut Tree Post" (where Piney Branch Road joined Seventh Street Road, and a tollhouse marked the spot). Long denoted as the farthest the Rebels got to taking the city for a command post by Colonel John F. Ballier of the Ninety-Eighth Pennsylvania before he was seriously wounded, this spot would attract fellow Pennsylvanian Lewis Cass White of the One Hundred and Second Pennsylvania after the war. He would buy the location and live the rest of his life there. With John B. Gordon's and Stephen Ramseur's reinforcements and Wright's VI Corps veterans plus other reinforcements converging to possibly expand the battle, the future course of action remained to be determined.[40]

By midafternoon, Gordon later boasted, "I rode to a point on those breastworks at which there was no force whatever." "The unprotected space was broad enough for the easy passage of Early's army without resistance," and "undoubtedly we could have ridden into the works." Post-hoc bravado or the actual fact at the time, possibly Gordon discovered the weak sector between forts Stevens and Slocum where meager trenches and unmanned battery positions beckoned. Cavalry scout John Opie would have agreed with Gordon's assessment. A yell, a shot, and a charge, and Washington was theirs, he said later. Union war correspondent Sylvanus Cadwallader, too, thought Early could have swept though the Federal positions "with the loss of a few hundred men" and was baffled by the lackadaisical approach of the enemy. Yet Sergeant John Worsham, Company F, Twenty-First Virginia Infantry, and Lieutenant Newman Feamster of the Fourteenth North Carolina stayed unconvinced that Washington was an easy take even at this point. "Their fort and fortifications are too strong and well guard[ed]," observed the Tar Heel. His Virginia comrade saw the hilltop forts near the Soldiers' Home (in the direction Gordon claimed to have visited), watched the linen dusters filing into the Yankee lines but later moved to the Silver Spring locale, and upon examining the lines at Fort Stevens he pronounced them "the most formidable looking I ever saw," with abatis and "a full sweep of the ground for at least a mile in their front." "If their works were well manned, our force would not be able to take them," he concluded.[41]

That, of course, was the catch in all this. Certainly when Wright arrived he was anxious to push ahead against the impetuous enemy only to be restrained by McCook and Augur. The five or six hundred dismounted troopers from Giesboro under Major George H. Briggs (Seventh Michigan Cavalry) stabilized the situation at Fort Stevens. "This was handsomely done about 1:30 p.m.," recorded McCook, the enemy's skirmishers thrown back and "our line well established at 1,100 yards in front of the works." Wright was told upon arrival around 3:00 p.m. merely to alert nine hundred men for picket relief during the night, and so Ballier's operation shut the door—at least temporarily—to Early's chances for a coup. Developments thereafter meant "constant skirmishing being kept up between the lines until after dark." To Early himself, however, "this defeated our hopes of getting possession of the works by surprise." Opie thought "Early was about the only man in that army who believed it impossible to accomplish."[42]

So it was left to veterans' reminiscences to recount incidents and impressions of that afternoon for our elucidation today. Isaac G. Bradwell, a prolific Georgia raconteur, later on recalled how his comrades from the Thirty-First halted and formed a line, threw out skirmishers, "and the usual preliminaries of battle began." Gordon then ordered a battery of Parrott guns, said Bradwell, which unlimbered at about four hundred yards in open view of the Federals and began knocking up "the red dirt around the muzzle of the big fellows in the fort while the enemy continued to aim at the moon and stars." Neither Rebels nor Federals ever really understood the functioning of the heavy artillery. The Confederates debunked their utility for accuracy, laughingly suggesting the Federals were "throwing flower barrels at us." Indeed, the heavy artillery was designed for distant fire, not close-in troop support, and it was used with good effect, disrupting Early's line of march, wagon parks, and bivouacs beyond Silver Spring. Beside each gun sat a table of ranges, carefully calculated almost by structure, prominent fence line, or tree trunk. The now-absent heavy artillerists had set the baseline. Eventually, even relative amateur newcomer gunners thrust into the northern lines made their presence felt, especially when more troublesome southern sharpshooters found sanctuaries in the houses of Richard Butts, W. M. Morrison, and W. Bell. Ohio guard colonel John M. C. Marble, commanding Fort DeRussy, Battery Smeade, and Fort Kearny to the west of Rock Creek, said how local citizenry later told him "the enemy were surprised at the accuracy of our [long distance] fire," and how this combination of artillery and skirmish line "contributed largely to deter them from making the intended assault on Monday night." Over the next twenty-four hours the fort guns along the line proceeded to blast any structure in front that could provide cover for enemy marksmen. But mainly by the evening of the eleventh—as on so many fields of strife in that war—the actions of a meeting engagement determined the battle space of the morrow. There would be a morrow for the fighting at Fort Stevens and the defense of Washington.[43]

Clarifying the Battle Space

The generals and colonels reconnoitered and conferred. The soldiery lounged by roadsides, under shade trees, by fence posts, and in bivouac or in the shadeless rifle pits. Behind Fort Stevens a makeshift hospital occupied a barracks building. Nobody seemed in a hurry except the skirmishers, sharpshooters, and gunners in those forts. Civilian spectators by the droves like everyone else watched and waited for something to happen. Time passed, opportunities slipped away, the two sides basically locked into position. Early's Confederates became tied to the high Silver Spring ridgeline a mile out and transected north to south basically by the Seventh Street Road. Bounded by the deep Rock Creek valley to the west (Rebel skirmishers crossed its upper reaches to harass the Federals all the way to link up with McCausland before Tennallytown), the ridgeline sloped off to the east. A spur line skirting a flattening upper Piney Branch Creek valley afforded a more salubrious approach to the Yankee defenses, and perhaps this was what John Gordon talked about. A "left fork" road (on contemporary U.S. Army engineer maps—Blair Mill Road to locals) slanted southeastward along the ridge before merging with a "right fork" leading in from a "Burnt Mills" beyond Sligo Creek in Maryland. The merger passed literally beneath the guns of Fort Slocum. Early's legions might have taken that approach to a weak sector—guarded meekly by rifle pits and unarmed field gun battery positions—or not, for Federal fortress guns commanded the ground, and the open space was well spotted by the signalers. Notwithstanding the urban landscape today, one can still study the basic terrain. Nonetheless, Early's attention remained transfixed by the Seventh Street Road approach to the city. Only that direct route downtown offered what he needed for that nine-mile wagon and booty train plus his artillery to make the passage. Here defensive works were hardly as formidable as those at Tennallytown or even at Fort Totten near the Soldiers' Home. But they were enough to give Early pause.[44]

On the Union side, forts Stevens, DeRussy, Slocum, and Totten were familiar to some of the newly arriving veterans from Petersburg. Many had helped construct them in the first place. Lieutenant Colonel George E. Chamberlin of the First Vermont Heavy Artillery had commanded Fort Totten earlier in the war, and his brother officer and now captain Aldace Walker told his father that week of returning, "I have a familiar dating place" for his letters home. Both had spent their term of service from October 1862 until departing for Grant's overland campaign in May 1864 overseeing the works progress, scouting the neighborhood, and young Walker had ingratiated himself with the Montgomery Blair family, enjoying meals and the daughter's piano music while chatting amicably about politics. Elisha Hunt Rhodes and Augustus Woodbury of the Second Rhode Island remembered that their line of battle now "was formed in the camps occupied by the brigade during the winter of

1861–1862." While the regimental officers fraternized with local families, their men often had raided barnyards and granaries, quickly identifying less than ardent Unionists. Three years of proximity, targeting of landmarks' artillery ranges, and mapping by army engineers bred familiarity with civilians such as D. Claggett, Grammer and W. Kurtz heirs, J. Carte, C. G. Coa, the Mooreland and Lay families, D. Colelazer (Coleglazer), T. Carberry, C. A. Shoemaker, a Dr. Noble, W. King, M. H. White, J. Selden, J. Pilling, Hoyl C. Bennett, L. Finchel, B. Jost, T. Mosher, Enos Ray, William Brooke Bell, McChesney, Reeve, Morrison, Mattimore, and Bladen. None of these folks anticipated that former camps and garrisons would become battlefields. In the name of protecting the capital and by implication presumably loyal citizenry of the neighborhood earlier, the fields, orchards, woodlots and structures, farm wells, ponds, and streamlets would become dark and bloody ground.[45]

And what of these Yankee positions? Situated generally on higher ground than land occupied by the attackers (the intervening swath notwithstanding), the defense line was that originally laid out by Major, later Major-General, John G. Barnard and his engineers. Perfected by teams of garrison soldiers and hired labor since 1861 as part of the large and sophisticated infrastructure of earthworks, roads, facilities, and manpower devoted to the defenses of Washington, they represented state-of-the-art field fortifications. Off to the west Fort and Battery Reno reflected an ever-improving military infrastructure. Then, coming east, Battery Rosell, Fort Kearny, Battery Terrill, and Battery Smeade had been added to control the countryside drained by Broad Branch. One of those unoccupied field gun batteries and ancillary rifle pits cut access to a particularly deep cleft where the stream flowed to Rock Creek.

Fort DeRussy next in line anchored the valley of Rock Creek. Built upon the farm of a "Mr. Swart" or Schwartz and first constituted as Camp Holt, the locale had hosted scores of weekend visitors because of picturesque surroundings and attractive creek bathing. Major-General Ambrose E. Burnside's wife and garrison ladies braved flies, bugs, and lizards to visit the posted Rhode Islanders there. The fort, named for either a former chief engineer of the army or colonel of the Fourth New York Heavy Artillery who had a hand in its construction, was trapezoidal, with a perimeter of 290 yards and well-defined rifle pits to the front and flanks still visible today in modern Rock Creek Park. Armament at different times included three 32-pounder seacoast guns (mounted in barbette), a crucial 100-pounder Parrott rifle (similarly mounted), five 30-pounder Parrott rifles (mounted in embrasure), a ten-inch siege, and a 24-pounder Coehorn mortar and two vacant gun platforms for field pieces. Battery Smeade to the west provided additional supporting fire covering the Milk House Road (a well-traveled east-west link between the Georgetown/ Rockville Pike and roads to Bladensburg to the east, crossing over Rock Creek beneath those watchful guns of the fort). Unarmed batteries Kingsbury (nine platforms) and Sill (nine platforms) east and west of these aforementioned works plus other unoccupied field gun positions and rifle pits could provide converging fire on attackers seeking to breach the debris-filled creek valley—if they were occupied. Of course, Fort Stevens's interlocking artillery fire added to the mix. On July 11, 1864, the position was garrisoned by the Sixth and Nineteenth Veteran Reserve Corps regiments of Colonel George W. Gile's First VRC brigade and Captain John Norris; the Second Provisional Pennsylvania Heavy Artillery had charge of DeRussy's guns. Battery Smeade held Captain Joseph Chaney's Company I, One Hundred and Fifty-First Ohio National Guard and one-half of Battery E, Ninth New York Heavy Artillery under Lieutenant French.[46]

More earthworks led up the western side to Fort Stevens. More such works stretched eastward to Fort Slocum constructed by the Second Rhode Island and named for its commanding officer, killed at First Bull Run (Manassas). A strong work of 653 yards perimeter, not only did it provide supporting fire to forts Stevens and Totten, but with twenty-five guns and mortars, it effectively shut down the left and right forks of Rock Creek Church Road as they entered the District. Two additional batteries intervened between forts Slocum and Totten (possibly the most visited position in the defenses by Commander-in-Chief Lincoln because of its proximity to the summer White House). Totten's heavy ordnance of twenty guns and mortars, including two eight-inch siege howitzers (en barbette), eight 32-pounder seacoast guns (en barbette), three 30-pounder Parrott rifles (en barbette), four 6-pounder James rifles (en embrasure), and one ten-inch and one 24-pounder Coehorn mortars would be invaluable to the defense. Most importantly, the fort mounted one of those 100-pounder Parrott rifles that could throw projectiles 6,820 to 8,453 yards. Perhaps a half-mile behind Fort Totten could be found the most crucial feature of all. Here was the signal station set up by Lieutenant P. H. Niles (under Augur's orders) atop of the castellated tower of the nearby Soldiers' Home. In Early's postwar wail: "We could not move to the right or left without its being discovered from a signal station on the top of the Soldiers' Home." Certainly between Yankee signal posts atop Fort Reno and the Soldiers' Home, if not Fort Stevens itself, Old Jube was right.[47]

The Soldiers' Home station was truly the linchpin in the system as authorities slowly extended their signalers to include sites at forts Slocum, Totten, and eastward to Bunker Hill and Lincoln. As captain/chief signal officer William B. Roe told his superior several weeks later, the Soldiers' Home station "proved to be of much importance, as communication could be held direct from provost-marshal's building in the city to any of the forts through it." Eventually signalers covered the whole northern front from Fort Sumner to Fort Lincoln since Confederate activity extended that whole distance. Sergeant Richards (Fort Sumner) and Captain Dillingham (Fort Reno, later Fort Slocum) linked with Lieutenant Asa T. Abbott (Fort Stevens), thence to Corporal William Wallace (subsequently Lieutenant E. H. Wardwell) at

Fort DeRussy and Sergeant Kintner (replaced by Lieutenant F. S. Benson on the twelfth and Lieutenant Strong switched from Fort Totten and eventually Slocum), at Fort Slocum, as "the latter fort being farthest in advance and more important" and on through Totten and Soldiers' Home to the city. Between such linkage and telegraph contact with the front and the War Department where Lincoln himself might read the "mail," the Union could more effectively control, manage, or even manipulate unfolding events better than Early could. The latter depended upon aides and scouts as his eyes and ears for communication and, again, lacked cavalry other than McCausland's band. How much Early could have used the presence and services of Bradley Johnson at Fort Stevens.[48]

The Fort Stevens Showplace

Above all, Fort Stevens remained the showplace for this drama. The 1864 fortification was an expansion of Fort Massachusetts, originally constructed adjacent to the Seventh Street Road by pulling down the Emory Methodist Chapel to make way for the work. Built by Brigadier General Darius B. Couch's Bay Staters in the wake of the First Bull Run debacle, the work was subsequently enlarged after the second battle at that site. The expanded work was renamed in honor of Brigadier General Isaac I. Stevens, killed at the battle of Chantilly on September 1, 1862. From the original 168 perimeter-yard work housing ten cannons and a two-hundred-man garrison, the new fort expanded to 375 perimeter yards with nineteen guns serviced by 423 officers and men. It was what engineers termed a *lunette* with a stockaded gorge or rear face. Deemed a "large enclosed work, situated on high ground" (321 feet above sea level and 5.2 miles from the Capitol Building, it overlooked terrain to its front for several miles), abatis of entwined tree branches at one point surrounded the work. Barracks, hospital, and other support facilities as well as a hollow that could mask large troop concentrations from enemy detection formed to the rear of the fort. Within the fort stood two magazines (one in each section of the enlarged earthwork), a bombproof for 423 officers and men, and the requisite whitewashed revetments and wooden gun platforms and a raised section at the northeast corner of the point of the two forts' linkage called "the lookout." Inspectors deemed the fort in "fair" combat readiness, but the outside grounds of Fort Stevens may not have been well prepared for an appearance of the enemy. Weeds and undergrowth covered fields of fire, although the generally cleared terrain that sloped northward to a brook and thence out to Silver Spring offered superb ground for her gunners. At the same time, intervening copses of trees, fences, and private structures gave habitats for enemy sharpshooters.[49]

Whoever manned the fort's guns that afternoon could avail themselves of range-tablets placed carefully beside each gun position. As of the previous May, the roster of cannon included four 24-pounder seacoast cannon (en barbette), six 24-pounder siege guns (en embrasure), two eight-inch siege howitzers (en embrasure), and five 30-pounder Parrott rifles (en embrasure). Lieutenant Colonel John N. Frazee of the One Hundred and Fiftieth Ohio National Guard commanded the post at the beginning of the action with Company K of his regiment (seventy-eight men under Captain A. A. Safford), seventy-nine men of the Thirteenth Michigan Battery under Captain Charles Dupont, and fifty-two convalescents commanded by Lieutenant Henry L. Turner of Company K, One Hundred and Fiftieth Ohio. But illustrating the confusion surrounding participants as well as commanders all along the northern lines, upon reaching this post and taking command about 2:30 p.m. that Monday, Colonel John M. C. Marble of the Ohio guardsmen later reported his units as Companies F and G of his regiment under Major J. L. Williams, Company A, First Wisconsin Heavy Artillery, Captain Wallace M. Spear, and one-half of Company L, Ninth New York Heavy Artillery under Lieutenant S. A. Howe.[50]

One of the delightful vignettes flowing through the Fort Stevens story has always been about a free black woman who originally owned the fort's land. Construction of one of the magazines in the old Fort Massachusetts portion had claimed the brick Emory Methodist chapel cellar. But the work's expansion to Fort Stevens tore into the house of Mrs. Elizabeth Proctor "Aunt Betty" Thomas to construct a second magazine. She and her husband, James, farmed the eleven acres that she owned in this locale. Aunt Betty recalled for years after the war how Union soldiers had removed her furniture and demolished the house, and that evening in 1862, she sat under a nearby sycamore tree (her only shelter), weeping with her six-month-old baby. A tall, slender figure, dressed in black, came to her side and gently stooped to comfort her. "It is hard, but you shall reap a great reward." Mrs. Thomas claimed it was President Lincoln himself. For decades until her death in 1917, she would claim wryly to all who would listen that she was still waiting for that reward. Had the president survived, she knew her claim would have been honored. At least she would become the featured attraction at veterans' reunions, where people would gather to hear her story. But on July 11 and most certainly the next afternoon, Aunt Betty, like other bystanders, hung about the fort. She and her benefactor would cross paths again at Fort Stevens.[51]

Lincoln under Fire—Was He There?

Just where was Lincoln all this critical day? Where was he that hot afternoon, in particular? We cannot be sure. No definitive evidence has emerged over the years beyond the diary note of presidential secretary John Hay. More reliance on memory attended postwar veterans' claims about seeing the great man that day. As perhaps the first true investigator of Lincoln under fire, historian John Cramer observed in

1948 that evidence comes "in the recollections of soldiers who participated in the defence of Washington, and in the reminiscences of civilians who were spectators at the scene of the battle." He went on to underscore the particular difficulty with marrying the sixteenth president to location that crucial afternoon. True, one un-identified artist depicted the president astride a horse in the company of Secretary of State William Henry Seward outside the fort, taking the salute of what appears to be reinforcing veterans while the skirmish rages in the background out toward Silver Spring. The woodcut was titled "night attack on Fort Stevens, July 11th, 1864, while President Lincoln was there." A destroyed house shell, dead center in the il-lustration, and the clearly defined skirmish and main lines of other combatants, in fact, may suggest the artist combined Lincoln and the fighting done on Tuesday, not Monday, when it was too early to fire those structures that provided safe haven to sharpshooters in front of the fort. Yet, Ohio guard colonels Marble and Frazee both attested to laying down artillery fire to suppress sharpshooters in the Rives and Carberry houses on the eleventh. Moreover, cavalryman James G. Crawford, when writing his father a week after the battle, proclaimed, "Uncle Abe was out nere [sic] whair [sic] we were fighting. O' how the Boys hollored and cheered when they saw him riding along the lines like a brave General." Crawford, however, failed to iden-tify which day he was talking about and just where he ostensibly saw the president.[52]

Further blurring of any timeline surfaced with Lucian C. Warner and James C. Cannon, both from the One Hundred and Fiftieth Ohio National Guard. They recalled their commander-in-chief arriving in a barouche about noon escorted by a troop of the Black Horse Cavalry—but on Sunday, not Monday. Perhaps some humble Sabbath gesture, Lincoln had hastily alighted from the carriage and entered Fort Stevens for what appeared to be a site inspection, wearing a yellowish linen duster. Cannon remembered that he had looked tired and more like a "care worn farmer in time of peril from drought and famine." Whether or not this might have been Monday, not Sunday, the days mixed up for excited men in the ranks like the Buckeye pair, we cannot be sure. The president's personal secretary John Hay was more certain, penning in his diary for Monday: "At three o'clock p.m. the President came in bringing the news that the enemy's advance was at Fort Stevens on the 7th Street road. He was in the Fort when it was first attacked, standing upon the para-pet. A solider roughly ordered him to get down or he would have his head knocked off." Apparently an exhilarated Lincoln then rushed next door to the War Depart-ment telegraph office where, according to operator Albert Chandler, he drew up a rough sketch and proceeded to explain, like some schoolboy, "the relative positions of the two bodies of troops and where the skirmish took place" to Major Thomas Eckert, Charles Tinker, and telegrapher David Bates.[53]

Hay jotted that Lincoln on Monday morning had determined "to desert his tormentors today & travel around the defenses." About 9:00 a.m. he had set off with his wife, Mary, and an entourage that may have also included other dignitaries, visited the front lines at Fort Reno, and then slipped eastward via a military road constructed specifically for the purpose of easing travel across the northern lines. He ended up at Fort Stevens when the skirmishing began. This may have been when the apocryphal stories commenced surrounding his coming under enemy fire. On the afternoon of the eleventh the presidential party ostensibly entered the work, Mr. and Mrs. Lincoln stopping at a filling field hospital after which Mary supposedly swooned, to which her husband remarked how poor a soldier she would make at the sight of blood, after which he and male companions escorted by the post commander ventured onto the parapet to see what was going on out front. At this point some-one—soldier, officer, civilian bystander—shouted to the striking figure to get down or get shot. We know Private John A. Bedient of the One Hundred and Fiftieth O.N.G. claimed that honor for one. Then too, young Frederick Seward recalled that he, his father, Secretary of the Navy Gideon Welles, as well as Mrs. Lincoln and the arriving General Wright were all part of the scene. Welles, himself apparently a "tourist" to the fort, recorded in his diary the next day that he had been informed during the weekly cabinet meeting at the White House that "the President said he and Seward had visited several of the fortifications" but that Lincoln was vague as to understanding exactly where the main body of Rebels could be located. The president's official party eventually exited the battle scene and returned downtown to the White House.[54]

Tireless presidential scribe Hay that night wrote in his notes that the day's events seemed an elixir to his boss. The chief executive even allowed his Soldiers' Home bodyguard to join unfolding frontline action. Neither Hay nor Lincoln nor anyone else at the time made much of the fact that here—at Fort Stevens on the afternoon of July 11, 1864—was (arguably) the first and only time that a U.S. presi-dent had suffered enemy fire while in office. In telegrapher Bates's words later (and perhaps more truthful to the next day's happenings), "His tall form must have been a conspicuous target for the enemy's sharp-shooters and it was a matter of remark at the time that he did not seem to realize the serious risk incurred in going to the front of our line while skirmishing was in progress." But this was said in retrospect and upon reflection of an aging veteran. In the view of one chronicler of the episode, Joseph Judge, "while accounts are muddled about his presence on the 11th, tradi-tion places him at Stevens." Had Lincoln been present, actually under Rebel fire, or merely an observer remains a mystery for July 11, 1864.[55]

Staying in Touch with Events

At 10:00 that evening, Assistant Secretary of War Charles Dana encapsulated the high points of the past two days in a telegram to General-in-Chief Grant. He never mentioned the president. Telegraph chief Eckert claimed in his report fifteen months later that the military telegraph line to Point Lookout "was the only line extending from the city any considerable distance, and for three days all telegrams for the army of Lieutenant-General Grant and for the North were sent to Point Lookout, and thence by dispatch boat to Fort Monroe, from which point they were transmitted to their destination." By this means, he claimed, "but little delay was occasioned in reaching the lieutenant-general by telegraph." Certainly Bradley Johnson's riders cut normal communications to the north via Baltimore, thereby increasing confusion and consternation for the Yankee home front. Yet aside from raising a dust-up in Baltimore's suburbs, his raid had little direct effect on the major scene of action at Washington. Grant was fortunate in thus keeping in touch with frontline action before the city compared with Lee's handicapped reliance on dispatch riders who proved of little value in monitoring his field lieutenant in Maryland. At any rate, Dana made no mention of Lincoln in his bulletin. What he did say, however, was more important to the stringency of the situation, if somewhat loaded with trivial detail.[56]

The assistant secretary opened with news of Johnson's Rebel cavalry activities north of Baltimore. Here local son, Colonel Harry Gilmor (one of Johnson's Marylanders), had attacked the Baltimore, Wilmington, and Philadelphia railroad bridge across the Gunpowder River, captured a train carrying Major-General William B. Franklin, and dispersed road guards and even a gunboat that belatedly came to the scene. Dana then mentioned Lew Wallace's headcount of Monocacy losses (two hundred to four hundred men) and a large enemy force in the Baltimore suburbs before turning to the threatened capital. Even then, Dana's observations were little more than tidbits—how Early, Breckinridge, and cavalryman Imboden had dined together at Rockville at 3 p.m. on Sunday, then how cavalry skirmished on the Tennallytown Road (as if Grant knew where that was), and the Rebels had merely one cannon trained on Union positions at Fort Reno. Clouds of dust, presumably from cavalry, enveloped the countryside, but post commander Martin Hardin "saw also a train of ambulances, which he judged to be about a mile in length, and a column of infantry, of another straggling character, moving in direction of Fort Stevens" (again presuming that Grant knew where that was). He closed those specifics with the fact that "nothing has occurred there to-day to demonstrate the presence of any such force, and the skirmishing has borne away to the right, in front of Fort Stevens."[57]

What Dana expected Grant to do with such intelligence remains unclear. More useful, of course, would be what Dana then specifically told Grant about the Fort Stevens situation. The pickets were very active that evening, "but they are composed mostly of 100-days men." While the fort's cannon had been at play "not a gun has been fired at the fort," and few of "our men have been wounded." The telegraph operator at the work "reports a considerable number of camp-fires visible in front."

The Washington-Baltimore rail link had not been interfered with yet, and five boatloads of the VI Corps and one of XIX Corps troops had arrived. Wright had taken his men to Fort Stevens, hospitals had been stripped of convalescents "collected and organized and sent to the trenches," while Quartermaster General Montgomery C. Meigs had taken 1,500 of his employees also to the northern lines and furnished guards to relieve the Veteran Reserves for similar duty from depots in Washington and Alexandria. Augur had also drawn upon the forts south of the Potomac of all garrison troops that could be spared.

Quincy Gillmore had arrived and "will take the chief command of the troops as soon as they are able to move out of the defenses." Dana found "General Halleck has very great confidence in this officer." With Alexander McCook in command at Fort Stevens and Augur very active in "getting these miscellaneous troops to the front," Dana admitted that he did not understand the precise relationship between the pair. He, too, hinted, as did others (presidential secretary Hay for one), that there were more generals present than could be usefully used, and he alerted Grant to future command and control issues. E. O. C. Ord, whom Grant wanted for overall command, had gone to Baltimore to somehow organize a field force there for operating on Early's rear (Wallace reverting back to administrative control of the department and city).[58]

Finally, Dana returned to bigger regional focus as he told Grant, "Washington and Baltimore are in a state of great excitement." Both cities had filled with "country people fleeing from the enemy." Damage to private property by the invaders "is almost beyond calculation," with mills, workshops, and factories of every sort destroyed. Twenty-four to fifty miles of John Garrett's Baltimore & Ohio railroad had been torn up; the houses of Governor Augustus Bradford north of Baltimore and the Blairs at Silver Spring burned. Nothing had been heard of Hunter in western Maryland, and "the force of the enemy is everywhere stated at from 20,000 to 30,000." An obviously weary and frustrated Dana sounded distinctly sour by ending his dispatch: "The idea of cutting off their retreat would seem to be futile, for there are plenty of fords and ferries now in their control where they can cross the Potomac and get off, in spite of all our efforts to intercept them, long before our forces can be so concentrated as to be able to strike an effective blow."[59]

Someone else spent invaluable time that day informing his superior on the situation in Maryland, even though a hundred miles or more away. Robert E. Lee, closer in proximity to Grant than to his own lieutenant besieging Washington, told President Jefferson Davis how his intelligence sources caught dispatch of Wright's corps away from Petersburg. "I had hoped that General Grant, rather than weaken his army, would have attempted to drive us from our position." "I fear I shall not be able to attack him to advantage," he continued, but "if I cannot I think it would be well to re-enforce General Early. In such fashion, it would oblige his enemy to further diminish his force." Lee also answered Early's week-old progress report, passing intelligence along about reinforcements going north (Ricketts plus other troops, possibly the rest of the VI Corps) plus what could be gleaned from Yankee newspapers about Hunter's tortoise-like movement to block Early's retreat route. Be on guard about all of this, Lee cautioned. Of course, by this point, Lee's enjoinder and information had been overtaken by events.[60]

Still, Lee told Early on the eleventh, "In your further operations you must of course be guided by the circumstances by which you are surrounded, and the information you may be able to collect, and must not consider yourself committed to any particular line of conduct, but be governed by your good judgment," advised Lee. If forced to retire from the operation then Early should do so by Potomac fords east of the Blue Ridge, a route through Loudon County that would afford the army provisions, a place to forage, and an advantageous position to continue to "retire into the Valley and threaten and hang upon the enemy's flank should he push on toward Richmond." Lee also alluded to a wild scheme now apparently dead that had envisioned Johnson's raiders teaming with a waterborne movement under John Taylor Wood to go all the way down to Point Lookout where the Potomac met Chesapeake Bay and to free a corps-size contingent of Confederate prisoners held there and return with them to Washington and hence back to the Army of Northern Virginia. "The subject was a matter of general conversation in Richmond, which may tend to frustrate it." It was Lee's considered opinion that if Early struck separately at any of his potential pursuers like Hunter, he could prevail and escape, which was what the Gray Fox distinctly expected Old Jube to do. Unbeknownst to either Confederate president or his army commander, Early that evening was conducting a council of war over Francis Blair's supply of naval rum. He was determined to see what the situation looked like before Fort Stevens at first light.

As for Lincoln, after regaling the telegraph operators with his day's experience, the president had walked calmly back to the White House that night. Hay recorded that "the President is in very good feather this evening." Unconcerned about the safety of Washington, penned the scribe, "with him the only concern seems to be whether we can bag or destroy this force in our front." One of these crafty war leaders was destined for disappointment. The more immediate problem, however, what to do about Washington, had not been resolved, and Lincoln knew it. And so did Jubal Early. Making his way to the rear by late afternoon, Old Jube was hot, irritable, and notably unhappy that his army had not been up to the task of mounting an assault. But he found the sylvan clime of Francis Preston Blair's Silver Spring mansion and nearby spring just the relief, quickly setting up headquarters in this lovely setting. And how inviting a setting it must have been. Silver Spring was the beautiful, country Gothic showplace of the senior Blair, and son Montgomery's Falkland mansion stood nearby, as did a third Blair property, Francis Preston Blair's son James's Mooring. All abutted the District of Columbia–Maryland line, and all now provided sanctuary for lounging Rebels in their owners' absence.[61]

War Council at Silver Spring

Family patriarch Francis and his daughter Elizabeth had discovered the setting some twenty years earlier during a country ride from their city home across from the White House. Ostensibly, one of their horses stumbled, throwing its rider to the ground on the edge of a fetching, bubbling, sunlit spring. The influential editor of the *Washington Globe* purchased the spot, developed a farm, and constructed his house in 1845. He improved the property with an artificial lake lined with flowers, a small honeysuckle-adorned island replete with a white marble statuette of a water nymph, and an acorn-shaped summer pavilion nearby. No wonder the Rebel generals were attracted to it like a magnet when they found it vacant save for some attendants on Monday morning. Everyone's ghosts today would be devastated were they to revisit the now urbanized scene. Only a replica of that acorn pavilion marks the site of the "silver spring" in a tiny triangular city park. Hardly a way to capture what would unfold there on the evening of July 11 for Early's war council with his chieftains. The former country gathering point for Washington's political and social gentry now became host to Jubal Early's stag party at Blair's liquor cellar.[62]

Of course, those present at the time included the Blair's Kentucky cousin and former vice president of the United States, John Cabell Breckinridge. As he explained to brother officers that Monday evening, his kin had succored him through formerly rough patches politically, and he harbored fond memories of the place and its people. Daughter Elizabeth Blair Lee later wrote her naval husband (after the dust of Early's intrusion had settled) that Breckinridge had been the one to vehemently protest Early's dismissive attitude toward one house "when we have lost so much" by the war. Early's deputy told him that "this place is the only one I felt was home to me on this side of the Mts." His commander probably knew nothing of this when earlier he had berated that riotous subordinate for disturbing the place rather than pushing on to the fort and taking it. But Early probably still fumed that if his vanguard had not lingered in the morning at the Blair mansion, they wouldn't have "ruined our whole campaign." He sensed Grant's reinforcements were now arriving, and "we can't take them without immense loss, perhaps 'tis impossible." At the same time now, Early and his generals had more pressing matters on their minds, and they were only too happy to ponder those while enjoying Blair hospitality via a well-stocked naval rum and wine cellar. Nearby Barnes Tavern probably accommodated the lesser classes in their army.[63]

The war council of Early, Breckinridge, Gordon, Rodes, and Ramseur, when not toasting the former vice president's return to the Senate chamber on the morrow or listening to his reminiscence of good times spent in the Blair household, had to face the facts. Intelligence had David Hunter's army closing off any retreat route whence the army had come from the upper Potomac. Bluecoats in force had retrieved Frederick. The arrival of Union veterans from Grant's army was imminent if not already in place. A dispatch received from raider Bradley Johnson (citing "a reliable source") affirmed that two corps from Petersburg, even perhaps "that his whole army," was probably in motion affected discussion. Possibly leaked purposely to Baltimore secessionists to affect Early's actions, it would replicate information en route from Lee but not yet in Old Jube's possession. At any rate, it sounded ominous and gave Early pause from any assault.[64]

John B. Gordon later recounted the story almost more reminiscent of Old Abe than Jubal Early's flock. What was to be done about Washington, everyone chorused? It reminded someone of the tale of Simon's dog. Asked wasn't Simon afraid of losing his dog since he chases every train that comes along, the dog owner replies, "No, but I wonder what the dog will do with that train once he catches it." In understandable hindsight, Gordon would claim later "there was not a dissenting opinion as to the impolicy of entering the city" (not necessarily reflected throughout the lounging army, however). Yet, somehow, failure to accomplish Lee's orders haunted everyone—especially Early. He heard out his senior officers, "determined to make an assault on the enemy's works at daylight next morning," but he concluded such a scheme was impractical "until I could examine the works again," according to his own postwar recollections. At the time, the Army of the Valley's senior leaders returned to more amenable pursuits.[65]

Upriver, Mosby's partisans had crossed at Conrad's Ferry and moved toward Poolesville, burning abandoned Union blockhouses on the way. Their nemesis, the Eighth Illinois Cavalry, was away scouting and harassing Early's columns at the time. Then the partisans turned to Seneca's Mills and to the Illini's abandoned Muddy Branch camp, where they further destroyed camp and cavalry equipage as well as yet another nearby cross-shaped blockhouse and frame storehouse. Thirty head of cattle and presumably quantities of fodder went back with the rangers across the river on the night of July 12. It was vintage Mosby. Did it aid Early then besieging Washington? Not in the least.[66]

According to what Patent Office examiner Horatio Taft wrote in his diary, Monday had been a surprise. Instead of near Baltimore, "today we find them in large force within four to six miles of this City." Considerable skirmishing had occurred but no general engagement, although an attack was expected for the morrow. "It seems that they abandoned the idea of taking Baltimore and have turned their attention to Washington," he suggested, adding, "but I think they have waited too long and have allowed troops to concentrate there in sufficient numbers within the past three or four days to defeat them in any attempt to take the City." Concerned like Secretary of State Seward for casualties suffered by the Ninth New York Heavy Artillery at Monocacy, Taft's nephew, Lieutenant Colonel E. P. Taft, was unaccounted for and presumed dead. Like Seward, Taft could get no information what with the disruption to the telegraph and railroads in the region. So, "I am soon going to bed but rather expect to be disturbed by the report of Cannon before my usual hour for rising," which was 6:00 a.m. "If the rebels make an attack on the Forts at all I think that it will be by tomorrow morning. Estimates now had the besiegers at "Forty thousand strong" in Maryland and threatening the city, but "should they make an attack it will be a bloody fight." If they did not attack on Tuesday, "I think it will be because their object is not so much Washington or Baltimore as to obtain Horses, Cattles, and provisions and then they will attempt to slide off over the Potomac into Virginia and escape." "We shall know soon," he sighed.[67]

Taft had worked in his office as usual all day. He noted the great excitement on the streets, "I never saw such a crowd of people on Pa. Avenue as on this afternoon." The excitable crowds listened to every tidbit from someone returning from the northern forts, "swallowing the most absurd stories from some sober faced wag." "The whole of the 6th Corps have come up now from the Army of the Potomac and many other troops have arrived." Most notably, Taft told how "Mr. Lincoln and Sec'y Stanton passed in a carriage thinking (perhaps) that it was necessary to show the people that they were not frightened." He "mentally wondered" why or how a Rebel army of thirty thousand or forty thousand could leave Richmond, get across the Potomac, and be almost knocking at the gates of the city and they know nothing about it, or at least think it only a "raid" of a few hundred troopers!

One of those "troopers" actually claimed later that he had infiltrated Union lines that hot July night. "Tiger John" McCausland bragged to Grant when the hero of the Union was later campaigning for president that the last time the Rebel had been in Washington had been in 1864 and had ridden with his staff into the defenses of Georgetown. Asked if he had been disguised, "Oh, no," McCausland answered, "your entire defending garrison had deserted!" "I sat there on a big gun and looked at the lights and wished I had men enough to go ahead and capture the place and end the damned war!" Apocryphal or plausible, McCausland supposedly used young aide and local scion Henry Loughborough and his knowledge of streamlet valleys and animal paths to penetrate the thinly held Union front lines in between forts Bayard and Reno. They would have visited Loughborough's family place, Grassland, on a ridge in that vicinity. The Loughboroughs were survivors—slave owning, southern sympathizing, but smart enough to patronize the nearby Fort Gaines garrison while son Henry was in Confederate service. On July 11, Fort Gaines may have been deserted or only had a corporal's guard. By this point in the war it was a rear echelon post whose understaffed and even unmanned guns had been supplanted by the newer defense line from Fort Sumner to Fort Reno, with Fort Bayard further down and in front of the ridge toward Tennallytown.

Recounted two years before his death in 1925, McCausland's "Grant story" may have been true or the figment of an aging warrior's imagination. If he did penetrate enemy lines, might he have simply seen the glow of the city? Could he have mustered even the smallest of raiding parties and knifed into the city to capture the president and slip off in the darkness with his prize? Why didn't he? Or as modern raconteur James Johnston puts it, "On a July evening in 1864, it would have been a lovely view—Capitol Hill aglitter with gaslight." Perhaps John McCausland, like his chief, Jubal Early, might also have missed a rendezvous with destiny but enjoyed the view![68]

Notes

1. Gideon Welles, *Diary*, volume 2 (Boston: Houghton Mifflin, 1909), 730–32; Howard K. Beale, editor, *The Diary of Edward Bates 1859–1866* (Washington, DC: Beale Press, 1933), 384.

2. A. B. Beamish, "Battle of Fort Stephens Near Washington, DC, July 12, 1864: A Little Different Version," *Grand Army Scout and Soldiers Mail* (Philadelphia) (Saturday, July 10, 1886).

3. U.S. War Department, *The War of the Rebellion: A Compilation of the Official Records of the Union and Confederate Armies* (Washington, DC, 1880–1901), Series I, Volume 37, Part 1, 202–3. Hereafter cited as *ORA*.

4. *ORA*, I, 37, pt. 1, 231, 236, and p. 2, 141, 162–70, 193, 203–4; Martin D. Hardin, "The Defence of Washington against Early's Attack in July 1864," Military Order of the Loyal Legion (MOLLUS), Illinois Commandery, *Military Essays and Recollections*, volume II (1894), 131–32.

5. *ORA*, I, 37, pt. 2, 170–71, 203–7.

6. Benjamin P. Thomas, editor, *Three Years with Grant as Recalled by War Correspondent Sylvanus Cadwallader* (New York: Knopf, 1955), 226–27.

7. *ORA*, I, 37, pt. 1, 231, 236, and pt. 2, 141, 162–70, 193, 203–5; see also Carol Bundy, *The Nature of Sacrifice: A Biography of Charles Russell Lowell Jr., 1835–1864* (New York: Farrar, Straus and Giroux, 2005), 394–96; James McLean, *California Sabers: The 2nd Massachusetts Cavalry in the Civil War* (Bloomington: Indiana University Press, 2000), chapter 6; Thomas E. Parson, *Bear Flag and Bay State in the Civil War: The Californians of the Second Massachusetts Cavalry* (Jefferson, NC: McFarland, 2001), chapter 8.

8. Edward Waldo Emerson, editor, *Life and Letters of Charles Russell Lowell* (New York: Houghton Mifflin, 1907; Columbia: University of South Carolina Press, 2005), 321–22, 407; *ORA*, I, 37, pt. 1, 249; pt. 2, 199–201.

9. *ORA*, I, 37, pt. 1, 236 and pt. 2, 199–202; J. Willard Brown, *The Signal Corps in the War of the Rebellion* (Boston: U.S. Veteran Signal Corps Association, 1896), Department of Wash-

ington chapter; Rufus Woolwine diary, July 11, 1864, Virginia Historical Society (VHS); T. A. Meysenburg journal, July 11, 1861, Duke University, Durham, NC.

10. See Benjamin Franklin Cooling and Walton H. Owen II, *Mr. Lincoln's Forts: A Guide to the Civil War Defenses of Washington* (Lanham, MD: Scarecrow Press, 2009), 137–47; Judith Beck Helm, *Tenleytown, D.C.: Country Village into City Neighborhood* (Washington, DC: Tennally Press, 1981), chapter 3.

11. George Perkins, *A Summer in Maryland and Virginia* (Chillicothe, OH: Sholl Printing, 1911), 52–53; Alfred Seelye Roe, *Ninth New York Heavy Artillery* (Worchester, MA: 1899), 318.

12. Cox, Randolph, Woolwine, and Lambeth diaries, all July 11, 1864, entries, VHS; John G. Young diary, July 11, 1864, North Carolina Historical Archives, Raleigh; John Worsham, *One of Jackson's Foot Cavalry* (Jackson, TN: McCowat Mercer, 1864), 141–42; G. W. Nichols, *A Soldier's Story of His Regiment* (Jessup, GA: Continental Book Company, 1898), 173; Mildred Newbold Getty, "The Silver Spring Area," *Montgomery County Story* XII (November 1968): 3–4; W. H. Farquhar, *Annals of Sandy Spring, Or Twenty Years of History in a Rural County in Maryland* (Baltimore: Cushings & Bailey, 1884), 13; Joseph Judge, *Season of Fire: The Confederate Strike on Washington* (Berryville, VA: Rockbridge, 1994), 231.

13. *ORA*, I, 37, pt. 1, 230–31, 236, 246, and pt. 2, 594; Edgar S. Dudley, "A Reminisence of Washington and Early's Attack in 1864," in Military Order of the Loyal Legion of the United States, Ohio Commandery, *Sketches of War History 1861–1865* (Cincinnati: Robert Clarke and Company, 1888), 107–27; William V. Cox, "The Defenses of Washington: General Early's Advance on the Capital and the Battle of Fort Stevens, July 11 and 12, 1864," *Records of the Columbia Historical Society, Volume IV*, (1901): 1–31; M. B. "Smokey," "Defense of the Capital—The Veteran Reserve Corps Experience," undated clipping, *National Tribune*, Lewis Cass White collection, Joseph and Sharon Scopin, Darnestown, Maryland.

14. *ORA*, I, 37, pt. 1, 236, 348.

15. Letter, George D. Jewett to Lewis Cass White, May 22, 1914, Lewis Cass White collection, Joseph and Sharon Scopin, Darnestown, Maryland.

16. *Washington Star*, July 15, 1864.

17. Abraham Kingsland to Thomas G. Kingsland, October 4, 1864, author's files; Letter, Jewitt to White, May 22, 1914, White collection.

18. A. G. Jacobs, "Getting There on Time—A Dismounted Cavalryman Tells about the Fort Stevens Fight," undated clipping, *National Tribune*, Lewis Cass White collection, Joseph and Sharon Scopin, Darnestown, Maryland; "B.O.B.," "Twenty-Fifth New York Cavalry, Washington, July 18, 1864," *New York Sunday Mercury*, July 24, 1864, in William B. Styple, *Writing and Fighting the Civil War: Soldier Correspondence to the* New York Sunday Mercury (Kearny, NJ: Belle Grove Publishing Company, 2000), 371.

19. "B.O.B," "Twenty-Fifth New York Cavalry Washington," and A. G. Jacobs, "Getting There on Time," ibid.

20. John H. Wolff, "Defending the Capital," *National Tribune*, November 9, 1899; Hardin, "Defence of Washington," 125–26; Edgar S. Dudley, "Reminiscence of Washington and Early's Attack in 1864," MOLLUS, Ohio Commandery, *Sketches of War History* (Cincinnati: Broadfoot Publishing Company, 1888), I, 10–115, 121; *Washington Star*, July 15, 1864; Note

for file, George E. Davis, Burlington, Vermont, August 24, 1891, Folder 2, George E. Davis collection, Monocacy National Battlefield, Frederick, Maryland; *ORA*, I, 37, pt. 1, 231.

21. Benjamin F. Taylor, *Pictures of Life in Camp and Field* (Chicago: S. C. Griggs and Company, 1888), 214–15.

22. Judge, *Season of Fire*, 235–36.

23. Ibid., 236; Lewis Cass White autobiographical sketch, June 16, 1880, 13, Lewis Cass White collection, Joseph and Sharon Scopin, Darnestown, Maryland.

24. George T. Stevens, *Three Years in the Sixth Corps* (Albany, NY: S. R. Gray, 1866), 372–73.

25. Thomas H. Scott (?), "War Reminiscences: Narrow Escape of Washington from Capture; Pen Pictures of the Late Civil Conflict by an Onondaga County Man Who Was on the Spot and Remembers What He Saw," Fayetteville (NY) *Weekly Observer*, July 3, 1890; Lewis Cass White, autobiographical sketch, 14, White collection, Joseph and Sharon Scopin, Darnestown, Maryland.

26. Beamish, "The Battle of Fort Stephens [*sic*] Near Washington, D.C., July 12, 1864; A Little Different Version," *Grand Army Scout and Soldiers Mail*, July 10, 1886.

27. Judge, *Season of Fire*, 238; FWMP; Stevens, *Three Years in the Sixth Corps*, 373; *ORA*, I, Volume 37, Part 1, 273, pt. 2, 193, 203, 207, 209, 210; Lewis Cass White, "Autobiographical Sketch," June 16, 1880, Lewis Cass White collection, Joseph and Sharon Scopin, Darnestown, Maryland.

28. Judge, *Season of Fire*, 233–34; "Lang, Life of," USAMHI; "Memorable Incidents of Old Fort Stevens," unidentified clipping, History files, Battleground Cemetery Lodge, National Park Service, Washington, DC (BC); John Clagett Proctor, *Proctor's Washington and Environs: Written for the* Washington Sunday Star *(1928–1949)* (Washington, DC: self-published, 1949), 348; *ORA*, I, 37, pt. 2, 208, 209.

29. Beamish, "The Battle of Fort Stephens [*sic*]," *Grand Army Scout and Soldiers Mail*, July 10, 1886.

30. Ibid.; *ORA*, I, 37, pt. 1, 231, 236, 243–44, 245, 262, 264.

31. Letter, John Earley-Sanborn, August 7, 1864, author's files; Young diary, NCHA, 40; I. G. Bradwell, "Early's Demonstration against Washington in 1864," *Confederate Veteran* (October 1914), 438, and "Early's March to Washington in 1864," *Confederate Veteran* (May 1920), 177; *ORA*, I, 37, pt. 1, 213, 238, 241–42; and XLIII, pt. 1, 602; Robert Park, "Diary," *Southern Historical Society Papers* I (1876): 379; Doree G. Holman and Gertrude D. Bradley, *Old Bethesda—Bethesda Not So Old* (Gaithersburg, MD: Franklin Press, 1956), 44; Atkins, "Evans Brigade Report" (HL); John C. Clevenger, "At Fort Stevens," *National Tribune*, June 19, 1900; A. F. Jackson, "Dismounted Cavalry," *National Tribune*, August 9, 1900.

32. Frank B. Wilkeson, *Recollections of a Private Soldier in the Army of the Potomac* (New York: G. P. Putnam Sons, 1898), 214; *ORA*, I, 37, pt. 1, 238–39, 241–43.

33. I. G. Bradwell, "On to Washington," *Confederate Veteran*, XXXVI (March 1928): 95; Cannon, *Memorial, One Hundred and Fiftieth Ohio, Company K* (Cleveland, 1907), 9; *ORA*, I, 37, pt. 1, 231, 236, 238, 241, 244–45, 348; pt. 2, 195; Frank Fuller, "At Fort Stevens," *National Tribune*, June 1, 1911; James M. Springer, "Lincoln at Fort Stevens," *National Tribune*,

February 8, 1912; Thomas, editor, *Three Years with Grant*, 227; "B.O.B.," "Twenty-Fifth New York Cavalry," July 24, 1864, in Styple, *Writing and Fighting the Civil War*.

34. Beamish, "The Battle of Fort Stephens."

35. Scott, "War Reminiscences," Fayetteville (NY) *Weekly Observer*, July 3, 1890.

36. *ORA*, I, 37, pt. 1, 231–34.

37. *ORA*, I, 37, pt. 1, 232–248 inter alia, and pt. 2, 195.

38. Letter, James G. Crawford to William Crawford, July 17, 1864, Copy, from the collection of Ron Meininger, Antebellum Covers, Gaithersburg, MD.

39. *ORA*, I, 37, pt. 1, 348, and "Letter from Gen. Jubal A. Early," December 14, 1874, in Baltimore *Gazette*, December 12, 14, 1874, copy, Peter Seaborg files, Fort Ward Museum and Park, Alexandria, Virginia; J. D. Bloodgood, *Personal Reminiscences of the War* (New York: Hunt and Eaton; Cincinnati: Cranston and Curts, 1893), 187.

40. Jim Leeke, editor, *A Hundred Days to Richmond: Ohio's "Hundred Days" Men in the Civil War* (Bloomington: Indiana University Press, 1999), 131–32; Judge, *Season of Fire*, 234–35; *ORA*, I, 37, pt. 1 and pt. 2, 195–200.

41. John N. Opie, *A Rebel Cavalryman with Stuart and Jackson* (Chicago: W. B. Conkey, 1899), 247; John H. Worsham, *One of Jackson's Foot Cavalry: His Experience and What He Saw during the War 1861–1865* (New York: Neale Publishing Company, 1912 and Jackson, TN: McCowat Mercer, 1964), 242; Cadwallader and Feamster quoted in Judge, *Season of Fire*, 235.

42. *ORA*, I, 37, pt. 1, 231, 246; Judge, *Season of Fire*, 236–37.

43. *ORA*, I, 37, pt. 1, 238, 242.

44. See John G. Barnard, *A Report on the Defenses of Washington to the Chief of Engineers, U.S. Army* (Washington, DC: Government Printing Office, 1871), Plate 10, and David V. Miller, *The Defense of Washington during the Civil War* (Buffalo, NY: Mr. Copy, 1976), sheet 171-100 for topographic comparisons.

45. Barnard, *Defenses of Washington*, Plates 1 and 10; *ORA*, Atlas, Plates 6:1, 7:1, and 89:1.

46. *ORA*, I, 37, pt. 1, 238, 241, Cooling and Owen, *Mr. Lincoln's Forts*, 164–72.

47. Jubal A. Early, *Autobiographical Sketch and Narrative of the War between the States* (Philadelphia: J. B. Lippincott, 1912), 391; *ORA*, I, 37, pt. 2, 563–64; Cooling and Owen, *Mr. Lincoln's Forts*, 185–92 and Appendix B, 253 and Appendix D, 261–62, for details on ordnance and signal stations.

48. *ORA*, I, 37, pt. 2, 532–64.

49. Cooling and Owen, *Mr. Lincoln's Forts*, 173, 174–75.

50. *ORA*, I, 37, pt.1, 241, 247.

51. Cultural Tourism DC, *Battleground to Community—Brightwood Heritage Trail* (Washington, DC, 2008), Stop 17.

52. Letter, James G. Crawford to William Crawford, July 17, 1864, from the collection of Ron Meininger, Antebellum Covers, Gaithersburg, MD; *ORA*, I, 37, pt. 1, 242, 246; also see John H. Cramer, *Lincoln under Enemy Fire: The Complete Account of His Experience during Early's Attack on Washington* (Baton Rouge: Louisiana State University Press, 1948; Knoxville: University of Tennessee Press, 2009), 24; Paul F. Mottelay and T. Campbell-Copeland, *The Soldier in Our Civil War, volume II* (New York: Stanley Bradley, 1885), 297.

53. David Homer Bates, *Lincoln in the Telegraph Office: Recollections of the United States Military Telegraph Corps during the Civil War* (New York: Century Company, 1907), 253; Tyler Dennett, *Lincoln and the Civil War in the Diaries and Letters of John Hay* (New York: Dodd Mead, 1939), 208; Lucian C. Warner, *The Story of My Life during Seventy Eventful Years* (New York, 1914), 47–48; John Cannon, *Record of Service of Company K, One Hundred and Fiftieth O.V.I., 1864* (Cleveland, 1903), 16, 26, and *Memorial, One Hundred and Fiftieth Ohio, Company K* (Cleveland, 1907), 8–10.

54. In addition to Cannon and Warner, see Isaac A. Hawk, "Fort Stevens," *National Tribune*, September 27, 1900; John B. Southard to sister, July 16, 1864, Southard Family papers, New York Historical Society (NYHS); John H. Bierck, "He Saw Lincoln under Fire," *Liberty Magazine* XIX (1937): 7; Welles, *Diary*, II, 72; Frederick W. Seward, *Reminiscences of a War-Time Diplomat and Statesman* (New York: G.P Putnam's Sons, 1916); Frederick C. Hicks, "Lincoln, Wright and Holmes at Fort Stevens," *Journal of the Illinois State Historical Society* XXXIX (September 1946): 329–30; Cramer, *Lincoln under Enemy Fire*, chapters 2 and 3.

55. Judge, *Season of Fire*, 239; Bates, *Lincoln in the Telegraph Office*, 252; Dennett, *Lincoln and the Civil War*, 208; Welles, *Diary*, II, 74.

56. *ORA*, I, 51, pt. 1, 262; I, 37, pt. 2, 192–93.

57. *ORA*, I, 37, pt. 2, 192–93; Mark A. Snell, *From First to Last: The Life of Major-General William B. Franklin* (New York: Fordham University Press, 2002), 326–33; Timothy Ackinclose, *Sabres & Pistols: The Civil War Career of Colonel Harry Gilmor, C.S.A.* (Gettysburg, PA: Stan Clark Military Books, 1997), chapter 6.

58. *ORA*, I, 37, pt. 2, 192–93; also Dennett, *Lincoln and the Civil War*, 209.

59. *ORA*, 194.

60. *ORA*, I, 37, pt. 2, 594–96.

61. Dennett, *Lincoln and the Civil War*, 209.

62. See Elbert B. Smith, *Francis Preston Blair* (New York: Free Press, 1980), 172–73; Aldace F. Walker to Father, October 25 and 29, 1862, July 13, 1864, especially with random other letters in the 1862 to 1864 timeframe, typescript copies, Vermont Historical Society, Montpelier (VHS).

63. Smith, *Blair*, 358–59; Virginia Jeans Laas, *Wartime Washington: The Civil War Letters of Elizabeth Blair Lee* (Urbana: University of Illinois Press, 1999), 404–13; Mildred Newbold Getty, "The Silver Spring Area, Part I," *Montgomery County Story* XII, Number 1: 2–3; Roger Brooke Farquhar, *Historical Montgomery County Maryland Old Homes and History* (Baltimore, 1952), 285–86.

64. Judge, *Season of Fire*, 241–42.

65. Jubal A. Early, *War Memoirs* (Bloomington: Indiana University Press, 1959 reprint), 392; Early to editor, *Richmond Gazette*, December 14, 1874, copy Defenses of Washington files (FWMP); Jubal Early, "The Advance on Washington," *Southern Historical Society Papers* 9 (August 1881): 309; *ORA*, I, 37, pt. 1, 348; John B. Gordon, *Reminiscences of the Civil War* (New York: Charles Scribner's Sons, 1904), 314–15; Henry Kyd Douglas, *I Rode with Stonewall* (Chapel Hill: University of North Carolina Press, 1940), 294–95; Cox, *Defenses of Washington*, 15–16; A. C. Fletcher, "At Fort Stevens," *National Tribune*, September 27, 1900; Charles Carswell, "Lincoln and the Sixth Corps," *National Tribune*, August 16, 1912.

66. James J. Williamson, *Mosby's Rangers: A Record of the Operation of the Forty-Third Battalion Virginia Cavalry* (New York: Ralph B. Kenyon, 1896), 189–91, 416.

67. Horatio Nelson Taft diary, July 11, volume 3, Library of Congress, Washington, D.C.

68. James H. Johnston, "The Man Who Almost Conquered Washington," *Washington Post*, March 18, 2001, and "If This Land Could Talk," *After Hours*, April 7, 2003.

Painting of President Lincoln at Fort Stevens, July 12, 1864, by Kiapp? [or Miapp?], *National Tribune,* **1912 Calendar.** *Author's Collection*

Fort Washington at the Beginning of the Civil War, *London Illustrated News,* **May 18, 1861.**

Unfinished U.S. Capitol, Symbol of the Federal Union. *National Archives and Records Service*

A Standing President Abraham Lincoln in 1864. *National Archives and Records Service*

Camp Brightwood, D.C., Evening Prayer Formation, Summer Encampment of Tenth Massachusetts Volunteers. Drawn by Edward Miller, Company E, printed A. Meisel, Boston. *Author's Collection*

Elizabeth "Aunt Betty" Proctor Thomas, "Owner of Fort Stevens," in Her Later Years. *Historical Society of Washington, D.C.*

Major-General John Gross Barnard, "Father of the Defenses of Washington" as Chief Engineer for the System. *Library of Congress*

Interior of Restored Northwest Bastion, Headquarters Replica and Gate, Fort Ward Park, Alexandria, Virginia. *Fort Ward Collections, Alexandria, Virginia*

President Lincoln's Summer Cottage at U.S. Military Asylum, the Old Soldiers' Home. *National Trust for Historic Preservation/National Park Service*

Gun Drill on Heavy Artillery at Fort Totten. *Library of Congress*

Lieutenant General Jubal Early, the Confederate Who Came Closest to Capturing Washington, D.C., Abraham Lincoln, or Both. *U.S. Army Military History Institute/Heritage Center, Carlisle Barracks, Pennsylvania*

Major-General John C. Breckinridge, Early's second-in-command and "Protector" of Francis P. Blair's Silver Spring Mansion. *U.S. Army Military History Institute/ Heritage Center, Carlisle Barracks, Pennsylvania*

Brigadier General Bradley Johnson, Maryland Cavalry Raider and Leader of the Baltimore/Point Lookout Expedition. *U.S. Army Military History Institute/ Heritage Center, Carlisle Barracks, Pennsylvania*

Major-General Lew Wallace, Defender of Baltimore and Washington on the Monocacy. *U.S. Army Military History Institute/Heritage Center, Carlisle Barracks, Pennsylvania*

Brigadier General John "Tiger John" McCausland; Early's "Eyes" and Early's Cavalryman on the Washington Raid Who Claimed to Have Breached Washington's Defenses and Viewed the Lights of the City from above Georgetown. *U.S. Army Military History Institute/ Heritage Center, Carlisle Barracks, Pennsylvania*

Major-General John B. Gordon, Early's Intrepid Division Commander Who Shattered Ricketts and Wallace's Defense at Monocacy and Later Claimed to Have Ridden Unchallenged onto Washington's Earthworks. *U.S. Army Military History Institute/Heritage Center, Carlisle Barracks, Pennsylvania*

Major-General Henry
Wager Halleck,
Grant's Chief-of-Staff,
Lincoln's Advisor, and
Grant's Washington
Regional Defense
Coordinator. *U.S.
Army Military History
Institute/Heritage
Center, Carlisle
Barracks, Pennsylvania*

Major-General
Christopher Augur,
Commander of
the Department of
Washington/XXII
Corps, Responsible
for Defending the
Nation's Capital.
*U.S. Army Military
History Institute/
Heritage Center, Carlisle
Barracks, Pennsylvania*

Francis Preston Blair, Newspaperman, Entrepreneur, Political Adviser, Country Squire, and Owner of Silver Spring Mansion, Jubal Early's Headquarters during the Attack on Washington. *Library of Congress*

Francis Preston Blair's Silver Spring Mansion, Guarded by Union Troops after Early's Retreat. *Library of Congress*

Artist Edwin Forbes's Impression of Jubal Early's Cavalry Driving off Cattle and Plunder for Lee's Army, a Diversion Detrimental to Early's Main Mission of Capturing Washington, and Which Engendered Harsh Feelings among Maryland Citizenry. Paul F. Mottelay and T. Campbell-Copeland, editors, *The Soldier in Our Civil War*, volume II (New York: Stanley Bradley, 1885), 302–3.

Brigadier General Martin Hardin, the One-Armed Brigadier Who Rushed from Convalescence to Command the Sector of Washington's Defenses First Tested by McCausland's Confederates. *U.S. Army Military History Institute/ Heritage Center, Carlisle Barracks, Pennsylvania*

Major-General Quincy Adams Gillmore, under Censure for Faulty Leadership during the Richmond-Petersburg Campaign, He Was Thrust into Command of a Portion of the Northeastern Defense Line and Arriving Contingents of the XIX Corps. *U.S. Army Military History Institute/Heritage Center, Carlisle Barracks, Pennsylvania*

Brigadier General Montgomery C. Meigs, Quartermaster General of the Union Army and Brevetted Major-General during Early's Raid. Personally Led a Provisional Brigade of Government Clerks and Convalescents to Help Stop the Confederate Threat to Washington. *U.S. Army Military History Institute/Heritage Center, Carlisle Barracks, Pennsylvania*

Heavy Ordnance Like This 100-Pounder Parrott Gun at Fort Totten (and Others at Forts DeRussy and Reno) Greatly Disturbed Confederate Wagon Parks, Bivouacs, and Troop Concentrations Camps during Early's Appearance before Washington. *U.S. Army Military History Institute/Heritage Center, Carlisle Barracks, Pennsylvania*

SIGNAL TOWER
FORT RENO
D.C.

The Signal Station at Fort Reno First Detected the Rising Clouds of Dust on the Morning of July 11 Signifying Early's Change of Approach to Attacking Washington from the Frederick-Georgetown Turnpike to the Seventh Street Road and Alerted the Northern Defense Line, Significantly Altering the Battle for Washington. *Library of Congress*

Contemporary Sketch Labeled "Night Attack on Fort Stevens, July 11th, 1864, While President Lincoln Was There." The Precise Details of Lincoln's Presence during Early's Attack on Washington Remain Elusive, but He Apparently Was Present at Fort Stevens on Both Days of the Two-Day Battle. Paul F. Mottelay and T. Campbell-Copeland, editors, *The Soldier in Our Civil War*, volume II (New York: Stanley Bradley, 1885), 297.

Contemporary Sketch of Union Skirmish Line Bivouac in Front of Fort Stevens by E. F. Mullen. Paul F. Mottelay and T. Campbell-Copeland, editors, *The Soldier in Our Civil War*, volume II (New York: Stanley Bradley, 1885), 297.

Major-General Alexander McDowell McCook and His Staff on the Moreland Tavern Porch, Brightwood, D.C., His Headquarters during the Battle of Fort Stevens. Like Gillmore, McCook Was under War Department Censure for Leadership Deficiencies on the Battlefield (Chickamauga), but He Was Placed in Overall Command of the Northern Defenses of Washington during Early's Appearance. *Library of Congress*

Major-General Horatio Gouverneur Wright, Commander of the VI Corps That Relieved Besieged Washington Defenders during Early's Raid and Who Subsequently Conducted a Deliberate but Dilatory Pursuit of the Confederate Retreat Back to Virginia. *U.S. Army Military History Institute/Heritage Center, Carlisle Barracks, Pennsylvania*

Brigadier General Frank Wheaton Temporarily Commanded the VI Corps Division from Which Two Brigades Conducted the July 12 Sortie to Disperse Early's Sharpshooters and Skirmishers. They Incurred a Pitched Battle under Lincoln's Observation. Mitchell's Crossroads North of Silver Spring on the Seventh Street Road Renamed Itself Wheaton after the War. *U.S. Army Military History Institute/Heritage Center, Carlisle Barracks, Pennsylvania*

Colonel Daniel Bidwell, Forty-Ninth New York, Commanding Third Brigade, Second Division, VI Corps, Led the Sortie That Evicted Offending Confederate Sharpshooters and Skirmishers from the Ground between Fort Stevens and Today's Walter Reed Army Medical Center. *U.S. Army Military History Institute/ Heritage Center, Carlisle Barracks, Pennsylvania*

Only Known Photographs of Temporary Union Graves outside Fort Stevens behind the Hospital Following the Battle, Later Reinterred at Battleground National Cemetery. *Courtesy of Gil Barrett, New Bern, North Carolina*

Artist's Impression of Early's Escape across the Potomac on July 14, 1864, Near Leesburg, Virginia. Early's Escape Prompted Great Controversy and Had Political Ramifications for the Lincoln Administration on the Eve of the 1864 Election. Alfred H. Guernsey and Henry M. Alden, editors, *Harper's Pictorial History of the Great Rebellion*, part 2 (Chicago: McDonnell Brothers, 1868), 708.

Only Known Postbattle Photograph of Fort Stevens Battlefield Looking North toward Toll Gate and Corner of Seventh Street and Piney Branch Roads with Site of Battleground National Cemetery beyond on the Right, Photograph by H. T. Anthony. *Courtesy of Minnesota Historical Society*

Special Artist E. F. Mullen's Caricature "The Sack of the Blair Mansion: Rebels Carousing Near the Garden Vase." *Frank Leslie's Illustrated Newspaper,* August 6, 1864.

Postmaster General Montgomery C. Blair Was an Ardent Unionist Member of Lincoln's Cabinet. His Falkland Mansion Was Occupied and Ransacked during Early's Occupation of the Area. A Modern High School Honors and Perpetuates His Association with the Area. *Library of Congress*

Sightseers at the Ruins of Montgomery Blair's Mansion Falkland. The Structure Burned Mysteriously as Early's Army Evacuated the Area, and It Was Thought to Be Retribution for David Hunter's "Hard War" Conducted Earlier in the Shenandoah Valley. *Library of Congress*

Francis Preston Blair's Silver Spring as Union Soldiers and Sightseers Saw It after Confederate Departure and Prior to the Blairs' Return. Silver Spring Escaped with Minor Damage Thanks to John C. Breckinridge's Intercession based on Ties to the Blair Family and Earlier Association with the Manor. *Library of Congress*

An Improved Battleground National Cemetery, 1865, as Veterans and Families Would Have Seen It. *U.S. Army Military History Institute/Heritage Center, Carlisle Barracks, Pennsylvania*

Third Massachusetts Heavy Artillery Officers and Men in Fort Stevens, 1865, with the Battlefield in the Background. Note: Lincoln and His Party May Have Stood and Been Fired upon on the Gabioned, Elevated "Lookout" in the Foreground Where Fort Massachusetts Linked to Fort Stevens. *Library of Congress*

Third Massachusetts Heavy Artillery Officers and Men in Fort Stevens, 1865, with Horatio Wright's Identified Parapet Where Lincoln Stood When Fired upon and Marked Today by the Lincoln Boulder/Stone and Battlefield in the Background. *Library of Congress*

Postwar General View from Fort Stevens, Showing the Battlefield Looking toward the Site of Carberry Farm, Walter Reed Army Hospital, Battleground National Cemetery, Site of Union Sorties on July 12 with Union and Confederate Skirmish Lines of July 11 and 12 in the Immediate Foreground, *Washington Times* Clipping circa 1915. *Lewis Cass White Collection, Joseph and Sharon Scopin, Darnestown, Maryland*

A Fort Stevens Survivor, the Famous "Sharpshooter's Tree," a Feature on the Carberry Farm/Walter Reed Army Hospital Grounds That Reputedly Served Confederate Sharpshooters during the Battle, Although It Is Uncertain If Any Shot Fired at Lincoln Came from This Sniper's Nest. It Remained Standing until a Windstorm after World War I. Photograph by Arthur R. Colburn. A Marker Today Stands on the Site. John Clagett Proctor, *Proctor's Washington and Environs: Written for the* Washington Sunday Star (Washington: self-published, 1949).

Other Fort Stevens Survivors: "Aunt Betty" Thomas Joins Veterans Seeking to Preserve Fort Stevens, Posing in Front of the Lincoln Boulder/Stone, 1911. *Historical Society of Washington, D.C.*

Burial of the Last Fort Stevens Veteran: E. R. Campbell in Battleground National Cemetery, 1936. *National Archives and Records Service*

The Monument to the Last Confederate Killed at Fort Stevens, Photographed in 1926. Plaque reads "Unknown Confederate Soldier Killed at the Spring by a Shell from Fort Stevens, July 12, 1864." The Monument, Erected by the Blair Family and Embellished with a Plaque and Parrott Shell, Has Since Disappeared, as Have the Grave and Its Occupant. *Library of Congress*

Confederate Dead Monument, Grace Episcopal Church, Silver Spring, Maryland, the Final Resting Place of Seventeen of Early's Men Killed before Fort Stevens and Interred in a Private Churchyard Where, Ironically, the Blair Family Were Parishioners. *Fort Ward Collections, Alexandria, Virginia*

Monument Row at Battleground (Left-Right): Company K, One Hundred and Fiftieth Ohio; One Hundred and Twenty-Second New York; Ninety-Sixth Pennsylvania; Twenty-Fifth New York Cavalry; with Superintendent's Lodge in the Background. *Courtesy National Park Service, Rock Creek*

Union Grave Circle, Flagstaff, Rostrum at Battleground National Cemetery. *National Park Service, Rock Creek*

Marker on Site of Famous Sharpshooter's Tree, Walter Reed Army Medical Center Reservation with Two Fort Stevens Cannonballs from Carberry/Lay Farm. *Fort Ward Collections, Alexandria, Virginia*

Front of Fort Stevens Restored Parapet. *Fort Ward Collections, Alexandria, Virginia*

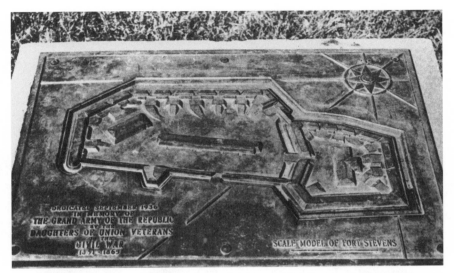

Bronze Scale Model of Fort Stevens, Dedicated by Sons of Union Veterans in Memory of the Grand Army of the Republic, September 1936. *Fort Ward Collections, Alexandria, Virginia*

The Lincoln Boulder/Stone atop Fort Stevens Parapet Today. Note Fac-simile Gun Embrasure and Revetment. *Courtesy National Park Service, Rock Creek*

Lincoln under Fire at Fort Stevens, Bronze Relief by Jakob Otto Schweizer Erected by Associated Survivors, Sixth Army Corps, July 12, 1920. *Fort Ward Collections, Alexandria, Virginia*

Artist Eugenie de Land Saugstad's Painting of Lincoln and Wright under Fire at Fort Stevens, July 12, 1864, as It Now Hangs in Superintendent's Lodge, Battleground National Cemetery. *Courtesy National Park Service, Rock Creek*

THE PRESIDENT IS ALMOST SHOT, JULY 12

Tuesday, July 12, 1864, was cabinet meeting day at the White House. Presidential secretary John Hay wrote that his boss "seemed in a pleasant and confident humor today." Word had come from Western theater commander William T. Sherman "that the enemy intend to desert Atlanta." That was not the case, although nobody knew it at the time. Lincoln was pleased, and the cabinet meeting convened at noon. The president, Secretary of State William Henry Seward, Secretary of the Navy Gideon Welles, Interior Secretary John Palmer Usher, Postmaster General Montgomery Blair, along with Attorney General Edward Bates, were in attendance. Blair, with his father, Francis Preston Blair, had taken a Northern Central train from Harrisburg on Sunday, and "the communications were not touched until Monday," wrote his sister Elizabeth to her admiral husband, Samuel Phelps Lee. Secretary of War Edwin M. Stanton was not there, much to Welles's chagrin. He had questions to ask about the major issue on their minds.[1]

At the moment, Stanton was solicitously trying to get Christian Commission staffers "to work their way around to Monocacy and look after the wounded in Saturday's battle" as well as placate Pennsylvania business and political leaders wishing to send more men and supplies. Lacking communication with Frederick, Maryland, thanks to the Rebels, and no means to ensure the wounded were relieved and the dead buried (perhaps accomplished by Harpers Ferry forces, he said), "I am anxious to know that it has been done." In any case, nothing of importance came before the cabinet anyway. The commander-in-chief seemed preoccupied with signing commissions and wondering about affairs in the suburbs. In fact, that was what Welles intended asking Stanton about.[2]

Stanton pretty well described the situation in an 11:00 a.m. telegram to Thomas A. Scott, president of the Pennsylvania railroad in Philadelphia. Supplies were sufficient but thanks for the offer, said the secretary. Plans to conscript manpower from all but essential war industries—as proposed by Susquehanna department commander Major-General Darius Couch and Governor Andrew G. Curtin, did not seem useful. "The apathy in the public mind is fearful," hence short-termers "could not be relied upon." As to the crisis generally, "The enemy have not made any assault on the forts, but are believed to be massing against Fort Stevens." Skirmishing was going on at other points. "There appears to be no doubt that the main force of the enemy is now around Washington, under Early and Breckinridge." Indeed, when Welles had asked Lincoln during the cabinet meeting where the Rebels were in force, the president replied that he did not know with certainty, but thought it was the main body at Silver Spring. "The President did not respond further than to again remark he thought there must be a pretty large force in the neighborhood of Silver Spring," recorded Welles. The fog of war pervaded everything. Had not Lincoln at 8:00 a.m. wired Grant by "cipher" suggesting vague rumors had been reaching the capital for two or three days "that Longstreet's corps is also on its way to this vicinity"? The president cautioned, "Look out for its absence from your front." Soon, some of these fretful public figures would again make their way to see what was actually happening at "the front." That front lay mainly at Fort Stevens.[3]

Moving to the Culminating Event

Curiosity also attended Jubal Early's Silver Spring headquarters that morning. The Confederate commander had decided to await developments when his muster of an assault column had failed so miserably on Monday. "As soon as it was light enough to see," recorded Early later, "I rode to the front and found the parapets lined with troops." Perhaps less enthusiastic than he had been the day before due to Blair's salubrious hospitality, a situational reality check in the clear light of dawn reconnaissance, and the psychological as well as physical fatigue catching up with the commanding general as it had his men, or receipt of intelligence, Early later reported to Lee that the assault, even if successful, would have been attended "with such great sacrifice as would insure the destruction of my whole force before the victory could have been made available." Had it proven unsuccessful, it definitely would have caused the destruction of his whole army, he added, catching the narrow margin of maneuver room in the tight situation. A sobered Early resolved to continue demonstrating before the capital during the daylight hours of July 12, and then to retire toward the Potomac after dark. Early said his infantry force now numbered only ten thousand men and characteristically mentioned "a considerable part of the cavalry has proved wholly inefficient."[4]

Yet what about "Tiger John" McCausland's postwar claim to have infiltrated Yankee lines and actually looked down upon a ruffled capital from the heights above

Georgetown? Had he not conveyed that feat to Early and suggested a beckoning opportunity? Moreover, Brigadier General Armistead Long's field guns when concentrated might well have suppressed counterbattery fire from the forts enabling either a surprise night attack (however unlikely given Civil War–era doctrine and practice) or a dawn assault. True, many artillery rounds had been expended while prying Lew Wallace out of his position on the Monocacy. Long, like his colleagues, depended upon getting to the Washington Arsenal for resupply from Yankee caches. Other reasons suggest themselves—the excessive heat and jaded condition of Early's men (a reason advanced by Stephen Ramseur to both wife and brother before his death in September), the disquieting impact of Monocacy losses and the day lost getting across that river, the Blair wine cellar, stiffening resistance from the reinforced Federals, Lee's imprecise and discretionary directives siphoning off manpower and focus, Confederate proclivity for foraging and straggling—or there was a basic failure of nerve on the part of Early and his lieutenants (possibly even common sense given a predictable bloodbath). The fact remained: the Confederates shrank from their planned assault on Tuesday morning, possibly saving Washington from capture and sacking. The day's action would settle once more into skirmishing, sharpshooting, and desultory long-distance artillery fire from the forts while waiting for something to happen or for covering nightfall to escape. As G. W. Nichols of the Sixty-First Georgia disgustedly phrased it: "We lay around all day (the 12th) and skirmished, and pretended like we would charge the enemy's works, till night." Colonel E. N. Atkinson (replacing the wounded Clement Evans as brigade commander in Gordon's division) similarly wrote petulantly in his after-action report that they lay in line during the whole day while "nothing of importance transpired."[5]

In fact, the initiative had passed to the Federals. Lincoln was ready, as was Grant. The generals and their men at Washington were less so. Chief-of-Staff Henry Halleck's word to Grant sometime that day sounded more like normal administrative trivia as to who would command the arriving XIX Corps or the Middle Department at Baltimore and other general army arrangements rather than resolving the major unresolved crisis on his doorstep. Only halfway through his dispatch did Halleck note the presence of only half the VI Corps and one transport of the XIX Corps, so that "till more arrive and are organized nothing can be done in the field." He thought Washington now to be "pretty safe, unless the forces in some part of the intrenchments, and they are by no means reliable, being made up of all kind of fragments, should give way before they can be re-enforced from other points." He carped that defending a thirty-seven-mile line "with an inferior force" was very difficult. He wavered as to just who the Rebels had brought before the capital, while "the boldness of this movement would indicate that he is stronger than we supposed" and that the enemy was massing "to attack us to-morrow" (however unclear that was given the date of dispatch). A subsequent prod by Assistant Secretary of War Charles Dana a half-hour before noon would prove more effective in getting the general-in-chief's attention at City Point headquarters.[6]

Grant and Lincoln had reached an accord that never would have occurred two years before with George McClellan in command. But such accord—mutual respect and understanding, no obvious political threat from a popular top general to a re-nominated president, and the ardent focus of both men to quickly defeat Lee and end the rebellion—translated to Lincoln's vote of confidence, and carte blanche for Grant to carry the war to the Confederate capital seemed dubious in the days between their last correspondence in the wake of Monocacy and the situation on July 12. It took the ever-fretful Stanton and then his alert assistant Dana, both skeptical of the army's energy and that of Halleck in particular, to jog things a bit that second day Early remained before Washington. It was more Dana than Halleck who ensured Grant understood the situation as well as the dysfunctional command setup that plagued the effort. In Dana's 11:30 a.m. wire, he assured Grant that no attack was being made on either Washington or Baltimore. McCook's artillery had been firing all night from forts Reno and Stevens (Dana called it by its old name "Massachusetts"). Wright had relieved McCook, who remained with his command and "is about to drive the rebel skirmishers away from his front, after which the artillery will cease." Then Dana got to the crux of the issue.[7]

Dana, an excellent fact-finder for the Union government, shed a spotlight since "nothing can possibly be done here toward pursuing or cutting off the enemy for want of a commander." In his often-quoted telegram that Tuesday, the assistant secretary of war noted how Christopher Augur commanded the defenses of Washington, Alexander McCook, "and a lot of brigadier-generals under him," but he is "not allowed to go outside." Horatio Wright commanded his own corps, Quincy Gillmore was assigned temporary command of those XIX Corps men who actually arrived in Washington, and E. O. C. Ord was sent to supersede Wallace running the VIII Corps and all other troops in the Middle Department while Wallace retired to Baltimore desk duties. "There is no one head to the whole, and it seems indispensable that you should at once appoint one," said Dana. Hunter would be the ranking officer, "if he ever gets up, but he will not do," especially since Stanton had declared "Hunter ought instantly to be removed, having proven himself far more incompetent than even [Franz] Sigel."

Dana even more strongly told Grant that Stanton "also directs me to say that advice or suggestions from you will not be sufficient." "Halleck will not give orders except as he receives them; the President will give none," and until Grant specifically "direct positively and explicitly what is to be done, everything will go on in the deplorable and fatal way in which it has gone on for the past week." An hour later, Dana sent a second wire raising the question about Longstreet moving down the Shenandoah to join Early's effort. "It is possible that the inactivity of the rebels in this vicinity is because they are waiting for re-enforcements," he raised. Given the uncertain state of communications, Grant's reply would not be received for over twenty-four hours. Washington's defenders were on their own for a second day.[8]

Tuesday at the Front

Meanwhile, events out on the lines set the pace. Roving *Chicago Evening Journal* reporter Benjamin Taylor thought that up to that time and, indeed, all the second morning of the crisis for that matter, "there had been no battle; only skirmishing and dashes of cavalry and soundings of our line." Confederate cavalry under Robert Ransom and John Imboden as well as John Mosby's partisans "had broken out in spots all over the country, like a case of malignant rash, but nothing tangible" as they soon "melted out of hand like a wisp of smoke." Meanwhile, our men were ready, said Taylor laughingly, citing Rear Admiral Louis Goldsborough's mobilized blue jackets "taking a hitch in their pantaloons and smoking their pipes and keeping a jolly eye out for squalls, with as much composure as if they were in the forecastle" rather than posted to Washington's forts in the Bladensburg sector.[9]

Still, the situation was this—the battlefront now stretched across the northern suburbs from west of Tennallytown almost to the Potomac, eastward beyond Fort Lincoln on the Baltimore Road, and almost to the Anacostia. The epicenter lay at Fort Stevens. In a sense, the situation on Tuesday morning had stabilized on the northern lines. The one-armed brigadier Martin Hardin reported from Fort Reno at 5:25 a.m. some firing on the picket line during the night and that a "rebel band heard playing, otherwise quiet." He needed some good troops for picketing and skirmishers and had heard nothing from the VI Corps. All that was quickly quashed by 6:15 a.m. when XXII Corps headquarters brusquely told him, "Fort Stevens is the real point of attack, the enemy's movement in front of Reno being but a feint." Therefore the VI Corps was being sent there. Hardin might "call for assistance from your right," but that was that. Not to be denied, Hardin kept asking and commenting how his cavalry reconnaissance went out on the River Road, how there were no indications of McCausland entrenching in his front, why he needed two battalions of heavy artillery as substitutes for light batteries ordered to Camp Barry (presumably to prepare to take to the field as such), and why "I think the citizens living within the range of the guns of the forts should be notified to go into town with such articles as they can take."[10]

Hardin had also strengthened pickets on the Brookeville Road toward Rock Creek overnight Tuesday as he reported Rebel horsemen trying to turn his position's right. Still, his surgeon in charge, R. Reyburn, would report only five killed and twenty wounded in this sector all day. So the action, while steady and sustained, could not have approached anything serious in nature. Sometime during

Tuesday Colonel Charles Lowell with two squadrons and Lieutenant Colonel Casper Crowninshield would escalate affairs by attacking and driving McCausland's horsemen back about a mile and a half. Ironically, Halleck's original misdirection of Wright the day before might have paid off had the VI Corps not been needed so desperately on the Seventh Street artery. They might have massed and gotten a head start via the River Road for intercepting Early's line of communication and retreat route. The decisive second day in Washington's suburbs might have been battle at Rockville or somewhere between there and Silver Spring. Or there might have been a delay until both sides massed near Darnestown or even Poolesville. However, the dire situation before Fort Stevens dictated events and the decision to hold on any counteroffense. Hardin's position at Tennallytown on Tuesday remained of secondary consideration.[11]

While predawn reports of general quiet also came in from the northeast and southern Maryland sectors, activity picked up as the day wore on, particularly when Bradley Johnson's raiders passed westward across the northern perimeter, seeking to regain Early's fold. They were moving rapidly now, having accomplished only portions of their mission. They had unnerved Baltimore authorities and ripped apart Union rail and telegraph infrastructure. They had set down at Beltsville on the Baltimore & Ohio link with Washington, deciding a dash to Point Lookout was impossible, and they would clash with Major C. Durland's Seventeenth Pennsylvania Cavalry detachment about three miles above Bladensburg toward Beltsville at the Paint Branch crossing of the main highway to Baltimore. In all of this, Johnson and Harry Gilmor raised feverish brows within Washington's fortifications. Navy Yard personnel rushed to Fort Lincoln, joining an ersatz band of XIX Corps arrivals, clerks, convalescents, government clerks, and citizenry from the Loyal Legion political bands in manning the forts across the northeast and beyond the Anacostia portions of the defenses. But that was about all.

Energetic scouting and reconnaissance by Federal commanders supplied better information on Early than he obtained on his opponents. Colonel William Gamble commanding the cavalry division at Camp Stoneman reported mounting nearly eight hundred riders on Monday and dispatching a twenty-six-man reconnaissance team "outside of this camp from the Potomac to Eastern Branch [Anacostia River], with orders for three men to guard the upper Eastern Branch bridge, arrest all suspicious persons prowling about, and collect information." Similarly, south of the Potomac, departmental cavalry actively patrolled the early warning lines with "scouts well out toward the gaps and towards Manassas," so spooked were they by Mosby's rangers. Yet the higher command knew the real danger zone lay in none of these places.[12]

Specific sites such as Fort DeRussy would see their share of activities as the second day wore on. Active in shifting his Veteran Reserve Corps soldiers around to relieve strain and fatigue, Colonel John Marble (One Hundred and Fifty-First Ohio

National Guard covered forts DeRussy and Kearny and Battery Smeade) advanced small contingents in front of his portion of the main defense. Subordinate George Gile, in fact, had half his men under arms at 3:00 a.m, ready and willing to take on all comers! Renewal of skirmishing and sharpshooting brought into question a barn belonging to the local Clagett family about 1,700 yards in front of the fort over a second ridge (now incorporated into modern Rock Creek Park). Like virtually every structure forward of the fortifications, the barn provided cover to Rebel marksmen. Marble had warned superiors John Warner and Martin Hardin the day before about this situation. In fact, he had determined the Confederates planned to unlimber a battery there. So Captain John Norris (Second Provisional Pennsylvania Heavy Artillery) had the fort's 100-pounder knock the barn to pieces.

Still, as time passed, it became necessary to send out a sortie from Captain Ezra Clark's Company H, Sixth Veteran Reserve Corps (VRC) regiment. They "advanced gallantly" until near the building when the enemy repulsed them from behind an ersatz log and brush breastwork. When the walking wounded succeeded in evicting the offenders, the Confederates sent reinforcements from the neighborhood of the Wilson farm to the north only to have them blasted again by DeRussy's cannon fire. "We opened on them, when they commenced retiring in considerable confusion," noted Marble, "were rallied by a field officer, but finally obliged to desist." One of the Sixth VRC claimed years later, "Through slashing [abates] by flank—drove 400–500 Confederates back to house," and "got every man of the forty back with bullet holes in clothing." Quite satisfied with their performance, the VRC boys might have sympathized more with Giles's particular concern about a high casualty rate sustained in this particular operation. This sharpshooter threat, in fact, became the salient feature of the "Battle of Fort Stevens" all day.[13]

McCook, Augur, and Wright themselves had spent the night trying to sort out the division of labor given conflicting orders and arrangements emitting from departmental headquarters. Five batteries of New York, Massachusetts, Pennsylvania, Rhode Island, and U.S. artillerists from Washington's defenses were redirected to Camp Barry, where they would reconstitute as four-gun batteries, three of light 12-pounders, and two of three-inch ordnance rifles. This implied preparation for the VI Corps counteroffensive field action. Eventually even Halleck saw fit to give Wright some latitude as dawn broke "bright and glorious," in the words of surgeon participant George Stevens. Renewed efforts took place on the skirmish line, with sharpshooters popping away at one another (if either had ever really ceased overnight) and the elevated booming of artillery from the principal forts. McCook simply reported later that the Rebels had begun it all once again, "opening fire upon our skirmish line, which had been intrenched during the night." But there was much lounging around waiting for something to happen. With Old Jube up and about and dissuaded from the planned assault, the moment of Confederate success had passed.

But the promised day of watchful waiting on both sides meant little more than what they labeled "demonstrating" in Civil War parlance. Still, not all in the Rebel ranks were content to have merely scared Old Abe but not taken his capital. And VI Corps veterans chafed for action. On the other hand, by this stage of the war, few soldiers wished to unduly risk life and limb, especially in the heat.[14]

Some overnight orders were specific, however. McCook's special order, in fact, directed Quartermaster General Montgomery Meigs to take charge of the defense sector from Fort Stevens to Fort Totten. He organized his 1,500 armed and equipped departmental "brigade" who, like Marble's people, "lay upon their arms all night." Moreover, 2,800 hospital convalescents took position in makeshift camps just to the rear. Of Meigs's three makeshift brigades, Brigadier General Daniel H. Rucker's (composed of QM men from the Washington depot, with a detachment of the Provisional Brigade) occupied the entrenchments between forts Slocum and Totten. Brigadier General Halbert Paine's second such brigade (Twelfth VRC, Second D.C. Volunteers, and three companies of the Washington QM depot men) similarly occupied the entrenchments from forts Slocum to Stevens. Undoubtedly these were the linen-duster-attired chaps that Rebels would jibe at for years thereafter. The third brigade (first commanded by Colonel Francis Price Jr., Seventh New Jersey, then Colonel Addison Farnsworth, Twelfth VRC, and finally Colonel Charles M. Alexander) collected the leavens from the department's hospital, convalescent, and distribution camps and encamped behind Fort Slocum.[15]

Although Lieutenant Colonel Joseph A. Haskin commanded the garrisons in forts Slocum and Totten, Meigs interfered when he found "the garrison of Fort Slocum was not as strong as it should be." He tapped Price to strengthen Fort Slocum, and 105 such specialists sprang to that task. "We got up wagons, rations, shelter-tents, cooking utensils, entrenching tools, axes, and worked to perfect the defenses and clear the timber and brush from our front," enthusiastically reported Meigs. All this bustling about subsequently earned the quartermaster general a brevet for a second star for meritorious field service on July 13. Thanking Lincoln and Stanton profusely, Meigs would record in a second official report how "the commission happened to find me exercising a full major general's command," with command of the right wing of that portion of the army that was directly in front of the enemy; "My command extended in line of battle two miles, and was 5,000 strong." Montgomery C. Meigs was prepared to make the most of his chance for glory when Jubal Early came to Washington.[16]

Skirmishing continued as "the day wore away." Even one telegraph operator in Fort Stevens wired a colleague, H. H. Atwater at Fort Reno, that "I am going out to take a shot at the rebels." But east of Fort Totten the rifle pits and other entrenchments were generally empty, recorded Meigs. He sent two thousand quartermaster personnel that way toward evening when Gillmore at Fort Saratoga became fidgety

THE PRESIDENT IS ALMOST SHOT, JULY 12

about Johnson's passage across his front. They encamped for the night near Fort Thayer, but by then the raider threat had passed. He detached four hundred more men to the skirmish line near Fort Stevens under McCook's order. "But two casualties" were reported among civilians from his department, he noted proudly, one a former employee shot and killed and to be buried "in the cemetery set apart by order of the Secretary of War for those who fell in the defense of the capital on the 12th of July." Meigs's efforts and the efforts of the men may have been an exception to the general languor displayed by both generals and privates for much of the day.[17]

Breaking up the Monotony

Sergeant A. G. Jacobs, Company B, Sixth Ohio Cavalry, one of the previous day's "first defenders," recalled brisk skirmishing kept up all night and Tuesday. About noon, he had spread his pup tent on the fence in front of an ersatz breastwork and sat in its shade to write in his diary. Soon an enemy bullet whizzed close to his head, and shortly thereafter one struck the fence within a foot of him. He looked up to see where the shots were coming from as another ball struck the ground a foot in front and plowed through and stopped directly under where he sat. "Yes, I drew in the flanks and retreated in good order," he recorded, and later "went and dug up that ball and kept it for 20 years and I looked at it [,] even then my nerves trembled to think what might have been."[18]

The *Washington Star* more matter-of-factly reported on July 13, "The soldiers not engaged in that skirmishing did not appear to be at all concerned about what was going on." Some joking and laughing in groups, others picking blackberries, "taking a chance of a compliment from the tube of a rebel sharpshooter"; a few such as artilleryman Frank Wilkeson watched from Fort Totten as Rebel cavalry rode aimlessly to and fro along the edge of a wood some five miles distant. He also spotted artillery glistening out there in the sun. Ohio sergeant Jacobs swore, "I positively know the enemy did not fire a cannon shot during the time they were threatening [Fort Stevens]." Everything seemed at a standstill except for the pop-pop of skirmishers and sharpshooters. The monotony seemed broken only by a seemingly endless stream of noisy, curious onlookers. For the most part, the road to Fort Stevens from Washington "was literally blockaded by pedestrians, horses and vehicles." By 4:00 p.m. guards would be posted "on the hill near the first tollgate to prevent civilians from going nearer the scene of the conflict. Those who got through were treated to the cat-calls of sarcastic half-drunken soldiery sneering at the unwelcome sightseers." "Skedaddle white livers," they chorused. Occasional humorous moments blossomed, as when Captain A. B. Beamish of the Ninety-Eighth Pennsylvania remembered commandeering a young couple's carriage to take a supply of ammunition forward to the skirmish line.[19]

Apparently at first rebuffed for help in Fort Stevens, an irritated Beamish then offered to show the civilian couple a close-up view of the spectacle from the tollhouse at Piney Branch Road. Only they backed out when "they heard a Minnie ball singing one of its peculiar songs." Undaunted, Beamish finally got the fort's ordnance officer to open the magazine and secured five boxes of ammunition "after a spirited parley" supposedly within hearing of President Abraham Lincoln's party, by this time present. How to get the ammo boxes back to his skirmishers, however? Spotting the carriage with lady and gentleman occupants, Beamish requested its use only to be rejected once more, especially because of possible injury to the invaluable horse. Beamish prevailed finally. They unhitched the horse, although who helped the captain push the ammunition carriage out to the battle line remains unclear. Beamish at least remembered, "We had a lively time before we reached our skirmish line, the enemy receiving us with a grand salute, the little Birds (balls) sang sweetly about us, and the way the dust flew was a caution."[20]

Treasury registrar Lucius Chittenden recorded how when he arrived at Fort Stevens in the early afternoon he was told that the Rebels still intended storming the place and "had filled the clusters of buildings" and occupied high ground to the north. There were sharpshooters "behind every stump and log and boulder," as close as "a hundred yards of our lines." Their fire had been quite effective, a Vermont captain friend from back in Addison County assured him—before the VI Corps arrived. Chittenden himself could see blue-clad skirmishers arrayed all across the front of the place in orchards and fields. Men in the rifle pits between forts Stevens and Slocum jumped up, fired randomly, and dropped back quickly into the pits for safety. Not a counterpart Rebel was visible, he added. "But from every square rod of it," he thought, "we could see the smoke and hear the report of the musketry." The Confederates, whether using Whitworths, P53 Enfields, or even short two-banded versions, had the upper hand over the Union-equipped Springfields or the even more rapid-firing Spencers and other breech-loading carbines.[21]

Chittenden found one bystander using a heavy American target rifle and field glass. "He was firing as deliberate as firing at a mark," noted the Treasury official. Singling out one fallen tree nest, the marksman fired and grunted satisfactorily that he "winged" the Rebel counterpart who had been firing all morning, killing two and wounding other Federals. That evening, Chittenden, roaming the battlefield, would discover that dead offender. The target rifle had indeed "winged him." But those sharpshooters in the buildings were what most worried the men on the skirmish line and in the forts. There wasn't anything strange about why the houses and barns were still there. Absent a defined threat prior to Early's arrival, there had been no reason to willfully destroy private property (some owned by loyal Unionists). Now, on July 12, there might be.

Fear of spy and secessionist collaboration was rife. Security became so critical that Colonel Moses Wisewell, the provost marshal, received orders to prevent citizen passage of the lines. Even Meigs reported small bodies of civilians milling around outside Union lines at Fort Slocum, seeking "places of refuge." He took stock of earlier reports from his procurement officers that in Prince George's County, Maryland, "a large proportion of the men only want opportunity to take up arms against the United States." Saner heads prevailed when Martin Hardin at Fort Reno simply suggested how "citizens living within range of the guns of the forts should be notified to go into town with such articles as they can take," regardless of any infiltration threat. Surprisingly, all this came despite the fact that Halleck himself had announced the patently obvious. As of 6:15 a.m., "Fort Stevens is the real point of attack," with enemy movements to the west at Tennallytown "being but a feint," and anything eastward equally so.[22]

The Fort Stevens sector remained the most volatile point. The offending sharpshooters, their untouched safe havens as well as the continuous taking of casualties—that was what remained uppermost. The generals talked all morning about repeating the previous afternoon's pushback of enemy pickets, but nothing happened. No artillery exchanges took place. No surging and recessional by either side developed. Civilian Lewis Chittenden, who had pulled up in a light wagon drawn by matching gray Morgan horses, recalled how his captain friend carefully chaperoned him to a safer location lest sharpshooters pick off both him and the steeds. After his observation of sniper marksmanship, Chittenden had entered Fort Stevens and found a viewing platform to be "a large stick of square timber [that] lay on top of the earth-work, raised a little above it, thus leaving a space through which the whole region beyond was visible."[23] Thus, the former Vermont judge glimpsed enough to provide posterity with a handsome word picture of what the Fort Stevens battlefield looked like from inside the point of maximum danger. From the bushes and logs hiding sharpshooters in the little valley to the front, he described the zing of the minie bullets and the cluster of buildings belonging to owners Selden, Reeves, and Carberry within a thousand-yard range providing ideal habitats for the Rebel marksmen. A game was going on between rival shooters, he thought—a deadly cat-and-mouse, life-threatening game with ample use of special marksmen's rifles and contingents of such warriors especially blessing the Rebel side. But the high point was not Chittenden's appearance or description of the standoff. Rather, it was the return of the president's party for a second afternoon of curiosity. "Leaving the ditch, my pass carried me into the fort," Chittenden recounted, "where to my surprise, I found the President, Secretary Stanton, and other civilians."

Lincoln under Enemy Fire

Many observers once again claimed after the fact to have seen Lincoln's tall figure return to the bullet-swept Fort Stevens parapet. The historical record for Tuesday

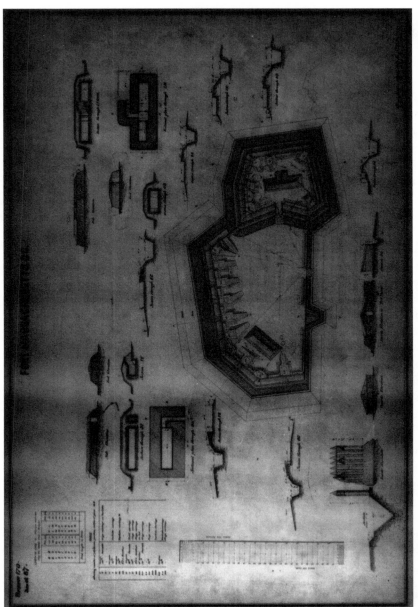

Fort Stevens/Massachusetts at the Time of the Battle, Engineer Drawing, 1864. *National Archives and Records Service*

remains almost as imprecise as Monday if only because of possible witness confusion of the two days in this regard. No doubt sometime after the Tuesday morning
cabinet meeting, Lincoln, accompanied by Mrs. Lincoln and Stanton (with cavalry
escort), joined the throng going out to the epicenter on the Seventh Street Road.
Somehow General Wright too appeared, for, according to one witness, the VI
Corps commander "in the forenoon . . . having made such disposition of his forces
as seemed desirable to him—rode into Washington some five miles away—to pay
his respects to the President and Secretary of War." Surgeon Daniel Holt of the One
Hundred and Twenty-First New York, arriving with his unit about this very time,
wrote his wife the next day that "Father Abraham, wife and son followed us in a
carriage to the walls of the fort and here I lost sight of the good man." But, "we have
learned to love him as well as he appears to love his boys in blue, and we all would
be willing to sacrifice anything for such a man and such a government."

All the while, "fighting continued more or less actively . . . but owing to the
forces in our immediate front, and the untiring activity of a considerable body of
sharpshooters occupying Blair's [Lay] Mansion, who picked off nearly every man
who raised above the parapets of earth that had been hastily thrown up—little of a
satisfactory character, was accomplished." At least that was the postwar observation
of Surgeon Cornelius V. Crawford of the One Hundred and Second Pennsylvania.
Present at the scene, he soon became a monumentally important figure in his own
right. Perhaps, along with Wright, this army doctor may have been the most creditable of all the witnesses. It was he who suffered wounding from a sharpshooter's
bullet while standing close to the commander-in-chief that fateful afternoon. Certainly no one, including reporter Ben Taylor noted any of this, although in dynamic
prose he told his readers, "The sun had burned its way clean through the day down
into Tuesday afternoon, and the enemy in that orchard you see yonder, was getting
saucy." There would be a lull, "and then, it was crack, bang and scatter; the gray and
blue skirmish lines, within short pistol shot in places, and elsewhere widening away
to rifle range, were playing 'balance to partners.'" It seemed like a battle to him, "very
much like the prefatory sparring of a couple of pugilists finding out the length and
muscle of each other's arms."[24]

Years later, Surgeon Crawford remembered also that "in the neighborhood
of five o'clock p.m., Wright, accompanied by Presdt. Lincoln—several cabinet officers, members of Congress—Mrs. Lincoln and several lady friends—returned to
the Fort." Crawford, like other observers that afternoon, wrote for others' benefit. In
this case, he recounted events as he remembered them to regimental comrade Lewis
Cass White thirty-six years after the fact. This would be the time when old soldiers
sought to place their deeds that day in context for the ages—especially to memorialize
Lincoln's presence under enemy fire on that parapet. Crawford regaled how Wright
(now in command of the operation), "after investigating the state of affairs which

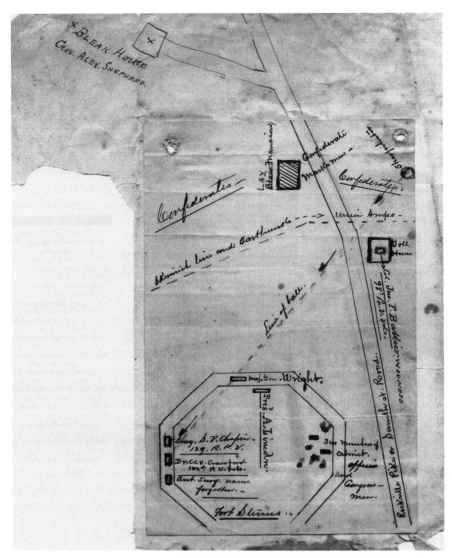

Surgeon C. V. V. Crawford's Sketch Diagram of His Wounding beside Lincoln at Fort Stevens, July 12, 1864. *Permission of Joseph and Sharon Scopin*

were not to his satisfaction," determined to shell buildings to drive out the large body of sharpshooters, "who had so greatly annoyed our line during the day, having during the forenoon, severely wounded in the right thigh Col. [John F.] Ballier of the 98th R[egt]. P[ennsylvania]. Vols. commanding the skirmish line and who was sitting in the toll house—his temporary headquarters [at the juncture of Piney Branch and

Seventh street roads].” Orders had gone to “the skirmish line to deploy right and left and to lie down until after the bombardment and then reform and charge the enemy.”

Wright, said Crawford, was dressed “in full uniform to his rank,” and laid down upon the front portion of the parapet of the fort, “reclining upon his left hand, face to the enemy and his field glass held in his right hand resting upon his right hip.” The president “stood within the Fort, directly back of Wright—his unusual height permitting a fair view of the movements in front.” On the side parapet of the fort, “left of front,” stood side by side as shown on an accompanying diagram to Crawford’s letter, Surgeon Samuel F. Chapin of the One Hundred and Thirty-Ninth Pennsylvania, then Crawford himself and a young medical officer from the Ninety-Third Pennsylvania. The rays of the July sun beamed full upon Wright’s belt and equipment, inviting sharpshooter retort from a distance to everyone’s right front.

“Armed with an English telescopic rifle,” suggested Crawford, “the prize awaiting his deadly missile—and so close was the bead he drew upon him, that the large conical ball passed between Wright’s fore arm and arm.” The “scream of such a ball as it rapidly pierces the air—so well known to any old soldier—and its dangerously close proximity impelled the President to involuntarily diminish the height of his personage—which he did by suddenly cracking his knees.” Wright, not to be outdone by his commander-in-chief, “quietly turned and rolled upon the sward inside the fortification.” “The dull ‘chunk’ quickly following the scream [of the bullet] evidenced very plainly the fact that some unlucky one had made too close an acquaintance with the unwelcome visitor,” drolly commented Crawford. He was that unlucky one, Crawford soon discovered. From that point, attended by his two medical comrades who cut the surgeon’s prized pair of riding boots, pants, and undergarment much to Crawford’s consternation, the witnesses all escaped a second sharpshooter’s bullet as the wounded officer was soon carried to the fort’s hospital building behind works “to the identical table which I had operated upon a number of other poor victims until about four o’clock.” The bullet extracted painfully, Crawford would then enjoy nine days of recovery at the Mount Pleasant Army Hospital downtown. Three months later, Crawford was discharged from the army, his term of service expired. Obviously, soon after wounding, Crawford had lost track of the president of the United States at Fort Stevens.

Crawford’s accompanying diagram with his letter to White showed his memory of where people stood and the general location of the prominent features of the battle, specifically the path of the particular sharpshooter who fired the offending bullets. His schematic drawing suggested more the shape of the original Fort Massachusetts portion as the location of the incident. The drawing could have been more abstract than literal, perhaps. Still, the ex-surgeon answered each of White’s questions forcefully and positively. He was shot at 5:30 p.m. on July 12, 1864, White recorded, and “Mr. Lincoln was within a few feet of me when wounded,” as

"I stood upon the parapet when shot." Mrs. Lincoln and accompanying lady friends were not permitted to enter the fort but sat outside in carriages that had conveyed the presidential party from downtown. They had come in open carriages, "the day being beautifully clear and very warm," said Crawford. He twice emphasized that only male members of the presidential party "came within the fort," for "none of the ladies were permitted inside," keeping to their carriages. Further, he stated, only Dr. Chapin had dressed Crawford's wound or ministered to his needs, and Crawford had no knowledge of the president's wife fainting, "and very much doubt if she did." News of his wounding so close to the president naturally spread, but Mrs. Lincoln at no time viewed his wound, "not having been permitted to enter the fortification in view of possible danger—and the outcome showed the wisdom of the commanding officer" in Crawford's mind. He admitted that he thought she had grown "faint and sick" when she heard Crawford had been hit, "simply, I think as a result of physical fear, and I believe Mr. Lincoln tried to rally her energies by telling her—'she would not make a good soldier, if she grew faint at the first sight of blood or scream of bullet.'" A perceptively caustic Mary Todd reputedly had replied, "But dear, suppose it had been you instead of Surgeon Crawford?"[25]

Crawford ended his epistle to White, "and now, my dear Comrade, the facts, as far as stated, are correct, and rest not only upon memory, but have been verified by careful reference to letters written my wife at the time these occurrences happened." She "has carefully preserved all my Army correspondence with great care," he added. "I am glad indeed to give you the solid facts in the matter." He repeated all of this a week later when White apparently pushed further, having in hand conflicting evidence from still another observer, but this time, while disclaiming "it is exceedingly easy to be in error after 38 years have elapsed, when memory also must be depended upon," Crawford would only add that he thought an assistant surgeon named Sturdevant of the One Hundred and Thirty-Ninth Pennsylvania may have been the young, unnamed surgeon "who stood immediately upon my right, and who kindly aided surgeon Chapin in removing me and examining and dressing my wound." Crawford could not comment about one vignette subsequent to his wounding. As he was carried off the parapet, Lincoln supposedly quipped how nobody now could claim that surgeons never got shot. Crawford's wound may even have come by ricochet off a cannon barrel before hitting the doctor.[26]

Where Did Lincoln Stand?

One might have expected more notice of Lincoln's presence in period diaries and letters. It was such a momentous event. Of course, that required close proximity to the scene. Among the very few who contemporaneously recorded Lincoln's presence was Elisha Hunt Rhodes, now commanding a veteran Second Rhode Island. Pointing to his unit's role in helping build Fort Slocum in 1861, while others in his brigade, such as the Seventh and Tenth Massachusetts, had constructed Fort Massachusetts, he noted afterward, "We did not expect in 1861 that these forts would ever be of service, but now we are glad that we helped to build them." As for Lincoln, "our column passed through the gate of Fort Stevens" late in the afternoon of July 12, together with their sister unit, the Thirty-Seventh Massachusetts, "and on the parapet I saw President Lincoln standing looking at the troops." Mrs. Lincoln and other ladies were sitting in a carriage behind the earthworks as Rhodes and his men marched in the line of battle out to a peach orchard in front of Fort Stevens, "and here the fight began." It was warm work, for a time, "but as the President and many ladies were looking at us every man tried to do his best." Rhodes added that "a surgeon standing on the fort beside President Lincoln was wounded." But this was hearsay, as Rhodes was off battling the Rebels at some distance from the parapet. Another contemporary, Private David T. Bull of the One Hundred and Forty-Seventh Ohio National Guard, wrote his wife two days after the battle that the president "and his doctor was standing up on the parapets." A sharpshooter perched in a house several thousand yards in front of the fort "shot the doctor through the left thigh, and Old Abe ordered our men to fall back." Typical, perhaps, of what observers heard, remembered, or simply thought they had witnessed, from this point the trail becomes distinctly reminiscent.[27]

Other observers later claimed to have seen Lincoln once more grace Fort Stevens's ramparts on July 12. Dr. George T. Stevens was sure the presidential party arrived at the barracks behind the fort about 4:00 p.m., "unattended, except by their coachman, the superbly mounted squadron of cavalry, whose duty it was to attend upon his excellency, being left far behind." According to Stevens, acting later as the VI Corps historian, the carriage stopped at the door of the hospital (set up specifically to service this battle's wounded), and "the President and his affable lady entered into familiar conversation with the surgeon in charge, praising the deeds of the old Sixth corps, complimenting the appearance of its veterans, and declaring that they, as well as the people of the country, appreciated the achievements of the wearers of the Greek cross." The party may have gone in and saluted the wounded, thus leading to the story that coming out of the building, Mary Todd Lincoln swooned, leading Old Abe to comment that she would never make a good soldier if she fainted at the sight of blood. One hospital volunteer, the Reverend Pliny Sanborne, that night recorded how he had labored all day in the hospital and grounds at Fort Stevens and witnessed plenty of casualties. But he never personally mentioned Lincoln. In any case, noted Stevens, "Thus for nearly an hour, they chatted of various things, when General Wright and his staff arrived on the ground, accompanied by several ladies and gentlemen from the city." Lincoln, Wright, and Dr. Stevens then walked to the fort's gate, where Sergeant Hiram Thompson of the Forty-Ninth New York challenged their entry. A ludicrous picture emerged of the commander-in-chief asking Secretary of War Stanton for a pass to do so, but once inside under Wright's invitation to see a battle (one that he regretted for the remainder of his days), the president's group (perhaps sans Mrs. Lincoln and the ladies) moved quickly to the parapet. Just where and when seems murky.[28]

Possibly, they moved around, the president seeking the best view. They may have stood momentarily atop part of the old Fort Massachusetts as suggested on the Crawford sketch map. Lincoln may have even been to the spot mentioned by Chittenden, which soldiers styled a "lookout" or raised portion of the wall joining the original Fort Massachusetts and expanded Fort Stevens. Here the extended fort blocked passage of a rudimentary Piney Branch Road extension toward the city. Of course, the ever restless, ever curious, lanky Lincoln may have been roaming even further along the exposed parapets. At any rate, high drama now attended the scene that afternoon. The blistering sun, the acrid smell of burning gunpowder, the hazy veneer of smoke, and the humidity-filled battlescape out front and the noise of gunfire all provided a backdrop for this tall man in a black suit and stove-pipe hat. Scarcely a mile away across the intervening gunfire was one of his 1860 presidential opponents, darling of the southern radicals, former U.S. vice president and something of a gadfly in Confederate flag ranks—fellow Kentuckian John C. Breckinridge. Even future leaders of a reunified country were present on that not-so-friendly field of strife—John B. Gordon of Georgia, Mark Hanna of Ohio, Edward V. Woolcott of Colorado, as well as Ohio philanthropist Lucian C. Warner and, perhaps, the future supreme court justice Oliver Wendell Holmes Jr.

Whether anybody besides Wright and Crawford truly saw Lincoln at a particular moment in history cannot be substantiated now. Supposedly, captured Rebels told Orderly Sergeant James H. Laird of Company K, One Hundred and Fiftieth Ohio National Guard, that they spotted him from the cupola of a house and fired at him. But Laird dated that incident as the eleventh, not the twelfth, so who knows? What is known is this. Many people were somewhere in the neighborhood as the minie balls sang and the cannon balls caromed while Lincoln took in the landscape. That is, until Wright became very, very nervous about how, in his own innocence, he had endangered the leader of the nation. Indeed, it may well have been Crawford's wounding that triggered Wright's sudden chagrin and anxiety. Crawford's misfortune may have even had a salutary effect on Old Abe's desire to see a battle or show his mettle before the men he so often sent to die for God and country. Recalled VI Corps veteran Thomas Hyde in 1895, "I saw the President standing on the wall a little way off"; an intervening officer between Hyde and the president "suddenly keeled over and was helped off." "Then a lot of people persuaded Mr. Lincoln to get down out of range which he very reluctantly did," he concluded. Beyond that, the record remains thin.[29]

Camp stories, postwar reminiscences, and the fading memories of old men years after the fact cloud the record. Pennsylvania color sergeant Lewis Cass White surely built upon others' accounts when he alluded that "the president was in the fort on the twelfth, standing on one side of a heavy cannon, Brigadier General Wheaton on the other when a sharpshooter in a cherry tree to the right of the road fired the ball passing near Genl Wright and the President" and wounding Surgeon Crawford of his regiment. White might have been in a position to personally know that "Pres. Lincoln and Stanton Secy of War came to Fort Stevens and Mrs. Lincoln with them." Beyond that fact, however, he had to rely on other accounts. White was guarding the colors while comrades manned the skirmish line. About noon, he went out "to the Toll Gate to the Picket line with mail for my co. (H)" and on the way back he and "two men on horseback and one walking under enemy fire and had to skedaddle." He added, however, that Mrs. Lincoln was "greatly alarmed when she heard Dr. C. had been wounded," a fact seemingly more memorable to him in 1880 than anything else, perhaps because that particular moment took place in closer proximity to where he viewed the day's action.[30]

Wherever Lincoln came under fire, a remorseful Wright apparently had difficulty "managing" the president, even with Crawford's wounding. The general informed his superior that he could not guarantee Lincoln's safety, and the two men may have haggled a bit about the constitutional prerogative of a chief executive to view combat in person. One account had Lincoln arguing that "as Constitutional Commander-in-Chief . . . he had a right at least to watch a battle fought by his own troops," with the general retorting respectfully but firmly that the sacred document said nothing about "authorizing the Constitutional Commander-in-Chief to expose himself to the enemy's fire where he could do no good!" Other accounts simply have Wright ordering the president off the parapet, and still others merely focused on the often-cited "Get that [damned] fool down." Indeed, that shocking utterance may have been emitted by almost anyone. Fort commander Lieutenant Colonel John N. Frazee (personally known to Lincoln), free black Aunt Betty Thomas (whom he had ostensibly met the previous year during her house demolition), and various lowly privates in the Ohio National Guard contingent numbered among those bystanders who later claimed credit for the suggestion (possibly without the expletive). Future Supreme Court justice and at the time one of Wright's junior aides (who happened to be transiting en route to discharge back to a Massachusetts civilian life), Oliver Wendell Holmes, loudly proclaimed authorship in his senior years. Holmes told select friends in later life how he had shouted "get that damned fool down." Yet his surviving diary lists no such utterance at the time. Probably Third Vermonter

George E. Farrington came closest to honesty. He said he knew the president was there but did not see him. "We were all busy watching the effects of the large shells from the fort and expecting to be ordered forward at any moment."[31]

In addition to Crawford's memory, two other accounts come close to completing the story of Lincoln's experience under Confederate fire at Fort Stevens. Both were by observer-participants at Fort Stevens: one emerged from the lowliest rank, the other via the top general on the scene. Private David T. Bull wrote to his wife simply on July 14, succinctly laying out the basic facts. "Old Abe and his wife was in the Fort at the time and Old Abe and his doctor was standing up on the parapets and the sharp shooter that I speak of shot the doctor through the left thigh and Old Abe ordered our men to fall back." Horatio Wright was perhaps the more authoritative commentator, although his official report contained no notice of Lincoln or Crawford's wounding. But in a reminiscence penned on the exact day of the event and subsequently sent by letter to doctor and VI Corps historian George T. Stevens for his 1866 corps history, Wright recollected the late afternoon hours when Lincoln stood under fire. The president "evinced a remarkable coolness and disregard of danger," said Wright. He then proceeded to explain why.[32]

Meeting the president while coming out of "my quarters," remarked Wright, "I thoughtlessly invited him to see the fight" without for a moment supposing the president would say "yes." Even so much as a moment later, Wright regretted the invitation, as Lincoln's life was too important to the nation to be placed in jeopardy by some chance sharpshooter shot. He might, for the corps commander should have known better. He owed his own position to the fact that predecessor John Sedgwick had been shot dead by a sharpshooter at Spotsylvania two months earlier while boldly proclaiming the enemy couldn't hit an elephant at that distance. But Wright's impetuous invitation now stood, and Lincoln took position by Wright's side on the parapet. All the general's entreaties failed to move him despite the passing shots indicating "the spot was a favorite mark for sharpshooters." When Crawford was shot and after Wright "cleared the parapet of everyone else," the president remained adamant. When the general told him, "I should have to remove him forcibly," the total absurdity "of the idea of sending off the President under guard seemed to amuse him."

Nonetheless, the commander-in-chief, realizing his subordinate's "earnestness in the matter," agreed to compromise by "sitting behind the parapet instead of standing upon it." Lincoln "could not be made to understand why, if I continued exposed, he should not." Wright's "representations that an accident to me was of little importance, while to him it could not be measured, and that it was moreover my duty" failed to impress a stubborn chief executive. Wright decided that Lincoln eventually left the parapet "rather in deference to my earnestly expressed wishes" rather than any consideration of personal danger to himself, however proven by

Crawford's wounding. Wright concluded that even after Lincoln departed the fire-swept point of greatest danger, "he would persist in standing up from time to time, thus exposing nearly one-half of his tall form." Some years later Wright embellished the wording of his remonstrance to his chief: "Mr. President, I know you are the commander of the armies of the United States, but I am in command here, and as you are not safe where you are standing, I order you to come down." That had raised a smile on Abe's face, humor hardly shared by Wright.[33]

Suffice to say, no contemporary account definitively identified the place where Lincoln came under enemy fire at Fort Stevens. Years after the fact, Surgeon Crawford suggested one location; Major-General Horatio Wright another. Perhaps their memory erred. Or perhaps an artistic sketch drawing was just that and no more. In the end, Wright's impression identified the spot where Lincoln stood and became the only sitting chief executive to have demonstrably come under enemy fire while in office. It would be there that VI veterans and their comrades from that momentous day would erect their boulder-stone monument. To this day, and beyond, Americans can visit that very spot for verification of the event if not the precise location.

Mr. Lincoln's Battle

We can be sure that not only was Abraham Lincoln shot at but also that as commander-in-chief, he was prevailed upon to actually issue an order during this battle. Again, who requested the order and at what moment this took place faded with the powder smoke. Certainly necessity existed—Rebel sharpshooters used civilian structures and treetops in the neighborhood. Victimized Union officers and their men wanted these noisome individuals taken care of. Months later, Lincoln substantiated that "I was present at Fort Stevens (I think) on the afternoon of July 12th 1864, when some houses in front were shelled by our guns, and understanding that the military officer in command thought it necessary, the shelling of the houses proper and necessary, I certainly gave my approbation to its being done." Guns from Fort Stevens and other works opened, the Carberry and Reeves suffered the fusillade of shells, and offending sharpshooters scattered like chaff. Shortly thereafter, the official party was treated to a "real" battle when Wright and other brass decided time had long since passed to push the Confederates back out of range and clear out sharpshooter nests once and for all. Perhaps "Mr. Lincoln's battle" never reached a stage comparable to the greatest engagements of the war. Yet a well-defined attack with artillery preparation, a textbook maneuver, all under the approving gaze of the highest official in the land, did take place.[34]

Lincoln's brush with death panicked everyone who had witnessed it. The orchard and shade trees on the Rives property plus Rives and Carberry or Lay houses on either side of the Seventh Street Road were festering nests of Rebel marksmen.

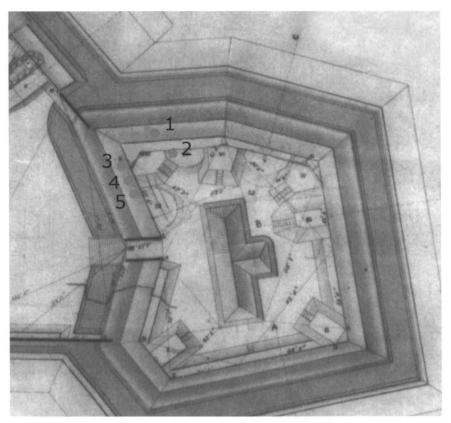

Overlay of Crawford Sketch Arrangement on Engineer Diagram of Fort Massachusetts Portion of Fort Stevens Suggesting Alternative Placement of Lincoln Party during the Crawford Wounding. 1 - Horatio Wright; 2 - Abraham Lincoln; 3 - Surgeon Chapin; 4 - Dr. Crawford; 5 - Name Forgotten; Graphics by Walton Owen. *Diagram, NARA*

The enemy simply lurked too close to Union works and skirmishers. The VI Corps had been "held well in hand," noted reporter Taylor, "for they chafed a little at hanging round the heavy artillery, and were eager to strike out." The Confederate's style "of rushing up, delivering his fire, dodging behind trees and scudding back to cover, making a rabbit-warren of the landscape, was not at all to their liking." Matters could not continue in this fashion. Under cover of darkness that night, "the enemy might advance his line, throw up breastworks within four hundred yards of the guns and pick off the gunners at his leisure." Union skirmishers were insufficient, and the invalids and others were not up to concerted assault. So McCook turned to Wright for more spirited and decisive action.[35]

In turn, Brigadier General Frank Wheaton (temporarily commanding Brigadier General George Getty's Second Division) received orders to deploy his own First Brigade with Colonel Daniel Bidwell's Third Brigade as instruments for a counterattack. Their mission—driving back the Rebels and occupying "if successful, two strong wooded hills in our front, the possession of which gave the enemy great advantage of position near our intrenched line," commented Wheaton. Nobody quite had the stomach for major combat in the fatiguing heat of late afternoon, Ulysses Grant's desire for annihilation of Early's threat notwithstanding. But what Bidwell encountered soon escalated. At first, cleaning out skirmishers seemed simple enough. Rounds from Fort Stevens guns penetrated sniper lairs and set those lairs afire. Dead and burned marksmen littered the yards, while less-heroic Rebels stampeded to the rear. Civilian Lucius Chittenden graphically captured the scene. Standing on the rim of rifle pits just east of Fort Stevens, he claimed to see almost two miles to Blair's Silver Spring mansion.[36]

Chittenden declared that the fields sloped gently down about one-half mile to a brook (later named Cameron Creek for its landowning Pennsylvania senator before this part of the battlefield became part of the Brightwood neighborhood and more especially Walter Reed Army Medical Center grounds in the twentieth century). The terrain then rose with similar gradient to a low ridge that provided the bivouac area for most of Early's foot soldiers. The slope immediately fronting the fort had been stripped of vegetation to facilitate defensive fire, and beyond the stream lay the fine, wooden Carberry house and outbuildings replete with cupola and owned by a member of the post office department, Richard Lay. A tulip tree subsequently became singled out (like the cupola) as a sharpshooter post (with a marker today still denoting the site). Slightly beyond lay the burnt-out shell of a house destroyed the previous day by the Federals. A small space around these two structures had been cleared, and then beyond that came a wide tract cover with oak scrub, six to fifteen feet high. Next came a large wheat field in which sizable numbers of Early's men could be seen, silhouetted against a larger woodland and the Roach house beside the road. The Blair properties stood further out, north of the District line in Maryland.

East of the Seventh Street Road, noted Chittenden, was "a large open space from which the timber had been first removed, and the stumps left standing." A recently constructed earthwork, probably for field guns, possibly for Gordon's battery, "stood a few rods from the rifle pits on a slight elevation." "To the left of this was a peach orchard in front of that a field of corn then an open space to the brook," he said. He also suggested that a few trees still stood in this area, while a field with ten- to twelve-foot-high scrub could be seen across the brook similar to that west of the road. The Piney Branch Road, which departed Seventh Street Road to the right at the tollhouse, cut across this sward, and a bridle path led to another well-appointed house surrounded by a large meadow and cultivated grounds (the McChesney property on John Gross Barnard's engineer map). According to Chittenden, a large virgin forest intervened between that structure and the Blair properties, although he must have meant the Carberry, not the McChesney, as Elizabeth Blair Lee reported the whole of their property stripped of forestland earlier in the war for fields of fire from Fort Stevens. By that point, Confederate soldiery filled the landscape, and skirmishers populated brushy sections on both sides of the Seventh Street Road. Today nothing but streets and houses of an aging city neighborhood and a derelict army facility fill the space. In 1864, Chittenden recorded that "not a man was visible but from every square rod of it as it seemed to me we could see the smoke and hear the roar of musketry." The "rapid discharges seemed peculiar as a brief spurt of smoke, gentle diffusion through the atmosphere and muted explosion due to distance were like a constant popping instead of the regular roll of musketry" to that civilian's eye.

Wright conferred with principals for the sortie and directed Bidwell "to move his command outside of the fort and, under cover of a ravine and woods, at trail arms, and every precaution taken to prevent the enemy discovering the movement, form in two lines in rear of [Wheaton's First] brigade (which was all deployed as skirmishers), and about 300 yards on the right of the [Seventh Street] pike, the position being entirely covered by scrub timber and underbrush." Bidwell was then told "to select three of his very best regiments at an indicated point a few paces in rear of our skirmish line and fronting the strong wooded position held by the enemy." The Seventh Maine, the Forty-Third New York (Lieutenant Colonel J. D. Visscher), and the Forty-Ninth New York (under Lieutenant Colonel George W. Johnson absent Bidwell) skillfully moved to their positions "without the enemy discovering the movement." Three other units, the Seventy-Seventh New York (Lieutenant Colonel Winsor B. French), the One Hundred and Twenty-Second New York (new to the brigade under Lieutenant Colonel Augustus W. Dwight), and the Sixty-First Pennsylvania stayed in reserve. As it turned out, elements from all these commands would eventually be needed in what turned out to be anything but an easy operation.[37]

Bidwell placed his units with the Seventy-Seventh New York, carrying a brand new flag at the right flank position on the first line with the Seventh Maine and Bidwell's own Forty-Ninth New York. A reserve picket of 150 men of the One Hundred and Second Pennsylvania and an eighty-man detachment from the Vermont brigade were to support the skirmish line immediately on the right and left of the pike. According to plan, Bidwell would signal his attack readiness by waving the Seventy-Seventh's flag, and the batteries of Fort Stevens and Fort Slocum would rake the houses harboring the nettlesome Rebel marksmen. Three salvoes would be fired, and after the thirty-sixth shot (equaling the stars in the national flag at the time), the brigade would charge forward. Meanwhile, the veterans lay upon their arms to avoid the enemy marksmen who began to claim victims as soon as the Federals moved beyond protection of the fortifications. The New Yorkers of the Forty-Ninth had camped upon this very ground in 1861, although only eighty-five survivors of the original one thousand stood to the colors. One survivor pointed out thirty years later, "This was the fourth battle that we had fought in defense of Washington—South Mountain, Antietam, and Gettysburg preceding." Eager to prove their mettle before their commander-in-chief as well as Invalid Corps and the 100-days men, they later considered none of the other battles provided "any harder fighting or heavier losses in proportion to numbers engaged," while "none was of more importance though scarcely known in history" than Fort Stevens.[38]

Bidwell's attack got off about 5:00 p.m. "In magnificent order and with light steps they ran forward up the ascent thru the orchard, thru the little grove on the right, over the fence rail, up to the road, making straight for this objective point, the frame house 'Carberry' in front," was the way Dr. Stevens regaled a VI Corps veterans' gathering at Fort Stevens in 1915. The Rebels at first stood their ground, then gave way "before the impetuous charge," and while "forced to seek safety in flight, turned and poured their volleys into the ranks of the pursuers." They surprised the Rebel picket line, which "skedaddled as fast as they could, leaving everything in their pits." As the Carberry mansion burned from incendiary shells and snipers dived from upper windows or were charred in the flames, the Down Easterners took the assigned ground and the Rives house before running into trouble. The fight lasted but a few minutes "when the stream of mangled and bleeding ones began to come to the rear." The divisional hospital set up just behind Fort Stevens soon witnessed "men leaning upon the shoulders of comrades or borne painfully on stretchers, the pall of their countenances rendered more ghastly by the thick dust which settled upon them" as they "were brought to the hospitals by scores." The Confederates rallied behind the Forty-Third and Fifty-Third North Carolina who rushed to the skirmish line and fought back fiercely. They were "found to be much stronger than had been supposed," Wheaton subsequently reported.[39]

The fighting continued well past day's end. Ohio cavalry sergeant A. G. Jacobs on the skirmish line remembered, "I think those hours from 6 to 9 o'clock were the noisiest I ever heard" since "the Sixth Corps got up and put in their work with a vengeance but then that was a way they had." There were anxious moments, and Napoleon smoothbore cannon from the First Maine Light Artillery joined the fortress guns bombarding Southern positions. Captain Charles Dupont of the Thirteenth Michigan Light Artillery claimed honors for "aiming the gun" that set one of the two targeted houses afire. Some two-dozen shots did the job on the Carberry place, claimed Daniel H. Bee of the Sixty-First Pennsylvania, who witnessed the barrage. Milton Evans, one of the Ohio national guardsmen present, said later that five men jumped from the upstairs windows but were all who escaped from an estimated thirty marksmen in the structure. "The balance burned up," he added matter-of-factly. The Federal guns then concentrated upon the survivors milling about in the road and surrounding fields as Bidwell's people swept forward. It was "as fine a bayonet charge as could be," wrote one gleeful participant. But Confederate resistance stiffened beyond the Carberry and Rives properties. Rodes sent line infantry and opened cannon fire on the victorious Federals, and a full firefight developed in the swale of the creek where Walter Reed Army Medical Center would later be established. Even the ridge to the north saw action, and Colonel Oliver Edwards (Thirty-Seventh Massachusetts) commanding the third brigade of the First Division, VI Corps, as well as Wheaton and Bidwell had to rescue the mission. Young William E. Ruggles from upstate New York recorded how his One Hundred and Twenty-Second New York ran out of ammunition, held position beyond the Rives place for twenty minutes, and then "fell back, rallied again, charged them without ammunition, and drove them back again" before finally securing more bullets from the rear.[40]

In Wheaton's words, "The enemy's stubborn resistance showed that a farther advance than already made would require more troops." So he pulled the Thirty-Seventh Massachusetts (Lieutenant Colonel George L. Montague) and Rhodes's Second Rhode Island to the battle line. The New Englanders were on familiar ground now, having encamped at Brightwood and vicinity three years earlier, and "as the President and many ladies were looking at us every man tried to do his best." "An old gentleman, a citizen in a black silk hat with a gun in his hand, went with us," jotted Rhodes in his diary, and "taking position behind a stump fired as cool as a veteran." But before Montague and Rhodes could arrive from Edwards's brigade, one of Wright's aides informed him "not to attempt more than holding of the position I had gained, as the object of the attack had been accomplished and the important points captured and held."[41]

The Confederates subsequently claimed to have repulsed Bidwell three times and retired from the field only after dark. Some Federals claimed similar rebuffs in counterattacking their opponents. Possibly Colonel E. N. Atkinson filed the most complete accounting of the Confederate side of the fight. Part of Evans's brigade of Gordon's division, his unit had been badly used up at Monocacy. Now, noting how the Federals had started the latest affair by firing at the houses protecting sharpshooters and then making "an attempt on our line," Atkinson noted that "they were driven back in our immediate front, but succeeded in driving the troops on our right back, which compelled the troops of this brigade or rather the Fifty-Third North Carolina Regiment and the sharpshooters, to fall back (the Thirty-Second North Carolina Regiment was watching the right flank), and immediately the Forty-Third North Carolina Regiment and the Forty-Fifth North Carolina were deployed as skirmishers and ordered to the front." They "went beautifully," said Atkinson, joining the Fifty-Third and the sharpshooters, and soon had a stable position established west of the Seventh Street Road. Those on the eastern side of the road, however, "could not succeed in going quite as far as their original line." His North Carolinians had fought well under heavy enemy artillery fire, he claimed. They lacked artillery fire support as they had enjoyed at Monocacy. Besides, "The enemy had decidedly the advantage in position, but our men went up cheerfully and confidently."[42]

Closing Down Lincoln's Battle

Nightfall brought a close to the brisk combat. The Federals retained the battlefield. District of Columbia militiaman Abraham Kingsland, present in the trenches, wrote his brother in California three months later how McCook "sent the sixth Corps on the advance while we were held as reserve [and] when we advanced they fetched up their Artillery and tried to get it in position but they failed for [the forts] were playing on both sides and in an hour and half time they were over the hill and out of sight." "I tell you," he continued, "it was a beautiful sight to see the shells flying with such rapid force and burst among the Rebs ranks. Next morning there [was] not a living Reb to be seen." "It took sixty minutes in all, and that was the end of it, and that was all of it," recorded Ben Taylor. Indeed, McCook and Wright had realized Wheaton and Bidwell's force was too small to accomplish much more and held the enthusiastic soldiery from bringing on heavier action. Besides, as Wheaton later observed, "this whole attack was as gallant as it was successful, and the troops never evinced more energy and determination." Still, he contended, "the losses were very severe, the brave Colonel Bidwell losing many of his most valuable regimental commanders."[43]

Casualties had been high for both sides. All of Bidwell's regimental commanders had been shot down, plus 250 to 375 were killed or wounded from a command numbering but one thousand brigade total (the authorized regimental strength at the beginning of the war). New Yorker S. A. McDonald observed after the war "that the percentage of killed was unusually large" shown in comparison to Antietam, Chancellorsville, and Gettysburg, where taken as a whole, Union losses in killed alone were "16.3 per cent of the aggregate killed and wounded." The Fort Stevens figure for Bidwell's command alone stood at 35.8 percent, he noted, with the Forty-Ninth New York alone losing twenty-six of eighty-five men in its ranks. Early never admitted much impact made by the late afternoon battle. He merely cited "a heavy reconnoitering force" sent out by the enemy and was never pinned down for total casualties over the two-day affair. Union quartermaster general Meigs was less charitable, claiming categorically that the sharp contest that afternoon cost "each party 300 casualties."[44]

There were certainly pockets of sharp fighting across the front lines, not just where Bidwell and Wheaton held forth. Indeed, the First and Sixth VRC regiments had had their own spirited engagement when they dislodged Confederate sharpshooters from Clagett family buildings west of Rock Creek. And apparently the tired, dismounted cavalrymen from the Twenty-Fifth New York also participated in the heavy skirmishing that day in front of Fort DeRussy. Effective fire from their Burnside carbines "began to be apparent in the number of stretchers which the Rebs began to bring into requisition on their side of the field." The cavalrymen kept up an incessant fire until six o'clock that evening, "when our lines of battle advanced, and attacked the Rebs in their chosen position, and after about three hours' hard fighting we drove them over three miles, the Rebels burning the farmhouses as they retreated." Far to the east, Gillmore's people may have placidly watched Bradley Johnson's Confederates ride across their front seeking to rejoin the main army. But civilian Lucius Chittenden claimed to have seen a last-minute spirited Rebel cavalry charge to bolster Rodes's position, but nobody else did. Monocacy captive William G. Browning of the Ninth New York Heavy Artillery and his mates watched the day from the Confederate lines, and at the close of Bidwell's attack they had been marched to the rear under heavy guard. Just then "the whole rebel army came pell mell, almost a stampede: with infantry and the drovers and their captured livestock pouring across the fields with artillery and cavalry seeking to escape by road." The final casualty of the Battle of Fort Stevens may have been a lonely, unknown Confederate sharpshooter, cut off in this retirement, shot, and buried where he fell on the edge of Preston Blair's Silver Spring estate. He would have been lost to history except that a member of the Blair clan eventually erected a small marker over his gravesite, although in twentieth-century development of the area, even that last small monument to the Confederate highwater mark has been erased from the landscape.[45]

Under withdrawal orders from Old Jube himself, very few of the cocky Rebel raiders ever admitted that they had been bested in the day's action. Most of them saw the events of July 12 as "little more than a heavy skirmish" and one "easily repulsed." Whatever the perspective, both sides were more than happy to let day slip into yet another hot night. Wheaton spoke for the Federal side: "The last shot was fired about 10 o'clock, and the remainder of the night was occupied in strengthening the position, burying the dead, and caring for the wounded, and relieving the skirmish line, which had been two days in front constantly under fire." That task would be accomplished by the Second Brigade of Vermonters by 4:00 a.m. Wednesday, the thirteenth. With the enemy reported "moving away from our front in the direction of Rockville" that next morning, continued Wheaton, the command in the afternoon "joined in the march on the new campaign, which culminated in the brilliant victories of the Valley of the Shenandoah." All in a day's work for the VI veterans. What had occurred at Fort Stevens would pale in comparison.[46]

So this was what Abe Lincoln had risked life and limb to see. Just how much he actually witnessed of the Bidwell assault and how much was obscured by smoke and haze eludes us. Afterward, the chief executive and his party undoubtedly congratulated the generals, took leave of the sweaty soldiery, perhaps consoled the wounded in the hospital behind the fort one final time, and perhaps passed the first makeshift graves just outside that structure's door. One Rhode Island cavalryman claimed years later that together with sixteen comrades he picketed a field just inside the District line, near the road when Lincoln's carriage drove up. Rear guard Rebel cavalry opened fire not thirty yards away. Simmons claimed he told Lincoln and his coachman ("no cowards," in their own right), "This is no place for you," and led him down a two-foot embankment, assisted him into the carriage, and they drove back to Washington. Perhaps it had been really Monday, not Tuesday evening; soldier memories were notoriously imprecise about Lincoln and the two days he appeared at Fort Stevens. In any case, after the battle on the twelfth, together with his wife and the other high officials, the president regained his carriage, his official escort, and returned to the White House. They had all seen their battle, the battle that saved their capital and government. A couple of days later, Mrs. Lincoln, who did not think much of the irascible Stanton anyway, would tell him bluntly that had she had "a few ladies with me" at the fight, Early and his troops would not have escaped, as they proceeded to do with impunity. Mrs. Lincoln, among many, had not been in awe of the military's performance. Luckily, the president had not been a casualty himself.[47]

As for their opponents, perhaps Major Henry Kyd Douglas of Early's staff captured the essence of the Bidwell-Rodes fight. He recounted an evening meeting with Early, Breckinridge, and Gordon at Blair's Silver Spring mansion. Whether in "a droll humor, perhaps one of relief," Early quipped in his famous twang, "Major, we haven't taken Washington, but we've scared Abe Lincoln like hell!" Unmoved, Douglas rejoined incautiously, "Yes, general, but this afternoon when that Yankee line moved out against us, I think some other people were scared blue as hell's brimstone!" Was that true, asked Breckinridge with a laugh? "That's true," muttered Old Jube, "but it won't appear in history!" Others in butternut and gray left Washington's suburbs with the same swagger they had come with.[48]

Early and his compatriots were not the only disappointed onlookers that night. Civilian patent office official Horatio Nelson Taft commented in his diary that night how "the day has passed away and no serious attack has been made upon the City." He cited constant skirmishing along the lines north of the city, cutting of the rail link with Baltimore, burning the bridge at Laurel, and occupying Bladensburg as highlights. So, too, was the report "that a rebel force has appeared on the Virginia side of the Potomac not many miles south of the City." He had listened to considerable heavy firing about sundown and later attributed it possibly to "some of our Forts getting the range by practice." He cited the militia and civilian government worker call-up. Reports of fighting near Tennallytown and Fort Reno had caused him to take a stagecoach up from Georgetown "in the hope of seeing something of the fight, a Shell burst &c." But he came away unfulfilled since "no fighting was going on there and consequently no Shells flying, and more than that I was not allowed to remain but a few minutes, all civilians being ordered presumptorily to leave forthwith." As he had not anticipated staying any longer than the stagecoach did itself, he was not too disappointed. Off to the east from one-half to two miles, "I could hear the constant report of musketry and see the puffs of smoke" of the Fort Stevens battle, but he got no closer than that to real combat. Returning to Georgetown about 5:00 in the afternoon, "after my return to this City I went on top of the Patent office with a good glass [telescope] but could see nothing."[49]

Notes

1. Tyler C. Dennett, editor, *Lincoln and the Civil War in the Diaries and Letters of John Hay* (New York: Dodd Mead, 1939), 209; Virginia Jeans Laas, editor, *Wartime Washington: The Civil War Letters of Elizabeth Blair Lee* (Urbana: University of Illinois Press, 1991), 403.

2. U.S. War Department, *War of the Rebellion: The Official Records of Union and Confederate Armies* (Washington, DC, 1880–1901) Series I, Volume 37, part 2, 256, hereinafter cited *ORA*, with appropriate volume, part, and page.

3. *ORA*, I, 37, pt. 2, 221, 223–24, 255–56; Gideon Welles, *Diary*, volume II (Boston: Houghton Mifflin, 1909), 74.

4. *ORA*, I, 37, pt. 1, 348.

5. E. N. Atkinson, "Report of Evans Brigade," July 22, 1864, Eldridge Collection, Huntington Library (HL), San Marino, CA; G. W. Nichols, *A Soldier's Story* (Jessup, GA: Continental Book Company, 1890), 172.

6. *ORA*, I, 37, pt. 2, 221–23.

7. *ORA*, I, 37, pt. 2, 223.

8. *ORA*, I, 37, pt. 2, 223–24.

9. Benjamin F. Taylor, *Pictures of Life in Camp and Field* (Chicago: S. C. Griggs and Company, 1888), 215.

10. *ORA*, I, 37, pt. 1, 236–37 and pt. 2, 237–41.

11. *ORA*, I, 37, pt. 1, 239.

12. *ORA*, I, 37, pt. 1, 245 and pt. 2, 241–45.

13. *ORA*, I, 37, pt. 1, 238–43, 344–45; "M.B. Smokey," "Defense of the Capital—The Veteran Reserve Corps Experience," undated clipping, *National Tribune*, Lewis Cass White Collection, Joseph and Sharon Scopin, Darnestown, Maryland.

14. *ORA*, I, 37, pt. 1, 232 and pt. 2, 208–9.

15. *ORA*, I, 37, pt. 1, 255–56, 258–59.

16. *ORA*, I, 37, pt. 1, 259.

17. See also *ORA*, I, 37, pt. 1, 258–63; and David W. Miller, *Second Only to Grant: Quartermaster General Montgomery C. Meigs* (Shippensburg, PA: White Mane, 2000), 238–39;

David Homer Bates, *Lincoln in the Telegraph Office: Recollections of the United States Military Telegraph Corps during the Civil War* (New York: Century Company, 1907), 254.

18. A. G. Jacobs, "Getting There on Time—A Dismounted Cavalryman Tells about the Fort Stevens Fight," undated clipping, *National Tribune*, Lewis Cass White Collection, Joseph and Sharon Scopin, Darnestown, Maryland.

19. Frank Wilkeson, *Turned Inside Out: Recollections of a Private Soldier in the Army of the Potomac* (Lincoln: University of Nebraska Press, 1997 edition), 214; *Washington Star*, July 13, 1864; Jacobs, "Getting There on Time," ibid.

20. A. B. Beamish, "Battle of Fort Stephens [*sic*] Near Washington, D.C., July 12, 1864," *Grand Army Scout and Soldiers Mail*, Saturday, July 10, 1886.

21. Lucius B. Chittenden, *Recollections of President Lincoln and His Administration* (New York: Harper and Brothers, 1891), 424–25; Fred L. Ray, *Shock Troops of the Confederacy: The Sharpshooter Battalions of the Army of Northern Virginia* (Asheville, NC: CFS Press, 2006), 161, 170, chapter 22.

22. *ORA*, I, 37, pt. 2, 224–44 inter alia.

23. Chittenden, *Recollections*, 411–15.

24. Taylor, *Pictures of Life in Camp and Field*, 216; Cornelius V. A. Crawford to Lewis Cass White, September 17, 1900, White collection, Sharon and Joseph Scopin, Darnestown, Maryland; James M. Greiner, Janet L. Coryell, and James R. Smither, editors, *A Surgeon's Civil War: The Letters and Diary of Daniel M. Holt, M.D.* (Kent, OH: Kent State University Press, 1994), 219–20.

25. Crawford to White, ibid.

26. Joseph Judge, *Season of Fire: The Confederate Strike on Washington* (Berryville, VA: Rockbridge Publishing Company, 1994), 251.

27. Robert Hunt Rhodes, editor, *All for the Union: The Civil War Diary and Letters of Elisha Hunt Rhodes* (New York: Orion, 1991), 171–79, and Bull's letter to wife, July 14, 1864, in John Henry Cramer, *Lincoln under Enemy Fire: The Complete Account of His Experience during Early's Attack on Washington* (Baton Rouge: Louisiana State University Press, 1948; Knoxville: University of Tennessee Press, 2009), 27, and Crawford to White, September 25, 1900, also White collection, Joseph and Sharon Scopin, Darnestown, Maryland.

28. George T. Stevens, *Three Years in the Sixth Corps* (Albany, NY: S. R. Gray, 1866), 374–75; Pliny Fiske Sanborne, "Diary" (Museum of the Confederacy), July 12, 1864, and "The Veterans Column," Fayetteville, NY *Weekly Recorder*, July 19, 1888, quoted in Marc Leepson, *Desperate Engagement: How A Little-Known Civil War Battle Saved Washington, D.C., and Changed American History* (New York: St. Martin's, 2007), 201.

29. On sources recounting Lincoln at Fort Stevens, see Thomas W. Hyde, *Following the Greek Cross* (Boston: Houghton Mifflin, 1895), 223; also C. H. Enos, "Fort Stevens," *National Tribune*, March 23, 1916; George E. Farrington, "Sixth Corps at Fort Stevens," *National Tribune*, July 12, 1913; B. T. Plugh, "Fort Stevens," *National Tribune*, September 23, 1915; Isaac A. Hawk, "Fort Stevens," *National Tribune*, September 27, 1900; John B. Southard to sister, July 16, 1864, Southard Family papers, New York Historical Society (NYHS); A. B. Beamish, "Battle of Fort Stephens [*sic*] near Washington, D.C., July 12, 1864, A Little Different Version," *Grand Army Scout and Soldiers Mail* (Philadelphia),

Saturday, July 10, 1886; Albert A. Safford, "Saw Lincoln at Fort Stevens," *National Tribune*, April 4, 1912; Oliver Edwards, "President Lincoln at Fort Stevens," *National Tribune*, August 20, 1903; Lewis Cass White, "President Lincoln at Fort Stevens," *National Tribune*, March 6, 1913; Lucien C. Warner, *The Story of My Life* (New York, 1914), 47–48; James Cannon, *Record of Service of Company K, 150th O.V.I.* (n.p., 1903), 16, 26, and *Memorial, 150th Ohio, Company K* (Cleveland: n.p., 1907), 8–10; John H. Bierck, "He Saw Lincoln under Fire," *Liberty* XIV (1937): 7; Frederick W. Seward, *Reminiscences of a War-Time Statesman and Diplomat* (New York: G. P. Putnam's Sons, 1916), 249; Stevens, *Three Years in the Sixth Corps*, 374–75; Penrose G. Mark, *Red, White and Blue Badge: History of the Ninety-Third Pennsylvania* (Harrisburg: Aughinbaugh Press, 1911), 280; Frederick D. Bidwell, compiler, *History of the Forty-Ninth New York Volunteers* (Albany, NY: J. B. Lyon Company, 1916); Howard Thomas, *Boys in Blue from the Adirondack Foothills* (Prospect, NY: Prospect Books, 1960), 227; Frederick C. Hicks, "Lincoln, Wright, and Holmes at Fort Stevens," *Journal of the Illinois State Historical Society* XXXIX (September 1946): 329–30; Dennett, *Lincoln and the Civil War*, 208; Augustus C. Buell, *The Cannoneer* (Washington, DC: National Tribune, 1890), 271; Jim Leeke, *A Hundred Days to Richmond: Ohio's "Hundred Days" Men in the Civil War* (Bloomington: Indiana University Press, 1999), 133–34.

30. Lewis Cass White, unpublished autobiographical sketch, June 16, 1880, Lewis Cass White Collection, Joseph and Sharon Scopin, Darnestown, Maryland.

31. Cramer, *Lincoln under Enemy Fire*, chapters 2 and 3, especially 26–27, 30–32; also John Y. Simon, editor, *The Papers of Ulysses S. Grant*, volume 11 (Carbondale: Southern Illinois University Press), 222, footnote 1.

32. Recounted in Cramer, *Lincoln under Enemy Fire*, 26–27, 30–31.

33. Ibid., 30–32.

34. "Lincoln's Order When under Fire," *Washington Herald*, May 31, 1908; A. G. Jacobs, "Getting There on Time—A Dismounted Cavalryman Tells About the Fort Stevens Fight," undated clipping, *National Tribune*, Lewis Cass White Collection, Joseph and Sharon Scopin, Darnestown, Maryland.

35. Taylor, *Pictures of Life in Camp and Field*, 216.

36. Lucius Chittenden, "A Chapter for My Children to Read," unpublished manuscript, copy, Defenses of Washington files, Fort Ward Museum and Park, Alexandria, Virginia (FWMP); see also John Gross Barnard, *A Report on the Defenses of Washington* (Washington, DC: Government Printing Office, 1871), plate 10; S. A. McDonald, "Fort Stevens Affair, Part 1," *National Tribune*, April 12, 1894, and "Part 2," April 19, 1894; *ORA* I, 37, pt. 1, 276.

37. *ORA*, I, 37, pt. 1, 276, also 271–72.

38. For firsthand accounts of the afternoon battle, in addition to those aforementioned, see *ORA*, I, 37, pt. 1, 230–79, 348, as well as I, 43, pt. 1, 603; Southard to Sister, July 16, 1864, NYHS; McDonald, "Fort Stevens Affair," ibid.; Milton Evans, "Fort Stevens," *National Tribune*, March 30, 1916; John D. Shuman, "War at Fort Stevens," *National Tribune*, March 7, 1912; Edward H. Fuller, "Fort Stevens," *National Tribune*, July 22, 1915; Stevens, *Three Years with the Sixth Corps*, 371–78; Mason W. Tyler, *Recollections of the Civil War* (New York: Badgley Publishing, 1912), 245; Welles, *Diary*, I, 75; Albert G. Riddle, *Recollections of War Times: Reminiscences of Men and Events in Washington, 1860–1865* (New York: G. P.

Putnam's Sons, 1895), 288; William V. Cox, "The Defenses of Washington: General Early's Advance on the Capital and the Battle of Fort Stevens, July 11 and 12, 1864," *Records of the Columbia Historical Society, Volume IV* (1901), 16–22, as well as his remarks in Cannon, *Record of Co. K*; Mark, *Red, White and Blue Badge*, 280; Bidwell, *Forty-Ninth New York*, 64–65; Alanson A. Haines, *History of the Fifteenth Regiment New Jersey Volunteers* (New York: Jenkins and Thomas, 1883), 226–27; James L. Bowen, *History of the Thirty-Seventh Regiment, Massachusetts* (New York: C. W. Bryan and Company, 1884), 352–53; Tyler, *Recollections of the Civil War*, 244–46; State of Maine, Adjutant Generals Office, *Report, 1864* (Augusta, 1864), 228, 233, 320.

39. *ORA*, I, 37, pt. 1, 276; Cary Whitaker diary, July 12, 1864, Southern Historical collection, University of North Carolina Library, Chapel Hill (SHC/UNCL); Leeke, *A Hundred Days to Richmond*, 136; "Reunion of the Sixth Corps," *National Tribune*, October 15, 1915, Lewis Cass White collection, Joseph and Sharon Scopin, Darnestown, Maryland; Dwight letter, "Veterans Column," Fayetteville (N.Y.) *Weekly Recorder*, April 12, 1888.

40. Robert Hunt Rhodes, editor, *All for the Union*, 170; David B. Swinfen, *Ruggles Regiment: The One Hundred and Twenty-Second New York Volunteers* (Hanover, NH: University Press of New England, 1982), 50–51; Daniel H. Bee, "Wounded at Fort Stevens," *National Tribune*, April 11, 1912; George S. Orr, "Death of Colonel Visscher," *National Tribune*, June 28, 1894; Beamish, "Battle of Fort Stephens [sic]," *Grand Army Scout and Soldiers Mail*, July 10, 1886, and Jacobs, "Getting There on Time."

41. *ORA*, I, 37, pt. 1, 276–77, 279; Rhodes, editor, *All for the Union*, 170.

42. E. N. Atkinson, "Report of Evans Brigade," Huntington Library, San Marino, CA.

43. Letter, Abraham Kingsland to Thomas G. Kingsland, October 4, 1864, author's files; Taylor, *Pictures of Life in Camp and Field*, 217–18; *ORA*, I, 37, pt. 1, 277.

44. *ORA*, I, 37, pt. 1, 37, 256, 259, 263, 277; Jubal A. Early, *A Memoir of the Last Year of the War for Independence: In the Confederate States of America* (Toronto: Lovell and Gibson, 1866), 65.

45. Swinfen, *Ruggles Regiment*, 51; McDonald, "Fort Stevens Affair, Part 2"; M. B. Aldrich, "Defense of the Capital," *National Tribune*, September 20, 1900; George Perkins, *A Summer in Maryland and Virginia, or, Campaigning with the One Hundred and Forty-Ninth Ohio Volunteer Infantry* (Chillicothe, OH: Sholl Print Company, 1911), 54; "B.O.B.," "The Twenty-Fifth New York Cavalry," *New York Sunday Mercury*, July 24, 1864, in William B. Styple, editor, *Writing and Fighting the Civil War: Soldier Correspondence to the* New York Sunday Mercury (Kearny, NJ: Belle Grove Publishing Company, 2000), 371.

46. *ORA*, I, 37, pt. 1, 277; Manly Wade Wellman, *Rebel Boast* (New York: Henry Holt, 1956), 172–73; Joseph T. Durkin, *Confederate Chaplain: A War Journal of Rev. James B. Sheeran, C.SS.R. Fourteenth Louisiana, CSA* (Milwaukee: Bruce Publishing Company, 1960), 95.

47. F. B. Carpenter, *Six Months at the White House with Abraham Lincoln: The Story of a Picture* (New York: Hurd and Houghton, 1867), 301–2; Letter to the editor, *National Tribune*, from James Simmons, Webster, Massachusetts, undated clipping, Lewis Cass White collection, Joseph and Sharon Scopin, Darnestown, Maryland.

48. Henry Kyd Douglas, *I Rode with Stonewall* (Chapel Hill: University of North Carolina Press, 1940), 295–96; Cramer, *Lincoln under Enemy Fire*, 69; Judge, *Season of Fire*, 257.

49. Horatio Nelson Taft diary, July 12, 1864, volume 3, Library of Congress, Washington, DC.

CHAPTER NINE
REBEL RECESSIONAL/YANKEE REPERCUSSIONS

P atent office examiner Horatio Nelson Taft wrote in his diary on July 13, "Another day and the reports and the general belief is tonight that the rebels have left or are leaving Maryland and crossing the River back into Virginia." Efforts were under way to intercept them. They "may prove partially successful." The raiders undoubtedly had made off with a large amount of plunder, cattle, horses, and such, and Taft was told that evening "by one who says he knows that the rebels numbered 22,000 men only." "It has been a great 'scare' for the Country amounting to a great foraging expedition if this is the last of it," Taft advanced, "and I am inclined to think it is." Many people still wondered if indeed that was true. Early's raid would linger for weeks in people's minds.[1]

About this time, too, Charles M. Yocum of the Fifty-Second Ohio National Guard once again wrote to his "Friend Bella" from Fort Reynolds in Washington's southern lines. Doubtless she had heard from the newspapers "of the Invasion of Maryland by the Rebs and their attempted dash on our Capitol." There was no use for him recounting the details, "but the activity of the entire mass of the populace simply illustrated what a people can do when driven to task." "Every citizen flew to Army brigades," he claimed. "One or two Corps were sent from the front and on Monday and Monday night, the streets were just completely filled with soldiers in every branch of the service: Infantry, cavalry and artillery." The previous day, "The excitement ran so high that citizens were not permitted to travel the streets for regiments—arriving all the time from the Potomac ran through the streets on the double quick to the scenes of action." "About 5 o'clock yesterday P.M., the ball commenced," he waxed. The battle was about eight miles from them. He continued, "We could plainly hear the musketry fire and could see the exploding shells." Still, they were not idle at Fort Reynolds, he assured her, for at noon an acting brigadier brought the order to fall in "for 5000 Rebs were within 4 miles." Every preparation was made despite the fact "we number about 150 men." But, "of course, we would have given them a warm reception."[2]

Rumor had Lee's old reliable general James Longstreet within twelve miles "on our side of the river with 12,000 or 15,000 men." Yet our troops always seemed "very mysteriously to spring up always prepared for every emergency," he contended. A sister One Hundred and Sixty-Ninth Ohio must have been near the battlefield even if not engaged, Yokum added. "From 40 to 60 of that regiment is said to have been captured while on a berrying expedition a few days ago," although he could not confirm the rumor. News was sparse because of "the wires being cut in so many places by the Rebs." "We think they have attempted to escape into Dixie for we can hear but little firing and only an occasional firing of buildings and bridges can be noticed by the ascending smoke from the heap of ruins." "I am afraid they will get away," he sighed.

The Confederates had held the South Mountain passes in order to escape, Yocum continued, "but I think they will have a heavy battle with General Hunter before they get back." Perhaps they proposed "to take our Capitol, which may and must forever be futile." He thought in a few days "we will have glorious news from the war-worn hero, Grant," so everything looked cheerful from Yocum's perspective, even though "no doubt a great many lives will now be sacrificed in a few days." He warned Bella his letter "will likely be a long time in reaching you as the railroads are almost all destroyed leading west and [mail must go by water to Philadelphia]." The next day, he added that "the morning papers contain very indefinite news" as "nothing of the rebs seems to be known." Apparently they were not entirely safe on the Virginia side, "as we are all the time preparing to meet them." Again, Longstreet seemed to be advancing with his entire corps, and "last evening trains of cavalry baggage passed our picket line for fear of capture," while "transports moved rapidly up and down the Potomac, and generally speaking everything seemed to be on the move." "I hope and pray," he concluded, "the Rebs will be captured for I tell you they evidently made a bold strike!" At that point, "I will leave military matters and resume my chat."[3]

First Impressions

The morning of Wednesday, July 13, according to news reporter Benjamin Taylor, found "the whole 'Front,' for miles out, was as empty as a drum." The invaders "came here hungry and active, every man's belt drawn up to the last hole, empty stomachs make light heels." Now their foraged "flocks and herds were well under way," he scoffed, "every nose of them all pointed toward the Antarctic," their booty wagons "laden with 'leather and prunella [a heavy woolen dress fabric or more appropriately here, perhaps, a heavy woolen fabric for upper parts of shoes],' and entertainment for man and beast, were stringing across the flat Potomac," the VI Corps close behind, and "there was no use knocking at the door [of Washington] any more." But for some, Early's departure was bittersweet. Rebel-sympathizing Marylander Floride Clemson could only witness the great raid on Washington from afar. But she was displeased.[4]

In troubled health, Clemson and her mother had taken up residence near Beltsville on the railroad between Washington and Baltimore. Settling into the local society to the point of enjoying the cultural lectures at the nearby Maryland Agricultural College, the neighborhood had been upset by Bradley Johnson's excursion so close to both Baltimore and Washington. Warming to possible liberation, Clemson tried to make sense of the myriad rumors and tales of raider accomplishments, the firing of musketry and cannonading, and even the distant battlefield smoke to the west when she and a companion rode to the college on the evening of July 11. "I suppose this puts an end to our sea excursion at least for the present," she jotted in her diary, dreaming like the Blair family women of a seashore respite from summer heat. Still, overjoyed at the Yankees' discomfort, Clemson enjoyed conversing with Johnson's cavaliers, who "are very strong, well clothed & expect to sweep the state." In turn, Johnson's "buttermilk rangers" (as Early derided his cavalrymen) had complained of newly requisitioned Maryland mounts being inefficient and too fat.

Most of all, however, Clemson underscored the fog of war for civilians when she decided that "there are so many hundred reports that one has no idea what to believe." Some observers said it was "a mere raiding party, others an organized movement to take Washington." Some "say the Soldiers' Home is burnt, others say not." "Ft. Totten is and is not taken. Blair's Home is & is not burnt. All is uncertain. Here we are nearly on the battlefield & know nothing." Eventually affairs returned to normal—drought until the first rain on the twenty-fifth since the beginning of June, crops ruined, tales of arrest of Rebel sympathizers all over Maryland in the wake of Early's audacious raid, and the reestablishment of Union control over the line of the Baltimore & Ohio railroad as well as the adjacent country by units such as Colonel Charles F. Johnson's Eighteenth Veteran Reserve Corps. To Johnson, it was a country where "all the rich are sechesh [sic] and all the poor are staunch union." Eventually, the Clemsons departed for Long Beach on the Jersey shore. It had been a highly exciting July outside the nation's capital.[5]

The *Washington Star* on July 16, 1864, carried letters from several local Confederates in Jubal Early's army. The letters had been left in the debris from Rebel presence around Silver Spring. "If any evidence is wanting that it was fully the intention of the rebels to make the attempt to take Washington, and that they were at one time confident of success in that attempt, such evidence is supplied in these letters," proclaimed the newspaper. One such letter dated Tuesday, July 12, to the writer's mother laconically proclaimed, "It seems hard that here I am within sight of my home and cannot get there." It was "like a pleasant dream to be in such a familiar place," he wrote. "I certainly expected to have been in Washington last night but fate decided otherwise, and for fear I will not get there, I will write." He was well, assured the writer, and unhurt despite fighting every day. His horse had been shot from under him, but he remained untouched. "I would give worlds to see you all again and I know you want to see me, but I suppose we will have to wait till a kind Providence grants our prayer." He had "fixed it up nicely to come to W. and if we do not get there it will be a sore disappointment to me; but, however, as a good soldier, I will have to trust in the sagacity of our general and valor of our boys." There would be no getting home to Washington for this lad in Early's army.[6]

Postbattle Cleanup in the Neighborhood

Early knew he would have to withdraw from Washington by dawn of July 12. Or so he claimed later. That afternoon's sharp combat had been unnecessary from his standpoint. By midnight, his threat to Mr. Lincoln's Washington was history. Confederate retirement proved orderly except that somebody burned Postmaster General Montgomery Blair's Falkland mansion on the way out. Flames similarly swept the nearby rented house of *New York Times* reporter E. A. Paul's family. Both were supposedly objects of Rebel retaliation for what had become hard war at David Hunter's instigation in the Shenandoah Valley. Whether attributable to unruly Louisiana "Tigers," Forty-Fifth North Carolina, disgruntled Marylanders in Early's ranks, or even Union artillery fire (that had incinerated parts of houses all the way out to Seventh Street Pike from Fort Stevens), blame was spread around. Certainly the retreating graycoats offered no harm to the Washington remodeler J. E. Turton, although, taking his change of clothing and on his remonstrating with them, they stated emphatically, "We can't help it, you're where you can get plenty, we can't." Preston Blair's Silver Spring escaped similar fate thanks to John C. Breckinridge and Early personally, although even that lovely house endured ransacking and destruction of furniture and personal property. Other destroyed houses on the battlefield included those of Richard Butts, W. Bell, J. McChesney, Abner Shoemaker, W. M. Morrison, Catherine Carberry, and Robert Lay.[7]

Secretary of the Navy Gideon Welles toured the Fort Stevens battlefield on July 18 and noted "chimneys of the burnt houses, the still barricaded road, the trampled fields and other evidences bear testimony to what had occurred." Just about everyone in the area had lost livestock, crops, even personal property to the vagabonds. Early and others would expend much ink through the years deploring such desecration while proclaiming it to have been just retribution for Yankee depredations elsewhere. In fact, some of those other Yankees probably praised the irrepressible

Major-General Benjamin Butler, who specifically sent a gunboat to burn the house and terrorize the family of Confederate secretary of war James A. Seddon near Fredericksburg on the lower Rappahannock. In truth, preparation of battle space before Fort Stevens and sister forts by Union soldiers and African American laborers from the city, Federals' artillery fire, and the general nature of combat had despoiled properties. Local residents, depending upon political sentiments, harbored grudges against Early's army or Lincoln's government in turn. As Chaplain F. C. Morse of the Thirty-Seventh Massachusetts wrote to home folks, "Piles of smoldering ruins now mark the place where happy union families dwelt in peace." "Shade trees of maple, locust and other varieties as well as trees heavily laden with fruit" had been simply hacked down by loyal, not Rebel, forces, he contended.[8]

Remarkably, the Silver Spring mansion and grounds of the elder Blair "was less injured than I had supposed," thought Welles, "and there must have been extra pains taken for the preservation of the shrubbery and the growing crops." In fact, he said, "Fields of the best corn I have seen this year were untouched." He was unable to ascertain "what depredation or plunder had been committed in the house," for the place was shut up. All that Welles had to go on was his son's observation as leader of the pickets the night before. Son Tom Welles told his father that Blair's personal papers had been scattered over the floor and "there had been crowds of persons there filling the house, sleeping on the floors, prying into the family privacy, but not more rudely, perhaps, than our own soldiers would have done, had the place been in their power." Blair's notably relieved daughter, Elizabeth, quite agreed, filling in details of Early's occupation for her absent husband, Rear Admiral Samuel Phillips Lee, as the status of things became clearer. Writing from Cape May, New Jersey, where she had taken her ailing mother during the episode, she recounted the subsequent return of family pets, tidying up the property by the caretaker and farmhands, and sorting out papers, clothing, and house furnishings.[9]

Elizabeth Lee relished that "our grapery was untouched & not a tree or shrub was injured," while specifically citing two indications of Confederate gallantry—inscriptions on mantle portraits about how "a confederate officer, for himself & all his comrades, regrets exceedingly that damage & pilfering was committed in this house, before it was known that it was within our lines, or that private property was imperiled." Especially regrettable to another intruder was "that Ladies property has been disturbed, but restitution has been made, & punishment meted out as far as possible" for "we wage no ignoble warfare for plunder or revenge, but for all that men hold dearest, & scorn to retaliate in kind the unmentioned outrages on our homes by federal Straps." And it had been Breckinridge who preserved Silver Spring according to Confederate officers who had dined at a neighbor's place, claimed Elizabeth Lee. He had "made more fuss about things there than if they had belonged to Jeff Davis."[10]

Silver Spring had been the Kentuckian's antebellum place of refuge and rest, Elizabeth Lee wrote her husband on July 16 and 31. Breckinridge had remonstrated with Early, who had snarled that it was "no use to fret about one house when we have lost so much by this proceeding." The former vice president (now Early's second-in-command) had vociferously disagreed. Silver Spring was spared, and "thus bread cast upon the waters came back to us to which I can say they were welcome in return for their good offices," she concluded. By the end of the month, a very tired Elizabeth told Phil, "yesterday finished my labors among the papers & piles of rubbish in the garret" in the wake of the invasion. "However they are now all separated & put in bundles—the useful taken out of the trash & Saturday night found this house in the same good order we left it on Saturday night three weeks ago but alas!! Minus some thousands in the way of valuables." She more pensively concluded on August 19, "Strange how zealous we are repairing damages—with so little security for the future." Even with a country squire's family, the scars of Early's violation of their home's sanctity left their mark.[11]

Treasury registrar Lucius Chittenden possibly left the clearest memory of the detritus-strewn Fort Stevens battlefield. Based on notes he jotted the next day, Chittenden recalled witnessing one last hurrah by a squadron of Confederate horsemen dashing by Bidwell's men. "Again had a charge of cavalry been resisted and defeated by infantry in line of battle," he recalled, "and the last armed rebel who was ever to look upon the figure of liberty on the dome of the Capitol had disappeared forever." Ensuring that his horses were well cared for by handlers that afternoon, Chittenden went out to inspect the battlefield. Men with stretchers were still carrying off the wounded and collecting the dead. The buildings in the valley that had been fired by Union artillery "burned very slowly and were only now fully aflame." On all the floors, on the roof, in the yards—anywhere within reach of the heat, "were many bodies of the dead and dying, who could not move, and had been left behind by their comrades." "The odor of burning flesh filled the air." He decided, "It was a sickening spectacle."[12]

Roaming around, Chittenden discovered near a large, fallen tree "one in the uniform of an officer." His sword lay by his side, but in his hand grasped a rifle. "What could have sent an officer here to act as a sharp-shooter?," asked the Vermont civilian rhetorically. Opening his clothing, Chittenden discovered boiler-iron body armor and "trusting to this protection, he had gone out that morning gunning for Yankees." Instead, quoting a Vernon, Vermont, headstone for a vaccination victim back home, Chittenden decided the Rebel officer suffered "the means employed his life to save, hurried him headlong to the grave." An artillery shard had cut through armor like a knife through butter. Chittenden also found the sharpshooter "winged" by the target-rifle-wielding Union marksman earlier. This enabled the Treasury official to study not just the body but the rifle and cartridge box of English make—"the only things about him which did not indicate extreme destitution." His feet wrapped in rags had coarse shoes upon them "so worn and full of holes that they were only held together by many pieces of thick twine." Ragged trousers, a jacket and shirt "of what used to be called 'tow-cloth,' a straw hat that had lost a large portion of both crown and brim, the sniper's hair was a mat of dust and grime as were his face and body which gave him the color of the red Virginia clay." His haversack's contents "were a jack-knife, a plug of twisted tobacco, a tin cup, and about two quarters of coarsely cracked corn, with, perhaps an ounce of salt, tied up in a rag." Chittenden deduced that the corn had been ground upon the cob, "making the provender which the Western farmer feeds to his cattle." Such was a complete inventory of the belongings of one Confederate soldier.

This was the first time that a civilian official like Chittenden had actually seen the enemy. He commented thirty-three years later how the Rebel dead looked as if they had been through six weeks of hard service. But "he was evidently from the poorest class of Southern whites," when on the evening of July 12, Chittenden "detached his haversack and its contents from his body and carried them away." He also noticed how many of the Confederate dead were clothed in blue, "and had it not been for the hats, which were of many shapes and sizes, they would have closely resembled our own men." He also noted the number of dead Federals and posited that their placement suggested "the time could not have been longer than ten minutes before they were all lying flat on the ground." Chittenden and other onlookers started their return to the city only after nightfall. They passed the victors' bivouacs in the fields, thus leaving the Seventh Street Road clear, whereby the invaders had made rapid departure. In the distance "a single heavy gun from a fort at intervals sent a shell, with a screaming rush, in the direction of the retreating Confederates, like some wild animal growling his anger at the escape of his prey." It was the last gun of the attack upon Washington, thought Chittenden, and they conveyed news of the Confederate's departure back to the city. "That night its inhabitants slept soundly, free from alarm or anxiety," was his opinion.[13]

Property owners on the actual battlefield certainly suffered more than the Blairs, as even Chittenden's comments suggested the two-day battle had been anything but a mere skirmish. Soldier correspondent "B.O.B." told *New York Sunday Mercury* readers on July 24, 1864, that "when daylight broke [on July 13], we advanced to the hills which the enemy had occupied in our front and found their dead lying around in great numbers." The party detailed for that purpose "buried about two hundred of them, and we have taken about four hundred prisoners, inclusive of 163 wounded, who were left in a house in charge of two of their own surgeons." Typical of all Civil War battlefields, Fort Stevens was its own showcase of carnage. Many militiamen and invalids had never seen such sights before, nor had the common citizenry who flocked to the site. Everyone wanted to see vestiges of the struggle—dead bodies, torn landscape, makeshift Rebel bivouacs, even perhaps some rudimentary breast-works to shield foemen against fusillades from one another. Stretcher bearers had borne the injured to the hospital just behind Fort Stevens, where already makeshift graves were captured by a photographer quickly on the scene. Perhaps Chittenden's comment about "a sickening spectacle" still was the case when President Abraham Lincoln's eldest son, Robert, visiting from Harvard, and his friend John Hay, the chief executive's personal secretary, engaged in their own sightseeing expedition on Wednesday morning.[14]

Young Lincoln and Hay encountered that rush of sightseers who had been held back for two days by provost guards. The duo joined Hay's friend Captain Oliver Wendell Holmes Jr. of General Horatio Wright's staff at the Crystal Spring encampment before making the rounds of the outer lines. The VI Corps troops seemed to be waiting for orders to move out against the retreating Confederates. They appeared in no hurry, lounging "in a loafer-like, gipsy style among the trees." Artillery batteries on alert, hitched and ready, said Hay, contrasted with listless infantry "diffused through the brush—dirty, careless, soldiery in all else" with "every variety of style and manner among officers." The trio then moved out to Fort Stevens and the parapet, where Robert's father had stood on various occasions during the two-day encounter. Apparently Holmes never mentioned shouting at the president. At least nobody in the group mentioned him doing so. The trio then rode on to Alexander McCook's headquarters for a round of lager with more friends and thence to Montgomery Meigs's command post for lunch with his deputy, Brigadier General Daniel Rucker.[15]

Well fortified with food and drink against the sights and stench of the battlefield, the trio meandered out with the secretary of the navy's son, Tom Welles, to bury the Rebel dead. They watched as an "old sapper and miner" and fifty black laborers moved down Seventh Street Road on this errand. The burial detail grabbed picks and shovels, while their chief told those bearing stretchers for the task, "Chief mourners, to the rear as pall bearers. Get out your pocket handkerchers" to counter the smell of dead bodies and animals in the stifling heat. Together they reached a bullet-decimated orchard where "our heavy loss took place." Young Lincoln, Hay, Holmes, and Welles also spotted a batch of "apparently hearty and well-fed of late" Confederates (a portion of some two hundred such prisoners) also pass to the rear, expressing themselves "anxious to get out of the Army." Tired, Lincoln and Hay took leave of Holmes (about to be discharged home to Massachusetts, his term of service expired). They returned to the city. Apparently, nobody mentioned Old Abe at Fort Stevens. At least nobody recorded doing so.[16]

Nonetheless, the elder Lincoln, it seems, had one more obligation toward Fort Stevens and the soldiery who had defended him there. Within a day or so, Union dead had been collected from both the battlefield and the temporary burial spot

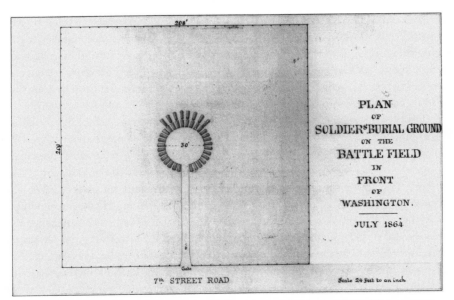

Battleground National Cemetery Plan, July 1864. *National Archives and Records Service*

behind Fort Stevens hospital. They were to be interred in a permanent, new cemetery actually on the field of strife. The War Department commandeered land from James Mulloy of the city's Metropolitan Police (who sought reimbursement two weeks later from the quartermaster department for damages done to his planned homestead, claiming the dead bodies contaminated his spring water, which made the property unfit for habitation). Forty Union veterans of the July 12 action found their final resting place on that open plain stretching out toward what would come to be known as Cameron Creek on the Lay farm. It was indeed all battleground—for which the new cemetery would acquire its name. At least some Confederates, buried mostly where they fell at the time, later would be exhumed and moved farther out on the Seventh Street Road, past the Blair mansions and the Sligo post office to the humble Episcopal Grace churchyard. This was the Blair's parish church, past which Early's marchers had come and gone on their way to Washington.[17]

Civil War burials were simple affairs for both sides, it seemed. Surgeon George T. Stevens of the Seventy-Seventh New York writing two years later rather bitterly suggested the initial interment was quite typical of battlefields generally. "We gathered our dead comrades from the field where they had fallen," he wrote, "and gave them the rude burial of soldiers on the common near Fort Stevens." "No one of those high in authority, who had come out to see them give up their lives for their country,

203

were present to pay the last honors to the dead heroes." No officer of state, no lady of wealth, no Washington citizen was there. "We laid them in their graves within sight of the capital, without coffins, with only their gory garments and their blankets around them." With the rude tenderness of soldiers, contended Stevens, "we covered them in the earth; we marked their names without pencils on the little head-boards of pine, and turned sadly away to other scenes."[18]

Dr. Stevens may have been mistaken. When final interment took place at Battleground, Abraham Lincoln was there. True, little fanfare apparently attended his appearance, what he said, and a brief dedication. According to veteran participant Third Vermonter Edward A. Campbell—himself to be Battleground's forty-first interee when he died in 1935—the burial party "had about finished the job, and who do you suppose came driving up?" It was Lincoln again. "I'll always remember what Lincoln looked like and what he said." He appeared sad, commented Campbell, and did not say anything for a minute. "We all stopped working," remembered Campbell. What came next hardly replicated the words for the ages rendered by the president the previous November at Gettysburg. "Mr. Lincoln held up his hand and said 'I dedicate this spot as the Battle Ground National Cemetery.'" Then the president and his aides rode away, Campbell claimed. Such simplicity belied the fact that Lincoln personally, and by implication the nation, owed more to the forty killed at Fort Stevens than the thousands interred at the small town in Pennsylvania.[19]

Fort Stevens, Controversy, and Lincoln

It seems that no one was quite satisfied after Fort Stevens. Ironically, at the height of the raid, Welles and Elizabeth Blair's husband tangled over the admiral's ostensible desertion of his Hampton Roads station to rush with his flagship USS *Malvern* to the defense of the capital. Occasioned by the Sunday panic and unfolding of difficulties with the Gunpowder River railroad crossing, as well as rumors of Confederate liberation attempts at Point Lookout, Admiral Lee responded appropriately by sending smaller flotillas to those endangered points. Frankly, he had acted when Welles had complained about inaction. Yet leaving his station to personally steam up the Potomac personally without orders was another matter. Welles dictated that he return to the station. Lee responded with displeasure about Welles's censure. All of this was because, in Lee's view, the emergency seemed to be nowhere "but here at the national capital."[20]

Lee reiterated all the facts regarding quiet on the James River front, his appropriate dispatch of vessels not only to Maryland but also chasing the Confederate raider *Florida* on the high seas. But "Old Greybeard," as the Blairs took to calling Welles, was unmoved by the admiral's "dash up the Potomac." Washington "was menaced, possibly in some danger," said Welles, in further condemnation on July

19. "But the principal object of the rebels was undoubtedly to create a panic, and by withdrawing our forces or a portion of them, to raise the siege of Petersburg." The secretary had a point, and Blair's "dash" equated with Grant's weakening of Meade's army for Lee's purposes. Still, by July 19, Welles knew better, carping that he thought Grant "understood the object and was immovable." Lee, "yielding to the panic that was created, and listening to the exaggerated and groundless rumors that were put afloat, left his station and proceeded to the capital, where neither himself nor his dispatch vessel could be of any service under any circumstances, while his absence from his post in a great emergency might have compromised the action and efficiency of the squadron intrusted [sic] to him and brought disaster upon the country." Welles downplayed communication difficulties between Washington and the field. He pressed Lee's specific orders and attributed the myriad of "sensational rumors and exaggerated statements that were put in circulation, many of them for mischievous purposes, and with a design of inducing our officers to leave their posts and withdraw our forces."

Then, Welles softened his tone. "No immediate bad results, other than the example, have followed," he told Lee. In what may have only further irritated the naval officer, however, the secretary preached, "To stand firm in such an exigency is important, and I regret that the rebels, or the rumors, should have moved you at such a time or led you to leave your post." He ordered Lee to mind the blockade and to visit stations and ships under his command. Whether or not this "Connecticut Yankee at King Abraham's Court," as Welles was once called, suspected Lee's actions were prompted by fears about Silver Spring or his wife, Elizabeth, and his family, others did. In any event, Elizabeth Blair Lee wrote her husband by mid-August about how her father counseled Welles's friendship and warmth to the admiral, especially as the situation on the battlefield and the Blair properties as well as failure of Early's strike came into better focus. Certainly everyone at the time of crisis would have been quite happy with the firepower of the eighteen-guns Malvern and Lee could have brought to bear if the Rebels had gotten into the city. They had not; officialdom remained hypersensitive to the close call, and Admiral Lee retired to a more conservative exercise of duty for the remainder of the war. Welles had spooked him. As late as December, he proved sluggish in risking a flotilla on Tennessee waters to interdict a Rebel army of Tennessee withdrawing from disaster at Nashville.[21]

Early's raid and Fort Stevens would shadow the president for some weeks, even months. Controversies over reimbursement for battle damages and government requisition of land hung over the scene at the most local level. Lincoln would be drawn into one such hassle later in October. In September both Catharine Carberry and Richard Lay submitted claims to the army for loss and damage to their properties sustained during the Confederate raid in July. Eventually, after the war, the matter made it all the way to Congress, only to have the House Judiciary Committee adversely deny the claims on the grounds that their submission fell under "the taking of private property for public use" rather that such claims "are for losses and damage by war." Such splitting of legal hairs, however, did not preclude the president of the United States giving testimony before the proceedings of a board of officers convened by Special Order Number 228, Headquarters, Department of Washington, September 13, 1864. That was when Lincoln clarified his role in the late battle. "I was present at Fort Stevens (I think) on the afternoon of July 12, 1864, when some houses in front were shelled by our guns, and understanding that the Military officers in command thought the shelling of the houses proper and necessary, I certainly gave my approbation to its being done." Just when and where the commander-in-chief issued the order remained a mystery.[22]

In addition, brouhaha within Lincoln's inner circle flared almost immediately after the battle. It involved a noticeably displeased postmaster general and Lincoln's war team. True, maneuvers were already under way to force changes among the cabinet of peers, and even the chief executive had his hidden hand at play concerning Secretary of the Treasury Salmon P. Chase, a political rival. But the focus of this particular furor was Montgomery Blair's tirade upon returning to find his country house in ruins. He exploded to Welles that "the house and furniture cost him just about $20,000 in losses." "Judge B," as Welles referred to him, then launched a scathing indictment of military incompetence, something to the effect (as relayed by Henry Halleck through his boss, Secretary of War Edwin Stanton) that "the officers in command about Washington are poltroons, that there were not more than five hundred rebels on the Silver Spring road and we had a million of men in arms; that it was a disgrace; that General [Lew] Wallace was in comparison with them far better as he would at least fight." An embarrassed chief of staff had protested that a large number of officers had devoted their time and energies on behalf of the government and that any guilty should be dismissed from the service or rather that the slanderous cabinet member should be sent packing. Lincoln's reply to Stanton reflected his usual posture of a headmaster dealing with troublesome schoolboys. The president disapproved any accusative remarks, although "I do not consider what may have been hastily said in a moment of vexation at so severe a loss, is sufficient ground for so grave a step" as dismissal of anyone. He proposed continuing "to be myself the judge as to when a member of the Cabinet shall be dismissed." Despite the departure of the Rebels, tempers and finger pointing remained after Fort Stevens.[23]

In the end, however, the greatest controversy lay with why Early's Confederates had escaped at all. The impact of the raid reverberated across the city. Patent Office examiner Horatio Nelson Taft vented his spleen in a diary entry on July 16. Very little had been heard of the Rebels in this vicinity for the past three or four days, he penned, as "they seem to have departed with their plunder (some eight thousand horses and two or three thousand head of cattle)" by his estimate. No information "has as yet been published that we have succeeded in recapturing a horse or cow or a rebel since they crossed the Potomac on their return." If this "'raid' does not prove the ruin of this Administration, it will be owing to successes in other quarters," he declared. "More stupidity could not well be manifested than it has been shown in this matter, with Washington in a defenceless condition and inviting the invader." Nobody was on alert, "and all we in stupid ignorance until an army of Twenty or Thirty Thousand were found knocking at our gates." "If they did not come in it was their own fault," was Taft's judgment. "They might have done it during three or four days." He was tired, weak in health, and had his bags packed to head north to his family for vacation. He complained about government pay in paper rather than gold, the former now worth "forty cents on the dollar," gold quoted at $2.50 when it had been $3.35, the expense of living increased to at least double, and his annual $1,600 salary hardly able to cover flour at $18.00 a barrel, coal at $13.00 a ton, oak wood $11.00, and pine at $8.00 per cord, cotton sheeting at sixty cents per yard with ham and beef at thirty-five cents a pound. Taft did not expect to be absent more than two or three weeks, "but I really do not care much if I never come back here to stay."[24]

One of the most bitter and even caustic commentaries on the debacle (and singularly overlooking the success at Fort Stevens) came from owner/editors of the Democratic newspaper, the *New York Sunday Mercury*. Their July 17 edition carried an excoriating damnation under the byline, "Were We Betrayed?" Administration papers represented the president as cheering the troops to give them confidence as they marched to defend Washington during the late attack, went the critique. "It is an insult to the already indignant people," claimed William Caldwell, Sylvester Southworth, and Horace P. Whitney, "who know that Lincoln is personally responsible for the whole raid." Attempts to "palliate his guilt by painting him as a buffoon, waving his title on a cane, and crying 'forward!' will fall this time," they noted. Once or twice might have prompted the public's patience, but this was "the thrice-told tale of murder, havoc, and configuration," with the added disgrace of the nation's capital "besieged and completely isolated" with no preparations for defense, and "the exact routes traversed by the raiders twice before" left unguarded. "This looks very like complicity between the White House and the Rebels," broadcast the accusers. In part disingenuously, they added that the newspaper advised Lincoln of the purpose of the Rebels and that General Grant added his timely warning. The paper's "always reliable Washington correspondent" said so, and "the President was implored to concern himself less with his own re-election and more with the border defence." "What to him," they queried, "was the integrity of the North, the tranquility of firesides, the safety of property and life?"[25]

Indeed, politics underlay the *Sunday Mercury*'s indictment. Lincoln did not wish to end the war upon which "his rich friends, the contractors are fattening." Grant might capture Petersburg and compel Richmond's evacuation, so to counteract such successes, "Lincoln left the back-door of the Capital open to the Rebel cavalry." That cavalry had swept Maryland "like a threshing-floor," thundering to the gates of Baltimore, stealing enough oxen "to feed their army for one year," destroying four railways, burning stacks, dwellings, and storehouses while also shooting Federal soldiers on the parapets of Washington's forts. They had "calmly re-crossed the river with all their plunder, leaving the North panic-stricken, humiliated, and indignant." All the while "the guardian of our destinies was waving his hat in the suburbs of Washington" as if the whole episode was only "a clever electioneering device to give him dramatic character." Maybe he wished to "appease the rising wrath of the people by moving their sympathies for his idiocy," railed the newspaper, but such subterfuges were played out. As with the Roman emperor Nero, cried the newspaper, "some people may be diverted by the picture of a grave Chief Magistrate waving his hat amidst the convulsions of a great nation in the pitch of danger, while on every hand the stern question of the grieved and thoughtful surges up 'Were we not betrayed?'"

Caldwell, Southworth, and Whitney concluded by bluntly suggesting that "twice before Southern armies gave battle upon Northern soil, and the people rose up, like the ocean, to overwhelm them." This time the North was not so prompt; "it demanded time for reflection and a change of rulers only will satisfy it that patriotism has any reward or loyalty any safeguard." Lincoln had to go. Their message was "he is arraigned as an incompetent, bad man, and the people have lost confidence in him." "He might receive the adulation of thieves and contractors who listen to his stories, and perhaps share their pickings with him." But not even their effrontery "can shield him from the just indignation of an outraged people." Time would certainly tell, and if Union success at Fort Stevens was evident (while incomplete) to the man who had stood on the parapet under hostile fire, it was certainly not so to his bitter opponents. Rebel host on the doorstep of the national capital, even while beaten back by Old Abe's boys, made headlines and shocked the northern public in the weeks following Early's raid.

Abraham Lincoln was indeed embattled after Fort Stevens. Personally returning to the Soldiers' Home cottage on the fourteenth after being assured Early's threat was ended, the personality differences in the cabinet prompted his sharp rebuke about "endeavoring to procure another's removal" as prejudicial to the public interest. Then came Horace Greeley's attempt by midmonth to develop policy on negotiations with the Confederacy. Two days later, Lincoln had to prod Grant to go forward with the general's promise to "make a desperate effort to get a position here which will hold the enemy without the necessity of so many men." Lincoln was glad to hear this but felt bound the next day to issue yet another proclamation calling for five hundred thousand more volunteers from the northern states. On July 19, Lincoln appointed government directors for a Union Pacific railroad clearly signaling his faith in the future of a United States. Yet, from surviving documentation, as the traumatic month of July closed, uppermost in Lincoln's mind were the dire situation of an unresolved war, the threat of peace without victory thanks to Confederate commissioners, a Democratic Party plank calling for the Union as it was and the Constitution as it is, and how to permanently ensure servile emancipation translated by permanent codification by law. And the administration teetered on the brink of defeat in November. A president who had escaped enemy bullets was not a contented man. On July 28, Lincoln wired Grant that he wished to confer with him at Fort Monroe. Militarily, one nagging issue remained on Lincoln's mind. It surfaced when Jubal Early's lieutenant, John McCausland, went north of the Potomac and burned Chambersburg, Pennsylvania, on July 30.[26]

The Unresolved Issue

The last two weeks in July displeased Lincoln as they displeased the nation. The *Washington Evening Star* headline on July 13 screamed, "The Rebels Have Disappeared from Our Front." Still, Union officials ran into problems stabilizing even the most basic of functions in the region. A party of telegraphers trying to reestablish the lines to Baltimore ran into Baltimore & Ohio agent George Koontz's refusal to provide an engine and car because he had no orders from the officer in charge of guards at Beltsville and other posts to permit passage. Only a direct order from Secretary of War Stanton permitted Captain Fred W. Royce, George W. Durity, Dal Cudlip, and Lon Stidbam out on the line to fix broken wires from Bradley Johnson's raiders. Ironically, it had been Royce who intercepted an attempt by one of Johnson's men to spread false intelligence on the line. Royce recognized the interloper for his distinctive use of Morse code. After the war, the culprit confronted his old friend Royce, "How in the Divil did you know that was me?" Royce smiled and said, "Oh, you couldn't disguise that old style of tangled foot Morse."[27]

There were other troubling signs. If, by the fourteenth, Jubal Early's army was gone, they showed no signs of defeat. Colonel Charles Russell Lowell's reconnaissance to Rockville, where he found John McCausland's rear guard still full of fight on July 13, sent that message. Authorities were so willing to let the raiders simply escape that Wright's eventually sluggish pursuit was soon a good day's march behind the fast vanishing Rebels. And those Rebels still seemed to be in the high spirits reflected by one ragamuffin in the Fifty-Eighth Virginia, who left a parting shot on the flyleaf of one of Blair's books at Silver Spring. It read, "Now Uncle Abe, you had better be quiet the balance of your Administration, as we only came near your town this time just to show you what we could do; but if you go on in your made career, we will come again soon, and then you had better stand from under." It was signed respectfully "the worst rebel you ever saw." Lincoln, of course, never saw it—but the sentiment was chilling. No wonder Quartermaster Montgomery Meigs wanted Halleck on the fifteenth to have engineer John Gross Barnard survey the late battlefield for Rebel breastworks and to publish them in the *Washington Intelligencer*. There were still "physical signs of a large force lying in ambush hoping to tempt an attack by our weak garrison to overthrow and follow them into the lines." Paranoia lingered in official circles as Early vanished.[28]

Sentiment in Early's ranks mixed relief of escape with the feeling that more could have been done and tasks had been left unfinished. Captain Francis M. Imboden of Company H, Eighteenth Virginia Cavalry (John Imboden's brigade), was one such individual. He wrote his mother in Fincastle, Botetourt County, on July 22, "I have returned from one of the hardest and most unsatisfactory trips of the war tho we have been very fortunate in loosing [*sic*] few men having but little fighting to do after crossing the river [Potomac]." "We were up to the fortifications of Washington," he said, "and could see the Capitol and the general impression in the Army is that we could have taken the City with small loss." They lay there "one day in sight of the Capitol and then fell back without any fight of consequence across the river near Leesburg." Imboden would go on to recount subsequent brushes with pursuing Federals before the army completed its return to the valley. Writing from near Strasburg, below Winchester, this member of the Imboden clan was most chagrined that while acquiring a horse from a "Maryland gentleman" that he sent home, "some goods" that he had likewise secured for his mother and himself had been lost in a disastrous raid on the army's wagon train shortly after leaving Leesburg on the final withdrawal back to the Shenandoah. Almost like Stephen Ramseur, at the time, they had accomplished a good deal and hoped for more good work for the cause. At least, young Imboden could assure his mother that he and kinsmen had themselves escaped harm.[29]

But others were less persuaded with the passage of time. C. A. Fondern of Carpenter's battery wrote, "It has been wondered why General Early at that time did not undertake the capture of Washington," but he opined that it was not in his province to "undertake to solve that problem." Most scathing was Fifth Virginia cavalryman John Opie. "The fact is, that a volley, a Rebel yell, and a vigorous charge, would have given us Washington," he later boasted. They should have captured that city under the circumstances, "had we all afterward perished in the flames." Having taken the city, he continued, "We could have easily marched across the high bridge to Alexandria and thence back to Virginia." "But, as so many Confederate generals did during the whole course of the war," stated this angry, former enlisted man, "Early sowed the seed but failed to reap the harvest." He did note that "while blustering in the eastern suburbs of the city, our undisciplined army committed a great many depredations, some stragglers burning several houses amongst them that of Postmaster Blair." Hence Opie admitted that if the army had entered Washington, he feared "they would have yielded to the great temptation to plunder." That city "would have been a scene of ruin"; thus, in his view, "it was best that it was not captured." Still, in all, "Early lost the golden opportunity afforded him of immortalizing himself by capturing the capitol of the nation." But Opie concluded venomously that Early himself "was about the only man in the army who believed it impossible of accomplishment."[30]

For the Union the problem was simply that Early had escaped. His raiding army had survived to fight another day. As the ever-dyspeptic yet perceptive Gideon Welles growled in his diary, "We have done nothing, and it is more gratifying to our self-pride to believe there were many of them, especially as we are likely to let them off with considerable plunder scot-free." John Hay recorded on the evening of the fourteenth, "This evening as the President started to the soldiers' Home I asked him quid nunc [what now?] & he said, 'Wright telegraphs that he thinks the enemy are all across the Potomac but that he has halted & sent out an infantry reconnaissance, for fear he might come across the rebels & catch some of them.' The Chief is evidently disgusted," thought Hay. Indeed, the strategic picture had changed little since before the weekend. Muddled command, lassitude or listlessness, or the old malady afflicting Army of the Potomac generals—inability to go for the jugular—all hung about the Union pursuit effort. Early remained within striking distance of Washington or further north.[31]

Welles also cited how the president and his cabinet as well as his military advisers were confused about the strength of the "Rebel invasion." Lincoln "wants to believe there was a large force, and yet evidently his private convictions are otherwise." Military leaders such as Halleck, senior policy adviser Ethan Allen Hitchcock, and those in the War Office "have insisted there was a large force," said the naval secretary. He had found few others that concurred—the Rebels "were defiant and insolent, our men were resolute and brave, but the Bureau generals were alarmed and ignorant, and have made themselves and the Administration appear contemptible." In fact, "*The National Intelligencer* commented with a good deal of truth and ability on our national humiliation," thought Welles. There was "no getting away from the statements and facts presented," he was convinced. Then, rising to a more strategic level, the naval secretary scribbled that "Grant and the Army of the Potomac are reposing in immense force near Richmond." Federal troops had been sent from Washington as well as other locales to reinforce "the great army, which has suffered immense losses in its march, without accomplishing anything except to reach the ground from which McClellan was withdrawn." While reinforced daily, Grant could push on to a given point, but "he seems destitute of strategy or skill, while Lee exhibits tact." Early's raid, which might have taken Washington and which had for several days cut off communications with the North, "was devised by Lee while beleaguered at Richmond, and, though failing to do as much as might have been accomplished, has effected a good deal."[32]

211

Early would continue to haunt Maryland and Washington for weeks. The weather continued hot. Hard marching to catch the raiders appealed to nobody either in Wright's VI Corps or David Hunter's Army of the Kanawha. Heat stroke claimed more victims than combat. Other Federal responses were more predictable throughout civilian Maryland, however. Middle Department commander Lew Wallace and Hunter harried up-country collaborators, imprisoning and confiscating their property. Baltimore businessman Samuel Van Elder wrote his son at school in Massachusetts how "we have had a very exciting time when the rebels was so near us. They stole a good many horses, cattle goods, and money when in our state." He was "sorry they got off so easy, if they should come again which some think they will to try to draw Grant from Richmond, I hope they will meet with a warmer reception than they did before." Business was generally dull as this was the dull season, but the Confederate raid only made matters worse. It would take a while for matters to settle down in the wake of Early's raid.[33]

Certainly, Old Jube himself could not afford to sit around Big Spring near Leesburg once he had recrossed the Potomac. Lee warned him as much in a dispatch written on the eleventh while Early "besieged" Washington. With as good or better an appreciation of the larger situation simply from reading northern newspapers, Lee warned his subordinate of Hunter's and Meade's forces sent to Washington combining against the raider. Strike and defeat them in detail, Lee pressed, then get back to the valley where Early should "threaten and hang upon the enemy's flank should he push on towards Richmond." The transit through John Mosby's Loudon County would permit the procurement of forage and provisions, thought Lee, and position Early for further mischief on the upper Potomac. Lee did not consider the raid ended or Early's work finished just because Washington had not been captured. Early offered to return to the main army by forced marches, something Lee distinctly did not have in mind at this point. In fact, as Lee conveyed Early's preliminary after-action report to the War Department on July 19, he told Secretary of War Seddon that "so far as [Early's] movement was intended to relieve our territory in that section [Lynchburg and the Shenandoah] of the enemy it has up to the present time been successful." He anticipated more; it was not yet time for Early to come home.[34]

Actually, Early nearly experienced disaster in his retirement through Loudon back to the valley. Local partisan ranger John Mosby may have claimed cooperation and harassment of Union outriders that he said kept pursuit confined to main thoroughfares. Nonetheless, Hunter's cavalry under brigadier Alfred Duffie, with Wright's pursuit not far behind, knifed into the retiring Rebel column at Purcellville, cutting out some eighty wagons, ambulances, and other conveyances, 117 mules and horses, as well as fifty or sixty prisoners. Admittedly, they did not completely interdict Early's marching column. They did cause havoc, and Captain Francis M. Imboden of Company H, Eighteenth Virginia Cavalry, wrote his mother that the disaster resulted from "some unaccountable neglect of Genl. Ransom or Genl. Johnson." He wanted to set the record straight because "the People of the [Shenandoah] Valley are disposed to put every thing of censure on our Brig[ade] that may occur in the Army." In truth, neither Hunter nor Wright effectively blocked Early's escape across the Shenandoah River at Snicker's Ferry. Both armies were now worn out, ragged in clothing and stamina, and in great need of rest and recuperation. The pursuers, at least, were not up to bagging the pursued.[35]

Early's Army of the Valley escaped to the vicinity of Berryville and rebuffed Wright's futile attempt to force river passage at the ferry and nearby Cool Spring. Wright presumptively told Halleck at 7:30 p.m. on July 17, "I have no doubt that the enemy is in full retreat for Richmond." He was still confident four days later when pushed by City Point if not Washington into his own retirement back to the city. In fact, Wright was more than ready to return to Meade's army. In his view, the object of the pursuit had been fully accomplished. He informed Halleck from Leesburg, "It was Early's intention, as expressed to the citizens, to hold the Valley and gather in the crops, and his rapid retreat southward occasioned them much surprise." Such sentiments conditioned Grant's previous predilection to secure the VI Corps's return as well as gathering the arriving XIX Corps (many, in fact, loitering around the streets of Washington awaiting orders at the time) to Petersburg for a big attack. One can sense some degree of perplexity among the soldiery themselves when Captain John William De Forest bridled at becoming a shuttlecock via riverboat *Winona* back to Petersburg on the eighteenth but then returning to Washington's Georgetown Heights a fortnight later to prepare to move to Harpers Ferry and to a buildup to chase Early. "Back again, and without knowing why, in the defences of Washington," was his comment. But frankly, suggests modern historian Jeffrey Wert, Wright's "whole expedition had become simply one of pushing Early's rear, a tactical reconnaissance in-force" anyway.[36]

Early teamed up against Hunter's Federals during the final days of July. Building upon the Snicker's Ferry/Cool Spring success, he battered George Crook at Second Kernstown near Winchester, completely panicked Hunter, and shocked the Union command that once more Rebels were loose on the upper Potomac, threatening John Garrett's railroad as well as undertaking incursions into western Maryland, Pennsylvania, even possibly the Washington-Baltimore region again. Overall, events after Fort Stevens resembled a cat-and-mouse game. Early toyed with Hunter. Two distant theater commanders—Grant and Lee—tried to orchestrate events from afar. Washington's intermediary high command only muddled communications, and that drew Grant's complaint about telegraphic transmittal delay. Wright's befuddlement and Hunter's ineptness bungled field operations. The fleet-footed Early proved not merely elusive but ever dangerous. The botched mine explosion and Battle of the Crater continued the Petersburg stalemate at month's end. Suddenly, Early unleashed McCausland's cavalry to burn Chambersburg, Pennsylvania, on July 30. It was a game changer. A paroxysm of fear once more shot through official Washington. With elections only three months away, Grant, for one, seemed oblivious to any urgency. No wonder Lincoln wanted consultation. It seemed like a repeat of McClellan two years before.[37]

Union Assessment

The Union army's top general always acted somewhat cavalier toward Washington's safety. He tacitly responded to Lincoln's concerns about the place. But did he truly understand that concern? Early was gone? Lee and Petersburg resumed priority in his mind. Halleck's nondecisional capacity hardly served the cause. On July 15, the general-in-chief told the chief-of-staff that should the Confederates raid northward again, "there should be an immediate call for all the troops we are likely to require." Washington, Baltimore, and Harpers Ferry should be designated as "schools of instruction," with all troops raised east of Ohio directed there. Union officials would then have all the capacity they needed, in Grant's view, with newcomers learning from being teamed with veterans. Grant still wanted Hunter to raid south and cut the Virginia Central Railroad, but if not then he should render all the mountain valleys south of the Baltimore & Ohio railroad "a desert as high up as possible." No, Grant did not want houses burned but merely wanted to remove "every particle of provisions and stock" and to warn the population to leave these areas. Scoffing at Confederate offensive capacities from Virginia to Georgia, he declared that "Early could never capture any important point with a force even of 30–50,000 men so long as the main union army is within thirty hours of the Capitol." At that point he saw no further reason for Wright to chase Early when the enemy was a full-day's march ahead of him. Grant clearly relied on Hunter and superior Union logistics for rushing reinforcements back to the capital region if needed. It sounded like McClellan's philosophy from 1862 all over again.[38]

Grant kept to this line of thinking for the next week or so. He envisioned Early turning west to reach the Ohio, possibly via Pittsburgh, but never venturing directly north of the Potomac again. He sent back to Washington some regiments due to leave the service and told Halleck to retain heavy artillery units previously sent to defend the city. Then, in the first real indication that he finally understood that the core of the problem lay with the lack of unified command, Grant sent a ciphered message designed "to prevent a recurrence of what has just taken place in Maryland." The Susquehanna, West Virginia, Middle, and Washington departments were to be consolidated under one single commander who would control "all troops that cooperate in any movement of the enemy toward Maryland or Pa." Perhaps he read the newspapers. Editor Henry Raymond of the *New York Tribune* had trumpeted this scheme with his old favorite George McClellan in charge. The administration would never agree to that ploy or even Grant's push to have Major-General William B. Franklin, late escapee from Harry Gilmor's clutches in the Baltimore raid and a veteran Army of the Potomac corps commander, put in charge. Franklin also bore the onus of McClellan's old clique. Stanton and Halleck sidetracked those notions, and the drama continued.[39]

In fact, Halleck played an intriguing role that summer. Grant's superior for much of the war, he now found himself ostensibly subordinated to him. Perhaps his role continued as it had been previously since Grant left the capital to oversee in the field. Halleck would be part of the Washington triumvirate with Stanton and Lincoln. But Lincoln placed great faith in Grant. So while "Old Brains" (his sobriquet among old army elite) was undoubtedly vainglorious and vindictive for all his perceived professional brilliance, he was conscious of two things. First, as a loyal professional, he recognized his hierarchical place (if it was truly, given the imprecise nature of "chief of staff" at this time). Second, he understood above all the need to protect Washington. "In my present position I cannot assume responsibility except in matters of mere administration or in way of advice," he wrote candidly on July 16 to William T. Sherman, another member of Grant's command team. Halleck might still dabble in strategic formulation, alter organizational arrangements, and subtly shape the war to his own view. But he also poured forth to Sherman that "I must be exceedingly cautious about making military suggestions not through General Grant." While "the general himself is free from petty jealousies, he has men about him who would gladly make difficulties between us." Was he referring to the vestiges of the McClellan clique among senior Army of Potomac leadership? In any event, "I think it well to act with caution," therefore making all suggestions to Grant and receiving only his orders. Still, Halleck was that indispensable link between Washington and the field on behalf of Grant and the administration. Halleck might interfere, muddle, and delay—or expedite—matters, and his obsequious tone may have been deceptive. Occasionally he offered sage advice, but in this period he couched so obliquely as to appear unhelpful or indecisive. It was in this vein that he wrote somewhat patronizingly to educate Grant on the political climate on July 19.[40]

The "recent raid into Maryland" seemed to have established several things that should be kept in mind, Halleck noted. First, as long as Grant operated south of the James with Lee between him and Washington, the Rebels could detach a fairly large contingent to either threaten Washington or to operate in the Valley—undetected by the Union. Second, Hunter's much-vaunted force—the only troops capable of field service aside from what Grant had in hand directly—was entirely inadequate for the diverse tasks of holding West Virginia, defending the line of the Baltimore & Ohio, while resisting any raid north of the Potomac. Third, reliance could not be placed upon mobilizing northern militia who might arrive late or not at all or prove unsatisfactory in numbers and capabilities. The Washington and Baltimore garrisons were entirely unfit for the field and inadequate for defense. Without the arrival of the VI Corps veterans, either or both cities would have been "in great danger" during Early's raid. Striking the same note as he had ever since the McClellan period (and, thus, reflecting the Lincoln administration's greatest fear), Halleck reiterated that as long as the Army of the Potomac stood between Lee and the national capital, he had been agreeable to stripping reserve garrisons of forts and camps serving Washington. As with McClellan's campaign two years before, the passage of Grant and Meade beyond direct supporting distance of Washington changed the equation. "I am decidedly of [the opinion] that a larger available force should be left in this vicinity [Washington]," Halleck argued. He was using the same argument used by Lincoln in holding back sizable reinforcements from Little Mac in the spring of 1862.[41]

Halleck methodically dissected the situation, as was his usual wont. Reinforcements might be sent from the James in an emergency, as had been done for Fort Stevens, but only if the government could determine the size and mission of the raiders. This would prove impossible without a superior cavalry force, not likely to appear since Early had stripped the country of animals and provisions, for such remount facilities lacked proper horseflesh. Furthermore, contended Halleck, if Early had used the Potomac crossings between Harpers Ferry and Washington—fordable in low-water season—and moved directly upon either Washington or Baltimore, or if the VI Corps had been delayed even by a day, then one or the other of those supply depots would have been in grave danger. Was it safe to repeat that risk, he queried? "Is not Washington too important in a political as well as military point of view, to run any serious risk at all?" As for Grant's vaunted idea of schools of instruction for recruits in an emergency, a skeptical chief of staff countered that the army wasn't receiving half the number of recruits as it discharged anyway, volunteering had virtually ceased, and Lincoln's latest call for five hundred thousand new men issued on July 18 was unpredictable of result. Unless the country braced for the adoption of an "efficient and thorough draft," then replacement for battle losses was unrealistic. As for the main problem, "so long as Lee is able to make any large detachments, Washington cannot be deemed safe, without a larger & more available force in its vicinity." Everyone except Grant, perhaps, had heard all this before.

It was unclear how Halleck's communiqués affected Grant. He was not far off the mark in his postwar conclusion: "It seemed to be the policy of General Halleck and Secretary Stanton to keep any force sent [to the Shenandoah] in pursuit of the invading army, moving right and left so as to keep between the enemy and our capital; and, generally speaking, they pursued this policy until all knowledge of the whereabouts of the enemy was lost." The pragmatic Grant wanted a single policy—

find, fix, and fight Early to the death. Halleck and Stanton seemingly counseled screening the capital region from invasion and mayhem. Everybody wanted Meade's army to concentrate on Lee. Halleck dutifully notified Grant on the twenty-second that Wright had broken off contact with the Rebels. He warned, "In my opinion raids will be renewed as soon as he leaves, but you are the judge whether or not a large enough movable force shall be kept there to prevent them." Assistant Secretary of War Charles A. Dana privately advised Grant on matters on the upper Potomac. Halleck suggested even President Lincoln looked to the general for a solution. Grant wrote an old political patron in exasperation, "Maryland raid upset my plans but I will make an attempt to do something before many days." John A. Rawlins, Grant's chief-of-staff, had asked Dana on the twenty-third, "How goes the pursuit after the enemy sum up?" Had "they been compelled to drop any of their plunder and have we killed, captured or scattered any of their forces to speak of"? Dana replied the next day that on the whole pursuit of Early "has proved an egregious failure." Wright and Crook had accomplished nothing. The VI Corps commander started back to Washington "as soon as he got where he might have done something worth while." Had Wright remained in the valley, "the combined forces might have made a fine campaign at least against the railroads and the crops." So it went, seemingly incapable of solution.[42]

Business as Usual

So Washington returned to business as usual; government officials were content to forget Early and return to running the affairs of state. Whether or not residents once more slept "free from alarm or anxiety," as Treasury registrar Lucius Chittenden observed, Quartermaster General Meigs kept his "troops" drilling just in case! He never quite forgot his two-day stint at field command. The D.C. militia returned to civilian pursuits, and normal schedules once again ensured rail service to the north. Transit system horse cars pulled through the heat on Pennsylvania Avenue, and a relieved Blair family returned to the salubrious charms of Silver Spring. Business-men such as Georgetown bargemen complained about lost revenue due to raider destruction of the Chesapeake and Ohio Canal upstream. And there were the usual naysayers who decided there never had been any actual threat but rather a hoax per-petuated by the newspapers. Even carefree and jaded soldiers were heard to declare of the famous equestrian statue of George Washington on Pennsylvania Avenue in the West End "that's wash-tub-a-ridin on a contract hoss!" The nation's capital had returned to form.[43]

Yet, nothing could erase the audacity and near success of the enemy. Nothing was being resolved that summer, that "wild howl of summer," in historian John Waugh's words. Even the president had to face facts. It did not look bright for his reelection, the war was hardly concluded much less won and word on the street may well have mirrored public building commissioner Benjamin B. French's July 17 jotting in his diary, "My friend Abraham has got to do something to retrieve this awful blunder, or he is 'a goner.'" Lincoln reacted to events, suggests historian Matthew Pinsker, by a certain hardening of his determination to finish the job of saving a besieged Union. With generals like Grant asking for more cannon fodder, he dutifully requested the half-million fresh young faces (figuring conscription might bring them out). Ironically, here was a stunning admission of inadequacy in and of itself to a war-weary public. Moreover, that same day, July 18, the chief executive stiffened his position on slavery. Cries for negotiation—a peace settlement—with the Confederacy were in high gear among people like newspaperman Horace Greeley. But, Lincoln stated unequivocally "to whom it may concern," that "any proposition which embraces the restoration of peace, the integrity of the whole Union, and the abandonment of slavery" would be the only terms he would entertain. Surely, even Rebel commissioners would understand that.[44]

Kate Lamson wrote to her naval husband from Mt. Vernon, Ohio, on July 13, "What do you think of the prospect for rebeldom capturing Washington before we capture Richmond?" She admitted that it may not be very patriotic, but she could not "help the feeling that even such invasions are better than stagnation." They "will keep us active and awake to the dangers surrounding us," she added. She hoped Early's invaders would be captured and felt Grant would not be diverted from his purpose as he has paid too great a price for his position before Petersburg and Richmond to relinquish it. She hoped there would not be anything more than "a little" left to be done by the next summer. Lieutenant Roswell Lamson commanded the USS *Gettysburg* off the North Carolina coast, and his wife assured him that "you know it is said to be 'always darkest just before day.'" Didn't her husband Roswell "think it is almost as dark now as it very well could be and that the 'day' must be coming soon?" Obviously if Lincoln was upset, the northern public was more than a little disturbed by the torpidity of events.[45]

Perhaps it was a dark and howling summer to the North—"the darkest of the many dark moments in the war," said Noah Brooks. The president and Congress seemed irrationally locked in opposition over the Wade-Davis harsh reconstruction legislation. Peace overtures butted war to the knife. To be sure, other items occupied the president's docket after Early's appearance before Fort Stevens. The furor about Confederate peace commissioners, David Hunter's burning of supposed Rebels' houses in the lower Shenandoah in retaliation for the incineration of Maryland governor Bradford's country house near Baltimore by Harry Gilmor's people, and the tottering political loyalty of Kentucky thanks to Unionist war hero Colonel Frank L. Wolford and his vehement opposition to the administration's emancipation policy all fretted Lincoln. He suspended the writ of habeas corpus when Kentuckians threatened insurgency. The ever-present, questionable trading in cotton in Union-occupied areas of the Deep South as well as equitability of wages paid to women workers in government munitions factories also intruded on the president's time. Yet, when Secretary and Mrs. Welles visited Lincoln and his wife at Soldiers' Home cottage on Tuesday, July 26, all the talk was about Early's apparent move toward southern Pennsylvania. The cabinet member warned his boss that energy and decision were called for "in getting behind them, cutting them off, and not permitting them to go back," directly reflecting Early's previous escape after Fort Stevens. Both men agreed that proactive, not reactive, action was called for instead of letting a crisis and scare and then escape with plunder define Rebel movements. Amid another heat wave striking the city, even Lincoln's coolness was tested as he repeatedly chided Hunter to get moving. He consoled the general that rumors of displeasure with Hunter's conduct had not come from the White House. When Hunter failed to act, the president made his move. The Hampton Roads meeting with Grant resulted.[46]

Resolution, Finally

Grant's plea for a unified regional command on the twenty-fifth finally caught hold in Washington. On the twenty-sixth, Stanton directed Halleck to organize and personally command a consolidated department of Middle, Susquehanna, Washington, and West Virginia entities for "the present emergency." But it was all still vague. Inside this "Division," the present departmental commanders still held sway. Halleck's latest biographer, Curt Anders, observes that Lincoln and Stanton "were in the position of cooks trying to restore a botched omelet to the pristine condition of the eggs," if not positioning Halleck once more as a lightning rod to absorb public wrath and to minimize additional political damage. Again, it seemed like 1862 all over again. And once again, the commander-in-chief decided it was time to personally confront his top general. A "cipher" message went from Lincoln to Grant on July 28. Meet him at Fort Monroe. Lincoln's wife, Mary Todd, and some of her friends could flee the heat wave for the sea breezes and accompany the president. But it would be Lincoln and Grant meeting alone for five hours on Sunday morning, July 31, that was the real focus of the trip.[47]

To this day we cannot be sure what the pair discussed. We may speculate, for Lincoln had scrawled on the back of Grant's July 20 acceptance telegram, "Meade & Franklin/McClellan/Md & Penna." Were these agenda items or talking points somehow involving generals or geography? Did they imply something about unity of command or perhaps the president's acquiescence to Halleck's new division as a stopgap measure? Were Franklin's and McClellan's names there because of political or military reasons? Perhaps, the pros and cons of bringing McClellan back aboard seemed a way to diffuse his political threat. Lincoln most certainly worried that Grant's attitude toward the ramifications of Early too closely reflected *New York Times* editor Henry Raymond's debunking of the late Confederate raid as the "annual 'scare,'" devoid of military value, with only what happened before Richmond and Atlanta as crucial to fall elections. Old Jube's name was absent from the president's cryptic note, but his presence in the war's equation most certainly was not. Grant had indicated a desire to discuss and not put anything in writing about his own consolidation scheme. The president surely viewed their consultation as leading to a resolution of the issues. Above all, the president expected action, quick action, when the two men returned to their respective corners of the war. That, too, was eerily reminiscent of the Lincoln-McClellan situation two years before.[48]

Grant wanted to introduce Phillip H. Sheridan, another young Westerner who had become part of the Grant clique now running military operations. Lincoln apparently acquiesced, for neither McClellan nor Franklin offered a viable alternative. Grant immediately wired Halleck on August 1 that he wanted Sheridan placed in command of the field troops in the Shenandoah "with instructions to put himself south of the enemy and follow him to the death. Wherever the enemy goes let our troops go also. Once started up the Valley they ought to be followed until we get possession of the Virginia Central Railroad." Grant once again left an escape for his old mentor and commander from a bygone period of service. David Hunter might retain departmental command if not actually continuing in the field dealing with Early. Lincoln reacted quickly as soon as he became aware of this move. At 6:00 a.m. on August 3, an obviously provoked commander-in-chief wired Grant that he agreed with the theory but "please look over the dispatches you may have received from here, even since you made that order, and discover, if you can, that there is any idea in the head of any one here, of 'putting our army South of the enemy' or of following him to the death in any direction. I repeat to you it will neither be done nor attempted unless you watch it every day, and hour, and force it." Finally, Grant got the message. On August 4, he traveled to personally see what was taking place. He found Hunter's army resting in camps along the banks of the Monocacy nearly three weeks after chasing back and forth responding to Early's feints. Grant still envisioned Sheridan and Hunter cooperating until he witnessed the lack of energy by a supine Hunter, who realized he was being shelved and asked for relief. Grant obliged, directing the army to move to forward positions around Halltown west of Harpers Ferry and prepare for active campaigning. Sheridan took over, and a young signalman, David Seibert, wrote his father from Harpers Ferry on August 7, "We expect some work is on hand and I expect something will be done now."[49]

Fate decreed that the story had come full circle. Grant's discussions with Hunter took place at Keifer Thomas's Araby house, and Sheridan's change of command came at the nearby Monocacy (Frederick) Junction station of the Baltimore & Ohio.

Both were key sites associated with Lew Wallace's battle of the Monocacy. So it was fitting that the resolution of Early's campaign against Washington would appear here. Still, somewhat surprisingly, the normally hyperactive Sheridan failed to move with expected speed. For one thing he needed to get a measure of his new position, the composite force he now commanded, and to allow the disparate elements a rest period for rehabilitation and establishment of cohesion as his new Army of the Shenandoah. Even when he moved, he sputtered at first against Early. This may have resulted as much from what Robert E. Lee had learned from Early's raid if not the continued parrying of Hunter. Lee never gave up on threatening Washington as a device to relieve Richmond-Petersburg pressure. On July 23 he wrote President Davis that "a mounted force with long range guns" might quickly and secretly penetrate the defenses of Washington south of the Potomac "and excite the alarm of the authorities at Washington." Notwithstanding what Early told him about the approach to the capital being detected by the enemy, hence those works "could be manned in time to prevent it," Lee kept searching all of August, reinforcing Early "should the enemy's forces move west of the Blue Ridge range, leaving Washington uncovered." Yet by September, just about the time Sheridan finally stirred, Lee realized the strategic game of threats to the nation's capital was at an end. He now told Davis on September 1, "As matters now stand, we have no troops disposable to meet movements of the enemy or strike where opportunity presents, without taking them from the trenches and exposing some important point." Grant, not Lee, was winning the resource war, thereby affecting the operational as well as the grand strategy of the war.[50]

With Time to Think and Reflect

Confederate leaders had to face reality. The cost incurred by Early's raid had been high. True, the booty and ransom seemingly offset losses. But whether or not direct military costs justified the expense (historians such as William C. Davis have concluded that they did), casualties and Early's eventual disasters in the fall raise the question. Recorded loss figures were never clear. Troops operating under John C. Breckinridge (as Early's second in command), reputedly amounted to just over one thousand or 15 percent of the corps, suggests Davis. Early mainly used Gordon's division to do the bulk of the fighting north of the Potomac, and his particular casualty figures reached 21 percent. Notwithstanding a campaign lasting less than three weeks and counting "but one small-scale battle," in Davis's view, that small battle, straggling and fatigue from hard campaigning, probably cost Early and the Confederacy their last chance to significantly affect the war's outcome. Davis may have been closer to the mark when he advanced that on the positive side, Early scared the North, the administration, possibly Lincoln "as they had never been frightened before." That Early had drawn almost two enemy army corps away from the Petersburg struggle is unarguable. That he had captured considerable supplies and "perhaps best of all," suggests Davis, showed the Union and the world "that the Confederacy could still mount a major threat to its antagonist" equally stands the test of time. Realistically, Old Jube probably gained Lee six months' respite. That same space might also have been obtained had Early never been dispatched in the first place. At the time, Lee, Jefferson Davis, or anyone else had little time to ponder those possibilities.[51]

Be that as it may, southerners thought much had been accomplished at the time. As historian Jason Phillips has written, reading the panic caused by Early's raid in Yankee newspapers, "and hoping this third invasion of the North would be the charm," Confederates in uniform and mufti "enjoyed weeks of good rumors and fantastic predictions." From the Petersburg trenches came comments about carrying the war to the enemy, exciting news of routed bluecoats, reliable and cheering word that Grant would give up his siege and return North to save Washington or Baltimore or both, and that POWs at Point Lookout had been liberated and Washington "had fallen into our hands & that Genl Early had mounted all of his men & was recrossing the Potomac." A more sanguine young gunner, Willy Pegram, regarded "it as a very brilliant & successful 'raid' so far; but hope Early may meet with no disaster in getting back, after having penetrated so far into the enemy's country." Early "should have been better satisfied if he had done less, but drawn Grant away from siege warfare and gotten back to field fighting once more." Given rumors and hopes, it might have seemed natural that another Rebel, Urban Owen, thought from Atlanta that "our prospects of final success were never more flattering than at present." Rather, observes Phillips, Early's operation "ended in ignominy not victory."[52]

The *Richmond Examiner* optimistically suggested that "Early is stumping the States of Maryland and Pennsylvania for the peace party." Thomas Goree, sometime aide to James Longstreet, wrote his mother from Lynchburg on August 26 with his diagnosis of affairs. "The chief points of interest now are Petersburg, Atlanta, Mobile and the valley of the Virginia." With seesaw affairs in the latter, "our force there is sufficient to contend successfully with that of the enemy wherever they may choose to give us battle." The situation at Petersburg was less favorable, and he mistakenly assessed that "our policy ought to be to risk no general engagement without it is necessary to hold a position of vital importance. Richmond and Petersburg were such places; Atlanta is not." President Davis thought differently, but Confederate focus did shift from Washington.[53]

The Final Howling

Ohio national guardsman Charles M. Yocum again wrote his friend, Bella, at the end of July. From Yocum's perspective at Fort Reynolds, "I need not say anything about the raid into Maryland and the danger to Washington" until "I can talk to you faster than in this way." He did unleash a tirade against "many of the [newspaper] editors [who] have lied wonderfully about I among whom the most indecent is the editor of the [Democratic New York] *World* [John Bennett]." He thought "if any man in the U.S. ought to wear a hempen cravat, that man is the editor and [the] correspondents of the *World*." "They seem aggravated because the Rebs did not take Washington," he railed. Meanwhile, Early's men were "making a good thing in the Shenandoah Valley" where "they are harvesting out the crops of the Union men." "Our fences do not seem able to overcome them," although by this time in the summer, news elsewhere "seems good enough" since "Atlanta is partly in hands of Sherman and he says he could make his headquarters in the city in 2 hours if he would."[54]

Yocum, as an astute observer of the political scene, did not reflect such optimism when it came to "Things National." "A great political campaign—perhaps the most agitating of any since the establishment of this Government—is pending, and soon that contest is to be and with it the direful throes of contention and even the most bitter hatred incident to such campaigns, and among those to whom the government must look for support and defense in this day of sorest trial," he predicted. Lincoln "is in a critical position, aye, most critical," he thought. Still, Yocum was pleased, "yea thrice happy," to see him sink his own political interests into the "patriot, the statesman, and the interests of his country." Lincoln's recent call for five hundred thousand more men "must weaken his political strength very materially"—although not among those who were true Union men, he was happy to say. "But there are too many who are Union just as long as others fight the battles, Union as long as they don't have to face the music." Old Abe would lose many such votes, Yocum went on, hence this autumn "we will be required to use double exertion to carry on the war and to elect our man." "If the Peace Party secures their man [McClellan], we may almost bid farewell to permanent peace." "Aye, I almost fear for the American Union," he wailed, except that the Democrats in postponing their convention from July 4 to August 27 demonstrated "they knew not what to do or how to do it." In Yocum's view, like those of most Americans both North and South after Early's surprising raid, events now hinged upon what Grant and Sherman might do at Richmond and Atlanta.

Student of the 1864 presidential election John Waugh speaks tellingly of how the "wild howl of summer" eventually dissipated via "three 'stump speeches,'" which he thought possibly the "most eloquent of the campaign" and were delivered by three nonpoliticians. Rear Admiral David Farragut damned torpedoes and closed Mobile Bay to Confederate use in Waugh's first declaration of Union power on August 5. Yet the political scene remained murky as War Democrats, Peace Democrats, Copperheads, Radicals, and ultra-Radicals all escalated their cacophony of criticism against the Lincoln administration, and McClellan acceded to formal opposition, as did disgraced general John C. Fremont for the radicals of the Republican Party.

Then, suddenly, the dark clouds broke apart. Uncle Billy Sherman finally "fairly won" Atlanta on September 2 for Waugh's second "stump speech," and Sheridan got his own juggernaut going with triple victories over the next month at Winchester, Fishers Hill, and Cedar Creek in the final of Waugh's three "stump speeches."[55]

More recently, David Johnson has also explained the important sequence. Farragut's breakthrough victory (without losing thousands of men) had thrilled northerners "coming after the Crater and Cold Harbor and the raid on Washington." David Alan Johnson, too, wove the sequence of events from the bleak chapter of Early's men at the threshold of the capital. But then from Mobile Bay through the fall of Atlanta to the washing of the spears with Sheridan in the Valley, Johnson's title, *Decided on the Battlefield*, features the relationship of Grant, Sherman, Lincoln, and the election of 1864. "Early's remnant continued to be a nuisance" thereafter, observed E. B. Long forty years ago in his still-classic *The Civil War Day by Day*, "but Federals controlled the Valley until the end." Early's threat to Lincoln and the capital clearly was no more. Momentum switched sides. Between northern state elections in October and the national presidential contest on November 8, Lincoln retained the White House with over 55 percent of the popular vote. Nowhere has any historian or contemporary correctly noted that the ending of this Civil War chapter began at a Confederate battle victory on the Monocacy that caused them defeat two days later at Fort Stevens. The specter of Monocacy, Fort Stevens, and Jubal Early hung over the period and has clouded the true nature of the epoch ever since. Eventually, Early's threat vanished, although possibly not until a final lurch at Waynesborough, Virginia, the following spring when Sheridan's veterans ultimately destroyed the remnants of Early's once proud and formidable Army of the Valley. But rather than disaster, Monocacy and Fort Stevens snatched Union strategic— hence political and military victory—from the jaws of defeat.[56]

Assigning Immediate Memories

Private George Perkins, Sixth New York Independent Battery, witnessed most of the Fort Stevens fighting from a supporting position near Fort Reno. He and his mates then had accompanied Lowell's sortie to Rockville, where they got a better taste of fighting to save the capital. Rather than going further with Wright's eventual pursuit, they returned to the defenses, and by July 14, they went back to the artillery camp at Camp Barry. Lateral passage behind the defenses brought his laconic, "this road ran through a beautiful glen musical with brook and waterfall, with an old mill and a farm house just peeping from a leafy nest." A rustic suspension bridge joined opposite banks of the stream, and "standing upon this swinging structure to gaze at the battery halting to water the steaming horses" proved "a picture worthy to be commemorated on canvas." Further march came to a ravine, which provided a magnificent view of the capital—a surprise "to find there was a point from which the city appeared so actually beautiful." Waxing for the benefit of hometown readers of the *Middlesex Journal* in Massachusetts, Perkins noted the distant mixing of "low wooden dwellings and dirty purlieus as indistinguishable, the distant blue of the Alexandrine hills turned softer by the nearer line of the river"—all a "fit background to the bossed green and white of the city, that circled the Capitol like jewels setting on a shining opal." In the end, he admitted, "about nightfall, after our arduous (?) and dangerous (?) campaign of three days we arrived in Camp Barry without the loss of a man—except a bag of pork, which unfortunately dropped off a caisson on our outward march." "We try to persuade ourselves that we did an immense deal of good, but cannot quite succeed." This is how Perkins remembered the battle in Washington's suburbs.[57]

Perkins wrote under the pen name of Hoplite. He was happiest recounting the state of feelings in civilian Washington during the Rebel visit. "It seemed to me that there was an amount of fear greatly above the cause." Men restlessly roamed to and fro looking feverishly into the faces of any passing column of soldiers. One lady was so nervous and trembling while passing water to marchers that "she scarce could ladle water from her pail into the tumbler" yet could not retire indoors, he recounted, and she had stood at her post all day in the dust and heat. Perkins doubted not the citizenry's "white faces, their tears and their tremblings, braced more than one stout heart to the conflict." To inspire the home front, he bragged that the arrangement of the defenders "was carried on in a very orderly and creditable manner," and a great many armed citizens aided in manning the trenches, so much so, in fact, that on the battery's return through the city it looked almost deserted. He quickly added, "This raid proved beyond a doubt that there are many secession sympathizers yet in the city." At least one Rebel flag was discovered in some state of fabrication, a dead citizen was found near Rockville "who had been fighting in the rebel cause," and even near where his unit had been positioned "there was a large house, the owner of which was engaged in fabricating a rebel flag while the fight was going on at Fort Stevens, as was learned from her negro laborer." Perkins concluded ten days after the event that "the rebels are safely across the Potomac, having accomplished the most successful and best paying raid of the war."

On September 10, a busy President Lincoln signed certificates of thanks for honorable service to "Ohio Volunteers for One Hundred Days." Their term of service had been short, read the wording, but distinguished by memorable events. "In the Valley of the Shenandoah, on the Peninsula, in the Operations on the James river, around Petersburg and Richmond, in the battle of Monocacy, and in the Entrenchments of Washington," as well as other important service, "the NATIONAL GUARD OF OHIO performed with alacrity the duty of Patriotic Volunteers," thus "warranting . . . the NATIONAL THANKS." Often maligned as "militia" by friend, foe, and posterity, these Buckeyes knew what they had contributed and were proud of doing "all that was required of us, and that was enough, in all conscience." "It was drill, fatigue and guard duty all the time, still all orders were cheerfully obeyed," said one, adding, "at Washington we manned three of the forts, could have defended them too." As witnessed by the president's own wording, the specifics of three days in July—at Monocacy and at Fort Stevens—would blur for the veterans, observers, and the future. In the aftermath, only the first group understood what had been accomplished by repelling Early from the ramparts.

Other reserve contributors similarly took up the cause of recognition. Quartermaster Montgomery Meigs praised his ersatz battalions. They had served sans reproach. Those on duty "relieved at least an equal number of trained soldiers and enabled them to go to the front, while those who were placed in the intrenchments extended the line of battle fully a mile to the right of the center of attack, and by their presence and bearing, standing upon the parapets and exposing themselves, perhaps, more than more experienced soldiers would have done, they convinced the enemy that the fortifications of Washington were not unmanned," he told the War Department on July 25. Of course, accomplishments at Fort Stevens merged with the chase of Early for VI Corps veterans. As Major Thomas McLaughlin observed, "From the landing at Washington until August 21 [we] marched over 400 miles, crossing the Potomac four times and the Shenandoah twice." If Early's words rang true, maybe Washington could never be taken "unless surprised when without a force to defend it." Nonetheless, nothing about Fort Stevens in those immediate commentaries quite resonated like Lew Wallace's strident cry about the Monocacy dead—"these men died to save the National Capital, and they did save it." Surely that same sentiment accompanied the Battleground Forty who went to their graves just as valorously defending Lincoln at Fort Stevens.[58]

Indeed, the afterglow could be seen in quips by the veterans. Private Benjamin Marshall of the First New Hampshire Heavy Artillery had witnessed Early's appearance from Fort Simmons, to the west of Tennallytown. "Don't know how many of [the rebels] were killed before it ended, but they got pretty badly whipped." Austin Fenn of the Tenth Massachusetts had been left behind at City Point when his unit went off to chase Early's corps "raising the devil" in Maryland. But he followed closely how the First and Third divisions of the VI Corps "helped chase the gray cusses out last year" and guessed "they will want to take their asses in their hands and get out this time" also. Vincent K. Tazlo of Company H, One Hundred and Fiftieth Ohio National Guard, and eight mates had gone to the battlefield without permission on July 13. Defending Fort Bunker Hill during the raid, they had naturally been disciplined for such actions. But Tazlo came back proud having saved a puppy from the scene of carnage. Perhaps the most poignant was the letter penned by a Christian

Commission volunteer to a young South Deerfield, Massachusetts, lass who had ten cents she had earned at some chore "to be spent in getting something for some brave soldier who might be in need." Henry M. Whitney wrote to her in November how he had purchased a testament and had taken it with him to Washington in July. He had become caught up in succoring the invalids at the 2,200-bed Mount Pleasant hospital at the very time of Early's appearance, but he never found the right match for the testament. Eventually, the right candidate emerged from the pool of Fort Stevens wounded. Elatedly, this Christian Commission delegate wrote young Mary Alice Munson that he finally found the right soldier for the testament so "that you approve of my disposal of my little trust."[59]

The following year, soldiers such as Color Sergeant Lewis Cass White, One Hundred and Second Pennsylvania, who had fought on the Fort Stevens skirmish line, went home. In between, Washington's static garrisons (such as the Third Massachusetts Artillery, captured on camera with the battlefield as a clear photographic backdrop) had drilled while engineers around the defense line continued to strengthen works, anticipating a threat that would come no more. Lincoln was shot on April 14, 1865, died the next morning, and, like Fort Stevens, now "belongs to the ages." Nine months after his escape from death on the ramparts of that fort, an assassin's bullet found its mark in a downtown theater. How would history had been changed if some Rebel minie ball had found its mark on July 11 or 12, 1864? Nondescript vice president Hannibal Hamlin would have succeeded Lincoln—to what result? Negotiating peace and trading away emancipation, McClellan vaulted into the White House? Would Lincoln as a military casualty have been different than being the victim of a zealot's political statement? Would the retribution that took hold after April 1865 have not occurred as a result of Lincoln's death or maiming at Fort Stevens? Ford's Theater, not Fort Stevens, produced retribution, not reconciliation, until a weary, reunified nation simply chorused forget it all, plow under the bleak memories, reinter the body pieces, and turn to new forms of progress. Through the succeeding decades, Decoration Day at Battleground meant more to the survivors than the dark and bloody ground that had claimed comrades and cause. Later people might appreciate the meaning of places like Monocacy and Fort Stevens in their own right. Perhaps not.

Notes

1. Horatio Nelson Taft diary, July 13, 1864, volume 3, Library of Congress, Washington, D.C.

2. Letter, Charles M. Yocum to friend, July 13, 1864, author's collections.

3. Charles M. Yocum to B. A., July 14, 1864, author's collections.

4. Benjamin F. Taylor, *Pictures of Life in Camp and Field* (Chicago: S. C. Griggs and Company, 1888), 218.

5. Charles M. McGee Jr., and Ernest M. Lander Jr., editors, *A Rebel Came Home: The Diary and Letters of Floride Clemson, 1863–1866* (Columbia: University of South Carolina Press, 1989), 52–59; Fred Pelka, editor, *The Civil War Letters of Colonel Charles F. Johnson, Invalid Corps* (Amherst: University of Massachusetts Press, 2004), chapter 8, especially 258, 259.

6. *Washington Star*, July 16, 1864.

7. J. G. Bradwell, "Reminiscences," chapter 3, 9, Maryland Historical Society (MS), "Burning of the Blair House," *Confederate Veterans* XIX (July 1911): 336; Jubal Early to Edmund Jennings Lee, September 26, 1872, Lee papers, DU; William C. Davis, *Breckinridge: Statesman, Soldier, Symbol* (Baton Rouge: Louisiana State University Press, 1974), 449; Jubal A. Early, "The Advance on Washington in 1864," *Southern Historical Society Papers*, 9 (July/August 1881), 310–11; Henry Kyd Douglas, *I Rode with Stonewall* (Chapel Hill: University of North Carolina Press, 1940), 296; Leonidas Lafayette Polk to wife, July 17, 1864, Southern Historical Collections, University of North Carolina, Chapel Hill (SHC/UNC); Robert E. Park, "Diary," *Southern Historical Society Papers* I (1876): 379–80; V. E. Watson, "Fifty-Fifth Regiment," in volume 3, 55, of Walter E. Clark, *Histories of the Several Regiments and Battalions from North Carolina in the Great War* (Raleigh: E. M. Uzzell, 1901); James McMurran diary, July 12, 1864, entry, Virginia State Library and Archives (VSLA); *ORA*, I, 42, pt. 2, 62; *New York Times*, July 22, 1864; Hudson Strode, *Jefferson Davis: Tragic Hero* (New York: Harcourt, Brace and World, 1964), 567; Alvin Green, "Burning of Blair Mansion," *National Tribune*, August 16, 1900; A. C. Fletcher, "At Fort Stevens," *National Tribune*, September 27, 1900; Virginia Jeans Laas, editor, *Wartime Washington: The Civil War Letters of Elizabeth Blair Lee* (Urbana: University of Illinois Press, 1991), 403–16 inter alia; *Washington Star*, July 15, 1865; Douglas, *I Rode with Stonewall*, 296.

8. Letter, F. C. Morse to "My dear bosom companion," July 13, 1864, F. C. Morse papers, Massachusetts Historical Society, Boston; Gideon Welles, *Diary*, volume II (Boston: Houghton Mifflin, 1909), 80.

9. Laas, ibid., 402–17.

10. Welles, *Diary*, 80; Laas, ibid.

11. Laas, *Wartime Washington*, 405, 411, 413–14.

12. L. E. Chittenden, *Recollections of President Lincoln and His Administration* (New York: Harper and Brothers, 1891), 418–19.

13. Ibid., 421.

14. David B. Swinfen, *Ruggles' Regiment: The 122nd New York Volunteers in the American Civil War* (Hanover and London: University Press of New England, 1982), 51; S. A. McDonald, "Fort Stevens Affairs, Part 2," *National Tribune*, April 19, 1894; Chittenden, *Recollections of President Lincoln*, 420, 421; "B.O.B," "The Twenty-Fifth New York Cavalry," *New York Sunday Mercury*, July 24, 1864, in William B. Styple, editor, *Writing and Fighting the Civil War: Soldier Correspondence to the* New York Sunday Mercury (Kearny, NJ: Belle Grove Publishing Company, 2000), 271; Letter, Vincent K. Tazlo to Friends, July 13, 1864, author's collection.

15. John H. Cramer, *Lincoln under Enemy Fire: The Complete Account of His Experience during Early's Attack on Washington* (Baton Rouge: Louisiana State University Press, 1948; Knoxville: University of Tennesse Press, 2009), 63–67.

16. Tyler Dennett, *Lincoln and the Civil War in the Diaries and Letters of John Hay* (New York: Dodd Mead, 1939), 208–10.

17. Letter, J. C. McFerran to Montgomery Meigs, March 17, 1870, relating to title, Battleground National Cemetery and Accompany Correspondence files, Rock Creek Nature Center, National Park Service, Washington D.C. (RCNC).

18. George T. Stevens, *Three Years in the Sixth Corps* (Albany, NY: S. R. Gray, 1866), 378.

19. Hoyt Barnett, "Recalls Gen. Early's Raid," *Washington Star*, July 14, 1935.

20. U.S. Navy Department, *Official Records of the Union and Confederate Navies in the War of the Rebellion* (Washington, DC, 1894–1927), Series I, Volume 10, 252–53, 254, 271–72, while on the individual vessels of the naval response, see Paul H. Silverstone, *Warships of the Civil War Navies* (Annapolis: Naval Institute Press, 1989), 28, 63, 75, 80, 90, 95, 99, 101, 203.

21. Ibid., 272, 284; Laas, *Wartime Washington*, 422–23.

22. Roy P. Basler, editor, *The Collected Works of Abraham Lincoln*, volume VIII (New Brunswick, NJ: Rutgers University Press, 1953), 42–43.

23. Basler, ibid., 439–40; Welles, *Diary*, II, 80.

24. Horatio Nelson Taft diary, July 16, 1864, volume 3, Library of Congress, Washington, D.C.

25. "Were We Betrayed?" *New York Sunday Mercury*, July 17, 1864, in William B. Styple, editor, *Writing and Fighting the Civil War*, 268–69.

26. Basler, *The Collected Works of Abraham Lincoln*, 439–74, inter alia; Fritz Haselberger, *Confederate Retaliation: McCausland's 1864 Raid* (Shippensburg, PA: Burd Street Press, 2000), chapters 8 and 9; and Ted Alexander et al., *Southern Revenge! Civil War History of Chambersburg, Pennsylvania* (Shippensburg, PA: White Mane, 1989), chapter 6.

27. Morgan Royce, "Account of Frederick W. Royce Regarding Reestablishing Communications on Baltimore and Ohio Railroad, July 13, 1864," Filson Club Archives, Louisville, Kentucky.

28. *ORA*, I, 37, pt. 2, 333–34; "Worst Rebel" quote in Allen Clark, "Abraham Lincoln in the National Capital," *Records of the Columbia Historical* Society 27 (1925): 60.

29. Letter, Francis M. Imboden to mother, July 22, 1864, author's collections.

30. John N. Opie, *A Rebel Cavalryman with Stuart and Jackson* (Chicago: W. B. Conkey, 1899), 246; C. A. Fonerden, *A Brief History of the Military Career of Carpenter's Battery* (New Market: Henkel, 1911), 48.

31. Dennett, *Lincoln and the Civil War*, 210; Welles, *Diary*, II, 77; *Washington Evening Star*, July 13, 1864.

32. Welles, ibid., 77–78.

33. Samuel Van Elder to Master Samuel Van Elder, July 28 and September 13, 1864, author's collections.

34. Clifford Dowdey and Louis Manarin, editors, *The Wartime Papers of Robert E. Lee* (New York: Brammel House for Virginia Civil War Commission, 1966), 819–20, 821–23.

35. Letter, Francis M. Imboden to mother, July 22, 1864, author's collections; on Mosby, see the partisan's report of September 11, 1864, in James J. Williamson, *Mosby's Rangers: A Record of the Operations of the Forty-Third Battalion Virginia Cavalry* (New York: Ralph B. Kenyon, 1896), 416.

36. *ORA*, I, 37, pt. 1, 268–74; Jeffrey D. Wert, "The Snicker's Gap War," *Civil War Times Illustrated* XVII (July 1978): 38; Benjamin Franklin Cooling, *Jubal Early's Raid on Washington, 1864* (Nautical and Aviation Publishing Company of America, 1989; Tuscaloosa: University of Alabama Press, 2007), 188–220; John William De Forest, James H. Croushore, editor, *A Volunteer's Adventures: A Union Captain's Record of the Civil War* (Baton Rouge: Louisiana State University Press, 1946/2001), 161–63.

37. Jeffrey D. Wert, *From Winchester to Cedar Creek: The Shenandoah Campaign of 1864* (New York: Simon & Schuster, 1987), chapter 1.

38. *ORA*, I, 37, pt. 2, 328–29, 350.

39. Ibid., pt. 2, 316, 373–74, 400.

40. Ibid., I, 38, pt. 5, 150–51; for further on Halleck, see Stephen E. Ambrose, *Halleck: Lincoln's Chief of Staff* (Baton Rouge: Louisiana State University Press, 1962), 176–77, and Curt Anders, *Henry Halleck's War: A Fresh Look at Lincoln's Controversial General-in-Chief* (Carmel, IN: Guild Press of Indiana, 1999), 590–98.

41. *ORA*, I, 37, pt. 2, 384–85.

42. Ibid., pt. 2, 408–12, 427; Ulysses S. Grant, *The Complete Personal Memoirs of Ulysses S. Grant, volume II* (New York: Empire Books, 1885), 317.

43. See P. J. Staudenrause, *Mr. Lincoln's Washington: The Civil War Dispatches of Noah Brooks* (South Brunswick: Thomas Yoseloff, 1967), 360; Mary Mitchell, *Divided Town: A Study of Georgetown, D.C., during the Civil War* (Barre, MA: Barre Publishers, 1968), 161–63; Chittenden, *Recollections of President Lincoln*, 421; Fred Smith, *Samuel Duncan Oliphant: The Indomitable Campaigner* (New York: Exposition Press, 1967), 163–67; Welles, *Diary*, II, 77; George R. Kimball to I. B. Upham, August 10, 1864, U.S. Army Heritage Center, Carlisle Barracks, PA.

44. Matthew Pinsker, *Lincoln's Sanctuary: Abraham Lincoln and the Soldiers' Home* (New York: Oxford University Press, 2005), 145; Donald B. Cole and John J. McDonough, editors, *Benjamin Brown French: Witness to the Young Republic: A Yankee's Journal 1828–1870* (Hanover, NH: University Press of New England, 1989), 453; Basler, *Collected Works of Abraham Lincoln, VIII*, 448–49, 451–52, 464–65; John C. Waugh, *Reelecting Lincoln: The Battle for the 1864 Presidency* (New York: Crown, 1997), chapters 19 and 20.

45. James M. McPherson and Patricia R. McPherson, editors, *Lamson of the Gettysburg: The Civil War Letters of Lieutenant Roswell H. Lamson, U.S. Navy* (New York: Oxford University Press, 1997), 189–90.

46. Basler, *Lincoln Collected Works, VIII*, 440–42, 445, 446–47, 457, 456, 459, 465, 466–67, 469–70, 471–72, 476, 480.

47. *ORA*, I, 37, pt. 2, 463, 492; Anders, *Henry Halleck's War*, 599.

48. *New York Times*, July 13, 16, 1864, and *Chicago Tribune*, July 20, 1864, quoted in Waugh, *Reelecting Lincoln*, 244; Basler, *Lincoln Collected Works, VIII*, 469–70, 476; Welles, *Diary*, II, 87–88; Pinsker, *Lincoln's Sanctuary*, 147–48.

49. David Seibert to his father, August 7, 1864, Seibert Family papers, Harrisburg CWRT Collection, U.S. Army Heritage Center; Grant, *Personal Memoirs*, II, 319–20; Basler, *Lincoln Collected Works, VIII*, 476 and note.

50. *ORA*, I, 37, part 2, 599; Dowdey and Manarin, *Wartime Papers of Robert E. Lee*, 832–35, 845–50, 852–53.

51. Davis, *Breckinridge: Statesman, Soldier, Symbol*, 445, citing Field Return, July 15, 1864, in James W. Eldridge collection, Huntington Library, San Marino, California.

52. Jason Phillips, *Diehard Rebels: The Confederate Culture of Invincibility* (Athens: University of Georgia Press, 2007), 128–29; letter, Urban Moore to wife, July 16, 1864, quoted in Enoch Mitchell, editor, "Letters of a Confederate Surgeon in the Army of Tennessee to His Wife," *Tennessee Historical Quarterly* 5 (June 1946): 172; "Letters from the Petersburg Trenches," from Collections of Virginia Historical Society, compliments cosmic.america@yahoo.com.

53. Thomas W. Cutrer and T. Michael Parrish, editors, *Longstreet's Aide: The Civil War Letters of Major Thomas J. Goree* (Charlottesville: University Press of Virginia, 1955), 133–35; Edward Younger, editor, *Inside the Confederate Cabinet: The Diary of Robert Garlick Hill Kean* (New York: Oxford University Press, 1957), 164.

54. Letter, Charles M. Yocum to "Very dear Bella," July 30, 1864, author's collections.

55. John C. Waugh, *Reelecting Lincoln*, 295–361 inter alia; for the fascinating sequel between Early and Sheridan, see George E. Pond, *The Shenandoah Valley in 1864* (New York: Scribner's, 1883); Edward J. Stackpole, *Sheridan in the Shenandoah: Jubal Early's Nemesis* (Harrisburg: Stackpole Books, 1961); Thomas A. Lewis, *The Shenandoah in Flames: The Valley Campaign of 1864* (Alexandria, VA: Time-Life Books, 1987); and Wert, *From Winchester to Cedar Creek.*

56. E. B. Long, *The Civil War Day By Day: An Almanac, 1861–1865* (Garden City, NY: De Capo Press, 1971), 585 and 549–94 inter alia; David Alan Johnson, *Decided on the Battlefield: Grant, Sherman, Lincoln and the Election of 1864* (Amherst, NY: Prometheus Books, 2012), 147.

57. Richard N. Griffin, editor, *Three Years A Soldier: The Diary and Newspaper Correspondence of Private George Perkins, Sixth New York Independent Battery, 1861–1864* (Knoxville: University of Tennessee Press, 2006), 260–61.

58. *ORA*, I, 37, pt. 2, 200, 257, 279, 349.

59. Letter, Henry M. Whitney to Mary Alice Munson, November 8, 1864, courtesy Chris Foard; Letter excerpt Austin Fenn to ?, July 8, 1864, Brian and Maria Green catalog, Kernerville, North Carolina; Benjamin Marshall to mother, July 11 (?), 1864, Jack Donahue auction catalog, Bayside, New York, Fall 1996; Letter, Vincent K. Tazlo to Friends, July 13, 1864—all copies in author's collection.

CHAPTER TEN

LINCOLN, FORT STEVENS, AND AMERICAN MEMORY

Some people in 1865 wanted to remember. Some people wished to forget what they had been through. Chaplain A. M. Stewart of the One Hundred and Second Pennsylvania was one of the former. Anxious to capture memories before they vanished, he penned his reminiscences even before the conflict ended and published them the next year. About the crisis over Early's raid, Stewart recounted, "It so happens that when any sudden emergency arises—and raid to be headed [off], any long and rapid marches to be made, or any reliable fighting to be done—our 6th corps is almost invariably selected." So in that late emergency, "Although our corps was farthest from City Point—miles south of Petersburg—[the] order came at dusk on Saturday evening July 9th to pack up and fall in." This was done none too soon, he said, "For a delay of twelve hours in the coming of our first and second divisions would to all human appearance, have given Washington into the possession of the rebels." It was a good base for similar veterans of the campaign to spring from later with their own impressions.[1]

On the other hand, Montgomery County, Maryland, farmer W. H. Farquhar wanted to forget. He alluded to the "slime and ugly crawling creatures"—Jubal Early's stragglers—who remained in his neighborhood after the raid. In fact, all over the South, the detritus of deserters and bandits spread terror and crime in the wake of regular military movements. Farquhar's Sandy Spring area witnessed irregulars under a "Captain Bowie" or Walter Bowie, ransacking stores and properties until hunted down, cornered, and killed in the fall of 1864. The end of the war brought no closure to local memories of Early's raid on Washington, and subsequently, Philip Sheridan's revenge on the Shenandoah Valley. Only slowly would Confederate and Union soldiers return home, restore the land, work on old and new endeavors, and bind up old wounds. Jubal Early, John C. Breckinridge, and John A. McCausland

SHOWING PROPOSED U.S. MILITARY RESERVATION

AT

FORT STEVENS D.C.

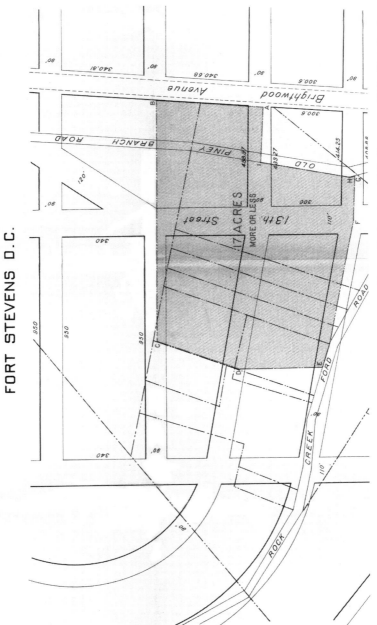

Proposed Fort Stevens Military Reservation, 1902, Plate by Henry B. Looker. U.S. Congress, 57th, First Session, Senate Document 433

all chose exile until the storm of Reconstruction passed. Still, the Kentuckian (like imprisoned Confederate president Jefferson Davis) fell prey to an indictment of high treason on May 26, 1865. Breckinridge's indictment stemmed from Old Jube's attack on Washington.

Survivor Benefits

Both Davis and Breckinridge were former U.S. officials. Yet it was Breckinridge who was charged with leading troops against the capital of the Republic, killing government soldiers and citizens, and destroying property during the July 1864 raid. Although the case never went to trial, signatories to the indictment had personal stakes in its settlement. Francis P. Blair, John P. Claggett, Thomas L. Maury, MD, George E. Kirk, John H. McChesney, and Martin D. Hardin were signatories directly involved with Early's occupation and the Battle at Fort Stevens. Ironically, of those names above, Hardin and McCausland lived to be counted among the oldest surviving officers of Early's raid—the one-armed Hardin dying in 1923 and McCausland four years later. And, of course, McCausland took great pleasure in telling Ulysses S. Grant that he had actually gotten into Washington in 1864.[2]

Others such as John Brown Gordon returned to Georgia, where he was elected senator and governor of the Peach State. He helped set up the state's Ku Klux Klan as well as organizing the United Confederate Veterans and became its first commander-in-chief. Robert Ransom became a government civil engineer in the New Bern, North Carolina, Brigade, and regimental commanders became postwar lawyers, businessmen, even clergymen. Former brigadier general Clement Evans edited a twelve-volume monumental *Confederate Military History*, thus contributing to the memory and understanding of the war. They would all recall, at some point, their devotion to the cause and would occasionally offer insights into Early's raid on Washington. As for their northern counterparts, generals such as Christopher Augur, John C. Barnard, Quincy A. Gillmore, Henry Halleck, Alexander McCook, Montgomery C. Meigs, and Horatio Wright stayed in the army. Ulysses S. Grant, of course, made it to the White House. Others such as Lew Wallace, Max Weber, Franz Sigel, and William Averill used wartime service to gain diplomatic or political positions after the conflict.

Lower officers and men used their service on the winning side to begin careers in politics, business, law, or education. Some, such as Joseph A. Goulden of the Twenty-Fifth New York Cavalry, went to the House of Representatives. George K. Nash, one of the "Oberlin College boys" in the One Hundred and Fiftieth Ohio National Guard, served as Buckeye governor from 1900 to 1904. Color Sergeant Lewis Cass White of the One Hundred and Second Pennsylvania never went home to Whitestown, Pennsylvania, but stayed in Washington. First as a government employee with the army's remount service, he passed to an honorable career with that massive U.S. government entitlement program, or veteran's benefits—the Pension Bureau (in its fabulously appointed red stone structure designed and built by none other than Montgomery Meigs). White's story would intersect again with Fort Stevens. Some would write reminiscences and memoirs. Many, like their Southern counterparts, would develop the politically influential apparatus of the veterans groups—the Grand Army of the Republic and the Military Order of the Loyal Legion. At some point in their lives, from Early down to the lowliest enlisted man, they would add to the body of knowledge about the abortive Washington campaign of 1864.[3]

Elizabeth Thomas, of "Aunty Betty" fame, like other property owners, got her Fort Stevens land back, but little else. She built a new and larger house. But gone were her prewar, two-story, six-room frame dwelling, a stable with a barn over it, a cow shed, a corn house, a hen house, a post and rail fence, her land, and a paling fence around a one-acre garden. Gone, too, were a small apple and peach orchard, damson plum trees, and many kinds of cherry trees together with much shrubbery. They had belonged to Thomas, her sister, Sarah Catherine Diggs, and George Proctor. Both of them would also be gone by the time a bill made its way up Capitol Hill in 1902, asking for $10,507 in reparations for such destruction and the subsequent erection of the three-acre Fort Stevens and rifle pits across their land that "greatly decreased the value for farming or any other purpose." Referred to the Federal Court of Claims two years later, the sum was reduced to $1,835 (perhaps $50,000 today), and it is by no means clear that payment was ever rendered either to Aunt Betty or her heirs.[4]

Honoring Fort Stevens's Confederate Dead

The story of the Confederate dead from Fort Stevens is part of local lore, the divided political sympathies of Marylanders residing in the Silver Spring area and "the progress of sectional reconciliation there during the decades following the war's end," believes one commentator, Gordon Berg. Based on parish records, legend, and family history, Grace Episcopal Church would become the final resting place for seventeen unknown (one would be eventually identified) Southern fallen from that battle. The year would be 1872, eight years after the battle, and presumably the humble, wooden-shingled structure would now have a roof, compliments of Early's donation of $100 sent to rector Dr. Joseph Harding. But a new priest, James Battle Avirett, himself a wartime chaplain with Confederate general Turner Ashby's cavalry in the Shenandoah, subsequently a chaplain in Goldsboro, North Carolina, and after the war headmaster of an Episcopal girl's school in Winchester, moved to Grace. Avirett recounted in 1902 how his frequent travels into Washington had passed a burial trench or mound in which the Confederate dead were buried. He determined this was on the dairy farm of Thomas Lay, soon to become part of the Walter Reed Army Hospital. Thus, they were not far from erstwhile enemies in Battleground National Cemetery.[5]

Avirett, of course, soon sought to remove his comrades-in-arms to the burial ground beside the church. At the time, all the parishioner Blairs were still alive, patriarch Francis Preston not passing until 1875, and in the process of securing vestry permission to reinter the Rebel bodies, Avirett received word that Montgomery Blair would fund "an eligible burying lot." Blair apparently remarked "that these gentlemen were entitled to a Christian burial." Supposedly, six coffins were originally procured, the funeral service was conducted on a "cold, but bright and clear" December 11, 1874, at 11:30 a.m. in the church, followed by interment. After that followed retirement to the parsonage for a poem read by William Pickney, bishop of Maryland, and thence to the church porch for a funeral oration by Dr. A. Y. P. Garnett, a resident of Washington who had been erstwhile surgeon general of the Confederacy, Jefferson Davis's personal physician, and was now president of the Southern Memorial Association in the city. As reported by the *Montgomery County Sentinel*, Garnett proclaimed that "the time had come when they could do justice to the memories of their friends, and perform such ceremonies unmolested and claimed that they should not perform the act coldly and with subdued spirits." Apparently he also mentioned the war's causes that had "justified the south for their action."

The story did not end there, however. Avirett identified Private James B. Bland of the Sixty-Second Virginia Mounted Infantry (one of the early arrivals before the fort on July 11, 1864). He claimed to ensure Bland's placement at the north end of the interment "to enable the friends and relatives to find it if they ever desire to remove the body." Equally interesting was the burial site for the final Confederate casualty in the battle on the Silver Spring farm. Discovered in the late 1890s, Avirett offered to place it with the others at Grace Church. But Admiral Lee, by now in retirement at the farm, determined to have the grave deepened, the remains placed in a terra cotta coffin, to "let him rest where he fell," was his determination. He promised to erect an appropriate grave marker, but, of course, time and commercialization of the farm in the twentieth century obliterated both. Fortunately, the other seventeen fared better. Resting in their sylvan repose for about twenty-two years and cared for by ladies of the local Women's Memorial Association, the plot eventually became neglected and overgrown. In February 1894, the Ridgley Brown Camp for Confederate Veterans began fund-raising for a monument to be placed over the common grave. The church proper burned to the ground the next year, but on November 14,

1896, five hundred spectators gathered for the unveiling of the monument—nine feet high and four feet square—still presiding over the graves today.

By 1896, efforts to mark and better preserve battle sites and graveyards from the war were in full spring. Grace churchyard was the culmination of such a Confederate effort for Fort Stevens. While Magnus S. Thompson read Robert E. Lee's General Order Number 9 from the Appomattox end, three young ladies recited the Mexican War–era poem "The Bivouac of the Dead" by Thomas O'Hara. A letter from Union veteran general and prime mover behind preserving Fort Stevens, William Van Zandt Cox, reflected the other spirit of the moment. Similarly, Judge Samuel S. Blackwell of Alabama, as orator of the day, "remarked upon the almost total obliteration of sectional lines" and urged that both north and south alike "should stand for the perpetuation of patriotism and the flag." Finally, Paul Jones, prominent Washington resident and Loyal Legion member whose father had died fighting for the Union "claimed the privilege of recognizing the valor of the Confederate soldiers by laying at the foot of the monument a large bunch of white chrysanthemums." But to further add to the mystery of the Commemorated Seventeen, the *Washington Evening Star* of the day announced that really only fifteen of the seventeen remained unknown. Supposedly two brothers, one a captain, the other a lieutenant named Butt from Augusta, Georgia, were the identified pair, with the legend that one of the mortally wounded brothers from the Fort Stevens fight asked an attending surgeon the condition of his sibling. "Your brother is dead," pronounced the medic, to which the surviving brother announced, "and in thirty minutes I, too, shall be dead, the last of five brothers who have given their lives to the cause." "He died just half an hour later," reported the newspaper. In the end, no Confederate battle monument to such sacrifice would ever appear on the Fort Stevens's field.[6]

Building a Body of Memory

The area of Early's encampments and wagon parks as well as the resting place for his Commemorated Seventeen came to be an incorporated town of Silver Spring after the war. The army had encamped across the fields and around the farmhouses of brothers Wilson, a Dr. Condit, and others, perhaps erecting rudimentary breastworks to ward off any Union cavalry forays. By 1872, quarryman Alfred Ray, whose farm Highlands was also part of the landscape of Early's raid, had presented the Blairs with a granite stone to mark the precise site of the silver spring. A year later, the Baltimore & Ohio railroad built a short-stem Metropolitan branch from Washington to Point of Rocks that would later become the main stem of the line west. The railroad would spawn suburbia—commuter communities such as Takoma Park and Silver Spring—cutting across the Blairs' properties, Confederate-occupied terrain, and the few surviving structures associated with Early's experience. Meanwhile, only human memories would fill the void.

It took awhile for veterans of the war to settle back into private pursuits, but it didn't take long to ponder what they had done. Surgeon George T. Stevens of the Seventy-Seventh New York, like Pennsylvania chaplain Stewart, numbered among the first to address the Fort Stevens fight in a significant way, including a chapter in his own memoir, *Three Years in the Sixth Corps*, published in 1866. In a way, however, it was Jubal Early who set the first real mark, the mantra that became dogma with his *Memoir of the Last Year of the War for Independence*, which appeared in 1867. Obviously with time in exile to perfect his story line and already feeling guilty for somehow failing his beloved commander, Robert E. Lee, with the disastrous Valley Campaign, the Confederate expeditionary commander unabashedly established what became Lost Cause dogma. Building upon what he had written to the *New York News* from Havana, Cuba, on December 18, 1865, Old Jube established his force as it appeared before Washington, which numbered but eight thousand muskets, three small battalions of artillery (forty pieces, none of them more than 12-pounder Napoleon smoothbores), and about two thousand badly mounted and equipped cavalry, "of which a large portion had been detached to cut the railroads leading from Baltimore north." The culprits for his failure to take the city had been heat, strength of the fortifications, superior Union signal communications, absence of friendly intelligence or help from Washington secessionists, and the arrival of Grant's veterans. His "small force" had been "thrown up to the very walls of the Federal Capital, north of a river which could not be forded at any point within 40 miles, and with a heavy force and the South Mountain in my rear—the passes through which could be held by a small number of [enemy] troops." He dismissed criticism for delays in the lower valley: "An examination of his narrative would show that not one moment was spent in idleness." He pointed out successful raids by Johnson and Gilmor to Baltimore, the acquisition of the large amounts of supplies and livestock taken back to Virginia, and flatly denied burning Montgomery Blair's house—"though I believe that retaliation was justified by previous acts of the enemy."[7]

Back in print with further rebuttals of critics, the feisty Early denied in 1874 any notion of a definite "attack" on the city. None had been ordered by Lee, and none was made, he announced. His commander's orders were "simply to threaten that city," since "my only chance of capturing it depended upon its being found without any garrison." While Lee "would have been gratified if I could have taken Washington," when Early had pressed that idea during talks with the general in late June, Lee had "remarked that it would hardly be possible to do so." Thus the mission to both army and expeditionary commander had been to simply cause Grant to withdraw from Richmond. Since by 1874 Lee was in his grave, who would dispute Old Jube's claim? To Union engineer John Gross Barnard for his 1871 expanded study of the defenses of Washington, Early merely "persists" in regard to numbers deployed before the city. Only by 1881 would Old Jube further refine his figures, prompted, in fact, by reading Barnard's report. His new total was 12,570, and arrayed against him were fifteen thousand in Washington's forts, fourteen thousand reinforcements from Grant, and over twenty thousand "in my rear at Harpers Ferry." It was obvious that the aging Rebel sought closure for his failure to take the capital.[8]

The battle of words over past deeds and intentions had begun. Rebuttal and clarification came with every publication or speech. Early's actions (if not precisely Fort Stevens) moved to center stage, especially in southern circles. Early's aide, Major Henry Kyd Douglas, and his old Lynchburg friend, John W. Daniel, would take up his cause. Early's "daring raid to Washington's doorstep displayed rapidity, audacity, and skill, [and] Early was justified in claiming 'it is without parallel in this or any other modern war,'" advanced Douglas. By 1894, Daniel's stirring apologia was gospel. Over only a month's duration and with less than fourteen thousand men, Early had (a) driven Hunter's army of 18,500 out of the field; (b) bottled up Sigel's force of six thousand at Harpers Ferry; (c) defeated Wallace's army of six thousand to seven thousand at the Monocacy and sent it packing to Baltimore; (d) diverted the VI and part of the XIX Corps from Grant's army, and (e) transferred the seat of war from central and Piedmont Virginia to the border on the Potomac, where it had begun three years earlier and occupied fully sixty thousand troops to oppose him. Again, even Daniels argued the notion that Washington's capture "was never either a design or expectation."[9]

Early and his actions (plus words) became a touchstone as the veterans themselves took up the pen to answer critics and to record their own observations. Kyd Douglas thought he "never has and never will receive the credit he deserves," since all the glory of that early and midsummer "were over-clouded and forgotten in the disasters of the autumn." Gordon, the man whose men had borne the brunt of the Monocacy bloodletting and who claimed that he had actually ridden onto the capital's fortifications at some point and found them empty, by 1904 could claim "undoubtedly we could have marched into Washington." While praising his old commander as "one of the coolest and most imperturbable of men under fire and in extremity," he also excoriated him for lack of "official courage, or what is known as the courage of one's convictions." Early would not act upon subordinates' suggestions and did not trust the accuracy of scouting reports (his "buttermilk ranger" cavalry?). Gordon implied that those traits applied generally to the Washington operation, and he admitted, "In the council of war called by General Early there was not a dissenting opinion as to the impolicy of entering the city."[10]

Others such as artillerist Armistead L. Long wrote that "this campaign is remarkable for having accomplished more in proportion to the force employed, and for having given less public satisfaction, than any other campaign of the war." In less than two months, Early's operations had carried more than four hundred miles, with a force "not exceeding twelve thousand men" and "had not only defeated but entirely dispersed two federal armies of an aggregate strength of more than double his own." Moreover, such operations invaded Maryland, and by bold and rapid movement upon Washington they had created a vital diversion in favor of Lee's defense of Richmond, had reentered Virginia, and had done it "with a loss of less than three thousand" men. As for Washington itself, Major Eugene Blackford of the Fifth Alabama and commanding Robert Rodes's division sharpshooters in the campaign claimed that "we could have gone into Washington with a loss of a thousand or two men from their Artillery." But what then? he asked. The Confederates "would have sacked the City—and have been drunk and unmanageable in an hour." Meanwhile heavy Yankee reinforcements would have arrived and "destroyed us in that field." He contended that "no private in our ranks ever had any idea that 'Old Jubilee' really intended to attack the place." Forts were "as thick as blackberries around the town," with plenty of artillery but no garrisons. Thus became enshrined Early's legacy in the memory and literature of the Lost Cause.[11]

Early also became the butt of those Confederate rankers who followed the plethora of commentaries fighting old campaigns. Former Rebel cavalrymen in particular took on the Early image of failure before Washington. John Opie of the Fifth Virginia Cavalry thought that Old Jube had lost a golden opportunity for immortality by taking the city. He "was about the only man in that army who believed it impossible to accomplish," Opie claimed. True, he admitted that if the army had entered Washington it would have plundered and left the city in ruin, so perhaps it was best that the eventuality had not materialized in the long run. Fellow Virginian Andrew Hunter thought it had been a mistake to ever put Early in charge anyway. "It shortened the war fully a year," was his conclusion. He especially rebuked Early for tippling in Francis Preston Blair's wine cellar— "he drank long and deeply from that keg, and sank into a deep slumber which lasted for hours, and from which nothing could rouse him; and that is why the order to advance was not given." Of all the participants, perhaps only Hunter directly contradicted Early's rendition of why Washington was not taken. "A steady stream of all kinds of emissaries of the Southern sympathizers came out from the city to greet the skirmishers," he commented. Black and white, adults and children all told one tale: "Come in at once, there are only Department clerks in the trenches. Don't delay, but come at once." Correct or not, Hunter thought the rank and file in the army never forgave Early for the failure to get them into Washington. From that day on, he claimed, the Confederates fought well, but "never with dash and firm determination to do or die." In Hunter's eyes, after Fort Stevens "they no longer displayed the spirit which had made them victorious on previous battlefields."[12]

In the end it fell to a Maryland cavalryman to categorically put a veteran's perspective on Early's raid, years after the event. George Wilson Booth, who had served with Bradley Johnson's column, flatly declared in 1907 that the army commander had failed in all three of his missions. "First and principally," he had failed to compel Grant to detach sizable numbers of troops and thus relieve pressure on Lee. Second, "if circumstances so turned out as to make possible the capture of Washington itself," Early failed to take advantage of that opportunity since it would have necessitated Grant's abandonment of the Richmond operations "with the possibility of creating an impression abroad which could be turned to our advantage." Finally, the inability to free the Point Lookout prisoners also was laid at Early's feet. By now, four decades after the fact, the litany was carved in stone. Wasted time on the upper Potomac getting into Maryland, the Monocacy battle delay, and the "altogether unforeseen" arrival of the VI Corps was "one of the accidental features which became prominent in war by reason of the great results which hinge on such occurrences," said Booth. "Once Early got to the capital," he observed, "to assault so superior a force behind strong entrenchments, on which the skill and labor of the federal engineer had been devoted for nearly three years, would have been rashness approaching to follow or madness." So prompt withdrawal proved the only option.[13]

Union veterans expended less ink rationalizing what they thought of Early's raid. They did not need to do so. Theirs was the winning side, and there were more controversial events than either Fort Stevens or Monocacy in their minds. If they sought scapegoats, aging Federals pointed to Hunter and Sigel. Grant delivered a deathbed exoneration of Wallace in 1885 for his supposed delays at Shiloh by suggesting, "if Early had been but one day earlier he might have entered the Capitol before the arrival of reinforcements," thus attributing the delay to Wallace's actions on the Monocacy. Cadwallader knew of "the esteem—or rather lack of esteem—in which Wallace had been held by Grant's inner circle since Shiloh." "Every member of Grant's staff at Shiloh were hot and outspoken whenever the subject [of Wallace's tardiness in reinforcing the beleaguered army at that point] was introduced." Apparently Grant always "assented to criticisms of Wallace's behavior," and while never entrusting him with any important command but "finding him commanding at Baltimore, he continued him, and gave him great credit for his conduct." Cadwallader thought perhaps Grant was so near the end of his life "his resentments were softened, and that he desired to make amends for any possible injustice in the past."[14]

Actually, Wallace had gained postwar fame on his own as governor of New Mexico, minister to Turkey, and acclaimed author of *Ben Hur: A Tale of the Christ*. Yet as late as 1904 some of his former soldiers felt obliged to preach his story. Monocacy veteran and Medal of Honor recipient Captain George E. Davis of the Tenth Vermont was one. He declared that year that Wallace's action at the battle was unique in seven specific ways worthy of remembrance and honor. First,

Wallace's force had been scraped together to repel invasion, and second, within twenty-four hours of such gathering "it had fought a memorable battle which saved our Nation's capital, and then dispersed never again to meet this side of the grave." Third, said Davis, Wallace's action was unique in that "we had no reserve ammunition; no trains of any kind." Fourth, the whole business of six thousand Federals "of whom probably 2,000 had never fired a gun in battle," with but seven pieces of artillery, "were so well posted in a strategic point of view that by God's special blessing they successfully resisted an attack of 20,000 to 25,000 [*sic*] of General Lee's veterans having 50 pieces of field artillery with abundance [of ammunition]." They did so from 8:30 in the morning to 4:30 p.m., "at which time our ammunition gave out and we retired." His fifth way held more bitterness. Halleck had sent Wallace "to his home in disgrace" because he had not driven off and dispersed Early, claimed Davis somewhat questionably. "This act of General Halleck was disgraceful, tyrannical, undeserved," as Wallace "did all that any man could have done under such limitations." Lightening a bit, Davis deduced a sixth point of Monocacy's uniqueness (albeit unrelated to Wallace specifically), which included "a genuine, sweet love story [that] was interwove with the battle," meaning the loving vignette of Araby Farm owner Keefer Thomas's daughter and her beau caught up in the maelstrom. Finally, Davis observed pithily for his seventh unique citation of Wallace's achievement at Monocacy, "because there were no newspaper reporters present," undoubtedly a two-sided coin had Davis thought about it more.[15]

Final victory shielded Grant, who nearly lost the capital because of myopia, or Horatio Wright, whose lackluster pursuit of Early had allowed the raider to escape. Wright made it plain to VI Corps historian George Stevens in 1870 that his invitation to Lincoln to ascend the Fort Stevens parapet on July 12 had been followed by telling the commander-in-chief to get down from the perch. Such was the extent of the mea culpa beyond official reports on the conduct of Union command on those July days. Montgomery Meigs fondly recalled his own battlefield command during the July crisis. Of course, from Martin Hardin as well as numerous junior officers and enlisted men and from Army of the Potomac veterans to Ohio "100-day" men, the old veterans exchanged stories about aspects of defending Washington and stopping Early's raid. They, like the aging Rebels, scolded one another on errors of fact and interpretation and gradually built memory into questionable remembrance. S. A. McDonald, late of the One Hundred and Twenty-Second New York, established Union dogma about Fort Stevens and Monocacy when he opined about the latter in 1894: "The whole affair was of no great magnitude as compared with Antietam, Chancellorsville, or Gettysburg, but the forces engaged outnumbered the combatants in the first battle of the Revolutionary war and the Union loss was far greater than that sustained by the Continental army at the historic battle of Bennington." The fighting had been sharp and lively, the percentage of casualties unusually heavy, "and the peculiarity of the surroundings was calculated to invest it with more of the dramatic than attached to any other minor engagement of the war."[16]

Relegated to Obscurity

By the close of the century, thinning ranks of veterans combined with newfound patriotism and the vaulting of America onto the world stage. The Spanish-American War and exuberant presidency of Theodore Roosevelt gave impetus to monumentation of Civil War battle sites, many of them already national military parks ostensibly invaluable to the War Department as public land for training and staging areas. Neither Fort Stevens nor Monocacy fit that category, although a significant portion of the Fort Stevens battlefield provided a new Walter Reed Army Hospital reservation in 1903. The fort itself—where Lincoln stood under enemy fire—did not. Battleground National Cemetery became the place for veterans to erect their monuments to the battle—Ninety-Eighth Pennsylvania (1891), One Hundred and Twenty-Second New York (1903), Company K, One Hundred and Fiftieth Ohio National Guard (1907), and Twenty-Fifth New York Cavalry (1914). Battleground, not Fort Stevens, would remain the gathering point for Memorial Day remembrance and veteran reunions just as the shaft to seventeen dead Confederates at Grace Church in the Woodside section of Silver Spring drew whatever visitors came from the South. Confederate remembrance at Monocacy similarly stayed with a beautiful memorial in Frederick's Mount Olivet cemetery holding ostensibly four hundred Southern fallen, although the United Daughters of the Confederacy erected a simple marker out on the battlefield for the fiftieth anniversary in 1914. Elsewhere on the Monocacy farmland, New Jersey erected the first monument in 1907 to its Fourteenth Volunteers, with Pennsylvania and Vermont following soon after. Eventually, Maryland completed such memorials in 1964 with a modest marker "to honor Maryland soldiers who fought for Union and Confederacy." Monocacy's physical landscape changed little over the years (except for the construction of the interstate highway bisecting principal farms of the battle site in the 1960s). A move to make it a national battlefield succeeded in the 1930s, then languished for funding implementation for another sixty years. The Fort Stevens story was different.[17]

Like other sections of the "battle in the suburbs" stretching from Fort Reno and points west to Fort Totten and beyond to the east, it took only two or three generations of Washington expansion to obliterate the Fort Stevens battlefield. True, country squires like the Blairs and former D.C. mayor Matthew Emery reoccupied their mansions, Emery returning to what had been a centerpiece for Camp Brightwood and a signal station thereafter for Fort Stevens. Apparently a telltale presence of relics and depressions as well as plateaus of earth for soldier campsites could still be seen decades later on the extensive grounds of Emery Place, according to Washington raconteur John Claget Proctor. Still, "memory" translated to the landscape and changed with property ownership with the introduction of trolley lines on major avenues such as Seventh Street Road (later Brightwood and Georgia avenues) or Wisconsin Avenue (formerly Georgetown or Rockville Pike) and even the postwar transition of Fort Reno land to squatter and later housing development.

Renaming of the small village of Leesborough for Brigadier General Frank Wheaton's success at thwarting the invaders set a precedent, while veterans Brigadier General George Getty, Pennsylvanian Lewis Cass White, and Vermonter Edward R. Campbell were induced to settle in what were parts of the greater Brightwood–Silver Spring neighborhood. Montgomery Blair rebuilt Falkland as his descendants like other Blairs lived on family properties until the lure of development money sent them packing by the 1950s. Whatever happened to the grave and poignant marker (with its mounted cannon shell motif) of Early's final casualty at the Fort Stevens battle remains a mystery. Sligo Crossroads assumed the name Silver Spring officially. The Metropolitan branch of the Baltimore & Ohio railroad skirted Blair properties and village, and a branch trolley linked Takoma Park station with the main stem on Brightwood or Georgia Avenue that passed the remains of Fort Stevens on the way. A gas station still graces the corner of Colesville Road and Georgia Avenue, replacing the country store where Old Jube's vagabonds liberated liquor. Acorn Park, resplendent with just such a pavilion, denotes the site of the silver spring. A new Emory Church edifice arose in 1911 and spelled an end to the site of Fort Massachusetts before it became the eastern bastion of Fort Stevens. Thus, a century of post–Civil War city expansion determined the fate and memory of the forts and the battlefield in the northern suburbs.[18]

Washington's prewar population of about seventy-five thousand added another one hundred thousand within twenty years of Appomattox. Even more people arrived over the next century as world conflict and the New Deal expanded government programs and employment, generating new configurations for places like Tennallytown, Brightwood, and Silver Spring. Sonorous-sounding city neighborhood names would encompass those sections of the Fort Stevens battlefield—Tenleytown, Shepherd Park, Takoma Park, Manor Park—enveloping the sacred ground. Available land and transportation transformed open farmland and orchards into neighborhood housing, city streets, and shopping facilities. As late as 1907, a Baltimore newsman claimed that "the country on either side of the [Brightwood/Georgia] avenue still retains many of its picturesque features—dairy cows still graze on the green slopes and agriculture is carried on in spots." Ten years later the caretaker for Washington's local lore, John Clagett Proctor, penned a glowing poem "Brightwood, D.C." that suggested the allure of that section to newcomers. In such context, the War Department paid $98,000 to convert the 43.5-acre Carberry (or

Lay) dairy farm, owned later by ex-senator J. Donald Cameron of Pennsylvania, whose name was attached to the meandering creek that passed through a ravine where some of the sharpest fighting occurred late in the afternoon of July 12, from the former battlefield to the Walter Reed Army Hospital reservation. It, too, would serve as a beacon for attracting newcomers beyond "the substantial homes" cited in the Baltimore newsman's report.[19]

Thus, perhaps as early as the 1920s the only unspoiled battlefield terrain was found in Rock Creek Park. The surviving topographical features at Walter Reed, like the Cameron's Creek defile or penny-packets of vacant lots, even the narrow strip of ground set aside as circumferential parkland by the MacMillan Commission at the turn of the century, qualified only by association. Although one observer had noted as early as 1873 that all the city's old forts had been dismantled, stripped of ordnance and appurtenances, and anything usable had been taken by their restored property owners or black migrants, a military guide to the nation's capital suggested in 1892 that there was still evidence of earthworks from Fort Sumner around to the Anacostia. Fort Slocum had been erased except for an old well and auxiliary works, and Fort Reno (where the emplacement surrounding the significant 100-pounder Parrott had been) would soon become the site of a city reservoir. Fort DeRussy happily was preserved as an obscure ruin in Rock Creek Park. Battleground Cemetery became an oasis in Brightwood. The eroding parapets at Fort Stevens took no special note. As to the battle site, "some of the buildings and fences here bear evidence of quite a lively time," with bullet holes still visible. But it was in this period that veterans rallied to ensure acknowledgment and care for the neglected work.[20]

To some degree it was a local effort. Elizabeth "Aunt Betty" Thomas reconstructed her modest home from materials salvaged from the enlarged Fort Stevens. She went on awaiting President Lincoln's promised "reaping of a great reward," but at least she got her land back. But then there were newcomers—veterans such as Lewis Cass White of the One Hundred and Second Pennsylvania, who as color sergeant had remained with "the colors" while his comrades went out on the picket line at Fort Stevens. In fact, when White, a former schoolteacher from western Pennsylvania and postwar civil servant in the pension office, returned to Brightwood and saw the old fort, he determined to resettle there and to preserve the ground over which he and his comrades had shed blood. He proudly purchased the site of the Toll Gate where Piney Branch and Seventh Street roads met, built a large house (and eventually two more for his children and grandchildren), and held forth to visitors about the battle and nearby fort and national cemetery. White now stood at what he and others always termed the "highwater mark" of Early's raid—the furthest penetration by sharpshooters and skirmishers on those fateful July days. Horatio Wright had already identified (as much as he could on the eroded remains of the front parapet of the fort) where he remembered Lincoln standing to an 1893

CHAPTER TEN

VI Corps reunion. In 1900, White, together with former generals Wheaton, Getty, Thomas M. Vincent, Fred C. Ainsworth, and others, formed a Fort Stevens-Lincoln National Military Park Association, designed to preserve the place where Lincoln had stood under Confederate fire.²¹

White explained their purpose to comrades elsewhere as endeavoring "to rescue from oblivion the only battlefield inside the District of Columbia, in sight of the dome of the United States Capitol, and the only battle of the Civil War in which the President of the United States took part or in which he was present when the engagement occurred." White intended a history of the battle and solicited veterans everywhere for their help. He recited in a solicitation letter how Crawford had been wounded, how he remained guarding the flag, "and consequently did not see as much of the battle as the boys on the skirmish line, and does not know so much of the details." In fact, White said he saw Lincoln but was unsure "whether he came in a carriage or on horseback, there being a number of carriages at the east entrance to the fort." What he did know was that "it is the purpose to have the immediate battlefield set apart as a park, with a statue of President Lincoln on the spot where he stood, and other appropriate tablets to mark the places where the different regiments were engaged." As the Pennsylvanian stated, the intent "will throw light on the history of this engagement, small in comparison with others, but fraught with great interest in saving the Capital at the most critical time in its history."²²

Building upon McMillan Commission recommendations the following year and especially its idea of a "fort drive" connecting the sites in a continuous, picturesque boulevard encircling the city, the Fort Stevens Lincoln Park association proposed in 1902 that Congress preserve the whole line of defense from Fort Reno to Fort Totten in three separate parcels of about 2.65 acres and tie in with Rock Creek Park (already preserving Fort DeRussy and adjacent battle site land), as well as Battleground cemetery. Fort Stevens would be the centerpiece. As association chairman Vincent suggested, War Department commissioners would supervise the development of the park, much as they were doing on battlefields elsewhere. They would also ambitiously "ascertain and definitely mark the lines of battle of all troops engaged in the battle of Fort Stevens and points of interest connected with the fortifications of defenses of the national capital during the Civil War." The open nature of upper northwest Washington at that time still seemed accommodating to the plan. Vermont senator, Civil War veteran, and sometime secretary of war Redfield Proctor introduced association-sponsored legislation. It went nowhere even when Senator William Warner of Missouri introduced a similar bill in 1906. William Van Zandt Cox, nephew of the influential Ohio congressman "Sunset Cox" and D.C. mayor Matthew Emery's son-in-law, then simply purchased the Fort Stevens site in order to save it and took charge of the historical committee of the Brightwood Citizens Association to spur things along. President Theodore Roosevelt at least attended an unveiling of a "Lincoln Stone" at Battleground National Cemetery on the fortieth anniversary of the battle, according to news reports of the time.[23]

The lack of recognition attended the rundown, debris-covered condition of old Fort Stevens irked both veterans groups and the association. Only a rude board nailed to a small, black locust tree ostensibly marked the site of Lincoln's appearance. In fact, a sycamore tree grew on the parapet where Lincoln had stood. A small street traversed the parade ground, and a row of small frame houses also covered the ground. Then, in early 1911, a "syndicate of capitalists" (as newspapers called them) purchased the site, and "the new owners have not concluded their plans; that is, as to whether they will hold the property as an investment or place it on the market," announced the *Washington Star* on March 22. Storm clouds of development threatened. About this same time, a flurry of concern over the nature and location of a suitable Lincoln Memorial joined the fray, with the preferred presidential commission site in West Potomac Park competing with a monumental highway scheme advanced by Maryland Sixth District congressman David J. Lewis and others to link Washington with Gettysburg. "If the Lincoln Highway was constructed, could there be a more appropriate place for the Archway that Senator John Walter Smith, of Maryland, favors or more fitting place for a Lincoln Memorial Monument than the battlefield on which he personally stood and saw men killed and wounded, and in which battle he, perhaps, would have been killed himself if not taken away?" asked the Fort Stevens Terrace Company (who as new owners would ostensibly have a stake in using all of this for promotional purposes and were constituents in Smith's district). The *Baltimore Sun* joined the bandwagon for the Fort Stevens project.[24]

Cox and White secured $250 by public appeal, and on November 7, 1911, they supervised the placement of a three-ton boulder (five-and-one-half feet high by three feet in diameter) drawn from Cameron's Creek on the new Walter Reed hospital grounds, formerly the battlefield. Hauled by wagon, it was now placed atop the parapet where Wright had identified Lincoln's position under fire. Four 32-pounder cannon balls recovered from the battlefield surrounded the base of the marker. They had been fired by Captain Jewitt's artillerists in the 1864 battle. Between four hundred and five hundred people witnessed the ceremony, led by army general Leonard Wood, the VI Corps Veterans Associations, and various patriotic societies. "Aunt Betty" Thomas appeared, still telling everyone she anticipated her reward, and the stone's sculptor, Tennessee Union veteran Richard Seek, was also present for the roll call of Union and Confederate dead and the unveiling of the homely boulder. Finally, Early's old artillerist and later Louisiana congressman Floyd King professed gladness that they had not taken the fort in 1864. Lincoln had been a friend of the South, he now claimed, suggesting a Damascus-road conversion. King would have been only too glad forty-seven years before had sharpshooters been able to pick off

Old Abe on the Fort Stevens parapet. The VI Corps Association then improved the Lincoln Stone's appearance by dedicating a bronze bas-relief on July 12, 1920, which depicted the president, Wright, and Surgeon Crawford under fire at the spot.[25]

Swiss-American and Philadelphia sculptor Jakob Otto Schweizer was commissioned that same year to improve the Lincoln Stone. Renowned for his seven military sculptures at Gettysburg and numerous other patriotic busts, bas-reliefs, and medallions, his bas-relief of Lincoln under fire at Fort Stevens offset the bland rock. But interest groups still could not secure federal legislation to preserve Fort Stevens. The situation took a downward turn after World War I. Developers nibbled around the very edges of the fort itself. Subdivisions of both apartment buildings and individual houses soon filled empty space, further corrupting the landscape. Despite preservation efforts, the fort's remains had become a public eyesore and dumping ground for trash. Many people simply assumed the government owned both the fort and national cemetery. Legislation went forward dutifully year after year but always foundered, as it did when Secretary of War John W. Weeks vetoed acquisition under the guise that while President Lincoln may have been there under enemy fire—hence, an "historically important and interesting" fact—he did not consider it sufficient to warrant government preservation. In what was almost a classic definition of a rationale for military parks (at the time under War Department administration), Weeks claimed, "I feel that a national military park should be a piece of ground of considerable extent, the site of an important military engagement in which a comparatively large number of troops was involved, the outcome of which had a definite military and political effect." Apparently the possibility that the president could have been killed, the battle lost, and the capital of the nation captured by an enemy did not fit Weeks's criteria. Nor, apparently, did Supreme Court Justice Oliver Wendell Holmes Jr.'s much-bandied claim to friends in this period that he was the one who shouted at that damned fool Lincoln to get down from his precarious perch.[26]

Perhaps for Holmes, it was some confluence of a final twinge of veteran's remembrance and the rush to preserve the physical remains where Lincoln stood under fire, or perhaps it was merely flirtations with the female sex over the place for his own final trial by fire and the closeness to the sixteenth president at the place. Writing to his old friend, economist Harold Laski, in the spring of 1921 and again in 1922, the elderly Holmes spoke of taking friends out to what he called his "little private show" of Fort Stevens. "It is an old earthwork hidden behind houses, but rather interesting for a last survivor to take a dame," claimed the old boy when involving a private tour for Mrs. John Chipman Gray and a Mrs. Asquith. In no case did he tell Laski that he yelled at Lincoln to get down from the exposed parapet. At least, he never told Laski that we know of. Still, the legend, the myth, the words have lingered over the decades as the truth—or that they might have been! At some point, finally by 1924, Congress set up a National Capital Parks Commission, and the first fort land, at Fort Stevens, was acquired on October 15, 1925. It was a start, followed by the acquisition of the linking greenway across the northern and eastern defenses of Washington. Concern about Fort Stevens, the surviving remains of all the units variously styled Fort Parks, and a circumferential scenic drive continued to percolate unabated through the succeeding years.[27]

Two Phoenixes Rising

Success finally came to fruition after World War I. The *Washington Star* reporter declared on January 15, 1934, that a "marker which etches Lincoln now symbolizes glory in the dust heaps." Before a monument to Lincoln graced the present site downtown as a bookend for the National Mall, some thought was even given to its erection at Fort Stevens. John Clagett Proctor, for one, composed an ode in 1920 that asked "what other place, pray tell me, has such claim? What other place has such immortal fame?" Finally, in a series of separate transactions between October 15, 1925, and May 13, 1933, the government acquired the eroded hummocks that remained of Fort Stevens. Supervised by a new National Park Service, Civilian Construction Corps workers carefully restored the western magazine of the fort and parapet upon which the Lincoln Stone rests to this day. Landscape architect Robert P. McKean would be proud that with periodic refurbishment, the idea of substituting concrete for the original wood in revetments, gun platforms, and magazines survives and accurately captures the style and detail of the Civil War works. Installation of a bas-relief diagram of the 1864 configuration of the fort occurred in September 1936 on a second base through the efforts of the Grand Army of the Republic and Daughters of Union Veterans of the Civil War. Private (postwar major) Edward R. Campbell, Second Vermont Volunteers, Second Division, VI corps, completed the roster of those interred in March 1936, age ninety-two, at Battleground. The famous Sharpshooter's tulip tree on Walter Reed grounds blew down just after World War I, but two 100-pound spherical case shot cannon balls fired either from forts DeRussy or Totten and found on the Thomas Lay or Carberry farm predating Walter Reed decorated a marker to the site of the tree. Whether or not this was the tree from which a sharpshooter fired the shot wounding Surgeon Crawford and missing Lincoln remains conjecture. Nonetheless, onlookers who can screen out intervening houses and apartment buildings will surely see the historical significance that appeared to elude Secretary of War Weeks.[28]

Today, the site of old Fort Massachusetts that reverted to Emory Church ownership after the Civil War may be recognized only as high ground serving modern uses. Present owners, the Emory-Beacon of Light congregation, intend to move forward with plans to erect a massive retail and residential edifice on the site. Thus, the possible location of Lincoln's viewing of the 1864 battle as suggested in Surgeon

C. C. V. A. Crawford's sketch drawing will be completely obliterated forever, however praiseworthy modern adaptive use of land may seem. Moreover, periodic National Park Service cleanup of the restored Fort Stevens portion and grounds mainly for an annual or semiannual commemoration, the remounting of replica cannon, or the reconstruction of gun platforms and emplacements as well as greater visibility for Battleground Cemetery show more promise. The superintendent's lodge at the cemetery became historic in its own right and hence buffed for administrative offices. The occasional erection of new interpretive signage contrasts with a palpable aversion to providing a distinctive Visitor Center either at the fort or the cemetery. Tourists simply have no dedicated contact point to talk with real people about events or personalities connected with Early's 1864 visit.

Similarly, inadequate interpretation and the absence of a dedicated visitor contact center for Washington's Civil War defenses as a whole has been abrogated to another jurisdiction altogether. The superb but distant Alexandria, Virginia, city government that administers Fort Ward Museum and Park only partly offsets neglect north of the Potomac. Over the years of enlightened stewardship, responsive facilities and staff address this challenge but in no way substitute for more comprehensive facilities for the Battle at Fort Stevens. Restoration of the Battleground Superintendent's Lodge by the National Park Service in 2010 plus an upgrade of attention to the Defenses of Washington through websites and brochures marginally suggest some recognition of a tourist-worthy attraction to Civil War sesquicentennial sites in the nation's capital. Public support groups exist to improve and enhance that central fact. Yet in a way, the private effort of D.C. Cultural Tourism affiliated with the city's neighborhood advocacy surpasses anything federal officials have done with interpretation and education. Cultural Tourism's street-side walking tour signs and brochures in Brightwood and Tennallytown, key neighborhoods relevant to the expanded Fort Stevens story, do add infrequent pilgrims to the sites associated with Lincoln under enemy fire. Of course, the National-Trust-owned-and-maintained Lincoln Cottage at Soldiers' Home has another mission and story, although they are tangentially associated with events of July 1864.

On the other hand, Monocacy's progress stands in stark relief to that of Fort Stevens. Human efforts in the 1930s also provided the impetus to do something about Monocacy as part of Early's campaign. The site came under federal jurisdiction and protection, although again the development of facilities languished until the last decade or two of the twentieth century. Then, the early efforts of boyhood battle observer and later judge Glenn Worthington and others of the Monocacy Battle Field Association of the 1930s reached fruition. U.S. representative Goodloe Byron and Senator Charles Mathias Jr. moved to upgrade the proper preservation of the principal land and historic structures and provide an adequate Visitor's Center (museum and library) as well as proper field interpretive devices. Despite continuous threats from the urban expansion of the city of Frederick and Frederick County and the traffic overload on the bisecting Interstate 270 since the 125th anniversary of the battle, it may be truly said that the belated fame and credit due this long-overlooked battle is reflected in annual visitation figures of forty thousand in 2011. National exposure to what Worthington saw as "the battle that saved Washington" was finally attained. The same cannot be claimed for Fort Stevens. Ominous ongoing challenges include not only the Beacon of Light activities but also the equally disturbing Defense Department Base Reduction Act (BRAC) disposal of public ground and facilities at Walter Reed for mixed public-private redevelopment designed to bolster upper Georgia Avenue. Significance of the Fort Stevens story for preservation and historical tourism much less civic understanding and local pride apparently continues to elude the community.[29]

Sesquicentennial Meaning and Opportunity

Fort Stevens and Monocacy stand as tributes to the passing of two great armies during Jubal Early's campaign to capture Washington in 1864. But it was Fort Stevens, not Monocacy, which formed the last obstacle to Confederate success. The Lincoln Stone or Boulder on the fort's parapet reflects a later French phrase associated with the great World War I battle of Verdun—"Ils ne passeront pas / On ne passé pas." "They shall not pass" applies just as aptly to the heroic defense mounted by Father Abraham's boys defending his city, his capital, and his government as well as that of the nation. Ultimately they were also defending him. He was there. Lincoln witnessed their deeds and their determination, and his presence inspired their pluck. He participated in their battle, issuing an order, and as a combatant he was almost shot. The enemy were veterans, Lincoln's army at Fort Stevens a mixed bag if there ever was one—veterans, short-termers, invalids, civilians. Union or Confederate soldiers were American citizen soldiers, and like Lincoln, they were amateurs in the best national tradition. Their actions were as crucial, even pivotal, as any other battle in American history. Their saga on those two July days will always leave as many questions as they answered. Those questions should be posed again after 150 years.

While counterfactual history is fashionable, it is not history. Still, it is useful to speculate. James C. Bresnahan's anthology of counterfactual scenarios and most especially David Johnson's epilogue about the "might have been" had Lincoln not been reelected in 1864 proves useful when linked to events at Fort Stevens. It is appropriate because Early could have taken Washington. He might have killed or captured Lincoln. What a difference that might have made. It was quite possible before early afternoon on July 11, just as newsman observer Sylvanus Cadwallader so vociferously argued in his memoirs. Said Cadwallader, "Our lines in his front could have been carried at any point, with the loss of a few hundred men." Washington "was never more helpless," as "several wide turnpikes led directly to it." Any such cavalry commander as Sheridan, Wilson, Hampton, or Stuart, claimed Cadwallader, "could have ridden through all its broad avenues, sabred everyone found in the streets, and before nightfall could have burned down the White House, the Capitol and all public buildings." And, again, Early "might have entered the capital at any time before midnight of July 11 (I think that the hour of Wright's arrival)," he added. He could have done so "without having the march of his columns delayed a half hour, and without any loss of men worth a moment's consideration, when playing for such a stake." Do such claims of a contemporary observer still hold as one assembles the pieces of a puzzle so long ago? And could Early's army have held Lincoln's capital had they smashed through the inadequately defended works in Washington's suburbs?[30]

Of course, did Early even need to hold on to his prize for very long? The symbolism of Early's achievement would have resonated around the world. Might Grant have returned with more men and ejected the impudent Rebel invaders? Quite probably, but the damage would have been done. The siege at Petersburg lifted, Grant would have had to hammer Early. Yet the momentum of the war would have shifted and a rejuvenated Lee, freed from the defense of Richmond and Petersburg, could have resumed the very offensive he dreamed of and talked about to Davis. Yet could he have done so as long as any Yankees remained close to the Rebel capital? Perhaps revived hopes in the west, not only involving Rebel armies but also occupied and suppressed, ever-truculent Southern people might have erupted in widespread partisan uprising. On the other hand, perhaps not, for three years of deepening stabilization and occupation efforts by Federal authorities had suppressed everything short of outright banditry and felony in Tennessee and Kentucky, for instance. Still, Early gained the reeling Confederacy another six months by his efforts in Maryland and subsequently the Shenandoah Valley. Even there, New York private John B. Southard seems quite on target when he wrote his sister during Wright's pursuit of Old Jube after Fort Stevens, "We are after the rebs that robed [*sic*] the Marylanders and they made a grate [*sic*] many union men that were rebs [for] about two thirds that they robed [*sic*] were C.S.A. and it turned them Union."[31]

If Early's raid and subsequent operations netted Lee and the Davis government breathing space, Fort Stevens gave Lincoln and his generals the watershed event to break military and political impasse. True, it would take all summer, the summer that was Lincoln's nadir, his darkest period—militarily going nowhere, economically turning downward, and politically moving in circles. It would take the tenacity of Grant and the patience of Lincoln (plus further prodding of the generals as the summer progressed), nay the passage of time, to ride out this storm. Perhaps it was dumb luck that combined with heat, dust, the heroic delay of Wallace on the Monocacy, Rebel proclivities to straggle and forage on the final leg to Washington, even the influence of spirits from old man Blair's liquor cellar—and, of course, those signalers atop Fort Reno to spot Early's ill-timed side-slip that contributed to the final event. Superior Union application of technology via river and rail steam transport and telegraphic communication also leveled the playing field. Southern valor and audacity could be met by application of those superior Union resources contributing to a holding action on the Monocacy and then a Thermopylaen stand in the Washington suburbs. The old days of Jackson's vaunted foot cavalry had been parried by the new age of steamboats and railroads in any race for the greatest prize.

Honestly, without Early's campaign, the war could have been over before Christmas. Richmond and Petersburg, Atlanta, as well as Savannah then would have fallen under Sherman's phrase of Yuletide gifts to President Lincoln. Or, had Fort Stevens turned out differently, perhaps a Christmas gift of Washington might have gone from Lee to Davis. Perhaps John B. Hood's lurch north in late fall in Middle Tennessee might have occurred earlier and been more successful for wintering in the upper heartland en route to a new war for the upper heartland. Quite probably, it would have meant Lincoln's eviction from the White House in November. Without Fort Stevens turning out as it did, the Civil War could have taken a different turn. Some Yankee veterans in old age reflected on the success of Old Jube's risky undertaking. One elderly veteran of the Twenty-Fifth New York Cavalry, who had been at Stevens, said in 1915, "If Gen. Early had the proper pluck, he could have gotten into Washington . . . our skirmish line was thrown out in single file over a large front." Lieutenant Frank Wilkeson, assigned to Battery A, Fourth United States Artillery, also a Fort Stevens witness, added, "I unhesitatingly answer, yes." The southern general could have taken the city without losing more than one thousand men. "But," continued this skeptical veteran, "if he had taken it, his poorly-clad, poorly-fed, impoverished men would inevitably have gone to plundering, would inevitably have gotten drunk, and stayed drunk, and he would have lost his entire army." That, of course, still is the bottom line for Early's escapade to Washington on what became the last Confederate invasion.[32]

The saga will always leave us with curiosity. President Theodore Roosevelt's secretary of the treasury, Leslie M. Shaw, in a later Memorial Day speech delivered at Battleground National Cemetery, caught that irony. "If it had been possible in those days to carry the news around the world by electricity, it is probable that the Southern Confederacy would have been recognized by some of the European powers." Early's army was within five miles of the Federal treasury and executive mansion, "but that fact was not known to the world for some time afterwards," he observed. In the meantime the Federal armies had been winning victories, he mused. What Shaw meant was not clear—Atlanta's capture and destruction in the Shenandoah yet lay on the horizon. Amusingly, uniformed Confederates actually did get to downtown Washington, and not just as a handful of prisoners in the wake of Fort

Stevens. The Confederate Veterans reunion in 1917 was the first held outside the boundaries of the former Confederacy. Supposedly it symbolized reconciliation as a grand parade traversed the same route as that of victorious Yankee armies a half-century before at war's end in Grand Reviews. It was not presided over by Jubal Early but rather the first southern-born president since the war, Democrat Woodrow Wilson. Whether this registered with participants or that any of those present remembered the battle in the suburbs or even took time to revisit the earlier scenes of Early's visit is unclear.[33]

The most tantalizing question of all is the question that has never gained traction, either with contemporaries or analysts. What if Confederates had gotten Lincoln (by capture or by bullet) at Fort Stevens? Different from what actually happened nine months later in Ford's Theater, what if Abraham Lincoln, the president of the United States, had been shot, captured, or forced to take to his heels and relinquish the Union's most cherished symbol—the nation's capital? Strategically, this issue remains the most abiding dilemma. Momentum shift, symbolism forever altered (in European capitals if not rural America), and an economic earthquake to the New York Stock Exchange remain possibilities. Lincoln dead or wounded; Vice President Hannibal Hamlin assumes the executive office, but to what end—negotiations with the Confederacy by Horace Greeley, the replacement on the Unionist ticket in the fall leading to defeat at the hands of well-known Union conservative military hero George B. McClellan, or even more inconceivably by radical Republican candidate John C. Fremont? All of these become possibilities. A separate, negotiated peace leading to permanent separation, an end to emancipation, even the far-fetched but provocative scenario in Ward Moore's 1955 classic *Bring the Jubilee* of a far different postwar America is plausible. Or, as it indeed turned out, would the Union boys in blue, old Abe's boys, along with a determined if fatigued Northern populace, have been as shocked, irate, and revenge seeking had Lincoln been simply killed in battle at Fort Stevens as when he was assassinated in time of peace? Would a combat killing of the commander-in-chief somehow have affected everyone differently from a political killing once the war ended? We shall never know. History comes from fact, not conjecture.[34]

Moot testament to actuality stands atop a preserved fort in northwest Washington. It resides less with studies of generalship or rumors of revels in Blair's deserted mansion. Even the apocryphal tales of who yelled at Lincoln to get down from the perch before he got shot pale before the monument that is still with us. Mankind's proclivity to desecrate the historical scene cannot totally eradicate the human dimensions of events such as Early's visit to the capital. The grave markers from Mount Olivet to Battleground and the tiny Grace Episcopal churchyard, the ever-sylvan farm fields beside the Monocacy, and the scattered monuments to New Jersey,

Pennsylvania, and Vermont memory, along with southern counterparts nearby are all still with us. Similar veterans' monuments at Battleground mark what New York, Pennsylvania, and Ohio young men accomplished. No counterpart memorial suggests what their opponents failed to do, although the still discernable swale of Cameron's Creek and the Sharpshooter Tree marker on Walter Reed come close. In the end, for our purposes, we might simply stand behind that restored rampart at Fort Stevens and imagine events. We look up at the rock, whether accurately or inaccurately placed for eternity, and conjecture about the sixteenth American president's presence and actions. Plucked from a local stream and as humble and homely as the man it memorializes—the Lincoln Stone or Boulder—and its bas-relief depiction of what he did there says it best. What it doesn't say—like Lincoln—also belongs to the ages.[35]

The restored Parapet, the circle of Forty-One Graves, the Seventeen Unknowns, the Sharpshooter's Tree marker—they all provide the last tangible reminders of those fateful July days when Abraham Lincoln almost met his fate. So, too, does John Henry Cramer's book *Lincoln under Enemy Fire: The Complete Account of His Experiences during Early's Attack on Washington*, however now dated from its original 1948 publication. In the end, our imagination of events comes not from the sites or even surviving words of memory. Rather, in this visual age of the twenty-first century it derives from pictures. Two depictions stand out—J. Otto Schweizer's bronze plaque is one; a painting by a relatively unknown World War I patriotic poster artist whose father knew Lincoln is the other. Schweizer's bas-relief on the Lincoln Stone seems the most artistic. Eugenie de Land Saugstad's painting *Abraham Lincoln at the Battle of Fort Stevens* by comparison seems more artificial, even stilted, the barrel of the heavy cannon next to the figures of Lincoln, Wright, and Crawford more amateurishly clunky. The painting hangs over a fireplace in the restored Superintendent's Lodge at Battleground. The Lincoln Stone resides three city blocks away atop the fort. These together—depictions and sites—give us the visual display by which to remember *The Day Lincoln Was Almost Shot: The Fort Stevens Story*.[36]

Notes

1. A. M. Stewart, *Camp, March and Battlefield: Or, Three Years and a Half with the Army of the Potomac* (Philadelphia: Kessinger Publishing, 1865), 406–7.

2. Indictments *United States vs. Jefferson Davis, United States vs. John C. Breckinridge*, District of Columbia Supreme Court, May 26, 1865, both Virginia Historical Society, VHS; Ezra Warner, *Generals in Gray: Lives of the Confederate Commanders* (Baton Rouge: Louisiana State University Press, 1959) and *Generals in Blue: Lives of the Union Commanders* (Baton Rouge: Louisiana State University Press, 1964), tell of postwar lives and careers of the general

officer participants in this campaign, See also James O. Hall, "Marylanders in the Civil War: The Death of Walter Bowie," *Maryland Line* [Montgomery County, Maryland, Civil War Round Table] (October 1989): 1–3.

3. Warner, *Generals in Gray* and *Generals in Blue*, while representative reminiscences, can be found in the bibliography of B. Franklin Cooling, *Jubal Early's Raid on Washington, 1864*. (Baltimore: Nautical and Aviation Publishing Company of America, 1989; Tuscaloosa: University of Alabama Press, 2007).

4. U.S. Congress, 58th, Third Session, Senate Document 53, Elizabeth Thomas, December 1904.

5. Gordon Berg, "The Graceful Dead: How Confederate Soldiers Came to Be Buried at Grace Episcopal Church," unpublished study, n.d., courtesy copy, author's files; Mildred Newbold Getty, *To Light The Way; A History of Grace Episcopal Church, Silver Spring, Maryland* (Silver Spring, MD, No Publisher, 1965), 9–10.

6. *Washington Evening Star*, November 14, 1896, recounted in Berg, ibid.

7. John G. Barnard, *A Report on the Defenses of Washington* (Washington, DC: Government Printing Office, 1871), 119, quoting Early's letter to the *New York News*, December 18, 1865; Jubal A. Early, *A Memoir of the Last Year of the War for Independence* (Toronto: Lovell and Gibson, 1866), 395 fn.

8. Barnard, *Report*, 122; Letter, Early to Editor, *Lynchburg Republican*, December 14, 1874, printed in *Richmond Sentinel*, June 1875, copy, Defending Washington files, Fort Ward Museum and Historic Site (FWMHS), Alexandria, Virginia.

9. John W. Daniel, "General Jubal A. Early," *Richmond Dispatch*, December 14, 1894, in *Southern Historical Society Papers* XXII (1894): 300; Henry Kyd Douglas, *I Rode with Stonewall* (Chapel Hill: University of North Carolina Press, 1940), 297.

10. John B. Gordon, *Reminiscences of the Civil War* (New York: Scribner's, 1904), 314–19; Douglas, ibid.

11. L. Minor Blackford, *Mine Eyes Have Seen the Glory: The Story of a Virginia Lady, Mary Berkeley Minor Blackford* (Cambridge: Harvard University Press, 1954), 237; Armistead L. Long, *Memoirs of Robert E. Lee* (New York: J. M. Stoddart, 1886), 359, 360.

12. Alexander Hunter, *Johnny Reb and Billy Yank* (New York and Washington: Neale Publishing Company, 1907), 649–52; John N. Opie, *A Rebel Cavalryman with Stuart and Jackson* (Chicago: W. B. Conkey, 1899), 247.

13. George Wilson Booth, *A Maryland Boy in Lee's Army: Personal Reminiscences of a Maryland Soldier* (Baltimore: Nabu Press, 1907), 126–28.

14. Benjamin P. Thomas, editor, *Three Years with Grant as Recalled by War Correspondent Sylvanus Cadwallader* (New York: Knopf, 1955), 228–29; see also Gail Stephens, *Shadow of Shiloh: Majr General Lew Wallace in the Civil War* (Indianapolis: Indiana State Historical Society Press, 2010), 232.

15. George E. Davis, "Battle of the Monocacy, Forty Years Ago," Burlington, Vermont *Daily Free Press*, July 19, 1904, clipping, Folder 11, Box 2, George E. Davis collection, Monocacy National Battlefield, Frederick, Maryland.

16. Examples of veteran comments can be found in the *National Tribune*, including S. A. McDonald, April 12, 19, 1894; Rufus R. Lord, February 22, 1900; R. Guyton, March 29,

1900; J. Fred Loeble, April 26, 1900; J. G. Bridaham, July 19, 1900; A. F. Jackson, August 19, 1900; Charles Porter, September 27, 1900; A. G. Jacobs, August 23, 1900; John H. Wolff, September 27, 1900; William G. Gleason, *Historical Sketch of the One Hundred and Fiftieth Regiment Ohio Volunteer Infantry* (Rocky River, OH: 1899), 17; and Russell F. Weigley, *Quartermaster General of the Union Army* (New York: Columbia University Press, 1959), 302.

17. See Benjamin Franklin Cooling and Walton B. Owen, *Mr. Lincoln's Forts: A Guide to the Civil War Defenses of Washington* (Lanham, MD: Scarecrow Press, 2009), 164–67, and accompanying research files FWMHP; *Maryland News*, July 9, 1907, and November 24, 1908; "Battle of Monocacy," vertical file, Frederick County Historical Society (FCHS); Getty, *Grace Episcopal Church*, 7.

18. Stuart Abramowitz, "The History of Silver Spring," unpublished paper, n.d., *Montgomery Journal*, October 21, 1983; *Washington Post*, May 29, 1955; *Maryland News*, May 27, 1955; Maryland National Capital Park and Planning Commission, "Silver Spring-Sligo Historical Trail," all in files of MCHS; Blair Lee, "The Day Confederates Marched into Montgomery County History," *Montgomery Sentinel*, June 28, 1989; Claudia Levy, "Capitol View Park: A Step Back in Time," *Washington Post*, May 13, 1989; Hoyt Barnett, "Recalls Gen. Early's Raid," *Washington Star*, July 14, 1935; John Clagett Proctor, *Proctor's Washington and Environs Written for the* Washington Sunday Star *(1928–1949)* (Washington, DC: by Author, 1949), 56.

19. Unidentified clipping concerning Walter Reed Army Hospital acquisition, *Baltimore Sun*, September 1, 1907, FWMP; also see Mary W. Standlee, *Borden's Dream: The Walter Reed Army Medical Center in Washington, D.C.* (Washington, DC: Department of the Army, 2009), chapter 1; John Clagett Proctor, "Brightwood D.C.," December 14, 1917, and "Georgia Avenue," June 18, 1919, in *Proctor's Poems* (Washington, DC, 1950), 44 and 50.

20. District of Columbia National Guard, Engineer Platoon of the Engineer Corps, *Guide to and Maps of the National Capital and Vicinity, Including the Fortifications* (Washington, DC, n.p., 1892), 20–22; Judith Beck Helm, *Tenleytown, D.C.: Country Village into City Neighborhood* (Washington, DC: Tennally Press, 1981), chapter IV especially; George Alfred Townsend, *Washington: Outside and Inside* (Hartford, CT: J. Betts and Company, 1873), 640; John Clagett Proctor, "Preservation of Historic Fort Stevens," *Washington Sunday Star*, July 8, 1945; Charles Moore, editor, *The Improvement of the Park System of the District of Columbia*, 57th Cong., First Session, Senate report 166 (Washington, DC, 1902), 7, 75, 91–93, 111–12, 167–69, D–288, 289; Frederick Gutheim and Antoinette J. Lee, *Worthy of the Nation: Washington, DC, from L'Enfant to the National Capital Planning Commission* (Baltimore: Johns Hopkins University Press, 2006), 119–43, 203–5, 300, 312.

21. U.S. Congress, 57th, 1st Session, Senate Document 433, Fort Stevens Lincoln National Military Park (Washington, DC, 1902), 2; District of Columbia Civil War Centennial Commission, Commemorative Ceremony Program One Hundredth Anniversary of the Battle of Fort Stevens, July 11, 1864; J. C. McFerran to M. C. Meigs, March 17, 1870, relating to title, Battleground Cemetery and Accompanying Correspondence, Rock Creek Nature Center, National Park Service, Washington, DC (RCNC).

22. Lewis Cass White to "Dear Comrade," August 10, 1900, copy, Lewis Cass White collection, Joseph and Sharon Scopin, Darnestown, Maryland.

CHAPTER TEN

23. *Washington Times*, June 26, 1904; Proctor, "Preservation of Historic Fort Stevens," other miscellaneous clippings, Fort Stevens files, RCNC. Sen. Doc. 433, ibid., 10–12.

24. Unidentified clipping, *Washington Star*, 1901; "Old Fort Stevens Sold," *Washington Evening Star*, March 22, 1911; "Fort Stevens," *Washington Evening Star*, March 27, 1911; "Wants Lincoln Highway," *Baltimore Sun*, August 5, 1911; Statement, The Fort Stevens Terrace Company, undated [1912]; U.S. Congress, 62nd, Third Session, Senate Bill 8142, "To acquire certain land between Peabody and Underwood Streets, east of Georgia Avenue for a public park, January 16, 1913," all Lewis Cass White collection, Joseph and Sharon Scopin, Darnestown, Maryland.

25. D.C. Civil War Commission, Fort Stevens Program, 1964; Lewis Cass White, "Fort Stevens and the Lincoln Boulder," in John H. Niebaum, *History of the Pittsburgh Washington Infantry, One Hundred and Second (Old Thirteenth Regiment), Pennsylvania Veteran Volunteers* (Pittsburgh: Burgum, 1931), 115; Lewis Cass White, "President Lincoln at Fort Stevens," *National Tribune*, March 6, 1913; Cooling and Owen, *Mr. Lincoln's Forts*, 161.

26. *Washington Star*, February 26, 1925; Ernst Jockers, *J. Otto Schweizer: The Man and His Work* (Philadelphia: International Printing, 1953).

27. Mark De Wolfe Howe, editor, *Holmes-Laski Letters: The Correspondence of Mr. Justice Holmes and Harold Laski, 1916–1925, Volume I* (Cambridge: Harvard University Press, 1953), 339–40, 410, 414. See also CEPH, *Civil War Defenses of Washington Historic Resources Study* (Chevy Chase, MD: National Park Service, 2004), part II, chapter III.

28. John Clagett Proctor, "Lincoln's Statue," *Washington Evening Star*, January 18, 1920, in *Proctor's Poems*, 47.

29. Collection of Memorial Day programs, miscellaneous clippings, and notes, Fort Stevens file, Defenses of Washington collection, FWMHS; *Washington Star*, December 22, 1212; *Washington Post*, July 5, 1964. On Monocacy preservation and park development see "Memorial Park on Monocacy Battlefield," *Confederate Veteran* XXXVI (February 1928): 44; U.S. 70th Congress, 1st Session, House of Representatives, Committee on Military Affairs, *Hearings—National Military Park at Battlefield of Monocacy, Maryland, April 13, 1928* (Washington, DC: Government Printing Office, 1928), 1–3, 6–14; Miscellaneous Clippings and data sheets, Monocacy vertical files, FCHS; Fact Sheets and Visitor Brochures, Monocacy National Battlefield, Monocacy file, Defenses of Washington collection, FWMHS, and Monocacy National Battlefield files, Visitor Center, Monocacy National Battlefield, Frederick, Maryland.

30. Benjamin P. Thomas, editor, *Three Years with Grant: As Recalled by War Correspondent Sylvanus Cadwallader* (New York: Alfred A. Knopf, 1955), 227, 228; David Alan Johnson, *Decided on the Battlefield: Grant, Sherman, Lincoln and the Election of 1864* (New York: Prometheus Books, 2012), epilogue; James C. Bresnahan, editor, *Revisioning the Civil War; Historians on Counter-Factual Scenarios* (Jefferson, NC: MacFarland, 2006), chapter 11, especially 192–95.

31. John B. Southard to sister, July 16, 1864, New York Historical Society, New York.

32. Frank Wilkeson, *Turned Inside Out: Recollections of a Private Soldier in the Army of the Potomac* (Lincoln: University of Nebraska Press, 1997), 219; Comrade Peterson, "Fort Stevens," *National Tribune*, December 2, 1915.

33. Charles Reagan Wilson, *Baptized in Blood: The Religion of the Lost Cause, 1865–1920* (Athens: University of Georgia Press, 1980/2009), 179–82; Shaw quoted in Smith D. Fry, "Two Critical Periods—The Capture of Washington in 1861 or 1864 Would Have Resulted in Foreign Recognition of Southern Confederacy," *National Tribune Scrap Book*, n.d., U.S. Army Heritage Center, Carlisle Barracks, Pennsylvania; also noted in a *Washington Star* editorial, March 27, 1911.

34. Ward Moore, *Bring the Jubilee: What If the South Won the Civil War* (LaVergne, TN: Wildside Press, 2010 edition).

35. Robert Engelman, "Fellowship of the Rings," *Washington Post*, June 25, 1989; Edward C. Smith, "When the Confederates Came to the Capital," *Washington Post*, July 9, 1989.

36. John Henry Cramer, *Lincoln under Enemy Fire: The Complete Account of His Experiences during Early's Attack on Washington* (Baton Rouge: Louisiana State University Press, 1948; Knoxville: University of Tennessee Press, 2010).

APPENDIX A: FORT STEVENS BATTLE IN THE SUBURBS: SELF-GUIDED MOTOR TOUR

Directions

Preferably begin your tour from the Monocacy National Battlefield—as did Jubal Early. Drive south on Maryland Route 355 through Urbana, Hightstown, and Gaithersburg to Rockville. This will be Early's historic route via the Frederick-Georgetown Road. Early's main force turned east at Rockville to gain Seventh Street Road (modern Maryland Route 97 to Georgia Avenue) via the precursor to modern Viers Mill Road. However, this tour suggests continuing on Maryland Route 355 (Rockville Pike, later Wisconsin Avenue) through Bethesda, following McCausland's historic route, which means that his cavalry arrived first to threaten Washington defenses at Tennallytown.

Thus, follow modern Wisconsin Avenue into northwest District of Columbia to Western Avenue, N.W. Turn right, go through four traffic lights, and turn left at River Road. Fort Bayard Park will be on the corner to your right after the turn. Turn right at the next street (Forty-Sixth Street, N.W.), right again (Fessenden Street, N.W.), and park on the street to visit the site of Fort Bayard.

Stop One: Fort Bayard

Historical Site

In a sense, the tiny fort (123 perimeter yards, six guns) anchored the active Union defense at Tennallytown, although the overall defense line extended west through forts Simmons and Mansfield to the formidable Fort Sumner with intervening and auxiliary battery positions. Named for Brigadier General George D.

Bayard, First Pennsylvania Cavalry, mortally wounded at Fredericksburg, December 13, 1862, the fort commanded the vital River Road, leading from Tennallytown upstream in Montgomery County, Maryland. Elements of several Ohio National Guard troops (100-day troops) manned the defense line in this sector. As you look north from the site of this fort, you can detect from topography that in conjunction with forts Simmons and Mansfield, Fort Bayard commanded a long sward of farmland emerging upward from Powder Mill Branch. None of the ground occupied by these works, forward-positioned by army engineers, replicated the stronger ridgeline to the south upon which Fort Gaines (now designed as a "secondary" or reserve fort to forestall an enemy breakthrough) was built in 1861.

A question remains. If, as Brigadier General John McCausland later claimed, he and his aide infiltrated Union lines personally on the night of July 11 through this general area (perhaps using the Powder Mill Run creek bed), then might have Early's whole army effected a breakthrough in this sector, despite the guns of forts Bayard, Simmons, and Mansfield—and especially Fort Reno at Tennallytown? Or was it never Early's intent to test the defenses of Washington at this point, relying instead upon that mysterious Hotchkiss Map or even intelligence from Southern sympathizers about a great weakness to the east at Fort Stevens? Instead, only active skirmishing occurred across this portion of Union lines in the "battle in the suburbs."

Directions

Return to Forty-Sixth Street N.W., turn right, go south to Massachusetts Avenue, N.W., turn left, and proceed to the top of the hill at Ward Circle. The site of Fort Gaines (171 perimeter yards, four guns, but essentially unoccupied at the time of the battle) stands to your left on the campus of American University at the circle. Next, proceed three-quarters of the way around the circle, turning east on Nebraska Avenue, N.W. This is the site of Grassland, the Loughborough family home possibly visited by a Confederate cavalryman and his aide, Henry Loughborough, by infiltrating the Union defense line. It lies on the right, where the NBC studio is now located. The circular drive in front of the mansion is replicated by the circular drive in front of NBC.

Continue east on Nebraska Avenue, N.W., past Tenley Circle (the site of historic Tennalleytown is to your left), noticing several remaining frame houses, then go past Woodrow Wilson High School to Chesapeake Street, N.W. Turn left, and proceed to the top of the hill. The site of Fort Reno/Battery Reno is to your right. Park on the street as directed. Proceed on foot to the highest attainable point—outside the reservoir fence—on the north side of the park.

Stop Two: Fort Reno, Battery Reno, Tennallytown

Historical Site

Occupying the highest elevation in the District of Columbia (409 feet above sea level), this sizeable fort is 517 perimeter yards, with twenty-seven guns. A "Double Covered way to an Advanced Battery" connected Fort Reno with Battery Reno (seven guns), further extending the frowning guns and fortifications on Tennallytown's heights. Together they commanded not only the intersection of River and Brookville roads with the Georgetown-Rockville Pike but also the open countryside northward to Maryland. Its 100-pounder Parrott particularly supplemented guns of companion forts in the defense line to the west from Fort Bayard to Fort Sumner as well as eastward at forts Kearny, DeRussy, and Fort Stevens. No wonder Confederate cavalryman John McCausland reported the strength and virtual impregnability of this position. However, the true importance of Fort Reno derived not from its firepower but rather its elevation. Here Signal Station personnel discerned the distant dust of Early's flank march to the Seventh Street Road on July 11. They alerted other stations along the line, thereby preparing a Union concentration at Fort Stevens for Early's arrival there.

Union cavalry engaged McCausland's advance several blocks further north on the Rockville Pike (Wisconsin Avenue, N.W.). The fort's artillery reputedly sent shells as far as what is now the Walter Reed National Military Medical Center (formerly Bethesda Naval Hospital) when Early's men withdrew on July 12. Colonel John Marble's garrison at the time of the battle included Ohio national guardsmen, heavy artillerymen from Wisconsin and New York, and Veteran Reservists and Provisional Brigade volunteers. Elements of arriving XIX Corps veterans were held in reserve behind the fort. Horatio Wright began his organized, if dilatory, pursuit of the departing Rebels from this vicinity.

After the war, landowner Giles Dyer (who recovered the property) sold the farmland to developers of "Reno City," which was soon to be inhabited by both white and black homeowners. Many of the African Americans had sought safety and work with the Union army at the Fort Reno fort and camps. By the turn of the century the Army Corps of Engineers had converted the fort site itself into a city reservoir, which you see today, with its distinctive red-brick tower (actually a water tank) denoting Fort Reno's pivotal (nay crucial) role in the "battle in the suburbs."

Directions

Return to Nebraska Avenue, N.W., turn left, and proceed east to the light at Fessenden Street, N.W., turning right and crossing Connecticut Avenue, N.W. A very substantially constructed Battery Rossell (named for Major Nathan B. Rossell,

Third U.S. Infantry, killed at Gaines Mill in June 1862 and sporting eight vacant platforms for field guns—hence possibly so armed on July 11 and 12, 1864) was located at the southeastern corner.

Now proceed three blocks to the merger of Fessenden and Linnean avenues, N.W., go right one block, and then go left on Ellicott Street, N.W., to Thirtieth Place, N.W. Turn left—you are now passing directly through the site of Fort Kearny (320 perimeter yards, ten guns). Together with Battery Rossell, this work covered the valley of Broad Branch (a tributary of Rock Creek) and provided a link between forts Reno and DeRussy. Random skirmishing may have occurred outward from these positions during July 11 and 12, 1864.

Next, turn left on Garrison Street, N.W. (noting Battery Terrill—seven unoccupied field gun emplacements, possibly manned—preserved on the grounds of the Peruvian Embassy; contact the embassy for possible access), then right on Linnean Avenue to Broad Branch Road. Turn left on Nebraska Avenue, and go right on Nebraska, proceeding one block to Military Road at the stoplight intersection.

Turn right. You are now approximating the historically named "Military Road" servicing the defense line in this vicinity. An unnamed, unarmed field gun battery remains on the east side of Broad Branch and provides a diversion; turn right at Twenty-Ninth and proceed to the fuse with Thirtieth Street, N.W. Otherwise, proceed approximately five city-block lengths (five traffic lights), past St. John's College High School on the left (site of the now nonexistent Battery Smeade, 170 perimeter yards, four guns, which commanded the Milk House Road/Ford to Brightwood further east). Rock Creek Park lies to your right (the location of the National Park Service Rock Creek Nature Center is a visitor contact point). Turn left at the Oregon Avenue, N.W., traffic light and park. The remains of Fort DeRussy are reachable via an unpaved bridle or footpath uphill to the right, behind the Fort DeRussy sign. Look for the National Park Service interpretive markers and the stone and plaque denoting the unrestored but preserved earthworks in the woods to your left from the bridle/footpath.

Stop Three: Fort DeRussy

Historical Site

This 190-perimeter-yard fort, boasting eleven cannon, commanded the deep valley of Rock Creek. Fort DeRussy's guns also provided a crossfire for the sector extending past Fort Kearny to Fort Reno at Tennallytown. Like Fort Reno, Fort DeRussy also boasted a 100-pounder Parrott rifled cannon which, during the battle in the suburbs (Fort Stevens), laid down rounds upon Confederate wagon parks north of Silver Spring. At the same time, garrison troops of Captain John Norris, including Wisconsin, New York, and Ohio national guardsmen, manned the works; Veteran Reserve contingents battled a Confederate attempt to construct breastworks and a battery position "two hills" over to the north-northwest; while VI Corps veterans bivouacked behind the fort in position to assist with its defense. The military road also lies in the rear. The site of Battery Kingsbury lay further east on the bridle/foot trail.

Directions

Proceed north on Oregon Avenue, N.W., to the vicinity of Bingham Drive on the right in Rock Creek Park (access limited to weekdays) and Beech Street, N.W., further north. The area of battle action on July 11 and 12 in front of Fort DeRussy roughly took place on the range of low hills in the park to your right and the city neighborhoods in the vicinity to your left. This, then, would be the approximate site of the Veteran Reserve Corps-Confederate skirmishing noted in dispatches.

Retrace the route via Oregon Avenue, N.W., to Military Road, turn left, and proceed eastward to Sixteenth Street, N.W., exit. Another existent unarmed field gun battery emplacement can be found off the Joyce Road exit at Ross Drive. But continue to Military Road and turn right on Sixteenth Street, N.W., and proceed south seven blocks to Kennedy Street, N.W. The Rock Creek Park tennis courts and recreational area is on the right.

Stop Four: Crystal Spring Racetrack/Rendezvous Area

Historical Site

Here, bounded by Kennedy Street, N.W., on the north, Fourteenth Street, N.W., on the east, and Colorado Avenue, N.W., on the south was located the half-mile-long Crystal Spring Racetrack. Established in 1859 on flat land long known to settlers and farmers for crystal spring waters, this area served as the reserve rendezvous or staging area supporting the defense of Fort Stevens at the time of the battle in the suburbs. The fort lay approximately a half-mile to the north. Repeated references to the Crystal Spring staging point appear in soldier reminiscences as well as official accounts. The location became even more famous when in 1894, Ohio businessman Jacob Coxey led an "army" of unemployed men from here to the Capitol to present the new idea of U.S. government job creation by building public facilities. Congress reacted negatively, Coxey was arrested, and his petition was never presented. "Coxey's Army" dispersed home.

Directions

Return via Sixteenth Street, N.W. (or alternate route Fourteenth Street, N.W.), to Military Road, turn right, and proceed east through two traffic signals to Georgia Avenue, N.W. Notice the old Military Road School (circa 1912) on the left, a legacy from the freedman's school conducted by the Fort Stevens garrison nearby and later a segregated D.C. public school.

Proceed via a dogleg at Georgia Avenue, N.W., where Military Road becomes Missouri Avenue, N.W.—headed east. Travel approximately 1.6 miles through nine traffic lights to North Capitol Street, N.W. Turn right on North Capitol, go three traffic lights, and bear right onto Rock Creek Church Road. Proceed through three additional traffic lights. A national cemetery lies on the left, Soldiers' Home is ahead, and Rock Creek Cemetery and Parish Church is on the right. At the traffic light at Upshur Street, N.W., turn left at Eagle Gate onto Soldiers' Home grounds. The Lincoln Cottage lies straight ahead, the old castellated tower building or Scott Hall is adjacent, and the Robert H. Smith Visitor Education Center and parking is on the left. (NOTE: If Eagle Gate is closed, proceed further on Rock Creek Church Road to Randolph Gate and follow the signs to the Lincoln Cottage.)

Stop Five: Lincoln Cottage and U.S. Military Asylum

Historical Site

President Lincoln's Cottage (as it came to be known) was the family summer retreat from 1862 to 1864. Built initially for this purpose in 1843 by banker George Washington Riggs, it became part of the first parcel of the U.S. Military Asylum for Mexican War veterans. It was renamed Anderson Cottage for cofounder Major Robert Anderson of subsequent Fort Sumter fame. Lincoln's predecessor, President James Buchanan, briefly used the Old Soldiers' Home and possibly recommended the locale to Lincoln. The brick house with stucco exterior reflects the Gothic revival architecture popular at the time and also seen in Francis Preston Blair's Silver Spring mansion just across the District line in Maryland. The Lincolns' residency witnessed transfer each year of some nineteen cartloads of family possessions. It was here that Lincoln drafted the preliminary Emancipation Proclamation as well as conducting other consultations. He often visited soldier encampments and the garrison at nearby Fort Totten. The Lincoln family had returned to the White House at the moment of Early's arrival.

Presidents Rutherford B. Hayes and Chester A. Arthur also used this salubrious retreat from Washington cares and heat during their administrations. By the twentieth century, the cottage faded from public view, and the Soldiers' Home administration adapted the structure for other use. It was designated a National Historic Landmark in 1973 and a National Monument in 2000. The National Trust for Historic Preservation restored and opened President Lincoln's Cottage to the public in 2008.

Adjacent to the cottage is the Scott Building, currently closed by the 2011 earthquake. It was named for General Winfield Scott who, together with Anderson and then-secretary of war Jefferson Davis, became the founders (using money from Mexican War tribute) of an asylum or secure and honorable retirement home for disabled and destitute veterans.

Begun in 1852, the uncompleted building served as a watchtower and signal station during Jubal Early's raid. Even now the Soldiers' Home grounds provide a panoramic view of downtown Washington to the south, hence the prominent tower can be appreciated as the vital communication link between defenders on the front lines relaying real-time information to the War Department adjacent to the White House.

Directions

Retrace the route via Rock Creek Church Road to North Capitol Street, and bear left but turn immediately right at the Buchanan Street traffic light (or if missed, the next street, Crittenden Street, N.E., will suffice). Proceed one block to Fort Totten Drive, N.E. Fort Totten Park lies straight ahead, with parking limited mainly to side streets. The preserved but unrestored fort lies in an overgrown, forested plot surrounded by parkland with a walking path closed to vehicles. Outlying Battery Totten remains to the left via the footpath.

Stop Six: Fort Totten and Battery Totten

Historical Site

A relatively small work (272 perimeter yards, twenty cannon) occupied a commanding height overlooking open country northward to the Maryland line. It also provided crossfire with intervening works (forts Slemmer, Bunker Hill, Saratoga, Battery Morris, and Fort Thayer) eastward to Fort Lincoln and the Baltimore-Washington rail and road axis. Across this whole sector rode Confederate raider Bradley Johnson's cavalry returning from Beltsville on his Baltimore raid to rejoin Early's army. Like similar 100-pounder Parrott rifles of forts Reno and DeRussy, Fort Totten's 100-pounder provided long-range harassing fire to support the fighting at Fort Stevens on July 11 and 12, 1864. At that time, its garrison comprised regular U.S. artillerymen as well as contingents of Ohio national guardsmen and a company of New Hampshire Heavy Artillery. Early may have later confused a station here with that at the Military Asylum (Soldiers' Home). Even today, visitors can easily see the castellated tower of the asylum while standing at the fort.

Directions

Next proceed northward on Fort Totten Drive, N.E. (Battery Totten lies in the woods to the right before the access route to Fort Totten Metro subway station), to the Riggs Road, N.E., traffic light. Turn left one block and then right again on North Capitol Street, N.E. Continue straight on North Capitol Street, N.E., through the traffic-light intersection with New Hampshire Avenue, N.E., for a total of five traffic lights (approximately 1.8 miles from Fort Totten) to Kansas Avenue, N.W. Turn left on Kansas Avenue. The site of Fort Slocum is on high ground on the left between Kansas Avenue, N.W., Nicholson Street, N.W., and Milmorson Street N.W. Parking will be limited. (NOTE: The misplaced "Fort Slocum Park" sign on the right actually denotes an interlocking rifle trench, and an unarmed field gun battery remains overlooking a broad Piney Branch Creek valley, which is the modern Third Street, N.W.)

Stop Seven: Fort Slocum

Historical Site

Like Fort DeRussy, this large work (653 perimeter yards, twenty-five guns) was a companion to Fort Stevens in the fighting of July 11 and 12. Reputedly, the opening shot in the "battle in the suburbs" or Fort Stevens came from a cannon at Fort Slocum under the order of Captain John N. Abbey, Second Pennsylvania Artillery, commanding the garrison. As with Fort Stevens and even Fort DeRussy, professional criticism of its location cited higher ground to the north upon which an enemy might establish position. Perhaps based on intelligence provided by Southern sympathizers or the Hotchkiss Map, Jubal Early chose these forts as the focal point for his attack. Nevertheless, Fort Slocum commanded the so-called Left Fork of Rock Creek Church Road as well as a country road leading out into Maryland. The latter road may even have been the lane from Bladensburg to Georgetown bearing the ignominious distinction of a militia retreat route from the 1814 disaster.

Like Fort Totten, Fort Slocum engaged roving bands of Confederate cavalry as well as deterred flank movements/attacks by Early's main force. Whether or not the sector between forts Slocum and Stevens (especially the weak line overseeing the Piney Branch creek valley) occasioned Confederate general John B. Gordon's remark about virtually unmanned rifle pits upon which he personally rode to ascertain weakness in enemy defense, Fort Slocum itself was never such a weak spot. Garrisoning for the battle came from New Hampshire, Michigan, and Pennsylvania artillerymen as well as the Ohio national guardsmen. Montgomery Meigs's Quartermaster Department clerks occupied adjacent rifle pits and two thousand hospital convalescents, representing perhaps most of the units in the Army of the Potomac encamped nearby as a reserve.

Directions

Continue south on Kansas Avenue, N.W., to Missouri Avenue, N.W. Proceed west through six traffic lights to Georgia Avenue, N.W.

Stop Eight: Camp Brightwood, Brightwood

Historical Site

To the south bordered on the west by Seventh Street Road (modern Georgia Avenue, N.W.) (Crittenden Street, N.W.) stood hilltop Camp Brightwood and the property of D.C. militia captain and builder/businessman Matthew Emery, whose postwar mansion dominated the scene. This site was a signal station and a transfer point for the wounded at the Battle of Fort Stevens. The intersection of Milk House Ford Road (now Rock Creek Ford Road, N.W.) and Seventh Street Pike (Georgia Avenue, N.W.) also boasted the site of Moreland Tavern, Major General Alexander M. McCook's headquarters for the Battle of Fort Stevens.

Directions

Turn right at the traffic light onto Georgia Avenue, N.W.—the hub of historic Brightwood. Proceed north two blocks to Quackenbos Street, N.W. (conamed Elizabeth Thomas Way) and turn left; Emory Church and Fort Stevens lie to the right and Nativity R. C. Church lies to the left. Park and move to the parapet section of the fort—facing the magazine on the left; Lincoln Stone or Boulder to the front. The original Fort Massachusetts portion is readily identifiable as the base for the Emory Church of Light property to the extreme right. (NOTE: D.C. Cultural Tourism has a superb Brightwood Neighborhood Heritage Tour, exemplified by their Stop 16 and 17 Heritage Trail Signs relating to the Lincoln and "Aunt Betty" Elizabeth Thomas stories associated with Fort Stevens. View them on Quakenbos Street, N.W., near Thirteenth Street, N.W., before entering the fort proper. Despite a misleading period map by Union soldier/cartographer Robert Sneden, visitors may gain a superb appreciation of the Lincoln-Fort Stevens story.)

Stop Nine: Fort Stevens

Historical Site

Despite the sparse National Park Service interpretation (see Wayside plus the bronze relief map of the fort on the pedestal), the visitor can concentrate on the principal parts of the story. The fort itself comprised the original 168 yards as expanded to 375 perimeter yards with ten original and finally nineteen cannon. Originally constructed by Massachusetts (hence its name) and New York troops (who in later years objected strongly to its naming), its expansion in the period from 1862 to 1863 derived from the story of landowner and free African American Mrs. Elizabeth Thomas and her first encounter with President Lincoln. Both were apparently in Fort Stevens on July 11 and 12, and Mrs. Thomas was one of those yelling to get the foolish commander-in-chief down off the parapet (marked with the Lincoln Stone-Boulder today). The site of the new magazine as restored supposedly marked the cellar of Mrs. Thomas's destroyed house.

The restored parapet where Lincoln stood and the magazine as well as concrete replicas of embrasures, revetments, gun platforms, and the stocked rear gorge of Fort Stevens conducted by the Civilian Conservation Corps in the 1930s as well as the preservation of the site by the National Park Service with its minimal replica artillery and interpretation today stand as a tribute to the pivotal event that occurred on this sacred ground in 1864. The question of "what if" as laid out in the main text of this book may serve as suitable discussion points when viewing the site. The main action of skirmish, sharpshooting, and clearing assault that constituted the two-day action can best be analyzed by standing on the parapet (like Lincoln when nearby Surgeon Crawford was shot) or through the gun embrasures looking north where the readily discernable modern Walter Reed Army Hospital (now in a state of redevelopment) indicate Confederate bivouac and battle position as well as the extent of the battle space.

Directions

Turn right on Thirteenth Street, N.W., and proceed to the Georgia Avenue, N.W., intersection—the historic site of Toll Gate and the furthest advance of Confederate skirmishers in the Battle of Fort Stevens. Turn left on Georgia Avenue, proceeding past the Battleground National Cemetery (to which we will return as Stop Ten) to the traffic light at Aspen Street, N.W. Turn left—the historic Sharpshooter's Tree location marker lies inside the now-inaccessible Walter Reed reservation on the right (inside the Butternut Street Gate entrance, actually, closed during post–Base Realignment and Closure Commission (BRAC) conversion activities on Walter Reed). Continue to the historic Cameron Creek ravine between Thirteenth Place,

N.W., and Luzon Avenue, N.W., on the right within Walter Reed and therefore inaccessible at present.

Turn left on Luzon Avenue, N.W., and proceed to Van Buren Street, N.W. Turn left on Van Buren and take it to Fort Stevens Recreation Center on your left.

Stop Ten: Fort Stevens Main Battlefield

Historical Site

Union veterans of the Battle in the Suburbs or Fort Stevens considered the Toll Gate confluence of Seventh Street Road (Georgia Avenue) and Thirteenth Street-Piney Branch Road, N.W., as the furthest point of Confederate advance on July 11 and 12, 1864. For this reason, one also might call it "the highwater mark of the Confederacy." Jubal Early's army got no farther than this in capturing Washington, dispersing the Union government, affecting the election of 1864, gaining yet reluctant European intervention, and ending the war on Confederate terms.

Moreover, the pitched battle that succeeded the two days of skirmishing and sharpshooter activity took place from this juncture northward on both sides of Seventh Street Road (Georgia Avenue) to the area later encompassed by the Walter Reed Army Medical Center and Butternut Street on the east. The area now covered with modern housing and commercial enterprises is difficult to visualize. For that reason, a brief tour of the neighborhood streets will provide some topographical sense of the broad, flat land of crops, orchards, and occasional woodlots over which the sharp and bitter fight took place as Bidwell's and Edward's reinforced brigade traversed the ground earlier contested by skirmish lines, makeshift breastworks, and sharpshooters (including the one who shot Surgeon Crawford standing near Lincoln atop the Fort Stevens parapet).

The hill/knoll at the Fort Stevens Recreation Center grounds probably comprised the final Union position after the intense seesaw battle on the late afternoon and early evening of July 12. The residue of a resolute Confederate defense across Cameron Creek now receded as Early began withdrawal and his eventual retirement back to Virginia. Jubal Early's threat to the nation's capital was over.

At this point in the tour, pause and reflect on the changed battle landscape before you. Vincent K. Tazlo wrote to friends what he found as a "tourist" from Company H, One Hundred and Fiftieth National Guard, to this area the day after the encounter with Early.

> I have been today to the battlefield at Fort Stevens. Our forces had about 2 hundred killed and wounded, it is a hard sight—all the farm houses in reach of the guns of the Ft had to be burned to keep them from sheltering the rebel sharpshooters, only

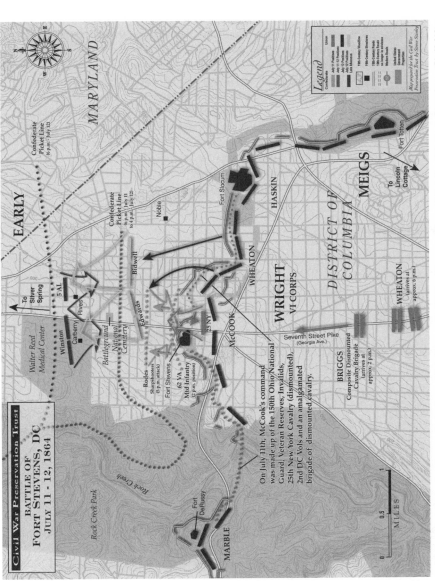

Battle Map Overlaid onto Modern Brightwood, D.C., Street Plan, Map by Steven Stanley. Civil War Trust

2 houses escaped, but the shot and shell almost tore it [sic] in pieces and killed 15 men and 1 lieutenant in one house. I counted 15 holes made by the shot and shell in one house and the bullet holes were too numerous to count, the house is almost covered with them. I saw today what I have read so much about. I saw men of both sides buried with not more than 4 inches of dirt to cover them their hands and feet sticking out. There were a great many pools of blood and I do not see how one man can bleed so much as I saw in one pile. I saw where 32 rebs were killed by one shell they were buried on the spot. The rebel loss must have been 5 times as great as ours. The trees and fences are all cut to pieces, in one little tree not more than 2 inches through I counted 21 bullet holes and I saw large trees cut down by cannon balls. I send you a splinter which was knocked out of a house by a shell which was sent to dislodge the rebel sharpshooters and went through the house and exploded in the rebel captain's tent, and sent him and his tent to the middle of next week.

War was Hell, even in so small a battle space as Fort Stevens. (Letter, Vincent K. Tazlo to Friends, July 13, 1864, Author's collections.)

Directions

From Thirteenth Street, N.W., at Van Buren Street, N.W., continue on Van Buren to the Georgia Avenue, N.W., traffic light; turn left on Georgia Avenue and go half of a block to Battleground National Cemetery on the right at 6625 Georgia Avenue, N.W.

Stop Eleven: Battleground National Cemetery

Historical Site

Here were gathered forty Union dead from the Fort Stevens battle after the fighting. Barely one acre in extent, President Lincoln's paltry dedicatory remarks hardly did justice to their sacrifice. Still, Battleground, not Fort Stevens, became the gathering point for reunion, remembrance, and monumentation of the historic events of July 11 and 12, 1864. Memorial Day ceremonies especially marked Battleground for neighborhood recognition as Brightwood demographics overtook the battlefield proper. The last veteran of the battle, E. R. Campbell, was interred in 1936, bringing the total gravesites to forty-one. Note the two 6-pounder cannons mounted on naval carriages at the entrance, the circular pattern of the graves, the bandstand, and the restored superintendent's house (after a design by Quartermaster Montgomery C. Meigs, himself a proud veteran of the battle in the suburbs). This structure now provides an ersatz Visitor Contact Station for those wanting more information from the National Park Service administration for the fort and cemetery.

Directions

The final leg of the tour begins from Battleground National Cemetery. Continue north on Georgia Avenue, past the former Walter Reed Army Medical Center (again, the site of Sharpshooter's Tree, Cameron Creek defile, and Confederate positions atop the ridge on the north side and battlefield action), and proceed 1.5 miles (eight to nine traffic lights) past the District/Maryland line into Silver Spring. The historic Jessup Blair mansion and park are on the right. Proceed to the next traffic light/major intersection marked "Thirteenth Street," but in reality it is Georgia Avenue and East-West Highway. Turn left on diagonal East-West Highway and proceed two blocks to historic Silver Spring Acorn Park on the left. Turn left onto Blair Mill Road; Acorn Park will be on the left.

Stop Twelve: The Silver Spring

Historical Site

The Francis Preston Blair Silver Spring mansion property was located approximately directly west on the left of East-West Highway; Montgomery Blair Falkland stood some distance ahead on the right of East-West Highway. No remnants exist except those names applied to the apartment complexes in the area.

Acorn Park humbly marks the famous water spot that attracted the elder Blair and his daughter Elizabeth and from which sprang his country property's name and later the town of Silver Spring, which is more properly located where Sligo Cross Road of Seventh Street Road (modern Georgia Avenue) and Colesville Road exist today. On July 11 and 12, 1864, Confederate soldiery lounged around the spring waters and fountain while their leaders held war council in the Silver Spring mansion. Perhaps it was the intercession of a Blair cousin, former U.S. senator and now Confederate major-general John Cabell Breckinridge, that saved the mansion from destruction. Son Montgomery Blair's newer Falkland enjoyed no similar reprieve, thereby tainting the memories of Early's raid for the Blair family long afterward.

Directions

Continue west on East-West Highway through two traffic lights to Colesville Road; proceed right through two traffic lights to Georgia Avenue; turn left and proceed seven blocks to Grace Church Road (historic Grace Churchyard/Church and Confederate Monument are on the right). Turn right and park. In this Woodside section of Silver Spring were the Confederate bivouacs and wagon parks close to historic Seventh Street Road and Sligo Creek to the east.

Stop Thirteen: Confederate Burial
Plot at Grace Church

Historical Site

Early's host marched past the modest wooden Grace Episcopal Church coming and departing from their appearance before Washington at Fort Stevens. The general reputedly later sent money to the rector to complete a roof for the structure. Perhaps he felt some remorse for the fallen from the battle that he left scattered across the countryside in the wake of his foray. In the postwar period, seventeen of the Confederate remains were gathered in the Grace Church burial yard having at first been deposited literally by the side of the Seventh Street Road until the extension of streetcar tracks occasioned the removal to the present location. They, like their erstwhile foe now eternally resting at Battleground National Cemetery, provide mute testimony to persons and events attending this crucial moment in our nation's history. Unlike Battleground, however, Abraham Lincoln proclaimed no epitaph to their sacrifice.

Directions

This concludes the tour—proceed north on Georgia Avenue to I-495 Beltway or to Wheaton, taking Viers Mill Road to the left to Rockville and replicating Early's approach to Fort Stevens as well as the Confederate retreat route to Darnestown, Poolesville, and the Potomac fords.

APPENDIX B: UNION ORDER OF BATTLE, JULY 11–12, 1864

Major-General Christopher C. Augur
Commanding XXII Corps/Department of Washington

Major-General Alexander McCook
Commanding, Northern Defenses of Washington

Cavalry Units

(Principally involved with Reconnaissance Tennallytown—Rockville)
Eighth Illinois Cavalry Regiment—Companies C and I, D, G (Wells and Hotopp)
Seventh Michigan Cavalry Regiment—detachment (Darling)
Second Massachusetts Cavalry Regiment—detachment (Lowell)
Provisional unit—Fry

Hardin's Division
Brigadier General Martin D. Hardin

Forts Sumner and Simmons
Twenty-Fourth United States Veteran Reserve Corps Regiment—Marsh

Forts Simmons, Bayard, Reno, and Kearny
First United States Veteran Reserve Corps Regiment—segment
Second United States Light Artillery—segment Battery I
Seventh United States Veteran Reserve Corps Regiment—Fyffe

Ninth New York Heavy Artillery Regiment—company
One Hundred and Fifty-First Ohio National Guard Regiment—Hughes

Fort Reno
Second U.S. Light Artillery—segment Battery I (Graves)
Ninth New York Heavy Artillery Regiment—Company B
One Hundred and Fiftieth Pennsylvania Regiment—Company K (Getchell)
One Hundred and Fifty-First Ohio National Guard Regiment—one company

Fort Kearny
Ninth New York Heavy Artillery Regiment—one company (Hough)
Twenty-Second United States Veteran Reserve Corps Regiment—Rutherford
One Hundred and Fifty-First Ohio National Guard Regiment—Company K
(Webb)

Fort Kearny to Battery Smead
First United States Veteran Reserve Corps Regiment—Trotter

Battery Smeade
Ninth New York Heavy Artillery Regiment—one-half Battery E
One Hundred and Fifty-First Ohio National Guard Regiment—Company I
(Chaney)

Battery Smeade to Fort DeRussy
Nineteenth United States Veteran Reserve Corps Regiment—Dayton

Fort DeRussy
First Wisconsin Heavy Artillery Regiment—Company A (Spear)
Ninth New York Heavy Artillery—one-half Battery L (Howe)
One Hundred and Fifty-First Ohio National Guard Regiment—Companies C, G
(Williams)

Fort DeRussy to Fort Stevens
First Maine Light Artillery—battery of two guns (Bradbury)
Sixth United States Veteran Reserve Corps Regiment—Palmer
Ninth United States Veteran Reserve Corps Regiment—Johnston
One Hundred and Forty-Seventh Ohio National Guard Regiment—Rosson
One Hundred and Fifty-Seventh Ohio National Guard Regiment—G. McCook

Meigs Division
Major-General Montgomery C. Meigs

Fort Stevens
Thirteenth Michigan Independent Light Artillery Battery—Dupont
Twenty-Fifth New York Cavalry Regiment—dismounted segment
One Hundred and Fiftieth Ohio National Guard Regiment—Company K
Frazee Provisional Brigade—segment

Fort Stevens to Fort Slocum
First Ohio Independent Light Artillery—battery of two guns (Gibbs)
Second District of Columbia Regiment—Alexander
Twelfth United States Veteran Reserve Corps Regiment—Farnsworth
Quartermaster Department—three companies

Fort Slocum
Second Pennsylvania Heavy Artillery Regiment—Abbey
Fourteenth Michigan Independent Light Artillery—Heine
One Hundred and Fiftieth Ohio National Guard Regiment—Company G (Nevins)
Provisional Brigade—segment

Reserve at Fort Slocum
Provisonal Brigade—segment

Fort Slocum to Fort Totten
Quartermaster Department
Provisional Brigade—segment

Fort Totten
One Hundred and Fiftieth Ohio National Guard Regiment—Hayward

Gillmore's Division
Major-General Quincy A. Gillmore

Forts Totten to Lincoln
Navy Yard contingent—Goldsborough
XIX Corps segments upon arrival

VI Corps, Army of the Potomac
Major-General Horatio G. Wright, Commanding

First Division
Brigadier General David A. Russell

First Brigade—Colonel William H. Penrose
Fourth New Jersey Infantry Regiment—Davis
Tenth New Jersey Infantry Regiment—Tay
Fifteenth New Jersey Infantry Regiment—Campbell

Second Brigade—Brigadier General Emory Upton
Second Connecticut Heavy Artillery Regiment—Mackenzie
Sixty-Fifth New York Infantry Regiment—Hamblin
Sixty-Seventh New York Infantry Regiment—Van Ness
Ninety-Fifth Pennsylvania Infantry Regiment—Randall
Ninety-Sixth Pennsylvania Infantry Regiment—Lessig
One Hundred and Twenty-First New York Infantry Regiment—Galpin

Third Brigade—Colonel Oliver Edwards
Second Rhode Island Infantry Regiment—Jenckes
Fifth Wisconsin Infantry Battalion—Kempf
Sixth Maine Infantry Battalion—Fuller
Twenty-Third Pennsylvania Infantry Regiment—Glenn
Thirty-Seventy Massachusetts Infantry Regiment—Montague
Forty-Ninth Pennsylvania Infantry Regiment—Wakefield
Eighty-Second Pennsylvania Infantry Regiment—Wetherill
Nine Hundred and Nineteenth Pennsylvania Infantry Regiment—Clark

Second Division
Brigadier General George W. Getty

First Brigade—Brigadier General Frank Wheaton
Sixty Second New York Infantry Regiment—Stewart
Ninety-Third Pennsylvania Infantry Regiment—Long
Ninety-Eighth Pennsylvania Infantry Regiment—Kohler
One Hundred and Second Pennsylvania Infantry Regiment—McLaughlin
One Hundred and Thirty-Ninth Pennsylvania Infantry Regiment—Munroe

Second Brigade—Brigadier General Lewis A. Grant
First Vermont Heavy Artillery Regiment—Warner
Second Vermont Infantry Regiment—Tray

Third Vermont Infantry Regiment—three companies (Pingree)
Fourth Vermont Infantry Regiment
Fifth Vermont Infantry Regiment—Barney
Sixth Vermont Infantry Regiment—Hale
Note: Second and Third Vermont positioned in support of the line between Fort
   DeRussy and Fort Stevens.

Third Brigade—Colonel Daniel D. Bidwell
Seventh Maine Infantry Regiment—Channing
Forty-Third New York Infantry Regiment—Van Patten
Forty-Ninth New York Infantry Regiment—Holt
Sixty-First Pennsylvania Infantry Regiment—Rodgers
Seventy-Seventh New York Infantry Regiment—French
One Hundred and Twenty-Second New York Infantry Regiment—Brower

APPENDIX C: BATTLE OF FORT STEVENS, JULY 11–12, 1864

Principal Involved Works and Armaments

(*) Principal involved works, west to east, with number of cannon/mortars, possible ammunition types, and ranges available.

Fort Bayard (123 yards / six guns)

Table C.1. *Fort Bayard*

Artillery Type	Projectile/Weight	Range
20-pdr. (3.67 in.) Parrott rifle *en embrasure* (4)	shell / 30 lbs.	4,400 yds.
12-pdr. field howitzer *en embrasure* (2)	shell / 8.43 lbs.	800–1,072 yds.
	case / 12.1 lbs.	

Fort Reno and Battery Reno (517 yards / twenty-seven guns)

Table C.2. *Fort Reno*

Artillery Type	Projectile/Weight	Range
Eight-inch siege howitzer *en embrasure* (2)	shell / 49.75 lbs. canister / 57.9 lbs. case / 59.5 lbs. shot / 65 lbs. grape / 75.5 lbs.	2,280 yds.
Two 4-pdr. howitzer *en embrasure* (9)	shell / 16.8 lbs. shot / 24.3 lbs. case / 24.6 lbs. canister / 21.25 lbs. grape / 30.6 lbs.	1,900 yds.
100-pdr. (6.4 in.) Parrott rifle *en barbette* (1)	hollow shot / 80 lbs. shell / 101 lbs.	6,820 yds. 2,080–4,250 yds.
30-pdr. (4.2 in.) Parrott rifle *en embrasure* (4)	shell / 30 lbs.	6,700 yds.
Ten-inch mortar (2)	shot / 127.5 lbs. shell / 88.42 lbs.	2,080–4,250 yds.
24-pdr. Coehorn mortar (2)	shell / 24 lbs.	1,200 yds.

Table C.3. *Battery Reno*

Artillery Type	Projectile/Weight	Range
20-pdr. (3.67 in.) Parrott rifle *en embrasure* (7)	shell / 30 lbs.	4,400 yds.

Fort Kearny (320 yards / ten guns)

Table C.4. *Fort Kearny*

Artillery Type	Projectile/Weight	Range
Eight-inch siege howitzer *en embrasure* (1)	shell / 49.75 lbs. canister / 57.9 lbs. case / 59.5 lbs. shot / 65 lbs. grape / 75.5 lbs.	2,280 yds.
32-pdr. seacoast gun *en embrasure* (3)	shot / 32.4 lbs. shell / 22.5 lbs. case / 32.7 lbs. canister / 37 lbs. grape / 39.8 lbs.	1,469–1,922 yds.
100- pdr. (6.4 in.) Parrott rifle en barbette (1)	hollow shell / 80 lbs. shell / 101 lbs.	6,820 yds. 2,080–4,250 yds.
24-pdr. siege gun *en embrasure* (3)	shell / 16.8 lbs. case / 24.6 lbs. shot / 24.3 lbs. canister / 29 lbs. grape / 30.6 lbs.	1,900 yds.
30-pdr. (4.2 in.) Parrott rifle *en embrasure* (3)	hollow shell / 80 lbs. shell / 101 lbs.	6,820 yds. 2,080–4,250 yds.

APPENDIX C

Battery Smeade (177 yards / four guns)

Table C.5. *Battery Smeade*

Artillery Type	Projectile/Weight	Range
20-pdr. (3.67 in.) Parrott rifle *en embrasure* (4)	shell / 30 lbs.	4,400 yds.

Fort DeRussy (190 yards / eleven guns)

Table C.6. *Fort DeRussy*

Artillery Type	Projectile/Weight	Range
32-pdr. seacoast gun *en barbette* (3)	shot / 32.4 lbs. shell / 22.5 lbs. case / 32.7 lbs. canister / 37 lbs. grape / 39.8 lbs.	1,469–1,922 yds.
100-pdr. Parrott rifle *en barbette* (1)	hollow shot / 80 lbs. shell / 101 lbs.	6,820 yds. 2,080–4,250 yds.
30-pdr. (4.2 in.) Parrott rifle *en embrasure* (5)	shell / 30 lbs.	6,700 yds.
Ten-inch mortar (1)	shot 127.5 lbs. shell / 88.42 lbs.	2,080–4,250 yds.
24-pdr. Coehorn mortar (1)	shot / 24.3 lbs. shell / 24 lbs. case / 24.6 lbs. canister / 29 lbs.	1,200 yds.

Fort Stevens (168–375 yards / ten to nineteen guns)

Table C.7. *Fort Stevens*

Artillery Type	Projectile/Weight	Range
Eight-inch siege howitzer *en embrasure* (2)	shell / 49.75 lbs. canister / 53.9 lbs. case shot / 59.5 lbs. grape / 75.5 lbs.	2,280 yds.
24-pdr. siege guns *en embrasure* (6) 24-pdr seacoast guns (2) *en embrasure* (2) *en barbette* (4)	shell / 16.8 lbs. shot / 24.3 lbs. case / 24.6 lbs. canister / 29 lbs. grape / 30.6 lbs.	1,900 yds.
30-pdr (4.2 in.) Parrott rifled guns *en embrasure* (5)	shell / 30 lbs.	4,800–6,700 yds.
Ten-inch mortar (1)	shell / 88.42 lbs. shot / 127.5 lbs.	2,080–4250 yds.
24-pdr mortar Coehorn (1)	shell / 24 lbs.	1,200 yds.

Fort Slocum (653 yards / twenty-five guns)

Table C.8. *Fort Slocum*

Artillery Type	Projectile/Weight	Range
Eight-inch siege howitzer *en embrasure* (1)	shell / 49.75 lbs. canister / 53.9 lbs. case shot / 59.5 lbs. grape / 75.5 lbs.	2,280 yds.
24-pdr. siege gun *en embrasure* (2)	shell / 16.8 lbs.	1,800 yds.
24-pdr. seacoast gun *en barbette* (2)	shot / 24.3 lbs. case / 24.6 lbs. canister / 29 lbs. grape / 30.6 lbs.	
24-pdr. howitzer *en embrasure* (4)	shell / 16.8 lbs.	1,200–1,300 yds.
30-pdr. (4.2 in.) Parrott rifle *en embrasure* (7)	shell / 30 lbs.	4,800–6,700 yds.
10-pdr. (2.9 in.) Parrott rifle *en embrasure* (6)	shell / 10 lbs.	3,200–5,000 yds.
Ten-inch mortar (1)	shell / 88.42 lbs. shot / 127.5 lbs.	2,080–4,250 yds.
24-pdr. Coehorn mortar (2)	shell / 24 lbs.	1,200 yds.

Fort Totten and Battery Totten (272 yards / twenty guns)

Table C.9. **Fort Totten and Battery Totten**

Artillery Type	Projectile/Weight	Range
Eight-inch siege howitzer *en barbette* (2)	shell / 49.75 lbs. canister / 53.9 lbs. case shot / 59.5 lbs. grape / 75.5 lbs.	2,280 yds.
32-pdr. seacoast gun *en barbette* (8)	shot / 32.4 lbs. shell / 22.5 lbs. case / 32.7 lbs. canister / 37 lbs. grape / 39 lbs.	1,469–1,922 yds.
30-pdr. (4.2 in.) Parrott rifle *en barbette* (3)	shell / 30 lbs.	4,800–6,700 yds.
6-pdr. James rifle *en embrasure* (4)	shot / 6.1 lbs.	1,523–1,700 yds.
Ten-inch mortar (1)	shell / 88.42 lbs. shot / 127.5 lbs.	2,080–4,250 yds.
24-pdr. Coehorn mortar (1)	shell / 24 lbs.	1,200 yds.

Sources

Barnard, John Gross. *A Report on the Defenses of Washington* (Washington: Government Printing Office, 1871).

Ripley, Warren. *Artillery and Ammunition of the Civil War* (New York: Van Nostrand Reinhold, 1970).

APPENDIX D:
CONFEDERATE ORDER OF BATTLE

Campaign against Washington—July 1864
Army of the Valley District
Lt. Gen. Jubal A. Early

Breckinridge's Corps
Maj.-Gen. John C. Breckinridge

Gordon's Division
Maj.-Gen. John B. Gordon

Evans's Brigade—Brig. Gen. Clement A. Evans
Thirteenth Georgia Infantry Regt.
Twenty-Sixth Georgia Infantry Regt.
Thirty-First Georgia Infantry Regt.
Thirty-Eighth Georgia Infantry Regt.
Sixtieth Georgia Infantry Regt.
Sixty-First Georgia Infantry Regt.
Twelfth Georgia Infantry Bn.

Consolidated Louisiana Brigade—Brig. Gen. Zebulon York
Hay's Brigade—Col. William R. Peck
(all fragmentary regiments)
Fifth Louisiana Infantry Regt.
Sixth Louisiana Infantry Regt.
Seventh Louisiana Infantry Regt.

Eighth Louisiana Infantry Regt.
Ninth Louisiana Infantry Regt.

Stafford's Brigade—Col. Eugene D. Waggaman
(all fragmentary regiments)
First Louisiana Infantry Regt.
Second Louisiana Infantry Regt.
Tenth Louisiana Infantry Regt.
Fourteenth Louisiana Infantry Regt.
Fifteenth Louisiana Infantry Regt.

Terry's Brigade—Brig. Gen. William Terry (consolidated)

Jackson's Old First or "Stonewall Brigade"—Col. J. H. S. Funk
Second Virginia Infantry Regt.
Fourth Virginia Infantry Regt.
Fifth Virginia Infantry Regt.
Twenty-Seventh Virginia Infantry Regt.
Thirty-Third Virginia Infantry Regt.

Jones's Old Second Brigade—Col. R. H. Dungan
Twenty-First Virginia Infantry Regt.
Twenty-Fifth Virginia Infantry Regt.
Forty-Second Virginia Infantry Regt.
Forty-Fourth Virginia Infantry Regt.
Forty-Eighth Virginia Infantry Regt.
Fiftieth Virginia Infantry Regt.

Stuart's Old Third Brigade—Lt. Col. S. H. Saunders
Tenth Virginia Infantry Regt.
Twenty-Third Virginia Infantry Regt.
Thirty-Seventh Virginia Infantry Regt.

Echols's Division (ex-Breckinridge, ex-Elzey)
Brig. Gen. John Echols

Echols's Brigade—Col. George Smith Patton
Twenty-Second Virginia Infantry Regt.
Twenty-Fifth Virginia Infantry Regt.

Twenty-Third Virginia Infantry Bn.
Twenty-Sixth Virginia Infantry Bn.

Wharton's Brigade—Brig. Gen. Gabriel C. Wharton
Forty-Fifth Virginia Infantry Regt.
Fifty-First Virginia Infantry Regt.
Thirtieth Virginia Infantry Bn. Sharpshooters

Smith's Brigade—Col. Thomas Smith
Thirty-Sixth Virginia Infantry Regt.
Sixtieth Virginia Infantry Regt.
Forty-Fifth Virginia Infantry Bn.
Thomas's Legion

Vaughn's Brigade—Brig. Gen. John C. Vaughn
(Acting as dismounted cavalry/mounted infantry with elements remaining in
    Shenandoah Valley)
First Tennessee Cavalry Regt.
Thirty-Ninth Tennessee Mounted Infantry (Thirty-First Tennessee Infantry Regt.)
Forty-Third Tennessee Mounted Infantry
Fifty-Ninth Tennessee Mounted Infantry
Twelfth Tennessee Cavalry Bn.
Sixteenth Tennessee Cavalry Bn.
Sixteenth Georgia Cavalry Bn.

Independent Divisions

Rodes's Division
Maj.-Gen. Robert E. Rodes

Grimes's Brigade—Brig. Gen. Bryan Grimes
Second North Carolina Infantry Regt.
Thirty-Second North Carolina Infantry Regt.
Forty-Third North Carolina Infantry Regt.
Forty-Fifth North Carolina Infantry Regt.
Fifty-Third North Carolina Infantry Regt.

Cook's Brigade—Brig. Gen. Phillip Cook
(all fragmentary regiments)
Fourth Georgia Infantry Regt.

Twelfth Georgia Infantry Regt.
Twenty-First Georgia Infantry Regt.
Forty-Fourth Georgia Infantry Regt.

Cox's Brigade—Brig. Gen. William Cox
First North Carolina Infantry Regt.
Second North Carolina Infantry Regt.
Third North Carolina Infantry Regt.
Fourth North Carolina Infantry Regt.
Fourteenth North Carolina Infantry Regt.
Thirtieth North Carolina Infantry Regt.

Battle's Brigade—Brig. Gen. Cullen A. Battle
Third Alabama Infantry Regt.
Fifth Alabama Infantry Regt.
Sixth Alabama Infantry Regt.
Twelfth Alabama Infantry Regt.
Sixty-First Alabama Infantry Regt.

Ramseur's Division
Maj.-Gen. Stephen D. Ramseur

Lilley's Brigade—Brig. Gen. Robert Lilley
Thirteenth Virginia Infantry Regt.
Thirty-First Virginia Infantry Regt.
Forty-Ninth Virginia Infantry Regt.
Fifty-Second Virginia Infantry Regt.
Fifty-Eighth Virginia Infantry Regt.

Johnston's Brigade—Brig. Gen. Robert D. Johnston
Fifth North Carolina Infantry Regt.
Twelfth North Carolina Infantry Regt.
Twentieth North Carolina Infantry Regt.
Twenty-Third North Carolina Infantry Regt.

Lewis's Brigade—Brig. Gen. William G. Lewis
(all fragmentary regiments)
Sixth North Carolina Infantry Regt.

Twenty-First North Carolina Infantry Regt.
Fifty-Fourth North Carolina Infantry Regt.
Fifty-Seventh North Carolina Infantry Regt.
First North Carolina Bn. Sharpshooters

Cavalry Division—Maj.-Gen. Robert Ransom

Imboden's Brigade—Brig. Gen. John Imboden
Eighteenth Virginia Cavalry Regt.
Twenty-Third Virginia Cavalry Regt.
Sixty-Second Virginia Cavalry Regt.
Unauthorized Virginia Cavalry Bn.

McCausland's Brigade—Brig. Gen. John McCausland
Fourteenth Virginia Cavalry Regt.
Sixteenth Virginia Cavalry Regt.
Seventeenth Virginia Cavalry Regt.
Twenty-Fifth Virginia Cavalry Regt.
Thirty-Seventh Virginia Cavalry Bn.

Johnson's Brigade—Brig. Gen. Bradley T. Johnson
Eighth Virginia Cavalry Regt.
Twenty-First Virginia Cavalry Regt.
Twenty-Second Virginia Cavalry Bn.
Thirty-Fourth Virginia Cavalry Bn.
First Maryland Cavalry Bn.
Second Maryland Cavalry Bn.

Jackson's Brigade—Brig. Gen. W. L. Jackson
Nineteenth Virginia Cavalry Regt.
Twentieth Virginia Cavalry Regt.
Forty-Sixth Virginia Cavalry Bn.
Forty-Seventh Virginia Cavalry Bn.

Horse Artillery (ten to fourteen guns)
Jackson's Virginia Horse Artillery Co. (attached to McCausland's Brigade)
McClanahan's (Staunton) Virginia Horse Artillery Co. (attached to Imboden's
   Brigade)

Baltimore Maryland Light Artillery (Second Maryland) (attached to Johnson's Brigade)
Lurty's Virginia Battery (attached to Jackson's Brigade)

Artillery (thirty-six to forty guns)

Brig. Gen. Armistead L. Long

Braxton's Battalion—Maj. Carter Braxton
Allegheny Artillery (Virginia)
Lee Artillery (Virginia)
Stafford Artillery (Virginia)

King's Battalion—Maj. J. Floyd King/Maj. William McLaughlin
Wise Legion Artillery (Virginia)
Lowry's Artillery, Centreville Rifles (Virginia)
Lewisburg Artillery (Virginia)
Monroe Artillery (Virginia)

Nelson's Battalion—Lt. Col. William Nelson
Amherst Artillery (Virginia)
Fluvanna Artillery (Virginia)
Milledge Artillery (Georgia)

Recapitulation
The Army of the Valley District nominally included sixty-seven infantry regiments, six battalions of infantry or fragments, eleven regiments, and nine battalions of cavalry as well as three battalions (nine batteries) of field and seven batteries of horse artillery. The total numbers between ten thousand and twenty thousand men at various times during the overall campaign and sustained casualties from 1,500 to 2,000 therein. Reputed number present for the Battle of Fort Stevens is approximately eight thousand to ten thousand.

Sources

Pond, George E. *The Shenandoah Valley in 1864* (New York: C. Scribner's Sons, 1883), Appendix D, 273.
Spaulding, Brett W. *Last Chance for Victory: Jubal Early's 1864 Maryland Invasion* (Frederick, MD: Thomas Publications, 2010), Appendix 1.
U.S. War Department, *The War of the Rebellion: A Compilation of the Official Records of the Union and Confederate Armies* (Washington: Government Printing Office, 1880–1901), I, 37, pt. 1, 1003–4.

APPENDIX E: MEMORIALIZATION AT BATTLEGROUND NATIONAL CEMETERY: REGIMENTAL MONUMENT INSCRIPTIONS AND ROLL OF HONOR OF BURIALS

Ninety-Eighth Pennsylvania
(on monument's obverse)

In Memory of our Comrades killed and wounded
in battle on this field July 11th and 12th 1864
98th Reg't P.V.
1st Brig. 2nd Div. 6th Corps.

(on monument's sides/reverse)

Killed in Battle July 11th and 12th, 1864

Frederick Walter	B
Bernard Hoerle	G
Sergt. George Marquet	E
Corp. Henry Pollser	F
Michael Bruner	F
Charles Schaus	K
George Merkle	K
Joseph Schnitzler	K

Wounded in Battle July 11th and 12th, 1864

Col. John F. Ballier	
Lieut. Col. John B. Kohler	
Capt. Wm. Wilson	K
Lieut. G. Schuler	G

Samuel Thompson	A
Corp. Charles Veneman	A
Sergt. Frank Reiner	G
Fredrick Denker	G
Corp. William Aberle	D
Jacob Reiner	D
George Klump	D
William Gaus	E
Daniel Kirsch	E
Corp. J. Schweitzer	E
Corp. Fred Loeble	E
Frederick Frank	G
William Fratz	G
1st Sergt. Christian Brandt	G
Frank Maier	G
Sergt. John Wagner	G
Sergt. John G. Greul	H
Arthur Corvan	H
Sergt. Jacob Goetz	K
Sergt. William Bayer	K
Frank Weingartner	K
Christian Wurster	K
Sergt. John G. Kaiser	K
John Gress	K

One Hundred and Twenty-Second New York
(on monument's obverse)

To the Gallant Sons of Onondaga County, N.Y.
Who Fought on this Field
July 12, 1864
In Defence of Washington
And in the Presence of Abraham Lincoln
122nd N.Y.V.

(on monument's reverse)

Served Three Years in Sixth Army Corps

Battles
Antietam   *Cold Harbor*

APPENDIX E

Fredericksburg   *Fort Stevens*
Mayres Heights   *Opequan*
Salem Church   *Fishers Hill*
Gettysburg   *Cedar Creek*
Rappahannock Station   *Fort Stedman*
Mine Run   *Petersburg*
Wilderness   *Sailor's Creek*
Spotsylvania   *Appomattox*

(on monument's sides)

Killed and Died of Wounds
John Bentley
Alanson Mosier
John Kennedy
George H. Richardson
Harvey P. B. Chandler
David L. Hogeboom
John Preston

Wounded
Capt. Davis Cossitt
Alonzo Fradenburgh
Loriston Adkins
Caius A. Weaver
Thomas H. Scott
Reed P. Buzzell
James Goodfellow
John Launpenthal
Thomas Thornton
Charles C. Snedeker
Miles J. McGough
Jethial Landphier
Peter Stebbins
William O. Swartz
Thomas G. Dallman
Merrick C. Smith
James Davidson
William Thompson

One Hundred and Fiftieth Ohio National Guard

(on monument's obverse)

150th O.N.G.I
Memorial to Co. K 150th O.N.G.I.
Which Took Part in the Defense of Fort Stevens, D.C.
July 12, 1864

Twenty-Fifth New York Cavalry

(on monument's obverse)

Sacred To The Memory
of our comrades who
gave their lives in
defence of the national
capitol July 11, 1864
Erected by the State of NY in honor
of the 25th NY Vol. Cav.

Roll Call

(Burial listing on National Park Service Tablet Marker)

Miscellaneous

(other graves—three children of Augustus Armbrechet, original superintendent)

Table E.1

Name	Age	Rank	Company	Origin	Grave	Commentary
Twenty-Fifth New York Cavalry						
Elijah Hufletin	28	Pvt	A	New York	17	
Wilhelm Frei	25	Pvt	D	Germany	19	Previously misidentified as William Tray
Alfred C. Starbird	31	Sgt	A	Pennsylvania	33	
Jeremiah Maloney	21	Pvt	K	Ireland	34	
Thomas Richardson	24	Sgt	B	Ireland	35	
Sixty-First Pennsylvania Infantry						
Edward Garvin	33	Corp	I	Pennsylvania	11	previously misidentified as Corp. George Garvin
Philip Bowen	34	Pvt	I	Pennsylvania	14	
Thomas McIntyre	19	Pvt	K	Ireland	15	previously misidentified as H. McIntyre
Andrew Ashbaugh	43	Pvt	H	Pennsylvania	26	
William Laughlin	28	2nd Lt	B	Maryland	28	
John Ellis	19	Pvt	A	Pennsylvania	36	
One Hundred Twenty-Second New York Infantry						
John Bentley	41	Pvt	B	England	4	
John Kennedy	34	Pvt	C	Ireland	13	previously misidentified as John Renia
David Hogeboom	35	Pvt	E	New York	16	
Alanson Mosier	20	Pvt	C	New York	32	
Harvey P. B. Chandler	18	Pvt	C	New York	31	
One Hundred Thirty-Ninth Pennsylvania Infantry						
John Milton Richards	22	Sgt	H	Pennsylvania	40	
Second Massachusetts Cavalry						
John Dolan	21	Pvt	D	Ireland	27	
Seventy-Seventh New York Infantry						
Alvarado Mowry	27	Pvt	K	New York	18	

Name	Age	Rank	Company	Place	No.	Notes
Ambrose Mattott	33	Corp	G	New York	25	
Andrew Manning	38	Pvt	H	Ireland	29	
Andrew J. Dowen	30	Pvt	H	New York	31	
Forty-Third New York Infantry						
Matthew J. DeGraff	32	Pvt	A	New York	1	
Richard Castle	25	Sgt	G	New York	2	previously misidentified as Mark Stoneham, posthumously promoted 1st Lt, July 15, 1864
John Davidson	32	Pvt	E	Ireland	3	
George W. Farrar	27	Corp	G	Canada	8	
Edward C. Barrett	21	Corp	E	United States	30	
Forty-Ninth New York Infantry						
William Ruhle	25	Corp	E	Prussia	22	
William Gillette	22	Pvt	D	New York	39	
Ninety-Eighth Pennsylvania Infantry						
George Marquet	30	Sgt	E	Germany	7	
Frederick Walther	29	Pvt	B	Germany	10	
Bernard Hoerle	46	Pvt	C	Germany	23	
Charles Seahouse	29	Pvt	K	Germany	24	
Ninety-Third Pennsylvania Infantry						
William Holtzman	35		A	Pennsylvania	20	
Seventh Maine Infantry						
John Poekett	19	Pvt	F	Maine	38	
Thirty-Seventh Massachusetts Infantry						
Patrick Lovett	39	Pvt	Unassigned	Ireland	12	
Second United States Artillery						
C. H. Christ	unknown	Pvt	G	unknown	5	
Veteran Reserve Corps						

(continued)

Table E.1. (continued)

Name	Age	Rank	Company	Origin	Grave	Commentary
George Gorton	19	Corp	D	unknown	6	1st Rhode Island Cavalry; transferred to Veteran Reserve Corps, April 1864; Hospitalized May–July 11, 1864
Quartermaster Civilian						
E. S. Bavett—civilian former employee who joined ranks with Quartermaster's Corps on July 11, 1864						
Third Vermont Infantry						
Russell Stevens	20	Pvt	D	unknown	27	
Second Vermont Infantry						
Edward R. Campbell	92	Pvt	Not known	Not known	41	Major, U.S. Army retired, interred March 1936

BIBLIOGRAPHY

NOTE: For a fuller bibliography, readers should consult the author's other works, including *Jubal Early's Raid on Washington, 1864*, *Monocacy: The Battle That Saved Washington*, and coauthored with Walton Owen, *Mr. Lincoln's Forts: A Guide to the Civil War Defenses of Washington._*

Primary Sources: Archival

Author's files to include original letters, other unpublished and published document copies deposited at Fort War Museum and Park, Alexandria, Virginia.
Chicago Historical Society, Chicago, Illinois
    John B. Gordon's Division Field Report
    William Terry Operations Report
Cosmic America Collections from Virginia Historical Society, cosmic.america@yahoo.com
    John Herbert Claiborne
    Peter Guerrant
    James
    Joseph Lyle
    Samuel Johnson MacCallough
    Willy Pegram
    Richard Watkins
The Filson Club, Louisville, Kentucky
    Morgan Royce Collection
Fort Ward Museum and Park, Alexandria, Virginia
    Defenses of Washington Collection
Frederick County Historical Society, Frederick, Maryland
    Miscellaneous Collections

BIBLIOGRAPHY

Huntington Library, San Marino, California
  Civil War Collection
  John Page Nichols Collection
Library of Congress, Washington DC
  Manuscript Division
  Robert Garrett Family Papers
  Joseph Warren Keifer Papers
  Horatio Nelson Taft Diary
  Prints and Photographs Division
  Subject Categories
Maryland Historical Society, Baltimore, Maryland
  Cary Miscellaneous Clipping Scrapbook
Monocacy National Battlefield, Frederick, Maryland
  Edwin C. Bearss Monocacy Documentation Study
  George Davis Collection
  Reference Files and Archival Collections
National Archives and Records Service, College Park, Maryland
  Still Pictures Branch
Rock Creek Nature Center/Battleground National Cemetery, Washington DC
  Vertical Files and Publications
Tennessee State Library and Archives, Nashville, Tennessee
  George W. Pile Memoir
University of North Carolina, Chapel Hill, North Carolina
  Southern Historical Collection
  Nimrod Porter Diaries
  Stephen Ramseur Papers
  Thomas Butler King Papers
  Lachlan C. Vass List of Confederate Wounded
  Zebulon York Papers
University of Virginia, Charlottesville, Virginia
  Buckner McGill Papers
  Robert E. Lee Papers
Washington and Lee University, Lexington, Virginia
  August Forsberg Memoir

Primary Sources: Printed

Newspapers and Periodicals
Fayetteville, New York, *Weekly Observer*
Frederick, Maryland, *Daily News*
Frederick, Maryland, *Examiner*
Washington, D.C., *Star*

Documents: Government

Barnard, John Gross, *Report on the Defenses of Washington*. Washington: Government Printing Office, 1871

CEHP Inc., for National Park Service, U.S. Department of the Interior, *A Historic Resources Study: The Civil War Defenses of Washington*. Chevy Chase, MD: CEHP Inc., 2004.

District of Columbia National Guard, Engineer Platoon, Engineer Corps. *Guide and Maps of the National Capital and Vicinity, Including the Fortifications*. Washington: no publisher, 1892.

Moore, Charles, editor. *The Improvement of the Park System of the District of Columbia*. United States Congress, 57th, 1st Session, Senate Report 166. Washington: Government Printing Office, 1902.

Stephens, Mrs. Gail. Monocacy Timeline (May 13–August 1864) typescript, Monocacy National Battlefield. , U.S. War Department.

United States Congress, 70th, 1st Session, House of Representatives, Committee on Military Affairs. *Hearings—National Battlefield at Monocacy, Maryland, April 13, 1928*. Washington: Government Printing Office, 1928.

Unpublished

Smith, Everard Hall III, "The General and the Valley: Union Leadership during the Threat to Washington in 1864." Unpublished doctoral dissertation, University of North Carolina, 1977. Ann Arbor, MI: University Microfilms, 1977.

Documents: Other

Basler, Roy P., editor. *The Collected Works of Abraham Lincoln, volume VII*. New Brunswick: Rutgers University Press, 1953.

Bates, Samuel P. *A History of Pennsylvania Volunteers*. Harrisburg, PA: B. Singerley, 1869–1871. 5 volumes

Dowdey, Clifford, and Louis H. Manarin, editors. *The Wartime Papers of Robert E. Lee*. New York: Brammel House for Virginia Civil War Commission, 1966.

Dyer, Frederick H. *A Compendium of the War of the Rebellion*. New York: Thomas Yoseloff, 1959 edition. 3 volumes

Freeman, Douglas Southall. *Lee's Dispatches: Unpublished Letters of General Robert E. Lee to Jefferson Davis and the War Department of the Confederate States of America, 1862–1865*. New York: G. P. Putnam's Sons, 1957.

Simon, John Y., editor. *The Papers of Ulysses S. Grant*. Carbondale, IL: Southern Illinois University Press, 1967.

Strait, Newton A., compiler. *Alphabetical List of Battles 1754–1900*. Washington, DC, by Author, 1905.

Illustrated Works

Adelman, Garry E., and John J. Richter, editors. *Ninety-Nine Historic Images of Civil War Washington*. Washington: The Center for Civil War Photography and the Civil War Preservation Trust, 2006.

BIBLIOGRAPHY

Frank Leslie's Illustrated Newspaper, August 6, 1864.

Guernsey, Alfred H. and Henry M. Alden, editors. *Harper's Pictorial History of the Great Rebellion.* Chicago: McDonnell Brothers, 1868. 2 parts.

London Illustrated News, May 18, 1861.

Mottelay, Paul F. and T. Campbell-Copeland, editors. *The Soldier in Our Civil War.* New York: Stanley Bradley, 1885. 2 volumes.

Memoirs, Diaries, Reminiscences—Civilian

Barker, Jacob. *Incidents in the Life of Jacob Barker.* Freeport, NY: Books for Libraries Press, 1858/1971.

Bates, David Homer. *Lincoln in the Telegraph Office: Recollections of the United States Military Telegraph Corps during the Civil War.* New York: Century Co., 1907; Lincoln, NE: University of Nebraska Press reprint, 1995.

Blackford, L. Minor. *Mine Eyes Have Seen The Glory, The Story of a Virginia Lady, Mary Berkeley Minor Blackford.* Cambridge, MA: Harvard University Press, 1954.

Brooks, Noah. *Washington in Lincoln's Time.* New York: Century, 1895.

Buck, William P., editor. *Sad Earth, Sweet Heaven: The Diary of Lucy Rebecca Buck during the War Between the States.* Birmingham, AL: Cornerstone, 1973.

Carpenter, F. B. *Six Months at the White House with Abraham Lincoln: The Story of a Picture.* New York: Hurd and Houghton, 1867.

Chittenden, L. E. *Recollections of President Lincoln and His Administration.* New York: Harper and Brothers, 1891.

Colt, Margaretta Barton. *Defend the Valley: A Shenandoah Family in the Civil War.* New York: Oxford University Press, 1994.

Dana, Charles A. *Recollections of the Civil War: With the Leaders at Washington and in the Field in the Sixties.* New York: D. Appleton, 1898.

Dicey, Edward. *Six Months in the Federal States.* London: Macmillan, 1863.

Donald, David, editor. *Inside Lincoln's Cabinet: The Civil War Diaries of Salmon P. Chase.* New York: Longmans, Green, 1964.

Ferguson, Sir James of Kilkerran. Ben Wynne, editor. *The Personal Observations of a Man of Intelligence: Notes of a Tour in North America in 1861.* Lambertville, NJ: True Bill Press, 2009.

Farquhar, William H. *Annals of Sandy Spring, Or Twenty Years History of a Rural Community in Maryland.* Baltimore: Cushings & Bailey, 1884.

Howe, Mark De Wolfe, editor. *Holmes-Laski Letters: The Correspondence of Mr. Justice Holmes and Harold Laski, 1916–1925.* Cambridge: Harvard University Press, 1953.

Laas, Virginia Jeans, editor. *Wartime Washington: The Civil War Letters of Elizabeth Blair Lee.* Urbana: University of Illinois Press, 1991.

Loughborough, Margaret, and James H. Johnston. *The Recollections of Margaret Cabell Brown Loughborough: A Southern Woman's Memoirs of Richmond, VA, and Washington, DC, in the Civil War.* Lanham, MD: Hamilton Books, 2010.

Mahon, Michael G., editor. *Winchester Divided: The Civil War Diaries of Julia Chase and Laura Lee.* Mechanicsburg, PA: Stackpole Books, 2002.

McGee, Charles M. Jr., and Ernest M. Lander Jr., editors. *A Rebel Came Home: The Diary and Letters of Floride Clemson, 1863–1866*. Columbia: University of South Carolina Press, 1989.

Mitgang, Herbert, editor. *Edward Dicey: Spectator in America*. Athens, GA: University of Georgia Press, 1989 edition; Chicago: Quadrangle Books, 1971.

Riddle, Albert Gallatin. *Recollections of War Times: Reminiscences of Men and Events in Washington, 1860–1865*. New York: G. P. Putnam's Sons, 1895.

Stoddard, William O. *Inside the White House in War Times: Memoirs and Reports of Lincoln's Secretary*. New York: Charles L. Webster, 1890.

Styple, William B., editor, *Writing and Fighting the Civil War: Soldier Correspondence to the New York Sunday Mercury*. Kearny, NJ: Belle Grove Publishing Company, 2000.

Taylor, Benjamin F. *Pictures of Life in Camp and Field*. Chicago: S. C. Griggs and Company, 1888.

Thomas, Benjamin P., editor. *Three Years with Grant: As Recalled by War Correspondent Sylvanus Cadwallader*. New York: Alfred A. Knopf, 1955.

Welles, Gideon. *Diary*. Boston: Houghton Mifflin, 1909.

Memoirs, Letters, Diaries, Reminiscences: Confederate Military

Blackford, L. Minor. *Mine Eyes Have Seen the Glory: The Story of a Virginia Lady, Mary Berkeley Minor Blackford*. Cambridge: Harvard University Press, 1954.

Booth, G. W. *A Maryland Boy in Lee's Army: Personal Reminiscences of a Maryland Soldier in the War between the States, 1861–1865*. Baltimore: privately published, 1898; Lincoln, NE: University of Nebraska Press, 2000 edition.

Briggs, Ward W., Jr., editor. *Soldier and Scholar: Basil Lanneau Gildersleeve and the Civil War*. Charlottesville: University Press of Virginia, 1998.

Clark, Willene B., editor. *Valleys of the Shadow: The Memoir of Confederate Captain Reuben G. Clark, Company I, Fifty-Ninth Tennessee Mounted Infantry*. Knoxville: University of Tennessee Press, 1994.

Cockrell, Monroe, editor. *Gunner with Stonewall: Reminiscences of William Thomas Poague*. Lincoln: University of Nebraska Press, 1998 edition.

Crow, Vernon H., editor. "The Justness of Our Cause: The Civil War Diaries of William W. Stringfield." *East Tennessee Historical Society Publications* 56/57 (1984–1985): 71–101.

Cutrer, Thomas W., and T. Michael Parrish, editors. *Brothers in Gray: The Civil War Letters of the Pierson Family*. Baton Rouge: Louisiana State University Press, 1997.

———. *Longstreet's Aide: The Civil War Letters of Major Thomas J. Goree*. Charlottesville: University Press of Virginia, 1955.

Dawson, Francis W. Bell I. Wiley, editor. *Reminiscences of Confederate Service, 1861–1865*. Baton Rouge: Louisiana State University Press, 1980.

Douglas, Henry Kyd. *I Rode with Stonewall*. Chapel Hill: University of North Carolina Press, 1940.

Durkin, Joseph T. *Confederate Chaplain: A War Journal of Rev. James B. Sheeran, C.SS.R. Fourteenth Louisiana, CSA*. Milwaukee: Bruce Publishing Company, 1960.

Early, Jubal Anderson. *A Memoir of the Last Year of the War for Independence: In the Confederate States of America*. Toronto: Lovell and Gibson, 1866.

BIBLIOGRAPHY

Gallagher, Gary W., editor. *Fighting for the Confederacy: The Personal Recollections of General Edward Porter Alexander.* Chapel Hill: University of North Carolina Press, 1989.

Gordon, John B. *Reminiscences of the Civil War.* New York: Charles Scribners, 1904.

Harding, French. Victor L. Thacker, editor. *Civil War Memoirs.* Parsons, WV: McClain Printing Company, 2000.

Hunter, Alexander. *Johnny Reb and Billy Yank.* New York: Neale, 1905.

Johnson, Pharris Deloach, compiler/editor. *Under the Southern Cross: Soldier Life with Gordon Bradwell and the Army of Northern Virginia.* Macon, GA: Mercer University Press, 1999.

Jones, Terry L., editor. *Campbell Brown's Civil War: With Ewell and the Army of Northern Virginia.* Baton Rouge: Louisiana State University Press, 2001.

———. *The Civil War Memoirs of Captain William J. Seymour: Reminiscences of a Louisiana Tiger.* Baton Rouge: Louisiana State University Press, 1991.

Koonce, Donald B., editor. *Doctor to the Front: The Recollections of Confederate Surgeon Thomas Fanning Wood, 1861–1865.* Knoxville: University of Tennessee Press, 2000.

Kundahl, George G. *The Bravest of the Brave: The Correspondence of Stephen Dodson Ramseur.* Chapel Hill: University of North Carolina Press, 2010.

Lee, Robert E., Jr. *Recollections and Letters of Robert E. Lee.* New York: Doubleday, 1904.

Lee, Susan P. *The Memoirs of William Nelson Pendleton, D.D.* Harrisonburg, VA: Sprinkle Publications, 1991.

Long, Armistead. *Memoirs of Robert E. Lee.* New York: J. M. Stoddart, 1886.

Montgomery, George F., Jr. *Georgia Sharpshooter: The Civil War Diary and Letters of William Rhadamanthus Montgomery, 1839–1906.* Macon, GA: Mercer University Press, 1997.

Mosgrove, George Dallas. *Kentucky Cavaliers in Dixie: Reminiscences of a Confederate Cavalry-man.* Lincoln: University of Nebraska Press, 1999 edition.

Northen, Charles Swift III, editor. *All Right Let Them Come: The Civil War Diary of an East Tennessee Confederate.* Knoxville: University of Tennessee Press, 2003.

Oates, Dan, editor. *Hanging Rock Rebel: Lt. John Blue's War in West Virginia and the Shenandoah Valley.* Shippensburg, PA: White Mane, 1994.

Opie, John N. *A Rebel Cavalryman with Stuart and Jackson.* Chicago: W. B. Conkey, 1899.

Skoch, George, and Mark W. Perkins, editors. *Lone Star Confederate: A Gallant and Good Soldier of the Fifth Texas Infantry [Robert Campbell].* College Station: Texas A&M University Press, 2003.

Runge, W. H., editor. *Four Years in the Confederate Artillery; Diary of Private Henry Robinson Berkeley.* Chapel Hill: University of North Carolina Press, 1956.

Williams, Edward B., editor. *Rebel Brothers: The Civil War Letters of the Trueharts.* College Station: Texas A&M University Press, 1995.

Worsham, John H. *One of Jackson's Foot Cavalry.* New York: Neale, 1912; Jackson, TN: McCowat-Mercer, 1964.

Memoirs, Letters, Diaries, Reminiscences: Union Military

Agassiz, George R. *Meade's Headquarters 1863–1865: Letters of Colonel Theodore Lyman from the Wilderness to Appomattox.* Boston: Atlantic Monthly Press, 1922.

Bender, Robert Patrick, editor. *Like Grass before the Scythe: The Life and Death of Sgt. William Remmel, One Hundred and Twenty-First New York Infantry.* Tuscaloosa: University of Alabama Press, 2007.

Blair, William Alan, editor. *A Politician Goes to War: The Civil War Letters of John White Geary.* University Park, PA: Pennsylvania State University Press, 1995.

Blanding, Stephen F. *In The Defences of Washington, Or, the Sunshine in a Soldier's Life.* Providence, RI: E. L. Freeman and Son, 1889.

Bloodgood, J. D. *Personal Reminiscences of the War.* New York: Hunt and Eaton; Cincinnati: Cranston and Curts, 1893.

Boaz, Thomas M. *Libby Prison and Beyond: A Union Staff Officer in the East, 1862–1865.* Shippensburg, PA: Burd Street Press, 1997.

Brinton, John H. *Personal Memoirs of John H. Brinton: Civil War Surgeon, 1861–1865.* New York: Neale, 1914; reprinted Carbondale, IL: Southern Illinois University Press, 1996.

Buell, Augustus. *The Cannoneer.* Washington: National Tribune,1890.

Chadwick, Bruce, editor. *Brother against Brother: The Lost Civil War Diary of Lt. Edmund Halsey.* Secaucus, NJ: Birch Lane Press, 1997.

Child, William. *Letters from a Civil War Surgeon: The Letters of Dr. William Child of the Fifth New Hampshire Volunteers.* Solon, ME: Polar Bear and Company, 2001.

Croffut, W.A., editor. *Fifty Years in Camp and Field; Diary of Major General Ethan Allen Hitchcock.* New York: Putnams, 1909.

De Forest, John William. James H. Croushore, editor. *A Volunteer's Adventures: A Union Captain's Record of the Civil War.* Baton Rouge: Louisiana State University Press, 1946 and 2001.

Drickamer, Lee C., and Karen D. Drickamer, compilers/editors. *Fort Lyon to Harper's Ferry: On the Border of North and South with "Rambling Jour," The Civil War Letters and Newspaper Dispatches of Charles H. Moulton (34th Mass. Vol. Inf.).* Shippensburg, PA: White Mane, 1987.

Dudley, Edgar. "A Reminiscence of Washington and Early's Attack in 1864." Loyal Legion of the United States, Ohio Commandery. *Sketches of War History 1861–1865, volume I,* 107–27. Cincinnati: Robert O. Clarke, Co., 1888.

Eby, Cecil D., Jr. *A Virginia Yankee in the Civil War: The Diaries of David Hunter Strother.* Chapel Hill: University of North Carolina Press, 1961.

Emerson, Edward Waldo. *Life and Letters of Charles Russell Lowell.* New York: Houghton, Mifflin, 1907; Columbia, SC: University of South Carolina Press, 2005.

Grant, Ulysses S. *Personal Memoirs.* New York: Charles Webster, 1889.2 volumes

Greiner, James M., Janet L. Coryell, and James R. Smither, editors. *A Surgeon's Civil War: The Letters and Diary of Daniel M. Holt, M.D.* Kent, OH: Kent State University Press, 1994.

Griffin, Richard N., editor. *Three Years a Soldier: The Diary and Newspaper Correspondence of Private George Perkins, Sixth New York Independent Battery, 1861–1864.* Knoxville: University of Tennessee Press, 2006.

Hecht, Lydia P., editor. *Echoes from the Letters of a Civil War Surgeon.* Long Boat Key, FL: Bayou Publishing, 1994.

Herdegen, Lance, and Sherry Murphy, editors. *Four Years with the Iron Brigade: The Civil War Journals of William R. Ray, Co. F., Seventh Wisconsin Infantry*. New York: Da Capo Press, 2002.

Howe, Mark De Wolfe, editor. *Touched with Fire: Civil War Letters and Diary of Oliver Wendell Holmes Jr., 1861–1864*. Cambridge: Harvard University Press, 1947.

Jones, Melvin, editor. *Give God the Glory: Memoirs of a Civil War Soldier*. Calumet, MI: Greenlee Printing Company, 1997.

Jordan, William B., Jr. editor. *The Civil War Journals of John Mead Gould, 1861–1866*. Baltimore: Butternut and Blue, 1997.

Leeke, Jim, editor. *A Hundred Days to Richmond: Ohio's "Hundred Days" Men in the Civil War*. Bloomington, IN: Indiana University Press, 1999.

McPherson, James M., and Patricia R. McPherson, editors. *Lamson of the Gettysburg: The Civil War Letters of Lieutenant Roswell H. Lamson, U.S. Navy*. New York: Oxford University Press, 1997.

Olcott, Mark, with David Lear. *The Civil War Letters of Lewis Bissell: A Curriculum*. Washington: The Field School Educational Foundation Press, 1981.

Patch, Eileen Mae Knapp, annotator. *This from George: The Civil War Letters of Sergeant George Magusta Englis, 1861–1865, Company K, Eighty-Ninth New York Regiment of Volunteer Infantry known as the Dickinson Guard*. Binghamton, NY: Broome County Historical Society, 2001.

Pelka, Fred. *The Civil War Letters of Colonel Charles F. Johnson, Invalid Corps*. Amherst, MA: University of Massachusetts Press, 2004.

Perkins, George, *A Summer in Maryland and Virginia Campaigning With The One Hundred and Forty-Ninth Ohio Volunteer Infantry*. Chillicothe, OH: Sholl Printin, 1911.

Petrie, Stewart Judson. *Bloody Path to the Shenandoah: Fighting with the Union VI Corps in the American Civil War*. Shippensburg, PA: Burd Street Press, 2004.

Priest, John Michael, editor. *One Surgeon's Private War: Doctor William W. Potter of the Fifty-Seventh New York*. Shippensburg, PA: White Mane, 1996.

Puck, Susan T., editor. *Sacrifice at Vicksburg: Letters from the Front*. Shippensburg, PA: Burd Street Press, 1980.

Rhodes, Robert Hunt, editor. *All for the Union: The Civil War Diary and Letters of Elisha Hunt Rhodes*. Lincoln, RI: A. Mowbray, 1985; New York: Orion, 1991.

Rosenblatt, Emil, and Ruth Rosenblatt. *Hard Marching Every Day: The Civil War Letters of Private Wilbur Fisk, 1861–1865*. Lawrence, KS: University Press of Kansas, 1992.

Silliker, Ruth L., editor. *The Rebel Yell & the Yankee Hurrah: The Civil War Journal of a Maine Volunteer*. Camden, ME: Down East Books, 1985.

Simon, John Y., editor. *The Papers of Ulysses S. Grant, volume 14*. Carbondale/Edwardsville, IL: Southern Illinois University Press, 1985.

Smith, Fred, *Samuel Duncan Oliphant: The Indomitable Campaigner*. New York:Exposition Press, 1967.

Sneden, Robert Knox. Charles F. Bryan Jr., James C. Kelly, and Nelson D. Lankford, editors. *Images from the Storm [300 Civil War Images by the Author of Eye of the Storm]*. New York: Free Press, 2001.

Stevens, George T. *Three Years in the Sixth Corps*. Albany, NY: S. R. Gray, 1866.

Wickman, Donald H., editor/compiler. *Letters to Vermont: From Her Civil War Soldier Correspondents to the Home Press*. Bennington, VT: Images from the Past, 1998.

Wilkeson, Frank. *Turned Inside Out: Recollections of a Private Soldier in the Army of the Potomac*. Lincoln, NE: University of Nebraska Press, 1997 edition.

Unit Histories: Confederate

Alexander, John H. *Mosby's Men*. New York and Washington: Neale Publishing Company, 1907.

Fonerdern, C. A. *A Brief History of the Military Career of Carpenter's Battery*. New Market, VA: Heakel and Company, 1911.

Gannon, James P. *Irish Rebels, Confederate Tigers: A History of the Sixth Louisiana Volunteers, 1861–1865*. Campbell, CA: Savas Publishing Company, 1998.

Hubbs, G. Ward. *Guarding Greensboro: A Confederate Company in the Making of a Southern Community*. Athens, GA: University of Georgia Press, 2003.

Jordan, Weymouth T., Jr. *North Carolina Troops, 1861–1865: A Roster—Volume XIII Infantry*. Raleigh: North Carolina Division of Archives and History, 1993.

Swank, Walbrook D., compiler/editor. *Stonewall Jackson's Foot Cavalry: Company A, Thirteenth Virginia Infantry*. Shippensburg, PA: Burd Street Press, 2007.

Trout, Robert J. *Galloping Thunder: The Stuart Horse Artillery Battalion*. Mechanicsburg, PA: Stackpole Books, 2002.

Wallace, Lee. *Fifth Virginia Infantry*. Lynchburg: H. E. Howard, 1988.

Walters, John. *Norfolk Blues: The Civil War Diary of the Norfolk Light Artillery Blues*. Shippensburg, PA: Burd Street Press, 1997.

Williamson, James J. *Mosby's A Rangers: A Record of the Operations of the Forty-Third Battalion Virginia Cavalry*. New York: Ralph B. Kenyon, 1896.

Unit Histories—Union

Benedict, G. G. *Vermont in the Civil War: A History of the Part Taken by the Vermont Soldiers and Sailors in the War for the Union, 1861–1865*. Burlington, VT: Free Press Association, 1886.

Bonnell, John C., Jr. *Sabres in the Shenandoah: The Twenty-First New York Cavalry, 1863–1866*. Shippensburg, PA: White Mane Publishing, 1996.

Farrar, Samuel Clarke, *The Twenty-Second Pennsylvania Cavalry and The Ringgold Battalion 1861–1865*. Pittsburgh, PA: Regimental Association, 1911.

Gleason, William. *Historical Sketch of the One Hundred and Fiftieth Ohio Volunteer Infantry*. Rocky River, OH, no publisher, 1899.

Leeke, Jim, editor. *A Hundred Days to Richmond: Ohio's "Hundred Days" Men in the Civil War*. Bloomington, IN: Indiana University Press, 1999.

McLean, James. *California Sabers: The 2nd Massachusetts Cavalry in the Civil War*. Bloomington, IN: Indiana University Press, 2000.

Morrow, Robert F., Jr. *77th New York Volunteers: "Sojering" in the VI Corps.* Shippensburg, PA: White Mane Books, 2004.

Mudgett, Thomas B. *Make the Fur Fly: A History of a Union Volunteer Division in the American Civil War.* Shippensburg, PA: Burd Street Press, 1997.

Niebaum, John H. *History of the Pittsburgh Washington Infantry, One Hundred and Second (Old Thirteenth Regiment)Pennsylvania Veteran Volunteers.* Pittsburgh, PA: Burgum, 1931.

Parson, Thomas E. *Bear Flag and Bay State in the Civil War: The Californians of the Second Massachusetts Cavalry.* Jefferson, NC: MacFarland, 2001.

Roe, Alfred Seely. *The Ninth New York Heavy Artillery.* Worchester, MA: By Author, 1899.

Thomas, Howard. *Boys in Blue from the Adirondack Foothills.* Prospect, NY: Prospect Books, 1960.

Secondary Sources: Books

Ackinclose, Timothy. *Sabres & Pistols: The Civil War Career of Colonel Harry Gilmor, C.S.A.* Gettysburg, PA: Stan Clark Military Books, 1997.

Adams, F. Colburn. *Siege of Washington, D.C., Written Expressly for Little People.* New York: Dick and Fitzgerald, 1867.

Alexander, Ted. *Southern Revenge; Civil War History of Chambersburg, Pennsylvania.* Shippensburg, PA: White Mane, 1989.

Allardice, Bruce S. *Confederate Colonels: A Biographical Register.* Columbia, MO, University of Missouri Press, 2008.

_____. *More Generals in Gray.* Baton Rouge: Louisiana State University Press, 1995.

Allgor, Catherine. *A Perfect Union: Dolley Madison and the Creation of the American Nation.* New York: Henry Holt, 2006.

Ambrose, Stephen E. *Halleck: Lincoln's Chief of Staff.* Baton Rouge: Louisiana State University Press, 1962.

Ames, Mary Clemmer. *Ten Years in Washington: Life and Scenes in the National Capital.* Hartford, CT: Queen City Publishing, 1873.

Anders, Curt. *Henry Halleck's War: A Fresh Look at Lincoln's Controversial General-in-Chief.* Carmel, IN: Guild Press of Indiana, 1999.

Andrews, Cutler, *The South Reports The War.* Pittsburgh, PA: University of Pittsburgh Press, 1970.

Baker, Jean H. *Mary Todd Lincoln: A Biography.* New York: W. W. Norton, 1987.

Bean, W. G. *Stonewall's Man: Sandie Pendleton.* Chapel Hill: University of North Carolina Press, 1959.

Bearss, Edwin C. Brett Spaulding, editor. *The Battle of Monocacy: A Documented Report.* Frederick, MD: Monocacy National Battlefield, 2003.

Benjamin, Marcus, collector/editor. *Washington during War Time: A Series of Papers Showing the Military, Political, and Social Phases during 1861–1865.* Washington: Committee on Literature for the Thirty-Sixth Annual Encampment of the Grand Army of the Republic, 1902.

Bernstein, Steven. *The Confederacy's Last Northern Offensive: Jubal Early, the Army of the Valley and the Raid on Washington.* Jefferson, NC: McFarland, 2011.

Bickham, Troy. *The Weight of Vengeance: The United States, The British Empire and the War of 1812.* New York/Oxford, UK: Oxford University Press, 2012.

Bowen, Catherine Drinker. *Yankee from Olympus: Justice Holmes and His Family.* Boston: Little Brown, 1994.

Bundy, Carol. *The Nature of Sacrifice: A Biography of Charles Russell Lowell Jr., 1835–1864.* New York: Farrar, Straus and Giroux, 2005.

Bushong, Millard. *Old Jube: A Biography of General Jubal Early.* Boyce, VA: Carr, 1955.

Catton, Bruce. *Grant Takes Command.* Boston: Little, Brown, 1968.

Clark, Allen C. *Abraham Lincoln in the National Capital.* Washington: W. F. Roberts Company, 1925.

Coffin, Howard. *Full Duty: Vermonters in the Civil War.* Woodstock, VT: The Countryman Press, Inc., 1993.

Cohen, Eliot. *Supreme Command.* New York: Anchor, 2002.

Cole, Donald B. and John J. McDonough, editors. *Benjamin Brown French: Witness to a Young Republic.* Hanover, NH: University Press of New England, 1980.

Cooling, Benjamin Franklin. *Jubal Early's Raid on Washington, 1864.* Baltimore: Nautical and Aviation Publishing Company of America, 1989; Tuscaloosa, AL: University of Alabama Press, 2007.

———. *Monocacy: The Battle That Saved Washington.* Shippensburg, PA: White Mane, 1996/2000.

———. *Symbol, Sword and Shield: Defending Washington during the Civil War.* Hamden, CT: Shoestring Press; Shippensburg, PA: White Mane, 1975/1991.

Cramer, John H. *Lincoln under Enemy Fire: The Complete Account of His Experience during Early's Attack on Washington.* Baton Rouge: Louisiana State University Press, 1948; Knoxville: University of Tennessee Press, 2009.

Davis, William C. *Breckinridge: Statesman, Soldier, Symbol.* Baton Rouge: Louisiana State University Press, 1974.

———. *The South Besieged: Volume Five of The Image of the War 1861–1865.* Gettysburg, PA: The National Historical Society, 1983.

Eckert, Ralph Lowell. *John Brown Gordon: Soldier, Southerner, American.* Baton Rouge: Louisiana State University Press, 1989.

Federal Writers' Project, Works Progress Administration. *Washington: City and Capital.* Washington: Government Printing Office, 1937.

Feis, William B. *Grant's Secret Service: The Intelligence War from Belmont to Appomattox.* Lincoln, NE: University of Nebraska Press, 2002.

Flood, Charles Bracelen. *1864: Lincoln at the Gates of History.* New York: Simon & Schuster, 2009.

Fox, Arthur B. *Our Honored Dead: Alleghany County, Pennsylvania, in the American Civil War.* Chicora, PA: Mechling Bookbindery, 2008.

Furgurson, Ernest B. *Freedom Rising: Washington in the Civil War.* New York: Alfred A. Knopf, 2004.

BIBLIOGRAPHY

George, Christopher T. *Terror on the Chesapeake: The War of 1812 on the Bay.* Shippensburg, PA: White Mane, 2000.

Getty, Mildred Newbold. *To Light The Way: A History of Grace Episcopal Church, Silver Spring, Maryland.* Silver Spring, MD: Grace Church, 1965.

Goodwin, Doris Kearns. *Team of Rivals: The Political Genius of Abraham Lincoln.* New York: Simon and Schuster, 2005.

Gordon, Larry. *The Last Confederate General: John C. Vaughn and His East Tennessee Cavalry.* Minneapolis: Zenith Press, 2009.

Gutheim, Frederick. *Worthy of the Nation: Washington, DC, From L'Enfant to the National Capital Planning Commission.* Baltimore: Johns Hopkins University Press, 2006.

Haley, William D., editor. *Philip's Washington Described, A Complete View of the American Capital, and the District of Columbia: With Many Notices, Historical, Topographical, and Scientific, of the Seat of Government.* New York: Rudd and Caleon, 1961.

Haselberger, Fritz. *Confederate Retaliation: McCausland's 1864 Raid.* Shippensburg, PA: Burd Street Press/White Mane, 2000.

Hattaway, Herman, and Archer Jones. *How the North Won: A Military History of the Civil War.* Urbana: University of Illinois Press, 1983.

Hearn, Chester G. *Lincoln, The Cabinet, and The General.* Baton Rouge: Louisiana University Press, 2010.

Heidler, David S., and Jeanne T. Heidler. *Encyclopedia of the War of 1812.* Annapolis: Naval Institute Press, 1997.

Helm, Judith Beck. *Tenleytown, D.C.: Country Village into City Neighborhood.* Washington: Tennally Press, 1981.

Howard, Hugh. *Mr. and Mrs. Madison's War: America's First Couple and the Second War for Independence.* London, UK: Bloomsbury Press, 2012.

Hunt, Roger. *Colonels in Blue; Union Army Colonels of the Civil War: The Mid-Atlantic States: Pennsylvania, New Jersey, Maryland, Delaware, and the District of Columbia.* Mechanicsburg, PA: Stackpole, 2007.

———. *Colonels in Blue; Union Army Colonels of the Civil War: The New England States: Connecticut, Maine, Massachusetts, New Hampshire, Rhode Island, Vermont.* Atglen, PA: Schiffer, 2001.

Jockers, Ernst. *J. Otto Schewizer: The Man and His Work.* Philadelphia: Press of International Printing Company, 1953.

Johnson, David Alan. *Decided on the Battlefield: Grant, Sherman, Lincoln and the Election of 1864.* Amherst, NY: Prometheus Books, 2012.

Judge, Joseph. *Season of Fire: The Confederate Strike on Washington.* Berryville, VA: Rockbridge Publishing Company, 1994.

Kennedy, Frances H., editor. *The Civil War Battlefield Guide.* Boston: Houghton Mifflin, 1998 edition.

Kolker, Carole A., et al. *Top of the Town: Tenleytown Heritage Trail.* Washington: Cultural Tourism DC, 2010.

Konsoulis, Mary, et. Al. *Battleground to Community; Brightwood Heritage Trail.* Washington, DC: Cultural Tourism, 2008.

Lee, Richard M. *Mr. Lincoln's City: An Illustrated Guide to the Civil War Sites of Washington*. McLean, VA: EPM Publications, 1981.

Leech, Margaret. *Reveille in Washington 1860–1865*. New York: Harper and Brothers, 1941.

Leepson, Marc. *Desperate Engagement: How a Little-Known Civil War Battle Saved Washington, D.C., and Changed American History*. New York, St. Martins, 2007.

Lewis, Thomas A. *The Shenandoah Valley in Flames: The Valley Campaign of 1864*. Alexandria, VA: Time-Life, 1987.

Lockwood, Charles, and John Lockwood. *The Siege of Washington: The Untold Story of the Twelve Days That Shook the Union*. New York: Oxford University Press, 2011.

Long, David E. *The Jewel of Liberty: Abraham Lincoln's Re-election and the End of Slavery*. Mechanicsburg, PA: Stackpole Books, 1994.

Long, E. B. *Civil War Day By Day: An Almanac, 1861–1865*. Garden City, NY: Doubleday, 1971.

Lord, Walter. *The Dawn's Early Light*. New York: W. W. Norton, 1972.

Mahood, Wayne. *General Wadsworth: The Life and Times of Brevet Major General James S. Wadsworth*. New York: Da Capo, 2003.

Maney, R. Wayne. *Marching to Cold Harbor: Victory and Failure, 1864*. Shippensburg, PA: White Mane, 1994.

Marszalek, John F. *Commander of All Lincoln's Armies: A Life of General Henry W. Halleck*. Cambridge, MA: Belknap Press of Harvard University Press, 2004.

McCoy, Jerry A., and the Silver Spring Historical Society. *Historic Silver Spring*, Images of America series. Charleston, SC: Arcadia, 2005.

Miller, David W. *Second Only to Grant: Quartermaster General Montgomery C. Meigs*. Shippensburg, PA: White Mane, 2000.

Miller, Edward A., Jr. *Lincoln's Abolitionist General: The Biography of David Hunter*. Columbia: University of South Carolina Press, 1997.

Mitchell, Mary. *Divided Town: A Study of Georgetown, D.C., during the Civil War*. Barre, MA: Barre Publishing, 1968.

Moore, Frank. *The Rebellion Record: A Diary of American Events*. New York: D. Van Nostrand, 1871.

Moore, Ward. *Bring the Jubilee: What If the South Won the Civil War?* LaVergne, TN: Wildside Press, 2010; by the author, 1955.

Mouat, Malcolm Palmer. *Dr. Henry Palmer "The Fighting Surgeon," 1827–1895*. Detroit: Harlo, 1977.

Norton, Louis Arthur. *Joshua Barney: Hero of the Revolution and 1812*. Annapolis: Naval Institute Press, 2000.

Perret, Geoffrey. *Lincoln's War: The Untold Story of America's Greatest President as Commander in Chief*. New York: Random House, 2004.

Phillips, Jason. *Diehard Rebels: The Confederate Culture of Invincibility*. Athens, GA: University of Georgia Press, 2007.

Pinsker, Matthew. *Lincoln's Sanctuary: Abraham Lincoln and the Soldiers' Home*. New York: Oxford University Press, 2003.

BIBLIOGRAPHY

Pitch, Anthony S. *The Burning of Washington: The British Invasion of 1814.* Annapolis: Naval Institute Press, 1998.

Plum, William R. *The Military Telegraph During The Civil War in the United States.* Chicago: Jansen, McClurg, 1882. 2 volumes.

Pollard, Edward A. *The Lost Cause: A New Southern History of the War of the Confederates.* New York: E. B. Treat and Company, 1867.

Pond, George E. *The Shenandoah Valley in 1864.* New York: Scribners, 1883.

Power, J. Tracy. *Lee's Miserables: Life in the Army of Northern Virginia from the Wilderness to Appomattox.* Chapel Hill: University of North Carolina Press, 1998.

Proctor, John Clagett. *Proctor's Poems.* Washington: self-published, 1950.

———. *Proctor's Washington and Environs: Written for the* Washington Sunday Star *(1928–1949).* Washington: self-published, 1949.

Quimby, Robert S. *The U.S. Army in the War of 1812: An Operational and Command Study.* East Lansing, MI: Michigan State University Press, 1997.

Ray, Fred L. *Shock Troops of the Confederacy: The Sharpshooter Battalions of the Army of Northern Virginia.* Asheville, NC: CFS Press, 2006.

Roe, Alfred. *Monocacy.* Baltimore, MD: Toomey Press, 1996.

Schairer, Jack E. *Lee's Bold Plan for Point Lookout: The Rescue of Confederate Prisoners That Never Happened.* Jefferson, NC: McFarland, 2008.

Scharf, Thomas. *History of Western Maryland.* Philadelphia: L. H. Evarts, 1882.

Sedgwick, Paul. *The Shield.* Washington: District of Columbia Civil War Centennial Commission, 1965.

———. *The Symbol and the Sword: Washington, D.C., 1860–1865.* Washington: District of Columbia Civil War Centennial Commission, 1962.

Silverstone, Paul. *Warships of the Civil War Navies.* Annapolis: Naval Institute Press, 1989.

Simpson, Brooks D. *Ulysses S. Grant: Triumph over Adversity, 1822–1865.* Boston: Houghton Mifflin, 2000.

Snell, Mark A. *From First to Last: The Life of Major General William B. Franklin.* New York: Fordham University Press, 2002.

Spaulding, Brett W. *Last Chance for Victory: Jubal Early's 1864 Maryland Invasion.* Frederick, MD: Thomas Publications, 2010.

Stackpole, Edward J. *Sheridan in the Shenandoah: Jubal Early's Nemesis.* Harrisburg: Stackpole Co., 1961.

Stagg, J. C. A. *The War of 1812: Conflict for a Continent.* New York/Cambridge, UK: Cambridge University Press, 2012.

Standlee, Mary W. *Borden's Dream: The Walter Reed Army Medical Center in Washington, D.C.* Washington: Office of the Surgeon General, U.S. Army, Borden Institute, Walter Reed Army Medical Center, 2009.

Stephens, Gail. *Shadow of Shiloh: Major General Lew Wallace in the Civil War.* Indianapolis: Indiana Historical Society Press, 2010.

Thomas, Benjamin P., and Harold M. Hyman. *Stanton: The Life and Times of Lincoln's Secretary of War.* New York: Alfred A. Knopf, 1962.

U.S. Navy Department, Naval History Division, compiler. *Civil War Naval Chronology 1861–1865*. Washington: Government Printing Office, 1971.

Warner, Ezra J. *Generals in Blue: Lives of the Union Commanders*. Baton Rouge: Louisiana State University Press, 1964.

———. *Generals in Gray: Lives of the Confederate Commanders*. Baton Rouge: Louisiana State University Press, 1959.

Waugh, John C. *Reelecting Lincoln: The Battle for the 1864 Presidency*. New York: Crown, 1997.

Weigley, Russell F. *A Great Civil War: A Military and Political History 1861–1865*. Bloomington: Indiana University Press, 2000.

Wert, Jeffrey D. *From Winchester to Cedar Creek: The Shenandoah Campaign of 1864*. New York: Simon and Schuster, 1987.

Williams, John S. *History of the Invasion and Capture of Washington and of the Events Which Preceded and Followed*. New York: Harper and Brothers, 1857.

Williams, T. Harry. *Lincoln and His Generals*. New York: Vintage, 1952.

Wills, Garry. *James Madison*. New York: Henry Holt, 2002.

Wills, Mary Alice. *The Confederate Blockade of Washington D.C., 1861–1862*. Parsons, WVA: McClain, 1975.

Wilson, Charles Reagan. *Baptized in Blood: The Religion of the Lost Cause, 1865–1920*. Athens, GA: University of Georgia Press, 1980/2009.

Works Progress Administration. *Washington: City and Capital [WPA Guide]*. Washington: Government Printing Office, 1937.

Worthington, Glenn H. *Fighting for Time: Or, the Battle That Saved Washington and Mayhap the Union*. Baltimore, Day Printing, 1932; Shippensburg, PA: Burd Street Press, 1985.

Secondary Sources: Articles and Essays

Casemate Museum Staff, Fort Monroe, Virginia. "Is It a Fort or a Fortress?" *Tales of Old Fort Monroe* 5 (January 1972): 1–4.

Cooling, B. Franklin. "The Campaign That Might Have Changed the War—And Did." *North and South* 7, 5 (August 2004): 12–23.

———. "A Near Miss in Washington." *America's Civil War* 17, 3 (July 2004): 30–36, 72.

———. and Wally Owen. "Washington's Civil War Defenses and the Battle of Fort Stevens." *Hallowed Ground* 9, 3 (Fall 2008): 24–41.

Cox, William V. "The Defenses of The Capital and The Battle of Fort Stevens, July 11 and12, 1864," *Records of the Columbia Historical Society, IV (1901): 1–31*.

Dame, Bob. "The Man Who Was Touched with Fire." *America's Civil War* (March 2001): 22–28.

Dudley, Edgar. "A EMINISENCE OF Washington and Early's Attack in 1864." Loyal Legion of the United States, Ohio Commandery. *Sketches of War History 1861–1865*. Volume I, 107–27. Cincinnati: Robert O. Clarke, Co., 1888.

BIBLIOGRAPHY

Early, Jubal A., "Early's March to Washington in 1864," in Robert Underwood Johnson and Clarence Clough Buel, editors. *Battles and Leaders of the Civil War.* New York: Century, 1884, Volume 4: 492–99.

———. "The Advance on Washington in1864," *Southern Historical Society Papers.* 9 (July, August 1881), 297–312.

Feis, William B. "Neutralizing the Valley: The Role of Military Intelligence in the Defeat of Jubal Early's Army of the Valley, 1864–1865." *Civil War History* 34: 143–71.

Fitzpatrick, Michael F. "Jubal Early and the Californians." *Civil War Times* (May 1998): 51–60.

Hendrickson, Ed. "Defending Washington: The District of Columbia Militia, 1861." *Washington History* 23 (2011): 37–58.

Mitchell, Enoch L., editor. "Letters of a Confederate Surgeon in the Army of Tennessee to His Wife." *Tennessee Historical Quarterly* 5 (June 1946): 142–81.

Offutt, William M. "The Civil War in the Chevy Chase Area." *Chevy Case Historical Center Newsletter* (Fall 2011): 4–5.

Osborne, Charles C. "Jubal Early's Raid on Washington." In *With My Face to the Enemy: Perspectives on the Civil War*, editor Robert Cowley. New York: Berkley Books, 2001.

Pinsker, Matthew. "The Soldiers' Home: A Long Road to Sanctuary." *Washington History* 18 (2006): 5–19.

Platteborze, Peter L. "Crossroads of Destiny: Lew Wallace, the Battle of Monocacy, and the Outcome of Jubal Early's Drive on Washington, D.C." *Army History* 61 (Spring 2005): 5–19.

Ray, Frederick L. "Shock Troops of the South." *America's Civil War* (July 2002): 35–40.

Skidmore, Richard S. "Lew Wallace and the Old Wound of Shiloh." *North South Trader* IX, 5 (July–August 1982): 10–14, 34.

INDEX

INDEX

INDEX